UGANDA DISTRICTS
Information Handbook

Expanded Edition 2011 – 2012

FOUNTAIN PUBLISHERS
Kampala

Fountain Publishers
P. O. Box 488
Kampala
e-mail: publishing@fountainpublishers.co.ug
website: www.fountainpublishers.co.ug

First published 1992
Second Edition 1994
Third Edition 1995
Reprinted 1996
Fourth Edition 1997
Fifth Edition 1998
Sixth Edition 2002
Seventh Edition 2005
Eighth Edition 2007
Ninth Edition 2011

Researcher
Nathan K. Twinomujuni

Cartography and Design
Robert Asaph Sempagala-Mpagi

Layout
Senfuka Kasule Ronald

The publishers have made every effort to ensure the accuracy of information in this book at the time of going to press; but in the unlikely event of errors and omissions, we will be grateful to receive corrections.

ISBN 978 9970 02 492 6

_____

Cataloguing-in-Publication Data

Uganda Districts Information Handbook – Kampala: Fountain Publishers, 2011
__ p; __ cm.
Includes colour maps, alphabetical entries and index

ISBN 978-9970-02-492-6
1. Uganda – manuals   I. Handbooks
025.96761

Contents

Northwestern Districts   3

Northern Districts   29

Northeastern Districts   84

Southwestern Districts   260

Western Districts   300

Districts Index   341

Introduction

This is an expanded edition of the regular *Uganda Districts Information Handbook*. The handbook provides detailed information on all the country's 112 districts in a condensed form.

While many users found information in previous editions very useful, this expanded edition is even more comprehensive and user-friendly.

In this edition, up-to-date detailed colour maps have been introduced for each district. For ease of reference, the districts have been grouped into seven regional blocks: Northwestern, Northern, Northeastern, Eastern, Central, Southwestern and Western. A map of each one of these blocks enables the user to understand a district in terms of its regional context by showing the other districts that border it.

In addition to location, the book gives the size in terms of area of each district, administrative divisions down to the sub-county and parish levels, climate, vegetation, rainfall range and relief. It shows the lowest and highest points, including spot heights above sea level.

The book classifies the population into male and female, and population density. There is information about economic activities, industry, banking services and NGOs.

The book also gives information about road and railway networks, airfields, radio and television stations and telephone systems that serve each district. The book further highlights tourist attractions and information on tourist lodges located in different national parks and game reserves.

It also lists the number of educational institutions, the number of students/pupils and teachers that serve them as well as pupils' furniture status in the district (basing on 2009 statistics). It gives the number and category of health centres and services available in each district.

Finally, there is a list of district leaders, municipal leaders and Members of Parliament.

This book is useful for planners, NGOs, district officials, councillors in local government, MPs, diplomats, schools and tourists.

Editor

Acknowledgements

The publisher would like to thank Odrek Rwabwogo for compiling the original edition of the Uganda Districts Information Handbook, and Daniel Karibwije for updating and collecting new information used in the 2005-2006 edition, Mrs Speciosa Kabwegyere for the 2008-2009 edition and Mr Nathan Twinomujuni for this edition. Many government, ministries, departments, officials and organisations were helpful in providing information for this handbook. The following are specially acknowledged:

1. **Size, population, climate and minor/major towns (urban areas):** Courtesy of Statistics Department, Ministry of Finance, Planning and Economic Development, P. O. Box 13 Entebbe, Uganda. Population and Housing Census 2002, Uganda Population Projections 2006.

2. **Administrative headquarters, sub-counties, counties, district boundaries:** Courtesy of Ministry of Local Government, P. O. Box 7073 Kampala, Uganda.

3. **Languages and historical institutions:** Courtesy of Culture Department, Ministry of Gender, Labour and Social Development, P. O. Box 7136, Kampala, Uganda.

4. **Major food crops:** Courtesy of Ministry of Agriculture, Animal Industry and Fisheries, P. O. Box 2, Entebbe, Uganda.

5. **Area covered by forest:** Courtesy of National Biomass Study, Forestry Department, Ministry of Water, Lands and Environment, P. O. Box 1613, Kampala, Uganda.

6. **District Estimates of Animal Population:** Uganda Bureau of Statistics: Livestock Statistics.

7. **Primary and district co-operatives:** Co-operative Statistics – Mid-July 2002, Uganda Co-operative Alliance Ltd, P. O. Box 2215, Kampala.

8. **Industries:** The Directory of Manufacturing Establishments of Uganda, Ministry of Tourism, Trade and Industry, Technology Library, Technical Information Unit.

9. **Health:** Major hospitals and health units by district: Health Facilities Inventory, and the Registrar, Uganda Medical and Dental Practitioners Council.

10. **AIDS Prevalence:** HIV/AIDS Prevalence Report, June 2003, STD/AIDS Control Programme, Ministry of Health, P. O. Box 7272, Kampala.

11. **Tourist attractions and resort centres:** Courtesy of Ministry of Tourism, Trade and Industry, Wildlife and Antiquities, P. O. Box 4241 Kampala, Uganda; Uganda Tourist Board, P. O. Box 7211, Kampala, Uganda. Ministry of Tourism, Trade and Industry (PAMSU PROJECT) (2002): Exploited and Potential Attractions Report.

12. **Schools and tertiary education institutions:** EMIS data 2002, Ministry of Education and Sports, Embassy House, P. O. Box 7063, Kampala.

13. **Banks:** Annual Bank Census Report as at 30th September 2002, Bank of Uganda, P. O. Box 7120, Kampala, Uganda.

14. **Annual traffic accidents statistics by district:** Uganda Police and Uganda Bureau of Statistics, 2002 Statistical Abstract.

15. **Operational television and radio stations:** Uganda Communications Commisssioin, 12th Floor, Communications, House, Plot 1 Colville Street, P. O. Box 7376, Kampala.

16. **Transport - Aerodromes (airfields) in Uganda:** Entebbe International Airport, P. O. Box 5536, Kampala, Uganda. Civil Aviation Authority Website; www.caa.co.ug/aerodromes.

17. **District leaders**
    (i) Ministry of Local Government, 5th Floor, Workers' House, Kampala.
    (ii) Urban Authorities Association of Uganda (UAAU), H/Qs – Kampala City Council (KCC) City Hall, 1st Floor.
    (iii) Uganda Local Authorities Association (ULAA), 8th Floor, NIC Building, Kampala.

18. **Members of Parliament:** Public Relations and Information Office, Parliament of the Republic of Uganda.

19. **Non-Governmental Organisations**
    (i) Development Network of Indigenous Voluntary Associations (DENIVA), Kampala Uganda.
    (ii) Uganda National NGO Forum. Website: www.ngoforum.or.ug
    (iii) NGO Handbook 2004, Published by Donor News, Magazine Center, P. O. Box 9350 Kampala.

20. **Cartography and Symbols:** The symbols used in the maps in this handbook are original creations of the cartographer and are copyrighted.

Equator	Cheetah
National Park Headquarters	Chimpanzee
Park Sector Headquarters	Crocodile
Ranger Outpost	Giraffe
National Park Hut	Elephant
Campsite	Hippopotamus
Beach	Hyena
Hotel	Leopard
Hot Spring	Lion
View Sites	Monkey
Stone Age Site	Mountain Gorilla
Car Ferry	Ostrich
Lake Ferry	Rhino
Antelope	ShoeBill
Baboon	Warthog
Buffalo	Zebra

District Population Projections by end 2009

Abim 53,500	Kalangala 53,300	Mbarara 410,500
Adjumani 305,600	Kaliro 191,700	Mitooma 181,600
Agago 253,700	Kalungu 168,700	Mityana 291,500
Alebtong 201,000	Kampala 1,510,200	Moroto 101,600
Amolatar 114,900	Kamuli 281,800	Moyo 322,200
Amudat 93,500	Kamwenge 303,900	Mpigi 202,700
Amuria 310,700	Kanungu 232,500	Mubende 535,500
Amuru 161,700	Kapchorwa 98,100	Mukono 498,500
Apac 309,500	Kasese 658,400	Nakapiripirit 127,100
Arua 690,700	Katakwi 153,700	Nakaseke 169,300
Budaka 161,700*	Kayunga 331,500	Nakasongola 144,100
Bududa 157,602	Kibaale 571,000	Namayingo 197,600
Bugiri 362,700	Sheema 203,500	Namutumba 198,200
Bukedea 160,900	Kiboga 142,700	Napak 163,700
Bukomansimbi 146,700	Kibuku 160,200	Nebbi 314,100
Bukwo 63,500	Kiruhuura 265,500	Ngora 135,400
Buikwe 389,100	Kiryandongo 265,300	Buhweju 93,700
Bulambuli 113,800	Kisoro 239,000	Ntoroko 70,900
Buliisa 73,700	Kitgum 215,936	Ntungamo 438,900
Bundibugyo 220,800	Koboko 193,500	Nwoya 48,800
Bushenyi 232,200	Kole 205,800	Nyadri 178,100
Busia 268,500	Kotido 188,200	Oyam 335,300
Butaleja 195,800	Kumi 219,500	Otuke 76,600
Buvuma 50,000	Kyankwanzi 158,000	Pader 196,200
Buyende 235,600	Kyegegwa 140,300	Pallisa 319,900
Dokolo 162,000	Kyenjojo 337,000	Rakai 449,500
Gomba 143,900	Kween 88,800	Rubiriizi 115,000
Gombe 93,700	Lamwo 149,152	Rukungiri 301,100
Gulu 357,400	Lira 358,600	Sembabule 202,700
Hoima 466,700	Luuka 230,600	Serere 246,700
Ibanda 232,400	Luweero 399,900	Sironko 217,600
Iganga 442,200	Lwengo 122,600	Soroti 270,600
Isingiro 378,600	Lyantonde 74,100	Tororo 443,500
Jinja 454,900	Manafwa 325,600	Wakiso 1,186,900
Kaabong 316,500	Masaka 238, 700	Yumbe 423,000
Kabale 477,500	Masindi 294,700	Zombo 199,400
Kabarole 389,600	Mayuge 406,600	
Kaberamaido 172,400	Mbale 397,400	

Uganda Population growth since 1948

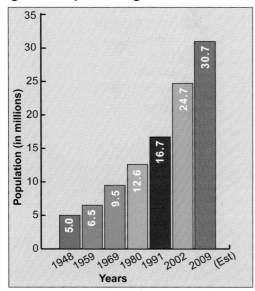

After every 10 years, the government of Uganda counts the people in the country. This exercise is called a Population Census. The graph on the left shows the number of people in Uganda according to census reports of different years. The population of 2009 is an estimate by the Uganda Bureau of Statistics (UBOS), which is responsible for carrying out census in Uganda.

Population Distribution

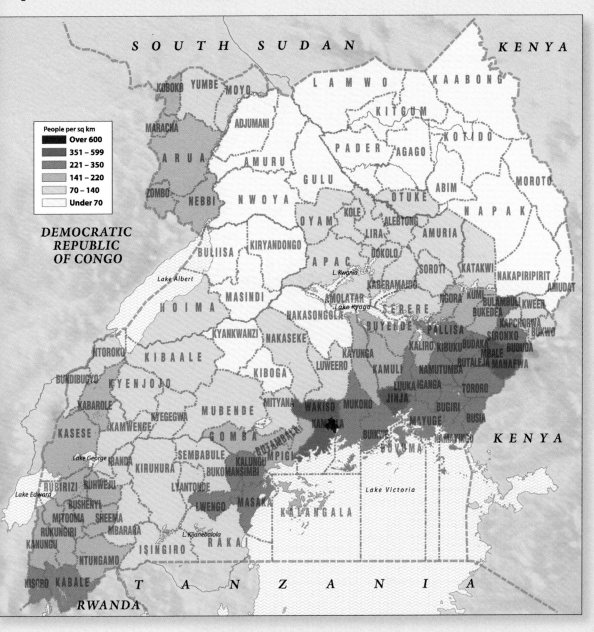

People per sq km
- Over 600
- 351 – 599
- 221 – 350
- 141 – 220
- 70 – 140
- Under 70

SOUTH SUDAN

KENYA

DEMOCRATIC
REPUBLIC
OF CONGO

KOBOKO   YUMBE   MOYO

MARACHA   ADJUMANI

A R U A   AMURU

ZOMBO   NEBBI   N W O Y A

L A M W O

KAABONG

K I T G U M

KOTIDO

P A D E R   AGAGO

GULU   OTUKE   ABIM   MOROTO

O Y A M   KOLE   ALEBTONG   N A P A K

LIRA   AMURIA

BULIISA   KIRYANDONGO   A P A C   DOKOLO

Lake Albert   L. Kwania   SOROTI   KATAKWI   NAKAPIRIPIRIT

MASINDI   KABERAMAIDO   NGORA   KUMI   AMUDAT

AMOLATAR   BULAMBULI KWEEN

Lake Kyoga   S E R E R E   BUKEDEA

H O I M A   NAKASONGOLA   KAPCHORWA

KYANKWANZI   NAKASEKE   BUYENDE   PALLISA   SIRONKO   BUKWO

ITOROKO   KALIRO KIBUKU BUDAKA   BUDUDA

K I B A A L E   KAYUNGA   KAMULI   MBALE   MANAFWA

BUNDIBUGYO   KIBOGA   LUWEERO   NAMUTUMBA   BUTALEJA

K Y E N J O J O   LUUKA IGANGA   TORORO

KABAROLE   MITYANA   WAKISO   MUKONO   JINJA   BUGIRI

NYEGEGWA   MUBENDE   KAMPALA   MAYUGE   BUSIA

KASESE   KAMWENGE   G O M B A   BUTAMBALA   BUIKWE   NAMAYINGO

KENYA

Lake George   IBANDA   SEMBABULE   MPIGI   BUVUMA

KIRUHURA   KALUNGU

RUBIRIZI RUHWEJU   LYANTONDE   BUKOMANSIMBI

Lake Edward   BUSHENYI   LWENGO   MASAKA   Lake Victoria

MITOOMA   SHEEMA   K A L A N G A L A

RUKUNGIRI   MBARARA   L. Kijanebalola

KANUNGU   ISINGIRO   R A K A I

NTUNGAMO

KISORO   KABALE   T A N Z A N I A

RWANDA

Road Distances

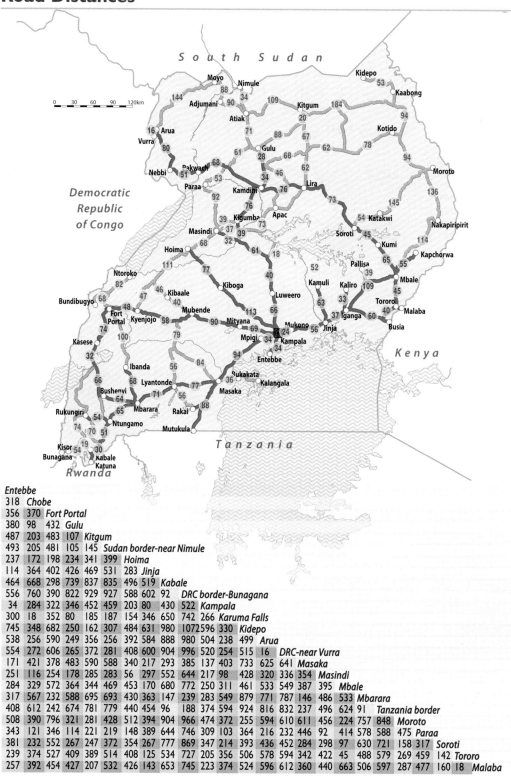

Entebbe
318 Chobe
356 370 Fort Portal
380 98 432 Gulu
487 203 483 107 Kitgum
493 205 481 105 145 Sudan border-near Nimule
237 172 198 234 341 399 Hoima
114 364 402 426 469 531 283 Jinja
464 668 298 739 837 835 496 519 Kabale
556 760 390 822 929 927 588 602 92 DRC border-Bunagana
34 284 322 346 452 459 203 80 430 522 Kampala
300 18 352 80 185 187 154 346 742 266 Karuma Falls
745 348 682 250 162 307 484 631 980 1072 596 330 Kidepo
538 256 590 249 356 256 392 584 888 980 504 238 499 Arua
554 272 606 265 372 281 408 600 904 996 520 254 515 16 DRC-near Vurra
171 421 378 483 590 588 340 217 293 385 137 403 733 625 641 Masaka
251 116 254 178 285 283 56 297 552 644 217 98 428 320 336 354 Masindi
284 329 572 364 344 469 453 170 680 772 250 311 461 533 549 387 395 Mbale
317 567 232 588 695 693 430 363 147 239 283 549 879 771 787 146 486 533 Mbarara
408 612 242 674 781 779 440 454 96 188 374 594 924 816 832 237 496 624 91 Tanzania border
508 390 796 321 281 428 512 394 904 966 474 372 255 594 610 611 456 224 757 848 Moroto
343 121 346 114 221 219 148 389 644 746 309 103 364 216 232 446 92 414 578 588 475 Paraa
381 232 527 267 247 372 354 267 777 869 347 214 393 436 452 284 298 97 630 721 158 317 Soroti
239 374 527 409 389 514 408 125 534 727 205 356 506 578 594 342 422 45 488 579 269 459 142 Tororo
257 392 454 427 207 532 426 143 653 745 223 374 524 596 612 360 440 663 506 597 287 477 160 18 Malaba

Uganda Districts

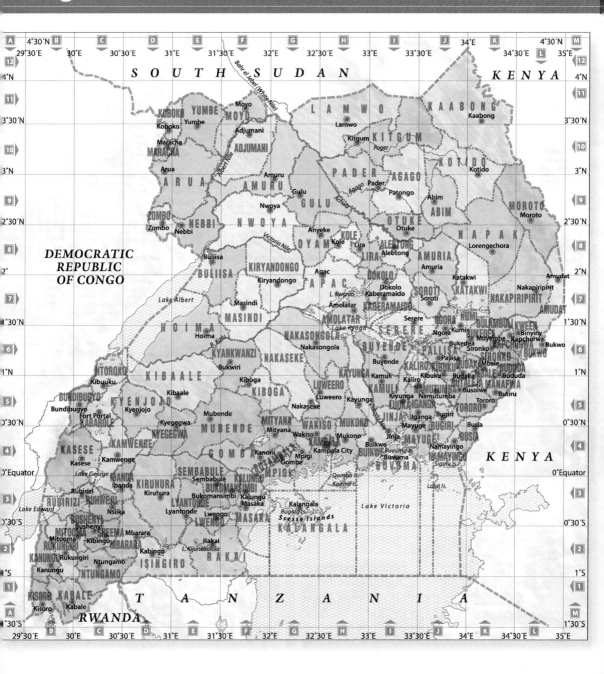

Uganda is made up of 112 districts as at December 2010. The Uganda Local Governments Association (ULGA), an organisation that brings together all local governments in Uganda, has grouped these districts into four main regions namely: Central, Western, Northern and Eastern. For ease of reference however, we have in this handbook, put the districts into seven groups, namely: Northwestern, Northern, Northeastern, Eastern, Central, Southwestern and Western.

Northwestern Districts

Adjumani Arua Koboko Moyo Nebbi Maracha Yumbe Zombo

The Northwestern districts cover the area originally known as West Nile. This is the area to the west of the Albert Nile, except for one district that is to the east of the river. The region borders both the Democratic Republic of Congo and the Sudan.

The People: The main inhabitants of these districts are the Lugbara, Alur, Kakwa and Madi. The Lendu, Okebu and Metu are other inhabitants of this area. The people are mainly cultivators and tobacco is the main cash crop produced.

Tourism: There are a number of tourist attractions in this region, which include wild game in East Madi and Ajai Wildlife Reserves.

How to get there: The area is accessible by road and air. The major access road to the region is paved (tarmac) up to Arua town. There are regular buses and other public service vehicles from Kampala.

Arua and Adjumani have airstrips and small aircraft fly the Entebbe-Arua-Adjumani routes on a regular basis.

There is also a ferry connection on Lake Albert to the region between Wanseko in Buliisa District and Panyimur in Nebbi District. The lake provides alternative access routes.

Left: An aerial photo of a village in Adjumani district. Right: Tobacco is a major crop in Arua district.

Northwestern Districts

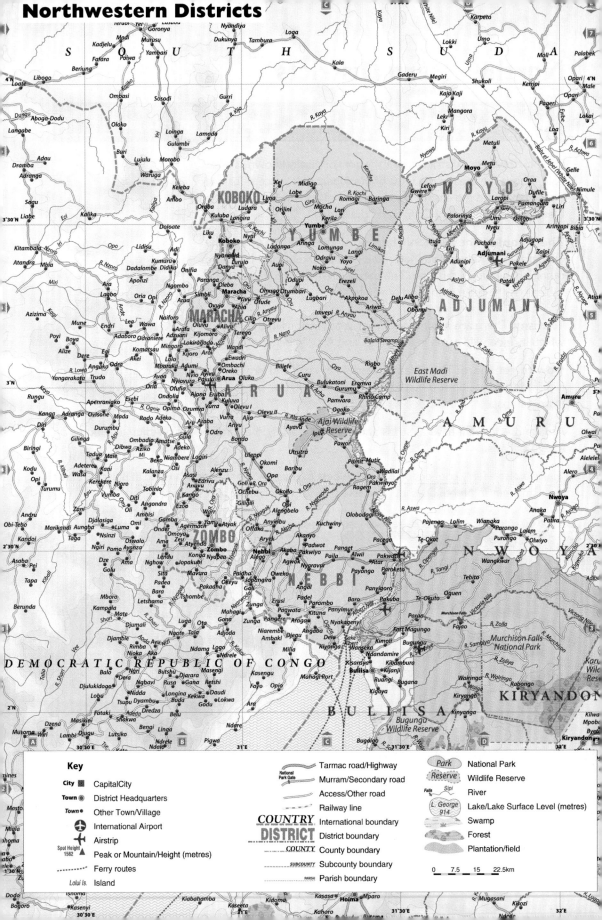

Adjumani District

Adjumani District was carved in 1997 from Moyo District, which at independence was known as Madi District. Adjumani and Moyo districts are separated by the Albert Nile.

Location: Adjumani District is bordered by the districts of Amuru to the east and to south; Arua to the southwest; Moyo to the west and north; and the Republic of South Sudan to the northeast.

Area: 3,086.0 sq. km.

Climate, Relief and Vegetation: The district lies on the low plateau of northern Uganda. The lowest point is about 600m at Nimule and the highest point is 1,300m above sea level. Adjumani District is an extensive savannah grassland with scattered woodlands and thickets. Rainfall is medium; ranging between 750mm – 1,250mm. The dry season is a longer one than in other places in the country.

Population: Based on the 2009 Projection - 305,600 people – 153,000 males and 152,600 females. The district has a population density of 99 persons per square kilometre.

Major Town: Adjumani (administrative headquarters); Trading Centres – Patali and Dzaipi.

Counties and Sub-counties: East Moyo County – Adjumani (Town Council), Adropi, Arinyapi, Dzaipi, Itrikwa, Ciforo, Ofua, Pakele, Pachara and Ukusuoni Sub-counties.

Main Language: Madi, Lugbara and Acholi.

People: Madi, Lugbara and Acholi.

Economic Activities: Agriculture with emphasis on:
- (i)   Food crops: Maize, millet, cassava and soya bean.
- (ii) Cash crops: Cotton and coffee.
- (iii) Fishing on the River Nile.

Industries: Oil milling, cotton ginning and flour milling.

Banks: Stanbic Bank Ltd – 1.

Area under Forestation: 151,119 hectares.

Animal Population: According to 2008 livestock census the district had 131,282 cattle, 7,449 pigs, 26,030 sheep, 26,030 goats, 391,626 chicken, 26,267 ducks, and 971 turkeys

Co-operative Societies: Adjumani and Moyo have 45 registered co-operative societies.

Education Services: Statistics 2009: Primary schools 77 – 69 government, 5 private, 3 community. Primary school enrolment: 40,332 pupils – 20,806 male and 19,526 female. Teachers: 727 – 493 male and 234 female. Available furniture is adequate for 31,509 pupils.

Secondary schools 15 - 4 Government, 8 private, and 3 community schools. Secondary school enrolment: 5,813 students – 3,826 male and 1,987 female. Teachers: 311 – 249 male and 62 female. Available furniture was not fully reported.

Health Services: I Black hospital (government) with 100 beds, 1 hospital (NGO), 1 health centre IV (government), 9 health centre III (5 government and 4 NGO), 12 government and 10 NGO health centre III, 22 health centre II (12 government and 10 NGO).

Transport Network: Adjumani has a murram road network linking some parts of the district as well as connecting the district with other districts. The traffic is however, very low. Sections of the Albert Nile are navigable. There is a ferry service linking Adjumani and Moyo districts across the River Nile. The district has an airstrip where scheduled and chartered flights are available.

Tourist Attractions: Its rather flat landscape adds to the beauty of the place blending in with the distant horizon. At night, the deep, inky, blackness of the landscape with bright stars is lovely. East Madi Wildlife Reserve offers a feel of Uganda's wild beauty. The River Nile which forms the eastern boundary of the district has potential for tourism along the banks.

Operational Radio Stations: Radio Paidha Limited

Additional Information: The district is sparsely populated and the land tenure system is generally customary, although in some parts it is communal. Agriculture is largely subsistence. Even though there are large tracts of land, extensive commercial farming is not widely practised in the district.

Key NGOs: MS Uganda, SNV Uganda, Adjumani Bee Keepers' Association, Adjumani People Living with HIV/AIDS Association, Finnish Refugee Council, National Union of Disabled Persons in Uganda, Nile Development Foundation, Basic Education Development Network, West Nile Women's Association, Nutrition Initiative for Rural Development.

District Leaders:	Members of Parliament:
District Chairperson – Mr Owole Nixon	Koboko County – Mr James Boliba Baba
Chief Administrative Officer (CAO)	District Woman MP
– Mr Okumu Christopher	– Ms Margaret Baba Diri
Deputy Chief Administrative Officer	
(DCAO) – Mr Martin Unzua	
Town Clerk (Adjumani Town Council)	
– Mr Samuel Lagu	

Arua District

At Independence, Arua was part of the then West Nile District, which consisted of present-day Arua, Koboko, Nebbi, Nyadri, Yumbe and Zombo districts. Under the 1974 Provincial Administration, West Nile District was divided into South Nile, Central Nile and North Nile districts. In 1980, North Nile and Central Nile became Arua District, while South Nile was renamed Nebbi District.

Location: It borders the Districts of Maracha to the northwest, Yumbe and Moyo to the north, Adjumani, and Amuru to the east (with the Albert Nile forming its border with the two

districts in the east), Nebbi and Zombo to the south, and the Democratic Republic of Congo in the west.

Area: 4,368 sq.km.

Climate and Relief: It lies at an approximate altitude of between 610m and 1,388m above sea level within a modified equatorial zone. It has heavy rainfall and moderately high temperatures all year round.

Population: Projected for 2009: 690,700 people - 330,000 males and 360,700 females. The district has a population density of 158 persons per square kilometre with Ayivu County having the highest density of 541 persons per square kilometre - one of the highest in Uganda.

Major Towns: Arua (administrative headquarters); Trading Centres – Rhino Camp, Terego, Vurra, Logiri, Utrutru, Baribu, Okollo, Otrivu, Utumbari and Mbaraka - a busy border trading centre.

Counties and Sub-counties: Ayivu County – Adumi, Aroi, Oluko, Pajulu, Manibe, Dadamu, Ayivuni Madi-Okollo County – Anyiribu, Ewanga, Offaka, Ogoko, Okollo, Pawor, Rhino Camp, Ulepi, Rigbo; Vurra County – Ajia, Arivu, Logiri, Vurra; Arua Municipality – Arua Hill, and Oli River. Terego – Ali-vu/Ajivu, Beliefe, Katrini, Omugo, Odupi and Uriama.

Main Languages: Mainly Lugbara

People: Mainly Lugbara

Economic Activities: Agriculture with emphasis on:
  (i)   Food crops: Cassava, simsim (sesame), peas, maize, beans, cow peas.
  (ii) Cash crop: Tobacco.
  (iii) Fishing on the River Nile.

Area under Forestation: 178,840 hectares.

Co-operative Societies: Arua and Yumbe have 90 registered primary co-operative societies.

Animal Population: According to 2008 livestock census the district had 117,157 cattle; 273,012 goats; 45,922 sheep; 22,927 pigs; 588,824 chicken; 21,468 ducks and 1,402 turkeys.

Industries: Cotton ginning, coffee processing, grain milling, tobacco curing, oil milling, carpentry and honey processing.

Banks: Stanbic Bank Ltd – 1, Centenary Rural Development Bank –1.

Education Services: Statistics 2009: Primary Schools: 209 schools - 180 government, 16 private, 13 community. Primary school enrolment: 263,334 pupils – 134,029 male and 129,305. Primary School Teachers 4,243 – 2,890 male and 1,353 female. Available furniture is adequate for 106,593 pupils.

Secondary Schools: 60 schools - 21 government, 24 private, 15 community. Secondary School Enrolment: 25,521 students – 15,162 male and 10,359 female. Secondary School Teachers: 1,478 – 1,189 male and 289 female. Available furniture is adequate for only 20,397 students.

Post secondary Institutions: 3 technical institutions, 2 teacher training colleges, and 1 Nationa hospitals (1 government – Arua Hospital with 278 beds, 2 NGO – Kuluva and Orijani with a total of 210 beds), 4 health centres IV (all government), 24 health centres III -(19 government, 6 NGO), 26 health centres II (21 government, and 5 II NGO).

Transport Network: The district has an inadequate road network. The existing roads are murram and are not well maintained except for the stretch between Arua - Nebbi towns. The poor road network has greatly hampered transportation in the district. The district has an airstrip and air transport which provides quick but expensive means to and from the district.

Arua Airfield – Arua Airfield is a designated entry and exit point. The murram surface runway is 1,707m x 30m and is in good condition. The terminal building was recently renovated. In order to cope with the increasing volume of passengers, the terminal building is planned for expansion. The airfield is equipped for airplane crashes, fire and has rescue services, as required for the safety of aircraft operations. Aviation security is complemented by the police at the airfield. The airfield is connected to the three national telecommunication services providers: Uganda Telecoms Limited (UTL), MTN and Airtel for mobile telephones. Public telephone call services are also available in town. The Civil Aviation Authority provides H.F. radio communication. The airfield is 5 km from Arua town. The White Rhino Hotel and other relatively smaller hotels offer reasonable accommodation with bed and breakfast. Transportation from the airfield to town can be provided by taxi.

Tourist Attractions: Ajia Wildlife Reserve which was formerly the home of the white rhino still attracts tourists. Other attractions include the Miri-Adua falls, the Obua falls, Kei and Wati Mountains, Mount Liru and the Albert Nile.

Rivers Ola, Kochi, Acha and Enyau traverse the district and flow into the Albert Nile.

Additional Information: Arua District is one of the districts in Uganda that was hit hard by the 1979 war that overthrew the Idi Amin regime. A large part of the population was uprooted from their homes and fled into exile. This crippled the district as all its infrastructure went to waste. The people in exile started returning to Uganda in 1988.

Arua town is strategically situated near the border of the Democratic Republic of Congo (DRC) and thus the people there benefit from cross-border trade. Given the lack of essential goods and manufactured products in eastern Congo, Arua is becoming a commercial centre that services the DRC. Gold from the DRC is exchanged for money and other goods in Arua.

In Arua, agriculture is largely subsistence. Tobacco is the leading cash crop. Poor roads limit access to markets.

Land tenure is customary. The population settlement pattern in the district is not uniform. Areas along the Nile are densely populated.

Operational Radio Stations and TV Stations: Capital Radio, Arua FM, Here is Life, Arua Hill FM, Homenet Radio Koboko, Radio Pasis, Born Free Technologies Network, UBC TV and Radio.

Key NGOs: African Network for the Prevention and Protection Against Child Abuse and Neglect Uganda Chapter, MS Uganda, World Vision Uganda, Family Planning Association of Uganda, Aids Information Centre, German Development Service, SNV Uganda, African Child Care Foundation, Ajai Rural Development Forum, Arua District Farmers' Association, CARE International in Uganda, Koboko United Women's Association, Lugbara Literature Association, United Humanitarian Development Association, Maracha Action for Development.

District leaders:
Chairperson – Mr Andama, Richard
Chief Administrative Officer (CAO)
    – Mr Vasco Sammy Ogenrwoth
Deputy Chief Administrative Officer
    (DCAO) – Vacant
Town Clerk (Arua Municipality)
    – Mr Martin Andua Drani
Mayor (Arua Municipality) – Charles Asiki

Members of Parliament:
Vurra County – Mr Okuonzi Sam Agatre
Madi-Okolo County
    – Mr Drito Martin Andi
Ayivu County – Mr Atiku Benard
Terego County – Mr Wadri Kassiano
    Ezati
Arua Municipality
    – Mr Ajedra Gabriel Gadison Aridru
Woman MP – Ms Christine Abia Bako

Tobacco is the leading cash crop in Arua district.

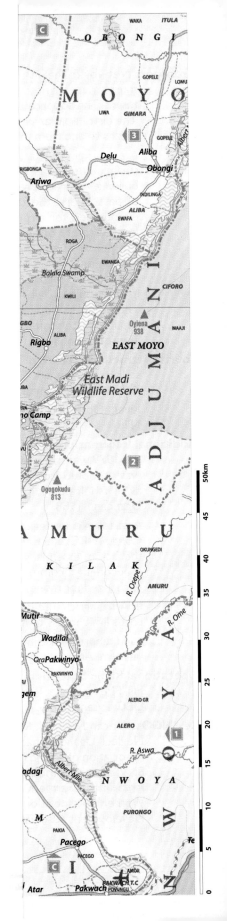

Koboko District

Koboko District was carved out of Arua District in 2005.

Location: Borders the districts of Yumbe in the east, Maracha in the south, Democratic Republic of Congo in the West and Sudan in the north.

Area: 660.94 sq. km.

Climate, Relief and Vegetation: District endowed with several rivers draining to the east and Albert Nile. Parts of the area are rocky which has led people to encroach on the wetlands.

Population: Basing on the 2009 projection, the district has 162,600 people - 82,300 females and 80,300 male with a population density of 246 persons per square kilometre.

Major Towns: Koboko Town Council; Trading Centres – Nyai Longira and Oraba, a busy border town.

Counties and Sub-Counties: Koboko County – Koboko (Town Council), Abuku, Dranya, Kuluba Lobule, Ludara and Midia.

Main Language: Kakwa

People: Mainly Kakwa

Economic Activities: Cross-border trade, timber production, tobacco growing and livestock

Animal Population: According to 2008 livestock census the district had 54,204 cattle, 101,602 goats, 33,250 sheep, 272 pigs, 209,513 chicken, 9,742 ducks and 648 turkeys.

Industries: Manufacture of furniture, textiles, metal products and grain mill products.

Education Services: Primary schools: 71 – 66 government, 4 private and 1 community. Primary school enrolment: 57,195 pupils – 29,733 male and 27,462 female. Primary school teachers: 765 – 591 male and 174 females. Available furniture is adequate for 30,540 pupils.

Secondary schools: 21 schools – 4 government, 10 private and 7 community. Secondary school enrolment as of 2009: 6,071 male and female not stated. Secondary school teachers: 392 –male and female not stated. Available furniture is adequate for only 5,861. Data on enrolment in private and community secondary schools not provided.

Health Services: 1 health centre IV (government), 2 health centre III (government), 1 health centre III (NGO), 5 health centres II (government).

Tourist Attractions (Developed and Potential): Ambitambe Crater Lake is found in Koboko County. Liru Historical Hill: Liru Hill is believed to be the first settlement of the early Luo tribes that migrated from Sudan. Up to now a number of traditional rituals are conducted at the hill by the Nubian tribe.

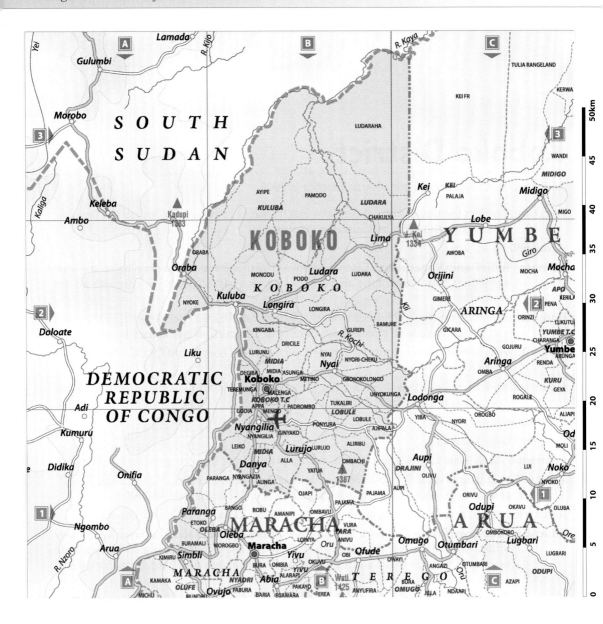

District Leaders:
District Chairperson – Mr Nginya Hassan S.
Chief Administrative Officer (CAO)
   – Mr Henry Harrison Makumbi
Deputy CAO – Vacant

Members of Parliament:
Koboko County – Mr Ahmed Awongo
District Woman MP
   – Ms Margaret Baba Diri

Maracha District

Up to July 2006, Maracha was a county in Arua District. When the county was elevated to a district status it was named Nyadri district. It comprised Maracha and Terego Counties. In 2010, Terego County was taken back to Arua District. The remaining district (Nyadri) was renamed Maracha.

Location: Maracha District borders the districts of Koboko to the north, Yumbe to the northeast, Arua to the east and south and the DRC to the west.

Climate, Relief and Vegetation: The district has heavy rainfall and moderately high temperature for most of the year.

Area: 443.0 sq. km.

Population: Based on 2009 projections, the district has 178,100 – 94,200 female and 83,900 male with a density of 402 persons per square kilometre.

Major Towns: Maracha Town Council. Trading centres: Oleba.

Counties and Sub-Counties: Maracha – Kijomoro, Nyadri, Oleba, Oluvu, Yivu, Tara and Olufe.

Main Language: Lugbara and Kakwa.

People: Lugbara, Madi and Kakwa.

Economic Activities: Agriculture with emphasis on food crops like cassava, simsim, maize, beans and cow peas. Communities along the River Nile engage in fishing as one of the livelihood activities. Tobacco is a major cash crop.

Animal Population: According to 2008 livestock census, Maracha district together with Terego county (before it transferred to Arua) had 123,640 cattle, 286,929 goats, 67,543 sheep, 29,222 pigs, 793,213 chicken, 32,534 ducks and 2,137 turkeys.

Education Services: Statistics of 2009: Primary schools: 66 - 58 government, 3 private, 5 community. Enrolment: 67,939 –male and female not stated. Teachers: 1,042 – male and female not reported.

Secondary schools: 11 secondary schools- 4 government, 3 private and 4 community schools. Student Enrolment: 4,385 –male and female not stated. Teachers: 216 –male and female not stated. Available furniture is adequate for 3,422 students.

Health Services: 1 hospital (NGO – Maracha Hospital with 160 beds), no health centre IV, 5 health centre III (all government), 5 health centre II (all government).

Transport Network: The existing road network is mainly loose surface (murrum), which is sometimes not in good condition; making transport within the district difficult.

Tourist Attractions: The district has tourism potential particulary of historical significance. Lugard's Fort is one of the few historical sites of the colonial government in Uganda. The site is of national significance and needs to be developed and protected. Other undeveloped sites are Alikwa Burial Monument, Ombo Historical Sites and Mount Vati.

Key NGOs: Same as Arua District

District Leaders:
Chair person – Achipio Emmanuel
Chief Administrative Officer (CAO)
    – Mr Ezaruku Kazimiro
Deputy Chief Administrative Officer
    (DCAO) – Vacant

Members of Parliament:
Maracha County
    – Mr Alex Aadroa Onzima
Woman MP
    – Ms Lematia Ruth Molly Ondoru

Moyo District

Present-day Moyo and Adjumani districts made up the former Madi district. Madi district was remaned Moyo in 1980. The district was reduced in size in 1997 when East Moyo county was elevated to a district status forming Adjumani District.

Location: Moyo borders the districts of Adjumani to the east and south, Arua to the west and the Republic of South Sudan to the north.

Area: 1,890.7 sq. km.

Climate and Relief: It lies at an approximate altitude of between 600m (at Nimule) and 1,586m above sea level, in a modified equatorial climatic zone with high temperatures and high rainfall.

Population: According to 2009 projections, there are 322,200 people - 167,600 female, 154,600 male with a density of 170 persons per square kilometre.

Major Town: Moyo (administrative headquarters).

Counties and Sub-counties: Obongi County – Aliba, Gimara, Itula; West Moyo County – Dufile, Metu, Moyo, Moyo (Town Council), Laropi, and Lefori.

Main Language: Madi.

People: Madi.

Economic Activities:
  (i) Mainly agriculture with coffee and cotton as the main cash crops.
  (ii) Fishing carried out on the River Nile.

Banks: Stanbic Bank Ltd – 2.

Area under Forestation: 70,719 hectares.

Animal Population: According to 2008 livestock census, the district had 103,873 cattle, 9,034 pigs, 37,742 sheep, 190,341 goats, 373,086 chicken 15,808 ducks and 776 turkeys.

Co-operative Societies: Moyo and Adjumani have 42 registered primary societies with Madi Union at the district level.

Industries: Coffee hulling, oil milling and cotton ginning.

Education Services: Statistics 2009: Primary schools: 75: 73 government, 2 private. Primary school enrolment: 33,262 pupils – 17,142 male and 16,120 female. Primary teachers: 674 – 464 male and 210 female. Available furniture is adequate for 24,926 pupils.

Secondary schools: 18 secondary schools - 6 government, 9 private and 3 community. Secondary school enrolment: 5,130 students – 3,413 male and 1,717 female. Teachers: 304 – 246 male and 58 female. Available furniture is adequate for only 4099 students.

Post secondary school: 1 technical institution, 1 teacher training college.

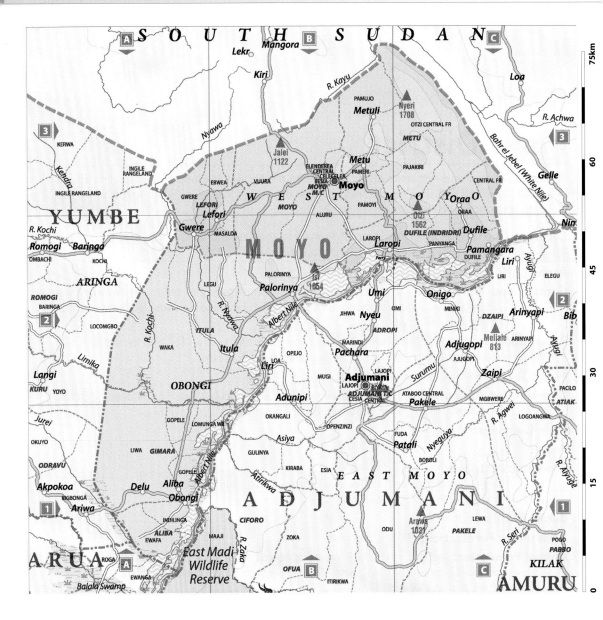

Health Services: 1 hospital (government- Moyo Hospital with 176 beds), 1 health centre IV (government), 9 health centre III (government), 3 health centre III (NGO), 20 health centre II (government) and 3 health centre II (NGO).

Tourist Attractions: It is a beautiful part of Uganda where the mountains of southern Sudan can be seen in the distance, standing out against the flat landscape all around. The River Nile which forms the eastern boundary of the district has potential for tourism along the banks.

Additional Information: The district is dependent on agriculture which is practised on a small scale. However, there are a few large scale farms. The number of livestock in the district is quite high. The main industries here are coffee hulling and cotton ginning

which do not employ many people. Telecommunication is only through radio and mobile phones.

Fishing has become a major employment sector in the district, but there are no fish processing plants. Most of the population is settled along the River Nile where the most agricultural activities take place. Land tenure is generally customary.

Key NGOs: Send a Cow Uganda SNV Uganda, Family Planning Association of Uganda, MS Uganda, Uganda Society for Disabled Children, Action against Domestic Violence, Action against Hunger, Africa Development and Emergency Organisation, Agency for Co-operation and Research and Development, Aktion Afrika Hilfe, Community Management Agency, International Aid (Sweden), Moyo Bee Keepers' Association, Moyo District Dairy Farmers' Association.

District leaders:	Members of Parliament:
Chairperson – Mr Jimmy O. Vukoni	West Moyo County – Mr AleroTom Aza
Chief Administrative Officer (CAO)	Obongi County
– Mr Aloysius Oloka	– Mr Hassan Kaps Fungaroo
Deputy Chief Administrative Officer	Woman MP – Ms Anne Auru
(DCAO) – Vacant	

Nebbi District

At Independence, Nebbi was part of the then West Nile District. In 1974, West Nile District was divided into North Nile, Central Nile and South Nile districts. South Nile became Nebbi District in 1980.

Location: Nebbi borders the districts of Arua to the north, Amuru to the east, Buliisa and Lake Albert to the southwest, the Democratic Republic of Congo to the south and Zombo to the west.

Area: 2,000.0 sq. km.

Climate and Relief: It lies at an altitudinal range of between 945m and 1,219m above sea level, with rainfall averaging 1,500mm and high temperatures of the modified equatorial climatic type.

Population: According to 2009 projections, there are 314,100 people – 165,500 female, 148,600 male with a density of 157 persons per square kilometre.

Major Towns: Nebbi (administrative headquarters) Pakwach Town Council; Trading Centres Agwok, Paroketto, Padwot.

Counties and Sub-counties: Jonam County – Pakwach (Town Council), Pakwach, Panyango, Panyimur, Wadelai and Alwi. Padyere County – Akworo, Atego, Erussi, Kucwiny, Nebbi (Town Council), Nebbi, Ndhew, Nyaravur and Parombo.

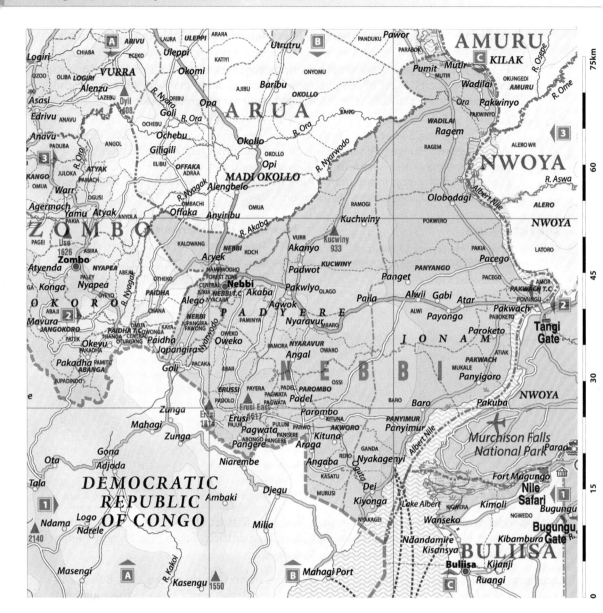

Main Languages: Alur and Jonam.

People: Alur.

Economic Activities: Mainly agriculture with emphasis on:
  (i)   Food crops: Cassava, maize, beans, sweet potatoes, cow peas, millet, sorghum and simsim (sesame).
  (ii) Cash crops: Coffee, cotton and sugar cane.
  (iii) Fruits and vegetables: Tomatoes, pawpaws, avocado, mangoes, oranges, lime, onions and cabbage.
  (iv) Fishing.

Banks: Stanbic Bank Ltd – 2.

Area under Forestation: 26,769 hectares (Nebbi and Zombo).

Animal Population: According to 2008 livestock census, Nebbi and Zombo had 101,952 cattle, 23 donkeys, 19,895 pigs, 46,084 sheep, 302,576 goats 583,704 chicken, 34,727 ducks and 1,304 turkey.

Co-operative Societies: Nebbi and Zombo districts have 69 registered primary societies with Okoro Co-operative Union and South West Nile Co-operative Union at the district level.

Industries: Coffee processing, cotton ginning, saw milling, pit sawing, furniture works and brick making.

Education Services: Primary schools: 185 – 163 government, 7 private, 15 community. Enrolment: 106,539 pupils – 56,263 male and 50,276 female. Teachers: 1,618 – 1,244 male and 374 female. Available furniture is adequate for 87,043 pupils.

Secondary schools: 24 secondary schools - 10 government, 7 private and 7 community schools. Student enrolment: 7,449 – 4,973 male and 2,476 female. Teachers: 431 – 359 male and 72 female. Available furniture was not reported.

Post secondary schools: 1 technical institution, 1 teacher training college.

Health Services: 2 hospitals (government), 1 health centre IV (government), 18 health centre III - (12 government and 6 NGO), 18 health centre II - (16 government and 2 NGO).

Additional Information: Nebbi District is located in the equatorial forest belt extending from the Democratic Republic of Congo. This is why activities like pit sawing and saw milling are common in the district. The district has reliable rainfall and fertile soils that support a wide range of crops. The climatic conditions favour arabica coffee.

There is also some banana growing in the area. Although the population is high, land is still adequate. The land tenure system is customary.

Transport Network: The district is linked to the neighbouring districts of Arua and Nwoya by the Arua-Kampala tarmac road that traverses the district from east to west. However, a poor feeder road network hinders the transportation of agricultural produce. Railway transport in the past alleviated the problem of transportation, but railway services have been halted for a number of years now.

Tourist Attractions: The district does not have a strong tourism base although the River Nile is a potential attraction.

Operational Radio Stations: Radio Paidha FM.

Key NGOs: Send a Cow Uganda, World Vision Uganda, MS Uganda. Actionaid Uganda, SNV Uganda, Action for Socio-Economic Development, CARITAS Nebbi, Kisa Womens' Group Kubbi Community Development Project, Nebbi District Muslim Development Association, Nebbi District NGO Forum, Nyapea Safe Motherhood & Child Care Association, Paidha Welfare Association, Uganda Society for Disabled Children, Youth Young Womens' Group.

District leaders:
Chairperson – Mr Esrom William Alenyo.
Chief Administrative Officer (CAO) – Mr Patric Otto Langoya
Deputy Chief Administrative Officer (DCAO) – Vacant
Town Clerk (Nebbi Town Council) – Mr Eric Fagayo
Acting Town Clerk (Pakwach Town Council) – Mr Nelson Oucha

Members of Parliament:
Padyere County – Mr Anywarach Joshua Carter
Jonam County – Mr Fred Mandir Jachan-Omach
Woman MP – Ms Acayo Christine Cwinya-Ai

Yumbe District

Formerly part of Arua District. In 2000, Aringa County of Arua District was given District status and named Yumbe district.

Location: It borders Moyo to the east, Arua to the south, Koboko to the west and the Republic of South Sudan to the north.

Area: 2,322.0 sq. km.

Climate and Relief: It lies at an approximate altitude of 945m and 1,219m above sea level and has high temperatures. Yumbe District has a modified equatorial climate.

Population: According to 2009 projections, there are 423,000 people – 207,600 females, 215,400 males with a density of 182 persons per sq. km.

Major Towns: Yumbe (administrative headquarters); Trading Centre – Aringa.

Counties and Sub-counties: Aringa County – Apo, Ariwa, Drajini/Arajim, Kei, Kerwa, Kochi, Kuru, Kululu, Odravu, Lodonga, Midigo, Romogi and Yumbe (Town Council)

Main Languages: Aringa, Kakwa and Madi.

People: Alur, Lugbara, Kakwa and Madi.

Economic Activities: Agriculture with emphasis on:
 (i) Food crops: Beans, cassava, maize, simsim, sorghum, groundnuts, bananas and peas.
 (ii) Cash crops: Tobacco.
 (iii) Fruits and vegetables: Pineapples, tomatoes and cabbage.

Area under Forestation: 138,573 hectares.

Animal Population: According to 2008 livestock census, the district had 223,649 cattle, 8 donkeys, 17,511 pigs, 151,356 sheep, 409,793 goats 709,483 chicken, 10,888 ducks and 1,097 turkeys.

Co-operative Societies Yumbe and Arua have 90 registered co-operative societies.

Industries: Craft making, tobacco curing, small scale brick making and carpentry.

Education Services: Statistics of 2009: Primary schools: 128 – 123 government, 3 private, 2 community. Primary school enrolment: 73,660 – 40,174 male and 33,486 female. Primary teachers: 1,552 – 1,215 male and 189 female. Available furniture is adequate for 50,750 pupils.

 Secondary schools: 13 schools- 3 government, 6 private and 4 community. Student enrolment: 7,437 – 5,081 male and 2,356 female. Teachers: 428 – 355 male and 73 female.

Health Services: 1 hospital (government - Yumbe Hospital with 108 beds) No health centre IV, 10 health centre III - (8 government and 2 NGO), 11 health centre II - (9 government and 2 NGO).

Key NGOs: SNV Uganda, Earth Care, Dragon Agroforestry Programme, Aringa Disaster Preparedness Forum, Aringa Association for Development Programmes, National Union of Disabled Persons in Uganda, Participatory Rural Action for Development, Uganda Change Agents Association, Islamic Medical Association of Uganda, Vocational Training Skill Development Centre – Yumbe.

District leaders:	Members of Parliament:
Chairperson – Mr Taban Yassin	Aringa County – Mr Achile Manoah Mila
Ag Chief Administrative Officer (CAO) – Mr Isa Mbooge	Woman MP – Ms Oleru Huda Abason
Deputy Chief Administrative Officer (DCAO) – Vacant	

Zombo District

At Independence, it was part of then West Nile District. In 1974, West Nile District was divided into North Nile, Central Nile and South Nile Districts. South Nile became Nebbi District in 1980. In 2009, Zombo District was created out of Nebbi district.

Location: Zombo borders the districts of Arua to the north, Nebbi to the east, and the Democratic Republic of Congo to the west and south.

Area: 899.0 sq. km.

Climate and Relief: It lies at an altitudinal range of between 945m and 1,219m above sea level, with rainfall averaging 1,500mm and high temperatures of the modified equatorial climatic type.

Population: According to 2009 projections, there are 199,400 people – 104,200 female, 95,200 male with a population density of 221 persons per sq.km.

Major Towns: Zombo (administrative headquarters) and Paidha; Trading Centres – Warr, Zeu, Kango and Nyapea.

Counties and Sub-counties: Okoro County – Abanga, Atyak, Jangokoro, Kango, Nyapea, Paidha, Paidha (Town Council), Warr, Zeu, Zombo (Town Council).

Main Languages: Alur and Jonam.

People: Alur.

Economic Activities: Mainly agriculture with emphasis on:
- (i) Food crops: Cassava, maize, beans, sweet potatoes, cow peas, millet, sorghum and simsim (sesame).
- (ii) Cash crops: Coffee, cotton and sugar cane.
- (iii) Fruits and vegetables: Tomatoes, pawpaws, avocado, mangoes, oranges, lime, onions and cabbage.
- (iv) Fishing.

Banks: Stanbic Bank Ltd – 2. Equity Bank.

Area under Forestation: 26,769 hectares (for Zombo and Nebbi).

Animal Population: Zombo and Nebbi have 101,952 cattle, 23 donkeys, 19,895 pigs, 46,084 sheep, 302,576 goats 583,704 chicken, 34,727 ducks and 1,304 turkeys.

Co-operative Societies: Okoro Co-operative Union and South West Nile Co-operative Union are the main societies.

Industries: Coffee processing, cotton ginning, saw milling, pit sawing, furniture works and brick making.

Education Services: Statistics of 2009: Primary schools: 96 – 86 government, 3 private, and 7 community schools. Enrolment: 56,130 – male and female numbers not stated. Teachers: 875 –male and female unreported.

Secondary schools: 11 secondary schools- 7 government, 1 private and 3 community schools. Student enrolment: 3,291 – male and female not stated. Teachers: 221 – male and female not stated. Available furniture is adequate for only 3,076 students.

Post secondary schools: 1 technical institution, 1 teacher training college.

Health Services: 1 hospital (NGO) with 121 beds, 5 health centre III (government), 3 health centre III (NGO), 7 health centre II (government) and 2 health centres II (NGO).

Additional Information: Zombo District is located in the equatorial belt extending from the Democratic Republic of Congo. This is why activities like pit sawing and saw milling are common in the district. The district has reliable rainfall and fertile soils that support a wide range of crops. The climatic conditions favour arabica coffee. There is also some banana growing in the district. The land tenure system is generally customary.

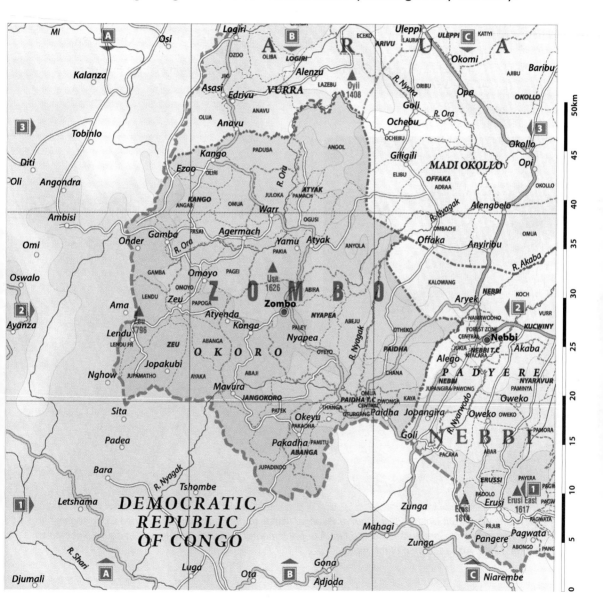

Transport Network: The poor transport network hinders the transportation of agricultural produce to urban areas and outside the district.

Tourist Attractions: The district does not have a strong tourism base.

Operational Radio Stations: Radio Paidha FM.

Key NGOs: Send a Cow Uganda, World Vision Uganda, MS Uganda. Actionaid Uganda, SNV Uganda, Action for Socio-Economic Development, CARITAS Nebbi, Kisa Womens' Group Kubbi Community Development Project, Nebbi District Muslim Development Association, Nebbi District NGO Forum, Nyapea Safe Motherhood & Child Care Association, Paidha Welfare Association, Uganda Society for Disabled Children, Youth Young Womens' Group.

District leaders:	Members of Parliament:
Chairperson – Mr Kakura Emmy K.	Okoro County
Ag Chief Administrative Officer (CAO) – Eliab Ntarwete Bagumya	– Mr Stanley Omwona Oribdhogu
Deputy Chief Administrative Officer (DCAO) – Vacant	Woman MP – Ms Kwiyucwiny Grace Freedom

Left: Alur king, Rwoth Ubimu Philip Olarker Rauni III listens to his Prime Minister, Prince Opar Angala Jalusonge during the inauguration of the first Alur parliament (Council of Traditional Chiefs) in Nebbi town in 2008. Right: Agwara dance of the Alur.

National Agricultural Research Organisation (NARO)

Introduction

National Agricultural Research Organisation (NARO) is an apex body established by the National Agricultural Research Act 2005 to coordinate, oversee and guide agricultural research in both public and private sector research institutions. NARO envisages a market-responsive, client-oriented and demand driven national agricultural research system comprising both public and private institutions working in tandem for the sustainable economic growth of Uganda. NARO's mission is to generate and disseminate appropriate, safe and cost effective techniques, while enhancing the natural resource base. Achieving the vision and mission will lead to sustainable agricultural productivity, sustained competitiveness, economic growth, food security and poverty eradication.

Evolution of Agricultural Research in Uganda

1898   Establishment of Botanic Gardens, Entebbe. Emphasis was on plantation crops such as rubber, coffee, tea and cotton for export to Britain.

1900   Establishment of Forestry and Scientific Department, and later transformed into Botanic, Forestry and Scientific Department in the Ministry of Agriculture between 1907 and 1910;

1919-1930   Establishment of Experimental Research Stations in Central (Bukalasa, Kikumiro, Kituza and Masaka); Eastern (Serere); and Western Uganda (Fort Portal and Naminage) as Makerere University was started in 1922;

1937   Relocation of research division to Kawanda and expansion of research under different ministries;

1992   Agricultural research remained as a department in the Ministry of Agriculture until NARO was set up by the 1992 statute as a body cooperates, semi-autonomous to coordinate and undertake research in crops, fisheries, forestry and livestock. All research came under one umbrella and 9 research institutes were established.

2000   Research decentralised to improve delivery of research service, and Agricultural Research and Development Centres (ARDCs) were established as part of the NARO outreach programme.

2005   NARO was reconstituted through the NARS Act 2005. This brought all institutions undertaking agricultural research using public resources under the coordination, oversight and guidance of NARO, including public agricultural research institutions, private sector, universities and civil society organisations.

Creation of NARO in 1992 resulted into considerable improvement in agricultural research service delivery and significant contribution to agricultural development. NARO become a strong well co-ordinated public agricultural research institution with a strong corporate image nationally, regionally and globally. Agricultural Research infrastructure was developed including a competent human resource capacity, physical and information resources.

Technical Achievements

Some of the technical achievements made by NARO at the time were:

- Control of the cassava mosaic pandemic
- Control of the water hyacinth which had paralysed fishing and power generation on Lake Victoria and Lake Kyoga
- Development of Newcastle Vaccine in poultry
- Development of clonal eucalyptus hybrid that matures in five years instead of 10 to 15years,
- Development of orange fleshed sweet potatoes varieties, very rich in Vitamin A
- Domestication of the Nile Perch,
- Development of high yielding cotton, maize, beans and sunflower; and fight against coffee wilt disease
- A study done by IFPRI in 2004 showed that investing in agricultural research was more paying than investment in feeder roads, education and health. For every 1 million shillings invested in agricultural research 58 people were lifted out of poverty as compared to 31, 13, and 5 invested in feeder roads, education and health, respectively.

However with the reform of 2005, NARO was again able to achieve some significant strides, and thus making agricultural research pluralistic comprising both public and private institutions working in tandem for the sustainable economic growth of Uganda.

Institutional set up and major programmes

The National Agricultural Research System (NARS) is governed by the NARO Council which is supported by a permanent Secretariat and has three committees of Finance and Administration, Science Committee and the user committee. At Public Agricultural Research Institute (PARI) level the Council is represented by the management committees. There are functions that cut across the institutes like procurement, audit, competitive grants scheme and management information system. The NARS is composed of six National Agricultural Research Institutes (NARIs), nine Zonal Agricultural Research and Development Institutes (ZARDIs) and Private Agricultural Research Service Providers (PARSP). The NARIs and ZARDIs are Public Agricultural Research Institutes (PARIs).

a) National Agricultural Research Institutes (NARIs)

I. National Crops Resources Research Institute (NACRRI)- Namulonge
II. National Fisheries Resources Research Institute ((NAFIRRI)-Jinja
III. National Forestry Resources Research Institute (NAFORRI)-Kifu, Mukono
IV. National Livestock Resources Research Institute ((NALIRRI)-Tororo
V. National Semi-Arid Resources Research Institute (NASARRI)-Serere, Soroti
VI. National Agricultural Research Laboratories-Kawanda

b) Zonal Agricultural Research and Development Institutes (ZARDIs)

i. Abi Zonal Agricultural Research and Development Institute-Arua
ii. Buginyanya Zonal Agricultural Research and Development Institute-Sironko
iii. Bulindi Zonal Agricultural Research and Development Institute-Hoima
iv. Mbarara Zonal Agricultural Research and Development Institute-Mbarara
v. Mukono Zonal Agricultural Research and Development Institute-Mukono
vi. Ngetta Zonal Agricultural Research and Development Institute-Lira
vii. Nabuin Zonal Agricultural Research and Development Institute-Nakapiripirit
viii. Kachwekano Zonal Agricultural Research and Development Institute-Kabale
ix. Rweitaba Zonal Agricultural Research and Development Institute–Kyenjojo

c) Some of the Private Agricultural Research Service Providers (PARSP) include:

i. AK-Oils and Fats Uganda Ltd, Kampala
ii. Uganda Rural Development and Training Programme (URDT)
iii. Enterprise Support and Community Development Trust (ENCOT)
iv. The Community Based Vector Control Organisation (COVECO)
v. Appropriate Technology Uganda Ltd (AT (U))
vi. Masindi District Farmers' Association (MADFA)
vii. Hoima Entrepreneurs Development Association (HODFA)
viii. OTTIS
ix. Environment Alert

The PARSP have been approved by the NARO Council and will be formerly registered when the appropriate statutory instrument is signed by the minister.

d) Some of the Universities and institutions that NARO work with include:

i. Makerere University
ii. Gulu University
iii. The Catholic University, Nkozi
iv. The Christian University, Mukono
v. Mbarara University of Science and Technology
vi. Civil society organisation

Staff Capacity

- NARO places lots of emphasis on the development of its human resource capacity, which comprises scientists , technicians and support staff
- NARO has established a staff capacity of 879, of which 248 are Scientists, 233 technicians and 398 support staff, and majority of them trained at master's and doctoral levels
- Collaborative linkages have been established with International Agricultural Research Centres, Fo¬rum for Agricultural Research in Africa (FARA), Association for Strengthening Agricultural Research in East and Central Africa (ASARECA)

Funding Mechanisms

Diversified and Sustainable Funding Mechanisms for the National Agricultural Research System Established

Funding for NARO 2005-2010 (Billions of shillings)

	2004/5	2005/6	2006/7	2007/8	2008/9	2009/10
Recurrent	2.0	2.3	2.4	5.5	2.9	4.5
Development	5.2	9.5	17.5	16.9	17.2	24.5
Donor	18.2	18.1	13.4	11.5	19.2	19.0
Total	25.4	29.9	33.3	33.9	39.3	48.0

NARO funding has steadily increased over the years

Future Plans

NARO's future plan is to have a robust, self-propelling, locally funded cohesive NARS that contributes to the development of Uganda. The NARS should be sustainably funded so as to tackle short and long term prob¬lems that affect agricultural development in Uganda. The private sector should be stimulated to participate fully and fund agricultural research. This in the long run will reduce the undesired donor dependency syndrome that has been the norm for a long time. Specifically the following will be done:

- Continue to support and back stop the NARO Council and its structures
- Support the new ZARDIs, Nabuin and Buginyanya   to take off
- Rwebitaba ZARDI in Kyenjojo District be operationalised
- Finalise the NARS Strategy 2007-2017
- Develop and implement a mid-term plan 2009-2014
- Mobilise financial resources for the research follow-up on project
- Push for legalising and operationalisation of ARTF
- Brand NARO as a real corporate concern on the African continent
- Promote public-private parternship in delivery of research services and products
- Support the PARIs and non-PARIs to carry out their work efficiently and effectively

Challenges

Despite good progress so far made, there are many challenges, which include the need to: strengthen and promote advisory and extension services so as to increase the flow of technologies to end users; empower the non-public agricultural research service providers to participate in the implementation and funding of agricultural research; develop capacity for market-oriented research; eliminate asymmetrical information flow within the value chain markets; empower clients to demand research services and; diversify sources of financial support foragricultural research, and sharing of knowledge and information within NARO and with other research service providers and end users. Although decentralisation of research is important for empowering stakeholders, and strengthening the process of feedback and institutional learning, there is need for boosting the capacities of ZARDIs for research and development processes in the different agro¬ ecological zones.

Location: NARO Secretariat, 11-13 Lugard Avenue, Entebbe
Chairperson: Professor Frederick I.B Kayanja
Director General: Dr. Denis T. Kyetere

Northern Districts

Agago	Alebtong	Amolatar	Amuru	Apac	Dokolo	Gulu	Kitgum	Kole	Lamwo
Lira	Nwoya	Otuke	Oyam	Pader					

The People: The districts are inhabited by mainly the Acholi and the Langi. Their main economic activity is cultivation and cotton is the region's main cash crop.

Tourism: There are many tourist attractions that include wild game in the Murchison Falls National Park. The park is inhabited by elephants, lions, crocodiles, hippos, birds and many other small animals. There are tourist lodges at Paraa and Pakuba.

How to get there: There is access by road and air. There is a tarmac road from Kampala to Gulu and Lira as well as from Kampala via Soroti to Lira. The rest of the roads in the region are gravel. There are regular buses and other passenger service vehicles to the region from Kampala.

There are airstrips at Gulu and Lira. The Gulu airstrip is tarmac and offers safe landing for large aircrafts. Eagle Air has scheduled flights to Gulu.

The Lira-Pakwach railway line is currently out of service.

Sub-divisions: This general region is divided into smaller regions of Acholi and Lango.

The "Devil's Cauldron", part of the stunningly beautiful Murchison Falls on the River Nile in Gulu district (left). The rich cultural history of the people as expressed through the Sir Samuel Baker fort in Gulu (right).

Northern Districts

Agago District

Formerly part of Kitgum District. In 2000, two counties of Kitgum District (Agago and Aruu) became Pader District. In 2010 Agago County was elevated to a district status.

Location: Agago District borders the districts of Lamwo and Kitgum to the north, Kotido and Abim to the east, Gulu to the west, and Otuke to the south.

Area: 3,494.0 sq km.

Climate and Relief: It lies at an approximate altitude of 351m – 1,341m above sea level, with rainfall ranging between 1,000mm and 1,500mm per annum and temperatures around 25°C.

Population: According to the 2009 population projection, the district has 253,700 people – 127,900 female, 125,800 male with a density of 72 persons per sq.km.

Major Towns: Kalongo (administrative headquarters), Lokole and Patongo.

Counties and Sub-counties: Agago County – Adilang, Arum, Lapono, Arum, Lira-Palwor, Lokole, Omot, Paimol, Parabongo, Patongo, Kotomor, Lamiyo, Omiya Pacwa, Wol, Kalongo (Town Council) and Patongo Town Council, Lokole (Town Council).

Main Languages: Luo and Acholi.

Economic Activities: Agriculture with emphasis on:
 (i)   Food crops: Sorghum, finger millet, groundnuts, sweet potatoes, bananas and rice.
 (ii) Cash crops: Cotton.
 (iii) Fruits and vegetables: Tomatoes, onions and cabbage.

Area under Forestation: 52,706 hectares.

Animal Population: Agago and Pader together have 57,087 cattle, 39,430 pigs, 6,298 sheep, 57,807 goats, 150,317 chicken 43,197, ducks and 1,144 turkeys.

Co-operative Societies: Agago, Pader and Kitgum have 128 registered co-operative societies.

Industries: Grain milling, cotton ginning, brick making and furniture making.

Education Services: Statistics of 2009: Primary schools: 116 – 111 government, 2 private and 3 community. Primary school enrolment: 70,456 pupils – 37,747 male and 32,709 female. Primary school teachers: 897 – 757 male and 140 female.

 Secondary schools: 8 schools - 5 government, 1 private, and 2 community. Secondary school enrolment: 3,669 – 2,700 male and 969 female. Teachers: 157 – 141 male and 16 female.

Health Services: – 1 hospital -Kalongo Hospital (NGO), 7 health centre III (government) and 10 health centre II (government).

Key NGOs: African Medical Research Foundation Uganda, World Vision Uganda.

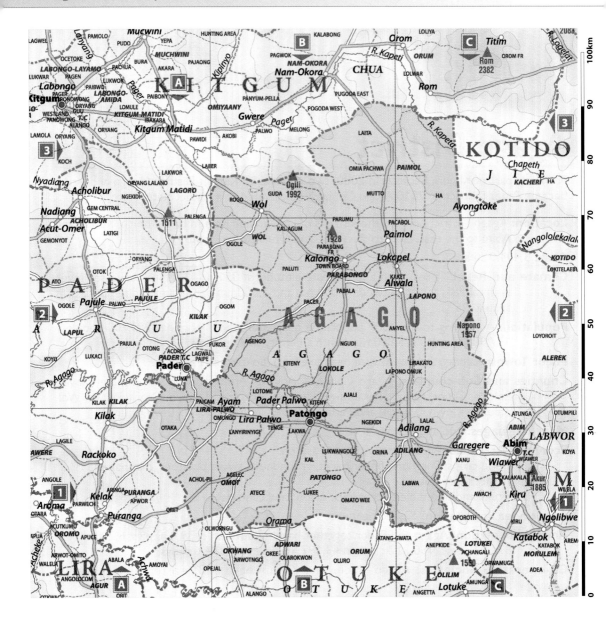

District leaders:
Chairperson – Mr Odok Peter W.
Ag Chief Administrative Officer (CAO)
    – Mr Mark Tivu
Deputy Chief Administrative Officer
    (DCAO) – Vacant

Members of Parliament:
Agago County – Mr Okot John Amos
Woman MP – Ms Akello Judith Franca

Alebtong District

Alebtong District was part of Lira District which was part of the former Lango District. Under the provincial administration, Lango was divided into West Lango and East Lango districts in 1974. In 1980, East Lango was renamed Lira District with Moroto as one of the counties. In 2009 Moroto was elevated to a district status with its headquarters at Alebtong, hence the name.

Location: It borders the districts of Dokolo and Kaberamaido to the south, Lira to the west, Otuke to the north, Katakwi to the east and Moroto to the northeast.

Area: 1,527.0 sq. km.

Climate and Relief: It lies at an approximate altitude of between 975m and 1,146m above sea level and the rainfall ranges between 1,000mm – 1,500mm, with high temperatures.

Population: Based on 2009 projection: - 201,000 people – 97,100 male and 103,900 female with a density of 131 persons per sq.km.

Major Towns: Alebtong (administrative headquarters); Trading Centres – Amugo and Omoro.

Counties and Sub-counties: Moroto County –Abia, Akura, Aloi, Alebtong (Town Council), and Apala. Ajuri County – Abako, Amugu, Awei, and Omoro

Main Languages: Luo and Lango.

People: Langi, Iteso, Acholi, Bagisu, Alur, Kumam, Baganda, Banyoro, Basoga, other Ugandans and non Ugandans.

Economic Activities: Mainly agriculture with emphasis on:
(i)   Food crops: Cassava, finger millet, maize, sorghum, pigeon peas, beans, simsim (sesame), groundnuts and sunflower.
(ii) Cash crops: Cotton, coffee and sugar cane.
(iii) Vegetables: Tomatoes, onions and cabbage.

Area under Forestation: 68,785 hectares.

Animal Population: According to 2008 livestock census, Alebtong, Lira, Kole, and Otuke had 159,533 cattle; 161,711 goats; 12,749 sheep; 28,631 pigs; 1,116,903 chickens, 30,927 ducks and 4,927 turkeys.

Co-operative Societies: 103 registered primary societies.

Industries: Oil and grain milling, cotton ginning, milk processing. Manufacture of food products and beverages, products of wood cork except furniture, articles of straw plaiting materials.

Banks: Stanbic Bank Uganda Ltd –1, Centenary Rural Development Bank –1.

Education Services: Primary schools: 78 – 76 government and 2 community. Primary school enrolment: 57,353 – 30,129 male and 27,224 female. Primary school teachers: 910 –male, female not reported. Available furniture is adequate for 19,509 pupils.

Secondary schools: 6 schools – 5 government and 1 community. Secondary school enrolment: 2,677 students – 1,338 male and 1,339 female. Teachers: 138 – 116 male and 22 female. Available furniture is adequate for 1,323 students.

Health Services: 1 health centre IV (government), 1 health centre IV (NGO); 1 health centre III (government); 13 health centre II (12 government and 1 NGO).

Transport Network: The district has a well distributed feeder-road network. The roads link up all the sub-counties and are all murram roads. The main means of transportation connecting the main town and other trading centres is taxi and pick-up trucks.

Tourist Attractions: The district has hardly any tourist attractions.

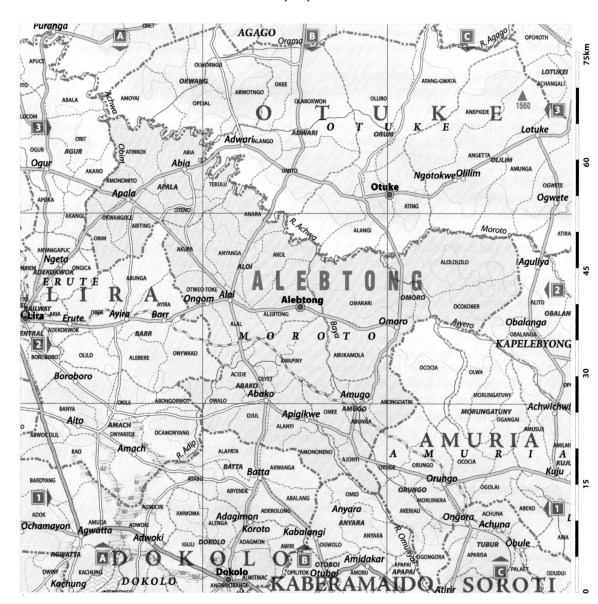

Operational Radio and TV Stations: Radio Apac based in Lira, Uganda Broadcasting Corporation Radio, Unity Investments, Rhino FM, Radio Management Services (U) Ltd, Radio Wa-Lira Diocese and Estalup Enterprises and Uganda Broadcasting Corporation Television.

Key NGOs: Same as in Lira District - Send a Cow Uganda, Uganda Project Implementation and Management Centre, Uganda Women's Effort to Save Orphans, Uganda Shelter Programme, ABOA Care for Children with HIV/AIDS.

District leaders:	**Members of Parliament:**
Chairperson – Odongo David K.	Moroto County – Mr Benson Obua Ogwal
Ag Chief Administrative Officer (CAO)	Ajuri County – Mr Obua Denis Hamson
– Mr Opio Leonard Ojok	Woman MP – Ms Amuge Rebecca Otengo
Deputy Chief Administrative Officer	
(DCAO) – Vacant	

Amolatar District

Amolator District was carved out of Lira District in 2005.

Location: It borders the districts of Kaberamaido to the east, Lira to the north, Apac to the west, Dokolo to the northeast, Kayunga, Kamuli and Nakasongola to the south.

Area: 1,760.0 sq. km.

Climate, Relief and Vegetation: Flat with savannah grasslands and the tributaries of Lake Kyoga to the south with the population distributed along the lake area.

Population: According to 2009 projections, there are 114,900 people – 56,800 males and 58,100 females with a population density of 65 persons per sq.km.

Major Towns: Amolatar, Akongomit, and Adonyimo.

Counties and Sub-counties: Kyoga County – Agikdak, Agwingiri, Akwon, Arwotcek, Aputi, Awelo, Etam, Muntu, Namasale and Amolatar (Town Council).

Main Language: Luo and Lango

People: Langi, Kumam, Iteso, Acholi, other Ugandans and non-Ugandans.

Economic Activities: Fishing, poultry, animal and crop production.

Animal Population: 81,269 cattel, 70,318 goats, 11,503 sheep, 34,293 pigs, 265,076 chicken, 15,780 ducks, and 1,189 turkeys.

Industries: Manufacture of grainmill products and other food products.

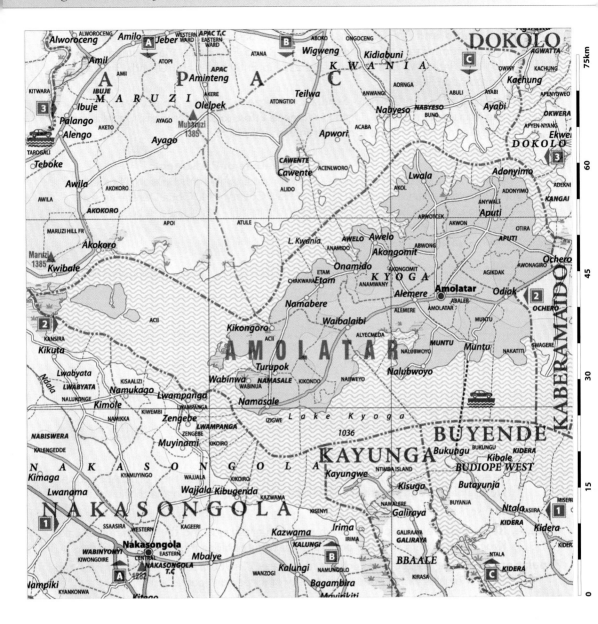

Education Services: Primary schools: 58 total – 49 government, 5 private and 4 community. Primary school enrolment: 41,984 pupils – 22,030 male and 19,954 female. Primary school teachers: 673 – 568 male and 105 female. Furniture available is adequate for only 22,347 pupils.

Secondary schools: 6 schools (all government). Secondary school enrolment: 2,224 – 1,443 male and 781 female. Teachers: 112 – 98 male and 14 female. Available furniture is adequate for 1,616 students.

Post secondary school institutions: 2 government and 1 NGO tertiary institutions.

Health Services: 1 hospital (NGO), 1 health centre III (government), 7 health centre II (government), 2 health centre II (NGO).

Tourist Attractions (Developed and Potential):

Lakes Kwania and Kyoga: These lakes comprise of open water surface, swampy papyrus shores and sandy landing sites. Fishing villages, canoeing, angling, bird watching and community tourism are some of the potential attractions. It is also possible to develop resort/picnic campsites and other hotel establishments at the shore areas.

Wetlands (Kyoga, Dokolo and Erute) are habitat to a variety of bird species with great potential as a major birding destination.

Gwata Forest Plantation – The forest provides opportunity for nature/forest walks. If combined with other tourism attractions in the district, such as community/market visits, it could promote development of eco-toursim.

District Leaders:	**Members of Parliament:**
District Chairperson – Mr Ongom Simon P.	Kioga County – Mr Okello Anthony
CAO – Joseph Balisanyuka	District Woman MP
DCAO – Vacant	– Mr Amali Caroline Okao

Amuru District

Amuru is one of the ten districts that were formed in July, 2006. Until then it was a county of Gulu District which then consisted of Kilak, Nwoya, Omoro, Aswa counties and Gulu Municipality.

Location: It borders the districts of Gulu to the east, Nwoya to the south, Nebbi and Arua to the west where River Nile forms the boundary, Adjumani to the northwest, Lamwo to the northeast and the Republic of South Sudan to the north.

Area: 3,625.0 sq. km.

Climate and Relief: It lies at an approximate altitude of 351m – 1,341m above sea level in a modified equatorial zone with high temperatures at a diurnal range of 4°C. Rainfall averages 1,540mm from April to November.

Population: Based on 2009 projections, there are: 161,700 people – 79,200 female and 82,500 male with a population density of 44 persons per sq.km.

Major Towns: Amuru Town Council.

Counties and Sub-counties: Kilak County – Amuru Town Council, Amuru, Atiak, Lamogi and Pabbo;

Main Language: Luo

People: Acholi

Economic Activities: Agriculture with emphasis on:
(i)   Food crops: Finger millet, maize, sweet potatoes, groundnuts, cow peas and pigeon peas, bananas, cassava and rice.
(ii) Cash crops: Tobacco, sugar cane, cotton and simsim (sesame).
(iii) Vegetables: Cabbage.
(iv) Fishing on the northern tip of Lake Albert and along the River Nile.

Animal Population: Amuru and Nwoya have 33,063 cattle; 67,092 goats; 9,773 sheep; 19,180 pigs; 142,121 chicken; 44,754 ducks and 2,558 turkeys.

Co-operative Societies: People still attached to associations in Gulu District.

Industries: There are no industries in the district.

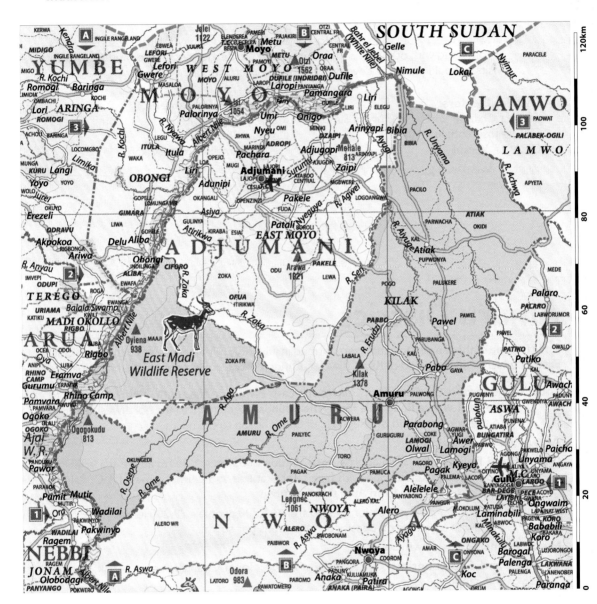

Education Services: Primary Schools: 56 total – 52 government, 2 private and 2 community. Primary school enrolment: 39,545 pupils – 21,212 male and 18,333 female. Primary school teachers: 564 – 421 male and 143 female. Available furniture is adequate for 17,735 pupils.

Secondary schools: 6 - 3 government, 1 private and 2 community. Secondary school enrolment: 2,320 – 1,703 male and 617 female. Teachers: 104 – 85 male and 19 female. Available furniture is adequate for 1,927 students.

Banks: The district is still dependent on the banks in Gulu District

Health Services: 1 health centre IV (government); 4 health centre III (2 government and 2 NGO); and 14 health centre II (all government).

Transport Network: All roads in the district are murram feeder-roads and are concentrated in the northern parts of the district. Transportation is provided by taxi and pick-up trucks.

Tourist Attractions: The district has no particular tourist attractions but its proximity to the East Madi Wildlife Reserve provides some tourism potential.

Operating Radio Stations: The district has the following radio stations: Radio Four Gulu, Norah Media Group Ltd, Uganda Broadcasting Corporation Radio, Radio Maria Uganda Association.

Key NGOs: AT Uganda Ltd, MS Uganda, Send a Cow Uganda, African Medical Research Foundation, Family Planning Association of Uganda, World Vision Uganda, Jamii Ya Kupatanisha, Peoples' Voice for Peace, Punena Child and Family Programme.

District Leaders:	**Members of Parliament:**
District Chairperson – Mr Atube Omach Anthony Louis	Kilak County – Mr Olanya Gilbert
Ag Chief Administrrative Officer (CAO) – Samuel Okot	Women MP – Ms Atuku Bigombe Betty
Deputy Chief Administrrative Officer (DCAO) – Vacant	
Town Clerk (Amuru Town Coucil – Mr Atube, Anthony Louis	

Apac District

Apac is part of former Lango District which existed at independence in 1962. Under the 1974 Provincial Administration, Lango was divided into West Lango and East Lango, which later became Apac and Lira districts, respectively.

Location: Apac lies north of Lake Kyoga and borders the districts of Masindi to the west, Lira to the east, Gulu to the north and Nakasongola to the south.

Area: 3,350.2 sq. km.

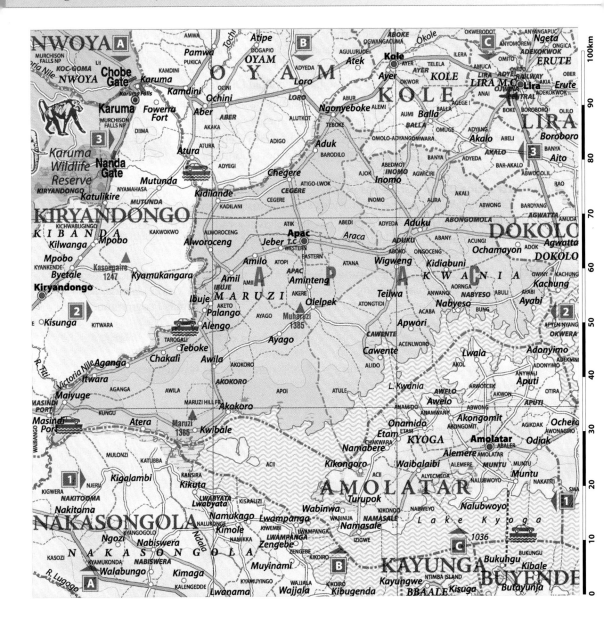

Climate and Relief: Rainfall averages between 1,000mm – 1,500mm per annum. Temperatures range over 25°C and vegetation includes woodlands, grass and thickets. The lowest point is about 700m above sea level at Karuma falls. The highest point is 1383m above sea level.

Population: Based on 2009 projections: 309,500 people – 151,100 male 158,400 female with a population density of 92 persons per sq.km.

Major Towns: Apac (administrative headquarters); Trading Centres – Aduku, Akokoro, Awia and Ibuje.

Counties and Sub-counties: Kwania County – Aduku Town Council, Aduku, Abongomola, Cawente, Inomo, and Nambieso; Maruzi County – Akokoro, Apac, Apac (Town Council), Chegere, Ibuje.

Main Language: Luo/Lango.

People: Langi.

Economic Activities: Agriculture with a bias towards:
  (i)   Food crops: Maize, finger millet, cassava, beans, simsim (sesame), pigeon peas, groundnuts, sunflower, cow peas and bananas.
  (ii) Cash crops: Tobacco, cotton and sugar cane.
  (iii) Fruits, vegetables: Tomatoes, cabbage, onions and sunflower.
  (iv) Fishing on Lake Kyoga.

Area under Forestation: 69,088 hectares.

Animal Population: 225,088 cattle, 28,442 pigs, 45,967 sheep, 279,649 goats, 939,652 chicken, 34,899 ducks and 4,043 turkeys.

Co-operative Societies: Apac and Oyam districts have 114 registered primary co-operative societies with Lango Co-operative Union as the umbrella co-operative union dealing mainly in cotton.

Industries: Small scale furniture work, engineering. The highest single employing company is an engineering firm with about 30 people.

Banks: Stanbic Bank Uganda Ltd – 1.

Education Services: Primary schools: 131 – 125 government, 4 community 2 private. Primary school enrolment: 100,390 – 50,268 male, 50,122 female. Primary school teachers: 1,541 – 1,224 male and 317 female. Data about furniture was not fully availed.

Secondary schools: 13 schools – 9 government, 4 private. Secondary school enrolment: 4,907 students – 2,894 male and 2,013 female. Teachers: 302 – 263 male and 39 female. Post secondary school: 3 technical institutions, 2 teacher training colleges, 1 business college – Uganda College of Commerce at Aduku.

Health Services: 1 hospital (government – Apac Hospital with a total of 100 beds); 1 health centre IV (government); 6 health centre III- (5 government and 1 NGO); 18 health centre II - (15 government and 3 NGO).

Transport Network: All roads leading to the district are murram roads. The district has a well distributed feeder-road network that links most parts of the district.

In the south, there is water transport linking Apac to Kiryandongo District via Masindi Port across the Nile and to Nakasongola and Soroti districts across Lake Kyoga.

Tourist Attractions: There are unexploited tourism opportunities in the district. Lake Kyoga, Lake Bisina and Lake Kwania have tourism potential, but there is no infrastructure to cater for tourism in the district.

Scenery viewing: The following scenic areas are unique to Lira and could become of national significance: the inselbergs at Ngeta and the monotonous shear tree vegetation in Otuke County. The rocky hills in the municipality provide a good view of Lira town and beyond.

Sporting activities: Lira town is one of the few in the country with a sizeable golf course. The pitch attracts the sports fraternity to visit Lira for days. If additional infrastructure such as swimming pools and tennis courts are developed they would promote tourism in the area.

Additional Information: There is little industrial activity. Even the informal sector – garages, metal and wood workshops operate on a small scale, they are few and their contribution is not visible.

But food production, especially millet, cassava, simsim and pigeon peas is high and are sold in the markets. Although the farmers themselves do not go to the markets in other districts, middlemen buy the foodstuffs from the farmers at cheap prices and sell them at higher prices in other parts of the country.

Operational Radio Station: Radio Apac.

Key NGOs: Send a Cow Uganda, Actionaid Uganda, MS Uganda, Traditional and Modern Health Practitioners, Apac Disabled Persons Union, Apac District Farmers' Association, Apac District Scouts Council, Campaign Against Domestic Violence in the Community, Apac Development Foundation Limited, Golgotha Orphanage Care, Care International in Uganda.

District leaders:	Members of Parliament:
Chairperson – Mr Okae Bob	Maruzi County
Chief Administrative Officer (CAO)	– Mr Akora Maxwell Ebong Patrick
– Mr Andrew Leru	Kwania County – Mr Ayoo Tonny
Town Clerk (Apac Town Council)	Woman MP – Ms Ajok Lucy
– Mr Dennis Egwel	

Dokolo District

Dokolo was one of the counties of Lira District, then consisting of Erute, Kioga, Moroto, Otuke and Dokolo counties as well as Lira Municipality. Dokolo County was elevated to district status in July 2006.

Location: Dokolo District borders the districts of Alebtong and Lira to the north, Kaberamaido to the east and southeast, Amolatar to the south and Apac to the west.

Area: 1,071.0 sq. km.

Climate, Relief and Vegetation: The rainfall ranges between 1000mm – 1,500mm and is accompanied by high temperatures.

Population: Based on 2009 Projections, there are 162,000 people – 82,800 female and 78,200 male with a density of 151 persons per sq.km.

Major Towns: Dokolo Town Council; Trading centres: Agwatta

Counties and Sub-counties: Dokolo County – Adekinno, Adok, Agwatta, Amwoma, Batta, Dokolo, Dokolo Town Council, Kangai Kwera, Okwalongwen and Okwongodul.

Main Language: Lango and Luo.

People: Langi

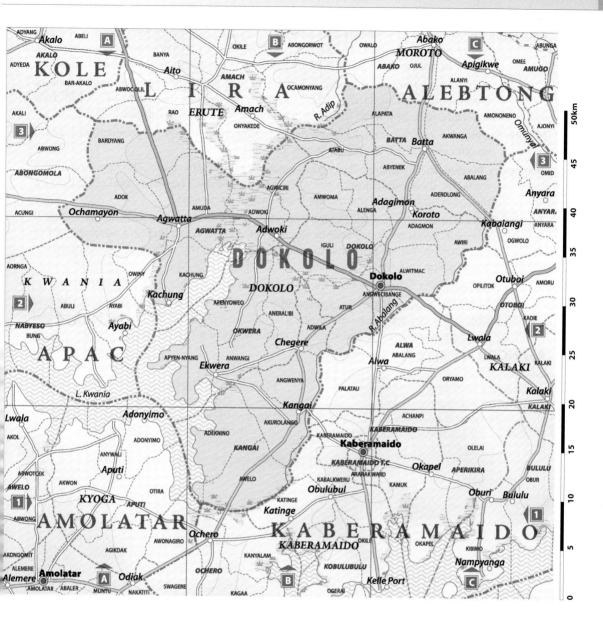

Economic Activities: Mainly agriculture with emphasis on food crops like cassava, finger millet, maize, sorghum, pigeon peas, beans, simsim, groundnuts and sunflower. In addition, vegetables like tomatoes, onions and cabbage are grown. Communites bordering the eastern arm of Lake Kwania engage in fishing.

Animal Population: 58,902 cattle, 71,815 goats, 16,361 sheep, 13,602 pigs, 291,027 chicken, 14,777 ducks and 623 turkeys.

Co-operative Societies: The new district still shares the Co-operative services of Lira District

Industries: Similar to those in Lira District.

Banks: As those in Lira District.

Education Services: Primary schools: 71– 54 government, 8 community and 9 private. Primary school enrolment: 49,434 – 24,978 male, 24,456 female. Primary school teachers: 725 –596 male and 129 female. Reported furniture is adequate for only 24,110 pupils.

Secondary schools: 7 schools – 5 government and 2 private. Secondary school enrolment: 2,488 students – 1,680 male and 808 female. Teachers: 147 – 128 male and 19 female. Reported furniture is adequate for only 1,987 pupils.

Health Services: 1 health centre IV (government); 3 health centre III (all government); and 8 health centre II - (6 government and 2 NGO).

Transport Network: The district has a good network of murram roads. The light intensity of traffic on these roads keeps them in good condition. The newly sealed Soroti-Lira tarmac road traverses the district from east to northwest.

Tourist Attractions: The Gwata Forest provides opportunity for nature/forest walks. If combined with other attractions like market visits, it could facilitate development of eco-tourism. Other potential tourist attractions are the expansive wetlands which are a habitat to a range of species.

Orweny Rice Scheme: Could be developed as an agricultural tourism attraction.

Historical sites/Antiquities: Located in the interior of the district is one of the few sites in the district that have historical significance because the Kings of Bunyoro and Buganda, Kabalega and Mwanga, respectively, were arrested there.

Key NGOs: As those in Lira District

District Leaders:	Members of Parliament:
District Chairperson – Mr John Baptist Okello-Okello CAO – Mr Julius Peter Odongkara	Dokolo County – Mr Felix Ogong Okot Woman MP – Ms Atim Ogwal Cecilia Barbara

Gulu District

Gulu is part of the former Acholi District which existed at Independence. In 1974, Acholi District was divided into East Acholi and West Acholi which later became Kitgum and Gulu Districts, respectively in 1980. Until July 2006, it comprised of Kilak, Nwoya, Omoro and Aswa counties as well as Gulu Municipality.

Location: It borders the districts of Lamwo in the northeast, Pader in the east, Oyam in the south, Nwoya in the southwest and Amuru in the west and northwest.

Area: 3,449.0 sq. km.

Climate and Relief: It lies at an approximate altitude of 351m – 1,341m above sea level in a modified equatorial zone with high temperatures at a diurnal range of 4°C. Rainfall averages 1,540mm from April to November.

Population: Based on 2009 Projections: 357,400 people- 175,600 males and 181,800 females with a density of 103 persons per sq.km.

Major Towns: Gulu (administrative headquarters); Trading Centres – Atiak, Awaka and Pabbo.

Counties and Sub-counties: Omoro County – Bobi, Koro, Lakwana, Lalogi, Odek, Ongako; Aswa County – Awach, Bungatira, Paicho, Patiko, Palaro and Unyama. Gulu Municipality – Bar-Dege, Laroo, Layibi, Pece.

Main Language: Luo.

People: Acholi.

Economic Activities: Agriculture with emphasis on:
- (i) Food crops: Finger millet, maize, sweet potatoes, groundnuts, cow peas and pigeon peas, bananas, cassava and rice.
- (ii) Cash crops: Tobacco, sugar cane, cotton and simsim (sesame).
- (iii) Vegetables: Cabbage.
- (iv) Fishing on the western end of the district in the River Nile.

Area under Forestation: 469,384 hectares.

Animal Population: Gulu has 40,130 cattle, 65,301 goats, 4,289 sheep, 26,569 pigs, 299,830 chicken 62,358 ducks and 5,211turkeys.

Co-operative Societies: The major societies are Middle North Tobacco Co-operative Union and West Acholi Growers Co-operative Union, both district unions.

Industries: Manufacture of ox-ploughs, saw milling, cotton ginning, furniture works and brick making.

Banks: Stanbic Bank, Centenary Rural Development Bank, Crane bank, DFCU Bank, Bank of Uganda (Regional Currency Centre).

Education Services: Statistics of 2009: Primary schools: 160 – 146 government, and 14 private. Primary school enrolment: 112,175 – 57,157 male and 55,018 female. Primary school teachers: 20,64 –1,218 male and 846 female. Reported furniture is adequate for only 76,592 pupils.

Secondary schools: 28 schools – 14 government, 1 community and 13 private. Secondary school enrolment: 16,132 – 10,156 male and 5,976 female. Teachers: 775 – 609 male and 166 female. Available furniture is adequate for 15,012 students.

Tertiary: 1 technical institution, 2 teacher training colleges and 1 national teachers' college – Unyama NTC. 1 University – Gulu University of Agriculture and Environmental Science.

Health Services: 2 government hospitals – (1 regional referral hospital – Gulu Hospital with 250 beds, 1 district hospital – Anaka Hospital with 104 beds and 1 private hospital – Gulu Independent with 80 beds); 2 health centre IV (government); 12 health centre III (11 government, 1 NGO) and 15 health centre II (10 government, 5 NGO).

Transport Network: The district is linked by a tarmac road to Kampala through Oyam, Kiryandongo, Masindi, Nakasongola, Luweero and Wakiso districts. The rest of the roads in the district are murram, feeder-roads many of which are in bad shape. The district is also connected to the railway network which crosses the middle of the district from Lira to Pakwach in Nebbi District. The district has lost this vital and cheap means of transport since the railway ceased operations following the suspension of train services along the northern railway line. Gulu has an airfield which facilitates air transport. Scheduled and chartered flights are available.

Gulu Airfield – Gulu Airfield is a designated entry and exit point. The runway is 3,110m x 45m and within acceptable operational limits. The terminal building is in good condition. The Civil Aviation Authority provides H.F. radio communication. The airfield is 1.9 km from Gulu town.

Communication – Telephone services are provided by UTL, MTN Warid and Airtel. Public pay phone services are available in town.

Operational Radio Stations: Radio Four Gulu, Norah Media Group Ltd, UBC (Radio), Radio Maria Uganda Association.

Key NGOs: AT Uganda Ltd, MS Uganda, Send a Cow Uganda, African Medical Research Foundation, Family Planning Association of Uganda, World Vision Uganda, Jamii Ya Kupatanisha, Peoples' Voice for Peace, Punena Child and Family Programme.

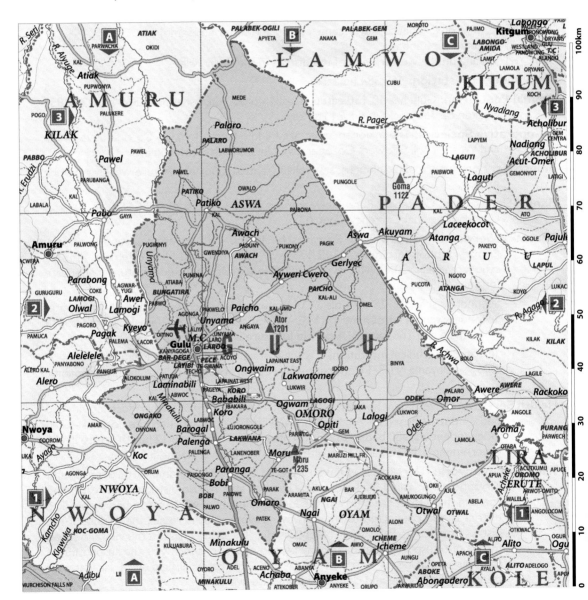

District leaders:
Chairperson – Mr Ojara Martin M.
Chief Administrative Officer (CAO)
　– Mr Abdallah Musobya Kiganda
Deputy Chief Administrative Officer
　(DCAO) – Vacant
Town Clerk　Gulu Municipality
　– Mr Augustin Bujara Rukiika
Mayor　Gulu Municipality
　– Mr George Labeja

Members of Parliament:
Gulu Municipality – Mr Acire Christopher
Aswa County – Mr Ronald Reagan Okumu
Omoro County
　– Mr Oulanyah Jacob L'okori
Woman MP – Ms Betty Ocan Aol

Kitgum District

At independence in 1962, Kitgum was part of Acholi District. Under the 1974 provincial administration, Acholi District was divided into two districts, West and East Acholi. The latter became Kitgum District in 1980.

Location: It borders the districts of Lamwo to the west, Pader to the south, Kaabong and Kotido to the east, Agago and Pader to the south, and the Republic of South Sudan to the north.

Area: 3,958.6 sq. km.

Climate and Relief: It lies at an approximate altitude of between 351m – 1,341m above sea level with temperatures of over 25°C per annum. Rainfall ranges between 1,000mm –1500mm annually.

Population: According to 2009 projections, there are 215,936 people – 109,616 female, 106,320 male with a density of 54 persons per sq. km.

Main Towns: Kitgum (administrative headquarters); Trading Centre – Kitgum-Matidi, Mucwini.

Counties and Sub-counties: Chua County – Akwang, Kitgum (Town Council), Kitgum-Matidi, Lagoro, Labongo-Amida, Labongo-Layamo, Mucwini, Nam-Okora, Omiya-Anyima, Orom

Main Languages: Luo and Acholi.

People: Acholi.

Economic Activities: Mainly agriculture with emphasis on:
　(i)　Food crops: Finger millet, sorghum, maize, groundnuts, beans, sweet potatoes, cassava, cow peas, pigeon peas, simsim (sesame), bananas and rice.
　(ii)　Cash crops: Cotton, sugar cane, simsim (sesame) and sunflower.
　(ii)　Vegetables: Tomatoes, onions and cabbage.
　(iii)　Cattle keeping.

Banks: Stanbic Bank Uganda Ltd – 1.

Area under Forestation: 475,309 hectares (for Kitgum and Lamwo).

Animal Population: Kitgum and Lamwo have 38,457 cattle, 276 donkeys, 38,444 pigs, 11,509 sheep, 54,815 goats, 1,109 rabbits 139,286 chicken; 31,949 ducks and 1,234 turkeys.

Co-operative Societies: Kitgum, Lamwo, Pader and Agago have 128 registered primary societies with East Acholi Growers Union at the district level.

Industries: Grain milling and cotton ginning.

Education Services: Primary schools: 130 – 118 government, 11 private, 1 community. Primary school enrolment: 66,712 – 34,706 male and 32,006 female. Primary school teachers: 951 – 663 male and 288 female.

Secondary schools: 16 schools – 6 government, and 10 private. Secondary school enrolment: 8,806 students - 5,456 male and 3,350 female. Teachers: 389 – 308 male, 81 female. Tertiary – 3 technical institutions, 3 teacher training colleges.

Health Services: 2 hospitals - 1 government – Kitgum Hospital with 185 beds, 1 NGO – St.Joseph's Kitgum with 250 beds. – 6 government health centre III - 5 government and 1 NGO, 10 health centre II - 9 government and 1 NGO.

Transport Network: The district has a well distributed feeder-road network. The roads are in fairly good condition. All the roads are murram.

Operational Radio Stations: Child Care International.

Additional Information: Agriculture is the district's biggest economic activity but is still on a small scale and specifically for subsistence. There are a few large scale farms. The district has a small population as compared to the land available. Some parts of the district are sparsely populated. Agricultural mechanisation is possible in the district because of its low altitude on the northern plateau.

Key NGOs: Actionaid Uganda, Oxfam GB in Uganda, SNV Uganda, AT Uganda Ltd, World Vision Uganda, African Medical Research Foundation, Meeting Point, Kitgum Private Sector Promotion Centre, Child Salvage Initiative, Bear Care Project, Concerned Parents' Association, Kitgum District NGO Forum, Agoro Community Development Association, Ibakara Child and Family Program – Affiliate of Christian Children's Fund, Youth Out of Poverty and AIDS.

District leaders:	Members of Parliament:
Chairperson – Mr Nyeko Luka M.P.	Chwa County – Mr Oryem Henry Okello
Chief Administrative Officer (CAO)	Woman Representative
– Mr Geoffrey Okaka	– Ms Beatrice Atim Anywar

Kole District

Kole district was carved out of Apac district in 2010 when Kole County was elevated to district status.

Location: Kole district borders the districts of Oyam to the west, Lira to the north and east, and Apac to the south.

Area: 763.0 sq. km.

Climate and Relief: Rainfall averages between 1,000mm – 1,500mm per annum. Temperatures range over 25°C and vegetation includes woodlands grass and thickets. The lowest point is about 700m above sea level at Karuma falls. The highest point is 1383m above sea level.

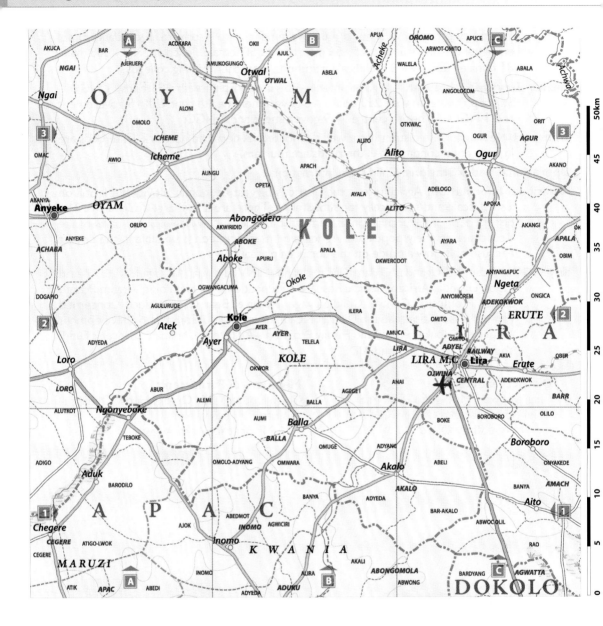

Population: Based on 2009 projections: 205,800 people – 99,300 male and 106,500 female with a density of 269 persons per sq.km.

Major Towns: Kole (administrative headquarters), Aboke.

Counties and Sub-counties: Kole County – Aboke, Akalo, Alito, Ayer, Balla, Kole (Town Council);

Main Language: Luo/Lango.

People: Langi.

Economic Activities: Agriculture with a bias towards:

    (i)   Food crops: Maize, finger millet, cassava, beans, simsim (sesame), pigeon peas, groundnuts, sunflower, cow peas and bananas.

(ii) Cash crops: Tobacco, cotton and sugarcane.

(iii) Fruits, vegetables: Tomatoes, cabbage, onions and sunflower.

(iv) Fishing on Lake Kyoga.

Area under Forestation: 69,088 hectares.

Animal Population: According to 2008 livestock census, Kole,Lira, Alebtong and Otuke had 159,533 cattle; 161,711 goats; 12,749 sheep; 28,631 pigs; 1,116,903 chicken, 30,927 ducks and 4,927 turkeys.

Co-operative Societies: Lira and Kole have 114 registered primary co-operative societies with Lango Co-operative Union as the umbrella co-operative union dealing mainly in cotton.

Industries: Small scale furniture works, and brick making.

Banks: Still use banks in Lira.

Education Services: Primary schools: 62 – 60 government and 2 private. Primary school enrolment: 63,333 –32,828 male and 30,505 female. Primary school teachers: 910 – 697 male and 213 female. Reported furniture is adequate for only 18,784 pupils.

Secondary schools: 9 schools – 3 government, 3 community and 3 private. Secondary school enrolment: 3,933 – 2,776 male and 1,157 female. Teachers: 246 – 204 male and 42 female. Reported furniture is adequate for only 2,771 students.

Health Services: 1 health centre IV (government); 2 health centre III (government); 8 health centres II (6 government, 1 NGO and 1 private).

Transport Network: A well distributed feeder-road network links most parts of the district. The district is linked by a tarmac road to Masindi, Gulu and Lira districts. A railway line crosses the northern parts of the district from Lira to Gulu District but railway services in northern Uganda were halted. In the south is water transport linking Apac to Nakasongola and Soroti districts.

Tourist Attractions: The district has little tourism potential.

Additional Information: There is little industrial activity.

But food production, especially millet, cassava, simsim and pigeon peas is high and the produce is sold in the markets. Although the farmers themselves do not go to the markets in other districts, middlemen buy the foodstuffs from the farmers at cheap prices and sell them at higher prices in other parts of the country.

Operational Radio Station: Radio Apac.

Key NGOs: Send a Cow Uganda, Actionaid Uganda, MS Uganda, Traditional and Modern Health Practitioners, Apac Disabled Persons Union, Apac District Farmers' Association, Apac District Scouts Council, Campaign Against Domestic Violence in the Community, Apac Development Foundation Limited, Golgotha Orphanage Care, Care International in Uganda.

District leaders:
Chairperson – Mr Ocen Peter
Ag Chief Administrative Officer (CAO) – Mr James Fred Okello
Deputy Chief Administrative Officer (DCAO) – Vacant

Members of Parliament:
Kole County – Mr Ebil Fred
Woman MP – Ms Acheng Joy Ruth

Lamwo District

Lamwo was one of the counties of Kitgum until 2009 when it was elevated to district status.

Location: It borders the districts of Gulu and Amuru to the west, Pader to the south, Kitgum to the east and the Republic of South Sudan to the north.

Area: 5,593.0 sq. km.

Climate and Relief: It lies at an approximate altitude of between 351m – 1,341m above sea level with temperatures of over 25°C per annum. Rainfall ranges between 1,000mm –1500mm annually.

Population: According to 2009 projections, there are 327,600 people – 164,700 female and 162,900 male.

Main Towns: Lamwo (administrative headquarters); Trading Centre: Kalongo and Lokung.

Counties and Sub-counties: Lamwo County – Agoro, Lokung, Madi-Opei, Paloga, Padibe East, Padibe West, Palabek-Gem, Palabek-Kal and Ogili.

Main Languages: Luo and Acholi.

People: Acholi.

Economic Activities: Mainly agriculture with emphasis on:
(i)   Food crops: Finger millet, sorghum, maize, groundnuts, beans, sweet potatoes, cassava, cow peas, pigeon peas, simsim (sesame), bananas and rice.
(ii) Cash crops: Cotton, sugar cane, simsim (sesame) and sunflower.
(ii) Vegetables: Tomatoes, onions and cabbage.
(iii) Cattle keeping.

Banks: Stanbic Bank in Kitgum.

Area under Forestation: 475,309 hectares.

Animal Population: Lamwo and Kitgum have 38,457 cattle, 38,444 pigs, 11,509 sheep, 54,815 goats, 139,286 chicken, 31,949 ducks and 1,234 turkeys.

Co-operative Societies: Kitgum, Lamwo and Pader have 128 registered primary societies with East Acholi Growers Union at the district level.

Industries: Grain milling and cotton ginning.

Education Services: Statistics of 2009: Primary schools: 73 – 71 government and 2 private. Primary school enrolment: 47,904 –25,136 male and 22768 female. Primary school teachers: 601– 494 male and 107 female.

Secondary schools: 4 schools - 2 government, 1 community and 1 private. Secondary school enrolment: 1,436 - 1,063 male and 373 female. Teachers: 56 – 48 male and 8 female. Available furniture is adequate for 835 students.

Health Services: 1 health centre IV (government), 6 health centre III (5 government and 1 NGO), and 11 health centre II (all government).

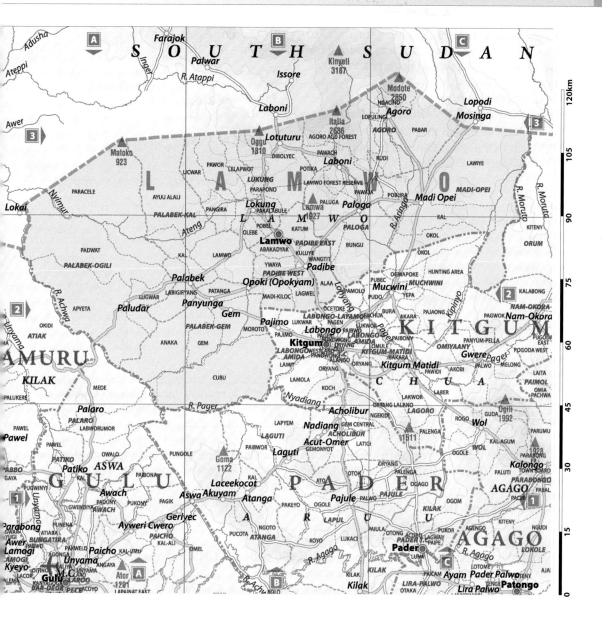

Transport Network: The district has a well distributed feeder-road network. The roads are in fairly good condition. All the roads are murram.

Operational Radio Stations: Child Care International.

Additional Information: Agriculture is the district's biggest economic activity but it is still practised on a small scale. There are a few large scale farms. The district has a small population as compared to the land available. Some parts of the district are sparsely populated. Agricultural mechanisation is possible in the district because of its low altitude on the northern plateau.

Key NGOs: AT Uganda Ltd, World Vision Uganda, African Medical Research Foundation, Actionaid Uganda, Oxfam GB in Uganda, SNV Uganda, Meeting Point, Kitgum Private Sector Promotion Centre, Child Salvage Initiative, Bear Care Project, Concerned

Parents' Association, Kitgum District NGO Forum, Agoro Community Development Association, Ibakara Child and Family Program – Affiliate of Christian Children's Fund, Youth Out of Poverty and AIDS.

District leaders:	Members of Parliament:
Chairperson – Mr Mathew Akiya Ochen	Lamwo County
Chief Administrative Officer (CAO) – Grandfield Omoda Oryono	– Mr Hilary Onek Obaloker
Deputy CAO – Vacant	Woman MP – Ms Lanyero Sarah Ochieng

Lira District

At independence, Lira District was part of the then Lango District which consisted of present-day Apac and Lira Districts. Under the provincial administration, Lango was divided into West Lango and East Lango districts in 1974. In 1980, East Lango was renamed Lira District.

Location: It borders the districts of Dokolo to the south; Apac, Kole and Oyam to the west; Gulu and Pader to the North; and Otuke and Alebtong to the east.

Area: 1,327.4 sq. km.

Climate and Relief: It lies at an approximate altitude of between 975m and 1,146m above sea level and the rainfall ranges between 1,000mm – 1,500mm, with high temperatures.

Population: Based on 2009 projection: 358,600 people - 184,500 female and 174,100 male with a density of 270 persons per sq.km.

Major Towns: Lira (administrative headquarters); Trading Centres – Ogur and Erute.

Counties and Sub-counties: Erute County – Adekokwok, Agali, Agweng, Amach, Aromo, Barr, Lira, Ngetta, and Ogur. Lira Municipality – Adyel, Lira Central, Ojwina and Railways.

Main Languages: Luo and Lango.

People: Langi, Iteso, Acholi, Bagisu, Alur, Kumam, Baganda, Banyoro, Basoga, other Ugandans and non Ugandans.

Economic Activities: Mainly agriculture with emphasis on:
(i)   Food crops: Cassava, finger millet, maize, sorghum, pigeon peas, beans, simsim (sesame), groundnuts and sunflower.
(ii) Cash crops: Cotton, coffee and sugar cane.
(iii) Vegetables: Tomatoes, onions and cabbage.

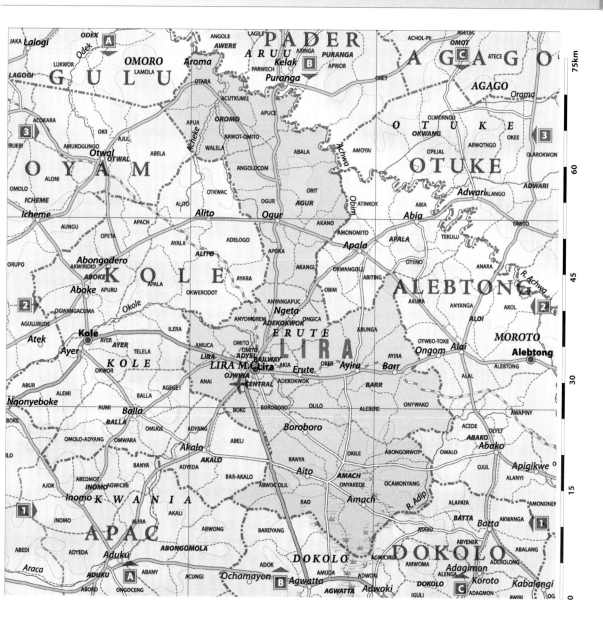

Area under Forestation: 68,785 hectares.

Animal Population: According to 2008 livestock census Lira, Kole, Alebtong and Otuke had 159,533 cattle; 161,711 goats; 12,749 sheep; 28,631 pigs; 1,116,903 chickens, 30,927 ducks and 4,927 turkeys.

Co-operative Societies: The district has 103 registered primary societies.

Industries: Oil and grain milling, cotton ginning, milk processing, manufacture of textiles, starch and furniture. Manufacture of food products and beverages, apparel, dyeing of fur, products of wood cork (except furniture) articles of straw plaiting materials, fabricated metal products (except machinery equipment) furniture manufacturing NEC, publishing, printing, reproduction of recorded media.

Banks: Stanbic Bank Uganda Ltd –1, Centenary Rural Development Bank –1, Crane Bank -1.

Education Services: Primary schools: 135 – 118 government, 15 private, and 2 community. Primary school enrolment: 109,839 – 55,418 male and 54,421 female. Primary school teachers: 2,065 – 1,359 male and 706 female. Available furniture is adequate for only 19,509 pupils.

Secondary schools: 24 schools – 8 government, 15 private, and 1 community. Secondary school enrolment: 11,274 students – 7,702 male and 3,572 female. Teachers: 777 – 612 male, 165 female. Available furniture is adequate for only 9,243 students.

Tertiary – 3 technical institutions, 3 teacher training colleges, 1 national teachers' college (Ngetta), 1 technical college (Lira).

Health Services: 2 hospitals – (1 government hospital – Lira Hospital with 254 beds and 1 NGO hospital - Uganda Protestant Medical Bureau – Amai Hospital with 80 beds); 3 health centre IV (2 government, 1 NGO); 7 health centre III (4 government, 3 NGO); 23 health centre II (all government).

Transport Network: The district has a well distributed feeder-road network. The roads link up all the counties and are in a fairly good condition. There are hardly any cars in some areas. A tarmac road links the district to Gulu-Kampala road at Corner Kamdini via Kole and Oyam districts. A newly contracted tarmac road (nearing completion) links the district to Kampala via the eastern region through Dokolo, Kaberamaido districts and Soroti. The district is also connected by a railway line running from Soroti to Gulu. However, the railway services have been non-existent for years now.

Lira Airfield – There is a 846m x 30m-grass runway and the airfield is equipped with portable fire extinguishers. The terminal building has the necessary passenger facilities. The airfield is 0.6 km from Lira town. Transportation from the airfield to town is provided by taxi. The Civil Aviation Authority provides H.F. radio communication. Mobile and public payphone servives are available in town.

Tourist Attractions: Situated in the north, 352 km from Kampala, the town of Lira has a public park with fine trees and a bandstand. Lira Hotel and Lira Rock Hills offer nice accommodation. Lira town is known for its sizeable golf course which attracts golf lovers to visit and stay for days.

Operational Radio and TV Stations: Radio Apac (Lira Station), Uganda Broadcasting Corporation Radio, Unity Investments, Rhino FM, Radio Management Services (U) Ltd, Radio Wa-Lira Diocese and Estalup Enterprises and Uganda Broadcasting Corporation Television.

Additional Information: Lira District is a fast growing district. This is partly because it has infrastructure in place and was not very destabilised by the rebels' insurgency in the northern region. This has enabled rehabilitation and reconstruction work to take off easily in the district. Agricultural production is still at subsistence level, but the surplus is sold. The only drawback is that cotton, which was once an important source of income, does not earn the farmer much anymore. But other crops such as simsim, peas and millet have market in other parts of the country, especially in Kampala. When railway transport was operational, transportation of produce to other parts of the country was cheaper.

Lira Spinning Mill, the main source of income in the town, has been renovated.

Key NGOs: Send a Cow Uganda, Uganda Project Implementation and Management Centre, Uganda Women's Effort to Save Orphans, Uganda Shelter Programme, ABOA Care for Children with HIV/AIDS, Northeast Chili Producers Association.

District leaders:
Chairperson – Mr ORemo Aiot Alex R.
Chief Administrative Officer (CAO)
   – Mr John Okolimo (On interdiction)
Deputy CAO – Mr Benson Rwanguha
Town Clerk (Lira Municipal Council)
   – Mr Paul Omoko
Mayor (Lira Municipal Council)
   – Mr Morris Odung

Members of Parliament:
Erute County North – Mr Omara Geoffrey
Lira Municipality
   – Mr James Michael Akena
Erute South – Mr Engola Sam
Woman MP – Ms Atim Joy Ongom

Nwoya District

Nwoya is one of the ten districts that were formed in July, 2010. Until then it was a county of Amuru District which was carved out of Gulu District in 2006.

Location: It borders the districts of Gulu to the east, Apac to the southeast, Kiryandongo and Buliisa to the south with the Victoria Nile forming its southern boundary and Nebbi to the west.

Area: 4,770.0 sq. km.

Climate and Relief: It lies at an approximate altitude of 351m – 1,341m above sea level in a modified equatorial zone with high temperatures at a diurnal range of 4°C. Rainfall averages 1,540mm from April to November.

Population: Based on 2009 projections, there are 48,800 people – 24,900 female and 23,900 male with a sparse population density of 10 persons per sq.km.

Major Towns: Anaka (administrative headquarters), Trading Centres: Purongo, Wianak, Wangkwar and Koc.

Counties and Sub-counties: Nwoya County – Alero, Anaka (Payira), Anaka (Town Council),Koch-Goma and Purongo.

Main Language: Luo

People: Acholi

Economic Activities: Agriculture with emphasis on:
(i) Food crops: Finger millet, maize, sweet potatoes, groundnuts, cow peas and pigeon peas, bananas, cassava and rice.
(ii) Cash crops: Tobacco, sugar cane, cotton and simsim (sesame).
(iii) Vegetables: Cabbage.
(iv) Fishing on the northern tip of Lake Albert and along the River Nile.

Animal Population: Nwoya and Amuru have 33,063 cattle; 67,092 goats; 9,773 sheep; 19,180 pigs; 142,121 chicken; 44,754 ducks and 2,558 turkeys.

Co-operative Societies: The district is still attached to those in Gulu District

Industries: Similar to those in Gulu District.

Banks: The people are still using banks in Gulu District.

Education Services: Statistics of 2009: Primary schools: 63 – 61 government and 2 private. Primary school enrolment: 23,547 pupils – 12,292 male and 11,255 female. Primary school teachers: 366 – 262 male and 104 female.

Secondary schools: 4 schools – 2 government, 1 community and 1 private. Secondary school enrolment: 2,102 – 1,461 male and 641 female. Teachers: 73 – 59 male and 14 female. Reported furniture is adequate for 2,102 students.

Health Services: 1 hospital – (government - Anaka Hospital); 3 health centre III (all government); and 5 health centre II (all Government).

Transport Network: The southern part of the district is traversed from east to west by the Karuma-Pakwach tarmac road. All other roads in the district are murram feeder-roads, which reach all parts of the district. The railway used to pass through the district to Pakwach in Nebbi District. Pakuba Airfield – Pakuba Airfield to the south along the River Nile is a designated entry and exit point. The murram surface runway is 1,585m x 30m and is in good working condition. The airfield's building is also in good condition. Mobile and public payphone services are available in town. The Civil Aviation Authority provides H.F. radio communication. The airfield is 8.6 km from Pakuba town. Transportation from the airfield to town can be provided by taxi.

Tourist Attractions: There are a variety of tourist sites such as Amoro Hot Spring which covers about 100 square metres and is the largest found in northern Uganda. If developed it has a lot of potential for tourism exploitation. The surrounding landscape is suitable for developing campsites and excursion grounds. Similar unexploited sites are Tochi Resort Beach on River Tochi and Guruguru caves. The caves are said to have been a safe haven during the Lamogi rebellion and historical inter-clan wars among the Luo. Kilak Hill is one of the many other hills that offer opportunity for climbing. Atiak Colobus Monkeys: A concentration of these rare monkeys is found in Atiak Forest Reserve near Lake Albert. In addition, the forest reserve is a sanctuary to a variety of bird species.

The district has a share of the Murchison Falls National Park, the largest national park in Uganda covering an area of nearly 4,000 sq km.

A boat trip operated by the Uganda Wildlife Authority to the falls is available. During the boat ride you are guaranteed to see hippos (there are reported to be 4,000 on this stretch of the river) and Nile crocodiles, buffaloes, giraffes and a wide range of antelopes.

The top of the falls is the most powerful rush of water. Game drives are available.

The best route for viewing animals is the Buligi Circuit, which includes the Buligi, Victoria Nile, Queens and Albert Nile tracks. During the game drive you can spot Rothschilds giraffes, lions, leopards, hyenas, elephants, buffaloes, Jackson's hartebeest, oribis, the Uganda kob and a huge variety of bird species.

Sport fishing can also be enjoyed. Fishing for Nile Perch and tiger fish attracts many anglers. The fast flowing waters above and below the falls are the best spots. Boat hire is available and permits costing $50 a day are required.

Accomodation facilites include Paraa Safari Lodge, Chobe Lodge, Sambiya River Lodge and Tented Camp, Paraa Rest Camp, Rabongo Forest Cottage and Baker's Fort at Patiko.

Operating Radio Stations: Same as Gulu.

Key NGOs: Same as Gulu.

District Leaders:
District Chairperson
– Mr Okello Patrick O.
CAO – Mr John Katotoroma
DCAO – Vacant

Members of Parliament:
Nwoya County – Mr Todwong Richard
Women MP – Ms Adong Lilly

Otuke District

Otuke District was one of the counties of Lira District until 2009 when the county was elevated to district status.

Location: It borders the Districts of Alebtong to the south, Lira to the west, Agago and Pader to the north, Abim and Napak to the east and Katakwi to the southeast.

Area: 1,549 sq. km.

Climate and Relief: It lies at an approximate altitude of between 975m and 1,146m above sea level and the rainfall ranges between 1,000mm – 1,500mm, with high temperatures.

Population: Based on 2009 projection: 76,600 people, 39,300 female and 37,300 male with a density of 49 persons per sq.km.

Major Towns: Otuke (administrative headquarters); Trading Centres – Ngotokwe.

Counties and Sub-counties:: Otuke County – Adwari, Ogor, Okwang, Olilim, Orum and Otuke (Town Council).

Main Languages: Luo and Lango.

People: Mainly Langi but other Ugandans like the Acholi and Iteso also live in the district.

Economic Activities: Mainly agriculture with emphasis on:
  (i)   Food crops: Cassava, finger millet, maize, sorghum, pigeon peas, beans, simsim (sesame), groundnuts and sunflower.
  (ii) Cash crops: Cotton, coffee and sugar cane.
  (iii) Vegetables: Tomatoes, onions and cabbage.

Area under Forestation: 68,785 hectares.

Animal Population: According to 2008 livestock census, Otuke, Lira, Kole, and Alebtong had 159,533 cattle; 161,711 goats; 12,749 sheep; 28,631 pigs; 1,116,903 chicken, 30,927 ducks and 4,927 turkeys.

Co-operative Societies: 103 registered primary societies.

Industries: Grain milling, cotton ginning, and articles of straw plaiting materials.

Banks: Still relies on banks in Lira.

Education Services: Primary schools: 47 – 45 government, 1 private, and 1 community. Primary school enrolment: 26,401– 14,098 male and 12,303 female. Primary school teachers: 413 – 349 male, 64 female. Reported furniture is adequate for only 15,848 pupils.

Secondary schools: 4 schools – all government. Secondary school enrolment: 2,530 – 1,813 male and 717 female. Teachers: 87 – 78 male, 9 female. Reported furniture is adequate for only 1,685 students.

Health Services: 1 health centre IV (government); 1 health centre III (NGO); 6 health centre II (government).

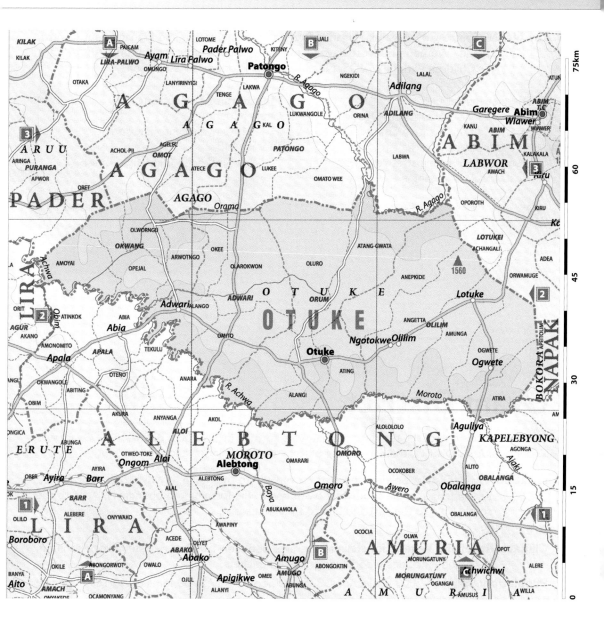

Transport Network: The district has a poorly distributed feeder-road network, which serves mainly the southern part of the district. One murram road links up all the sub-counties in the district and connects to the neighbouring districts, especially those to the west and east. Transportation in the district is provided by taxi, pick-up and other trucks.

Tourist Attractions: The district has no particular tourist attractions.

Operational Radio and TV Stations: Radio Apac (Lira Station), Uganda Broadcasting Corporation Radio, Unity Investments, Rhino FM, Radio Management Services (U) Ltd, Radio Wa-Lira Diocese and Estalup Enterprises.

Additional Information: Otuke District is a new district with inadequate infrastructure for administration at district level.

Key NGOs: Send a Cow Uganda, Uganda Project Implementation and Management Centre, Uganda Women's Effort to Save Orphans, Uganda Shelter Programme, ABOA Care for Children with HIV/AIDS, Northeast Chili Producers Association.

District leaders:	Members of Parliament:
Chairperson – Mr Ogwang Ogoog B.	Otuke County
Ag Chief Administrative Officer (CAO)	– Mr Ogwal Jacinto Deusdedit
– Mr Alex Kwizera	Woman MP
Deputy Chief Administrative Officer	– Ms Nyakecho Okwenye Annet
(DCAO) – Vacant	

Oyam District

Oyam District is one of the ten districts that were formed in July 2009. Before then, Oyam was a county of Apac District, then consisting of Kole, Kwania, Maruzi and Oyam counties.

Location: Oyam District borders the districts of Gulu to the north, Nwoya to the northwest, Kiryandongo to the southwest (with River Nile forming the boundary), Apac to the south, Kole to the east and Lira to the northeast.

Area: 2,189 sq. km.

Climate, Relief and Vegetation: Rainfall averages between 1,000mm – 1,500mm per annum. Vegetation includes woodlands grass and thickets.

Population: Based on 2009 projections: 335,300 people – 171,500 female and 163,800 male with a density of 153 persons per sq.km.

Major Towns: Oyam. Trading centres: Kamudini, Anyeke and Loro.

Counties and Sub-counties: Oyam County – Oyam (Town Council), Achaba, Icheme, Ngai, Otwal, Aber, Aleka, Abok, Loro, Kamdini, Myene and Minakulu.

Main Language: Luo/Lango.

People: Langi.

Economic Activities: Agriculture with bias towards food crops such as maize, finger millet, cassava, beans, simsim (sesame), pigeon peas, groundnuts, sunflower, cow peas and bananas.

Animal Population: Oyam and Apac have 27,288 cattle, 83,371 goats, 6,886 sheep, 4,497 pigs, 1,236 exotic chicken and 191,607 local chicken.

Co-operative Societies: The people are still attached to co-operatives in Apac District.

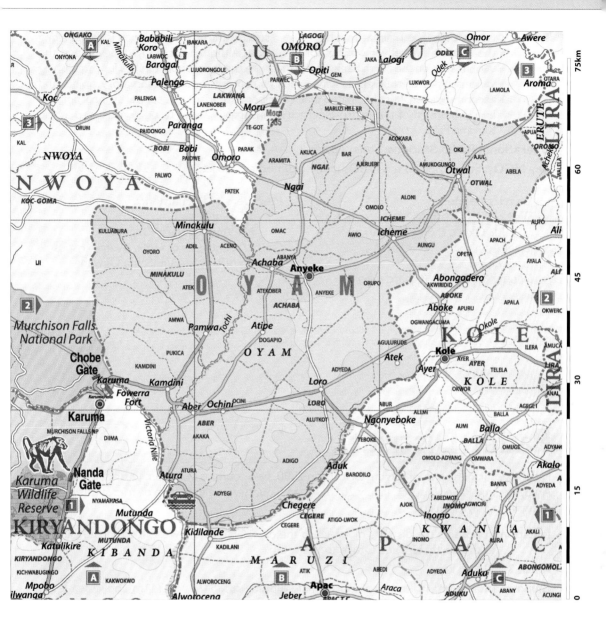

Industries: Small scale furniture works, engineering.

Banks: Still relying on the banks in Apac District.

Education Services: Primary schools: 113 – 108 government, 3 private and 2 community. Primary school enrolment: 114,424 – 59,205 male and 55,219 female. Primary school teachers: 1,664 – 1,331male and 333 female. Reported furniture is adequate for only 35,465 pupils.

Secondary schools: 9 schools – all government. Secondary school enrolment: 4,237 – 2,577 male and 1,660 female. Teachers: 184 – 162 male and 22 female. Reported furniture is adequate for only 3,843 pupils.

Health Services: 1 NGO hospital - Aber, 1 government health centre IV, 5 health centre III (3 government and 2 NGO); and 8 health centre II (all government).

Tourist Attractions: The main attraction in the district is Karuma Falls which is found along the Victoria Nile River on the northern side. Although currently undeveloped the various sites on the north banks of the River are potential opportunities for establishing various types of tourism activities such as campsites, bird observatory points and accommodation. It is anticipated that a number of tourism aspects will be incorporated into the design of the hydro-electricity dam that is about to be constructed at the Karuma Falls.

Operational Radio Stations: Radio Apac

Key NGOs: Still relying on the NGOs in the old/mother district.

District Leaders:	Members of Parliament:

District Chairperson
  – Mr Okello P. Engola Charles
Chief Administrative Officer (CAO)
  – Vacant
Deputy CAO – Mr Richard Okolli
	Oyam County South
	  – Ms Amongi Betty Ongom
	Oyam County North – Mr Ayena Krispus
	Woman MP – Ms Alum Santa Ogwang

Pader District

Pader was formerly part of Kitgum District. In 2000, two counties of Kitgum District (Agago and Aruu) became Pader District. In July 2010, Agago County was elevated to district status leaving Pader with only Aruu county.

Location: It borders the districts of Agago to the east, Gulu to the west, Kitgum and Lamwo to the north, Lira and Otuke to the south.

Area: 3,359.8 sq km.

Climate and Relief: It lies at an approximate altitude of 351m – 1,341m above sea level, with rainfall ranging between 1,000mm and 1,500mm per annum and temperatures around 25°C.

Population: Basing on the 2009 projections: 196,200 people – 98,000 female and 98,200 male with a density of 58 persons per sq.km.

Major Towns: Pader (administrative headquarters), Trading Centres: Atanga, Acholibur, Akuyam and Puranga.

Counties and Sub-counties: Aruu County – Acholi-Bur, Angagura, Laguti, Latanya, Atanga, Puranga, Awere, Pader, Pader Town Council, Lapul, Ogom and Pajule.

Main Languages: Luo and Acholi.

Economic Activities: Agriculture with emphasis on:
(i)   Food crops: Sorghum, finger millet, groundnuts, sweet potatoes, bananas and rice.
(ii) Cash crops: Cotton.
(iii) Fruits and vegetables: Tomatoes, onions and cabbage.

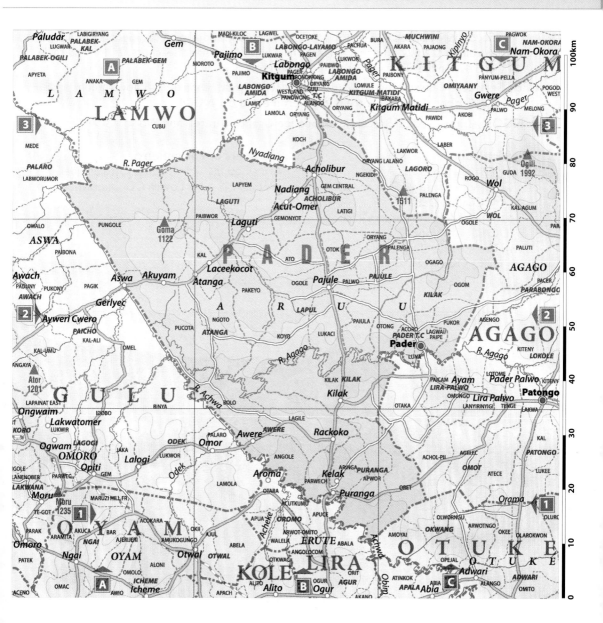

Area under Forestation: 252,706 hectares.

Animal Population: Pader and Agago together have 57,087 cattle, 39,430 pigs, 6,298 sheep, 57,807 goats, 150,317 chicken 43,197, ducks and 1,144 turkeys.

Co-operative Societies: Pader and Kitgum have 128 registered co-operative societies.

Industries: Grain milling, cotton ginning, brick making and furniture making.

Education Services: Primary schools: 111 – 109 government, 1 private, and 1 community. Primary school enrolment: 61,191 – 32,781 male and 28,410 female. Primary school teachers: 844 – 693 male and 151 female. Data about furniture was not fully available.

Secondary schools: 11 schools – 5 government and 6 private. Secondary school enrolment: 2,622 students – 1,756 male and 866 female. Teachers: 211 – 169 male and 42 female. Tertiary: 1 technical institute.

Health Services: 1 health centre IV (government); 9 health centre III (8 government and 1 NGO); and 7 health centre II (6 government and 1 NGO).

Key NGOs: African Medical Research Foundation Uganda (Amref) and World Vision Uganda.

District leaders:	Members of Parliament:
Chairperson – Mr Akana Alfred	Aruu County – Mr Odonga Otto Samuel
Ag Chief Administrative Officer (CAO) – Mr Charles Otai	Woman MP – Ms Lowila CD Oketayot
Deputy Chief Administrative Officer (DCAO) – Vacant	
Town Clerk (Pader Town Council) – Mr C. Oketayot	

Bwola dance of the Acholi.

Special Report on Northern Uganda's Gradual Road to Recovery

H.E. Yoweri Kaguta Museveni
President of The Republic of Uganda

Hon. Amama Mbabazi
Current Prime Minister

Professor Apolo R. Nsibambi
Former Prime Minister

Hon. Janet K. Museveni
First Lady and Minister for
Karamoja Affairs

Hon. David Wakikona
Former Minister of State for
Northern Uganda Reconstruction

Hon. Rebecca Amuge Otengo
Current Minister of State for
Northern Uganda Reconstruction

Mr. Pius Bigirimana
Permanent Secretary Office of the
Prime Minister

Office of the Prime Minister
Postel Building, Yusuf Lule Road,
P. O. Box 341, Kampala, Uganda.
Tel: +256414344839,
Email: lrdp.apm@gmail.cam

Special Report on Karamoja

Mrs. Janet Museveni, Uganda's first lady, is also the State Minister for Karamoja Affairs. Since her appointment as minister in February 2009 Mrs. Museveni has overseen a progressive change and development of one of Uganda's most backward regions. This is perhaps the most significant story of a region on a path towards rural transformation, decades after independence excerpts. Below are some:

Since your appointment as Minister for Karamoja Affairs, one of the areas your ministry has embarked on has been that of providing water for both human and animal consumption. What is the progress so far?

We have made some modest achievements although we haven't made a breakthrough yet. However, I and my team (ministry officials) took a trip to Israel recently to learn from them how to fully manage and harness water resources in a desert. We signed an MOU with them.

What did you learn from the Israelis that will benefit

Karamoja and Ugandans? What does the MOU entail?

Israel (which is smaller than Karamoja in land size) is a very dry country with little or no water. We learnt from the Israelis how to trap rain water in the desert. They trap water in big reservoirs and have managed to channel this water for agricultural projects like irrigation and also for animal and human consumption.

The Israelis have communities called Kibbutz where they have large farms that produce fruits, vegetables, flowers, dairy farms and have even started industries where produce from these projects is packed and sold locally and exported.

With the help of some of the Israeli expertise, we will see a complete transformation of Karamoja in the near future. Remember Israel is dryer than Karamoja.

Karamoja has a lot of water and all we need is to trap it and have it harnessed for irrigation, domestic use and for animals.

The other challenge has been that of food security. How are you doing in this area, since you launched a protracted food campaign last year?

Since we began the campaign last year, we have seen quite a dramatic turnaround in the food situation. First, we mobilised the people especially the youth and women who bought into the initiative. We then embarked on ploughing and sowing the ground. We planted hundreds of acres of land of mainly maize, sorghum, beans, cassava and very interestingly, matooke (bananas). I am thankful to God that the harvests were successful. There was a bumper harvest and we are now preparing to start planting at the end of next month and in December.

Out of 10 where would rate yourself in this agricultural season initiative?

I would put it at 8. In fact the World Food Programme (WFP) have reduced food aid to Karamoja by big margin. Previously, 70% of the region's people was receiving food aid. This has now dropped to 40%. This is a great achievement.

However, I would like to add that we still have challenges. After the insecurities which bogged the region (mainly rustling) many people moved into the small towns. These populations are still dependent on food aid. But we are working with the WFP to help people get organised farming, We are planning to get the people back to the land.

Your ministry also embarked on modern housing for the Karimojong people.

That is part of the initiative to get people back to the land. We embarked on an initiative to build organised settlements with proper infrastructure with water, solar power, modern toilets and where it has been implemented the people are appreciating. We engaged a company called Hydraform which produces reinforced bricks using local materials and can build multiple houses in one day. And so we need lots of cement, iron sheets and other inputs.

How is the programme progressing?

It is gradually taking shape. You see once we build homes, plant trees, and teach people to live in sanitised environments, we shall bring confidence to the people who will then leave violence. The Karimojong believe that once one is comfortable and lives in a secure environment, it brings durable security.

On the social scene, how is the programme of involving the elders, women groups and the youth in bringing progressive change to the region?

We have explored working with the elders in their different hierarchies. We are also working very closely with the churches and other religious institutions. The women groups have been the catalysts of development, especially agricultural production. They are very enthusiastic to work. The last bumper harvest has been an incentive to their labour.

How are you doing on infrastructure development?

In the last financial year, the Uganda National Roads Authority (UNRA) did set aside funds for tarmacking the Soroti-Moroto road. We are also working with the Local Government Ministry for the feeder roads. We are also working on power and electricity has been installed in Abim from Nakapiripirit (south-east Karamoja).

Where do you see Karamoja in the coming years?

I am very optimistic about developments in this sub-region. In the current progarmmes we have, we are building teachers houses, health workers houses in Abim and Moroto. We have embarked on the beutification and proper planned city and residential environments.

The biggest success which is also a challenge is the issue of changing mindsets. Once the local people and the leaders can grasp the vision, Karamoja will move to higher levels and will be a model for development for backward regions.

How is the security situation?

There are less cattle raids and optimism! Our security forces have really done a commendable job. We are about to roll modern methods of containing rustling. We shall announced this at the appropriate time.

Karamoja at a glance

Region - Karamoja; People - Ikarimojong; Language Ngakarimojong.

Land size: 27,900 square kilometres (about the size of Rwanda, Burundi, Belgium or Maryland State in the USA).

About one million people live in Karamoja, with more than a third of them being Karimojong.

Karamoja inhabitants are predominantly cattle keeping groups although some lead semi-nomadic lifestyle mixed with crop cultivation.

Mt. Kadam 3,063m, Mt. Napak 2,540m and Mt. Moroto 3,083 m.

Karimojong ethnic groups: Consist of three clans - Matheniko, Bokora and Pian. Other groups are Tepeth, Oropom, Pokot, Jie, Ik, Ethur and Jabwor.

Mineral resources: gold, copper, cobalt, chromite, iron ore, magnetite , columbite-tantalite, granite, gneiss, quartzite and sandstone, clay, limestone and marble.

Minister of State office of the Prime MInister in charge of Karamoja, Mrs. Janet Museveni.

Investment Opportunities: Horticulture, wheat farming, fruit growing, tourism, forestry, mining, education, fish farming, ranching, dairy and beef production.

Karamoja undergoes rejuvenation – Initiatives boost development

Karamoja undergoes rejuvenation

It used be said of the sub-region that "You cannot wait for Karamoja to develop." Today that perception is changing as the region is fast becoming a case study of rural transformation, thanks to the efforts of government and the leadership of the ministry charged with Karamoja - the Office of the Prime Minister (OPM).

Mr. Pius Bigirimana is the Permanent Secretary in the Office of the Prime Minister (OPM). He is confident this perception is changing. "Karamoja has changed in the last two years," he says.

"We are trying to change the wrong attitudes. Both the technical people and the leadership had denied the people services. Today, because of vision, planning, focus, accountability, hard work and great leadership, the sub-region is turning around," says Mr Bigirimana.

"We are determined to work 24-7 to see that this area is transformed. That is on top of the agenda, we shall see this come to pass," a confident and visibly positive Mr. Bigirimana told this reporter.

Karamoja is arguably Uganda's most backward region.

This underdevelopment is historical, having been neglected from colonial times to all post independence regimes until the National Resistance Movement (NRM) took power in 1986.

"We want to do more and the leadership is engaged at all levels," he says, thanks to the appointment of Uganda's First Lady as State Minister for Karamoja in February 2009.

NEW HOMES: The First Lady Mrs Janet Museveni at the launch of Hydraform houses

She and her team have had the herculean task of turning around the region.

The sub region's geographical size is slightly bigger than countries like Belgium, Rwanda, Burundi and the US state of Maryland. It is at the tip of north-eastern Uganda.

It borders Kenya to the east and Sudan to the north.

Administratively, Karamoja comprises Abim, Amudat, Kaabong, Kotido, Moroto, Nakapiripirit and Napak district.

It is sandwiched between a fast growing and developing world and decadent traditional cultural belief system and an unstable and harsh environment.

National Record Holder

Karamoja has some interesting statistics. The 2008 National Livestock Census produced by the National Bureau of Standards, puts Karamoja region as having the most cattle in Uganda. The same census shows that Karamoja has the highest number of donkeys in the country, 960 of the 1,590 donkeys are found in here.

About 32,000 of the 32,870 camels found in the country come from the sub-region.

The national sheep herd is estimated at 3.4 million. Karamoja region has the highest number of sheep, estimated at 1.69 million, while the western region had the least, at 0.27 million.

The census results show that the country has 12.5 million goats, with Nakapiripirit District having the highest number of goats at 547,370, closely followed by Kotido and Kaabong with 535,140 and 525,390 goats, respectively. The report, adds that the highest number of dog owners are found in Karamoja. The report recommended that these assets can be exploited to promote commercial livestock enterprise that can economically lift the region from poverty.

The region has great potential for tourism, sport hunting, wildlife enterprises, ranching, trade and tourism, craft sales etc.

Mineral exploitation also has a big potential in contributing to the development of Karamoja.

Statistics show that there are about 50 different minerals and precious stones in the Karamoja region. They include unknown large numbers of gold, silver, copper, iron, titanium, manganese, niobium, tantalite, chrome, rare earth and radioactive minerals.

The Minerals Department in Entebbe shows that the gold belt stretches from north to south Karamoja in the Upe region.

"This belt has one of the largest deposits in the world with the highest level of purity," according to a survey report.

Other mineral deposits in Karamoja are mica, green and red gannets, tin, marble, beryl, cuprites, haematite, limestone, talc graphite, columbite, magnetite and zircon.

There is one national park in the area, the Kidepo Valley National Park, one of Uganda's most spectacular parks. It covers 10 % of the total district area, and harbours scenery unsurpassed by any other park in East Africa. The other is Pian Upe Game Reserve – another bastion of flora and fauna.

But years of neglect, insecurity, rampant and traditional rustling tendencies using modern weaponry have wrecked havoc to the region, causing some of these potentials to remain unexploited.

While many of these negative factors have formed the headlines for many decades, a new chapter or era is being rewritten of the sub region.

With the appointment of Mrs. Museveni, things have changed for the better. That is exactly the same feeling Mr. Bigirimana said in a recent interview.

Food Security

"The region was chronically food insecure. About 37% of the people in Karamoja were receiving food aid. But now the situation has improved as a result of the massive campaign started by the First Lady," he says.

According to the latest World Food Programme (WFP) Food and Nutrition Survey, food assistance has dropped from 70% to 40% which is 30% difference in one and a half years. "We had two food production cycles in which we helped them cultivate 2,300 acres of land."

That has made the Karimojong harvest maize, sorghum, cassava and cow peas "Because of the First Lady's initiative, Karamoja now grows matooke. People are eating," Mr. Bigirimana adds.

The initiative has been very successful. We are trying to prepare early. Very soon, we shall do away with WFP in Karamoja," a confident PS says cheerfully.

"We are also trying to chase away wrong attitudes. Both the

BYE TO HUNGER: Government has engaged the locals in agricultural production. Bumper harvests like these are a testimony of hard work work, focus and determination

technical people and the leadership, in the past, who had denied people services," he insists.

Asked why this sudden change of fortunes or is it situation, Mr Bigirimana says it is a variety of reasons and strategies.

"He says it is timing, resource allocation, accountability that have turned the region around. "We want to move forward and do better. We are trying to get those who were skeptical to see the results and know there is a difference in this region. There were also others who missed out on the inputs like tractors that need help. For others we are trying to get ox ploughs to handle post harvest planting," he adds.

According to Bigirimana, Karamoja is intrinsically divided into three main areas.

IDENTIFICATION : Government is helping in branding animals to check rustling

Western Karamoja, is largely an agricultal area.

Then there is Middle Karamoja which is semi-agriculture/semi-pastoral. And then there is Eastern Karamoja, which is largely dry and predominantly a cattle keeping region.

The biggest challenges are faced by this last group. This is mainly a lack of water and is drought stricken during the dry spells of the year.

"That is why a delegation from the ministry specifically travelled to Israel to get a few lessons from a country which is predominantly a desert but which has successful strategies and with challenges of war and insecurity combined with commitment, Israel is a successful country.

"We have invited them here and with their expertise and know-how of water management, supply of deep wells engineering, cloud seeding. We agreed with them to come and expand operations, the Mekorof Company will be coming to help us get assistance in exploiting:

Drill water wells
Flood water handling
Development of irrigation infrastructure."

Hydrology and drilling of boreholes

"We are going to have clean water for human beings and animals.

In Israel we saw water stored in 200,000 litre tanks in many places. Huge tanks are pumped to a high place and sent down by gravity."

Cattle Branding

Cattle rustling has been a big problem in Karamoja. According to Mr. Bigirimana, "Rustling is going to stop. The good news is that government methods of using disarmament and psychological approach.

This will be done with punctuality and sensitivity through MPs, youth and women groups, churches, etc using a modern technology. As an effort, we have to solve cattle rustling holistically.

Cattle rustling takes on different forms, i.e.

Inter-tribal rustling
Intra-tribal rustling
International rustling

The warriors rustle from each other and then rustle Bokora and Pokot Kenyans, South Sudan and Ethiopia.

"We are going to brand 1,200,000 cattle using modern technology to be announced later. At the moment we are using tags and hot iron branding," says Mr. Bigirimana.

Jobs

We are employing the young men and women to build houses, housing estates, toilets and valley tanks for water.

Teachers Houses

"We have started building hydraform houses. For instance we have built in Napak, five schools and five primary health centres. In each school, we shall have six housing units, one for the headmaster, one for the the deputy headmaster and four for the teachers. This is the model we are replicating in other places,"

Self-Help

"We are mobilising women and youth groups - how to involve them in development of the area and self-help projects to boost household and community incomes. For instance, in Amudat, Nakapiripirit and Moroto we purchased ox ploughs and gave the women and youth groups capacity to produce food," he adds.

Mrs. Flavia Waduwa, the Underscretary in the ministry is also optimistic about the region. Agriculture is on the rise. "We are now growing bananas in the region, a thing that was un-heard of, thanks to the peace that has been restored."

Govt plots better agenda for North

TOGETHER WE CAN: President Yoweri Museveni (2nd left) poses with cultural leaders and chiefs who have received new houses from government as part of initiatives to help pacify Northern Uganda and help mobilise communities for development. (2nd right is Hon. Wakikona)

The people of northern and north-eastern Uganda are this year seeing results of nurturing peace and development. The restoration of peace has brought with it an economically viable region. A new boom and refreshment of the spirit of courage and determination is in place.

In their efforts to shake off the shackles of poverty in the once war torn area, the Acholi, Lango and Teso sub-regions, government has implemented various development projects in their respective areas.

As part of her Peace Recovery Development Plan, Government initiated the second Northern Uganda Social Action Fund (NUSAF2), following the collapse of NUSAF 1.

Launched early this year on February 8, by President Yoweri Museveni, NUSAF2 is financed by a specific investment loan of $100 million from the World Bank and 24 million pounds (about$40m) grant from the UK Department For International Development (DFID).

The five year multi-sectoral community driven project, part of a Peace Recovery and Development Plan (PRDP) implementation, covers 40 districts in Acholi, Teso, Lango, Bukedi, Bunyoro, Elgon and West Nile sub-regions.

Since its official launch, implementation has been on course. The systematic roadmap to roll out the project to the communities in the regions was development by the office of the Prime Minister.

Training

Key milestones already achieved include among others workshops to impart key messages of processes, modalities, and procedures of implementation. The NUSAF2 technical support team completed the comprehensive training of the region Expanded Participatory Rural Appraisal (EPRA) resource persons.

As part of the interventions, constructions of residential homes for Chiefs are ongoing and near completion.

"NUSAF 2 is designed based on the community demand for development, focusing on the livelihood improvement and access to quality basic socio-economic services. The project will contribute to the implementation of strategic

objectives of the PRDP, particularly rebuilding and empowering communities and revitalisation of Northern Uganda," a statement from the Office of the Prime Minister's Office says.

Improved incomes

NUSAF2 is expected to improve access of beneficiary households to income earning opportunities and better basic socio-economic services, and increase access and utilisation of basic services in underserved communities.

NUSAF officials contend that the target beneficiaries for the project will be the poorest households and service communities. District and sub counties, they said, will be responsible for targeting the community.

More Power

NUSAF2 was approved by the World Bank in May 2009 and Parliament in September 2009.

While launching the project, President Yoweri Museveni, said his main projects in the northern region were Karuma Dam power project, which he said will be funded by Uganda Government and Nyagak another proposed power project.

Without dwelling on NUSAF, Museveni emphasised the development of infrastructure in the region including a railway line from Gulu or Pakwach to Juba.

"Karuma will be funded by the Ugandan Government. If there are those who want to come, they are welcome, but we don't want them to come with their terms," Museveni said.

"After Karuma, the other big projects are Gulu-Atyak-Dibia road, Arua-Koboko-Oraba to be tarmacked, and Soroti-Dokolo-Lira".

The President also stressed the need for value addition processing for all products that can't be eaten fresh in the region once wrecked by civil strife. He cited the Bidco's Oil Palm project in Kalangala as some of the products that can help the country.

In 2003, the Government launched NUSAF1 to assist the north catch up with the rest of the country. The project was expected to close in March 2008 but it was extended to March 2009.

NUSAF1 raised a lot of concern from the public and legislators after it was marred with mismanagement.

Over 100 cases of theft and mismanagement are still pending at the Anti Corruption Court.

New NUSAF2

Tired of the nasty past experiences of corruption that marred the Northern Uganda Social Action Fund 1(NUSAF1), the World Bank

has now made it clear that it will monitor the new NUSAF2.

World Bank officials have stressed the World Bank's policy on zero tolerance for corruption saying project resources will be suspended where quick and appropriate action is not taken until culprits are brought to book.

"We will be closely monitoring this programme to ensure that all World Bank programmes achieve their intended purpose," said Mr John McIntire, World Bank Country Director for Tanzania, Uganda and Burundi, during the launch of NUSAF 2.

McIntire, said the World Bank is increasing its presence in northern Uganda and will undertake independent audits over and above the normal audits, set up transparency committees and take immediate measures to strengthen local government capacity to ensure that all resources are used efficiently and transparently.

Above: INFRASTRUCTURE GROWTH: State Minister for Northern Uganda, Hon David Wakikona participates in the hydraform training by police

Right, a new bridge at Bulkur in Paicho Sub-county in Gulu constructed under PRDR

Tractor hire scheme bolsters agric

MECHANIZATION: The government has put in place modern best practices like the tractorisation of farming. This has boosted production

With the end of the LRA conflict in northern Uganda and the containment of cattle rustling in the Karamoja region, the relative peace has facilitated the need to focus on development interventions in these two regions.

The poverty gap between the south and the north of the country which the PRDP is expected to bridge through various activities indicate that the agriculture sector is one area that greatly lags behind. For example, in 2009, in the northern Uganda and the Karamoja regions, the food security situation continued to decline as close to 90% of the populations needed food aid, and own food production contributed to less than 46% of household food need.

PRDP is supposed to facilitate activities that are over and above those implemented through the various government budget expenditure framework. Ministry of Agriculture, Animal Industry and Fisheries, through NAADS and direct disbursement to local governments, finances agricultural

activities including in the PRDP districts. However, in order to respond to the huge challenge of food insecurity caused by the above mentioned factors, OPM under the auspices of the PRDP developed a tractorisation programme on a pilot basis to establish the extent to which the existing agriculture interventions could be complemented to ensure food security within the regions.

The major objective of the scheme was to improve agriculture production and productivity in the northern Uganda and Karamoja regions through mechanised farming, use of improved seeds, better crop husbandry and mobilise the local populace to produce their own food in order to improve household food security and income.

There was the tractor hire scheme where firms were contracted to cultivate land and plant crops. All the districts of Karamoja, Acholi sub-region, Adjumani, Oyam, Dokolo, Kaberamaido and Amuria districts benefitted.

Working closely with Ministry of Agriculture Animal Industry

and Fisheries (MAAIF), the Office of the Prime Minister, contracted registered and reputed seed companies to supply certified seeds for planting under the scheme.

A total of 33,334 kgs of Maize (Longe V), 24,800 kgs of Sorghum (Sekedo), 16,600 kgs of Cowpeas (white CP), 61,000 kgs of Beans (K 132) and 2,150 bags of Cassava (2961) were delivered for planting.

The specific objectives of the scheme was to increase crop production and productivity, show case potential for agriculture production in the northern Uganda and Karamoja regions, improve availability of farming skills among the communities, and promote mechanised, improved farming technologies in the region.

Under the strategic objective No. 2 of the Peace Recovery and Development Programme (PRDP) for northern Uganda, government committed itself to rebuilding and empowering communities in the PRDP districts.

Following the full scale implementation of the PRDP in the FY 2009/2010, the OPM, in collaboration with local governments and line ministries has been carrying out a number of activities geared towards ensuring community rehabilitation and development for the people of northern Uganda, especially those who were affected by the LRA insurgency and the disruptive pattern of cattle rustling in the Karamoja sub-region.

Before the conflict in 1986, northern Uganda used to be the food basket of Uganda due to its fertile soils and hardworking people. The prolonged LRA conflict, however, reversed this agriculture potential as

people were forced to live in IDP camps and made to survive on relief hand-outs. In the case of Karamoja, the culture of cattle rustling that generated into communal conflicts, coupled with poor climatic conditions has made it difficult for the people to grow crops, leading to reliance on relief food, even though some green zones have potential to grow food.

Like any other projects, the tractor scheme also faced challenges in its implementation. Management of tractors was one of the issues.

While the OPM's initial interest was to procure tractors and give to districts to encourage mechanisation for purposes of sustainability, this approach did not work successfully as management of the tractors at the district level proved problematic.

Poor and late mobilisation of communities led to existence of tree trunks in virgin land, yet with the nature of the enterprise, there was need to expeditiously plough land and ready the gardens for early planting. This in some instances led to damage to equipment, raising the cost of production and causing relative delays.

Poor road infrastructure, unreliable and low rainfall in the arid pastoral zone also hampered the scheme.

Many areas of northern Uganda and Karamoja have very poor road networks, hence they are very difficult to access. Access to gardens is challenging, in some cases blocking delivery of inputs by trucks, necessitating the use of alternative, slow and small quantity delivery options.

The unreliable and characteristically low rains in the arid pastoral zones led to poor crop performance in some areas such as Moroto and Kotido in Karamoja, while Kaberamaido in northern Uganda registered flooding. Either phenomenon significantly affects crop production.

The OPM through FEIL and the district local governments of Karamoja has ploughed and planted 2,312 acres of gardens of cassava, sorghum, cowpeas and maize. Yields will begin to be realised in the coming months, and all indications point to expected good yields in all the wet agricultural zones of the region. The arid pastoral zone is expected to harvest some sorghum and cowpeas. The northern Uganda region was supplied with 23,334 kgs of Maize (Longe 4) and 61,000 kgs of Beans (K 132), with the initial allocation of 7,987 acres for ploughing.

There is renewed enthusiasm among the populace of the regions to undertake agricultural production and improve their livelihood, thus reducing the current dependence on relief food.

Through Private Public Partnership; OPM contracted firms with competence in management of equipment and machinery, and cultivation, and was able to register timely ploughing and planting of crops, and working closely with MAAIF, contracted reputed registered seed companies that timely supplied high quality seeds for planting.

Key Approaches for the OPM Tractor Hire Scheme

Involvement of key local leadership and stakeholders like Chief Administrative Officers at the district levels coordinated the implementation of the tractor hire scheme project, while technical backstopping was provided by the designated agriculture officers and the OPM.

This enabled active participation of all stakeholders, including the beneficiary communities themselves.

Through timely delivery of high value seeds and other inputs, Owaro said, 2,312 acres of land which was cultivated in the Karamoja region was harvested.

He said ploughing and planting of 7,987 acres is currently ongoing in the greater northern Uganda districts.

"Timely ploughing, especially in the Karamoja region and delivery of seeds enhanced success of the programme," Owaro added.

Pesticides (Dudu bullet) and Knapsack sprayers were provided to all the districts of Karamoja to control pest infestation.

The district production office, in close cooperation with the OPM, ensured that the seeds were planted according to specified spacing for maximum yields. FEIL provided approved planters to speed the work, and in some instances, farmers were encouraged to undertake own planting as a learning process.

Crop management up to harvest remained a responsibility of beneficiary farmers. Group crop management, including weed and pest control has been encouraged in areas where vulnerable farmers could not manage the crop on their own.

The district production officers with support from NAADs extension staff are to train farmers in post harvest management, including post harvest pest control, storage and price fluctuations.

The OPM tractor hire scheme for the Karamoja sub-region has demonstrated that mechanised farming using high quality seeds, good husbandry methods and working in close partnership with all stakeholders including the local beneficiaries themselves can significantly contribute to improved food production and productivity.

It is, therefore, recommended that the OPM, in partnership with other stakeholders, scale up the pilot tractor hire scheme to cover a significant amount of acreage, both in northern Uganda, West Nile and in the Karamoja region. Larger tractors may be used to speed up the process.

Farmers benefit from mapping

1.0 INTRODUCTION

Office of the Prime Minister (OPM) initiated a Tractor Hire Scheme in which it extended support to all the Karamoja districts to open up land for cultivation. Each of the then five districts of Karamoja, namely; Nakapiripirit, Moroto, Kotido, Kaabong and Abim districts benefited from the programme. The allocation was as detailed below:

District	Land allocation (acres)
Nakapiripirit	556
Moroto	400
Kotido	400
Kaabong	400
Abim	556

A team headed by Johnson Owaro (OPM agriculture expert) was sent to undertake mapping of the ploughed and planted gardens. The team established the geographical locations of samples of the ploughed and planted areas in the Karamoja region. This field report shows the mapped ploughed areas and reflects the opinions of beneficiary farmers to the tractor hire scheme.

The fieldwork was carried out to verify the areas ploughed by Farm Engineering Industries Ltd, with financing by Office of the Prime Minister and it was undertaken in the five districts of Karamoja region which include, Nakapiripirit, Moroto, Kotido, Kabong and Abim districts. Other members of the team included Christine Nyaruwa (GIS expert), Teddy Nakato (GIS expert) and Samuel Ntege (driver). The exercise was conducted from 9th to 16th of June 2010. This report summarises the activities and findings of the exercise.

1.1 General objective

The general objective of this study was to critically examine and map the areas ploughed and planted under the Office of the Prime Minister Tractor Hire Scheme in the Karamoja region.

2.0 PROJECT AREA

The Karamoja region is located in the north-east of Uganda and consists of five districts. The region is bordered by Kenya to the east and Sudan to the north.

3.0 METHODOLOGY

While in the field, a number of data collection methods were used. These included; interviews, observation and mapping which include generation of map of Uganda showing the ploughed areas.

3.1 Interviews

This was in the form of question and answer talk sessions; in which farmers were asked about the different crops grown and the challenges they faced. It was purely an open face-to-face dialogue. Key informants were as well interviewed.

Through this method, we were able to identify the various crops grown, the various areas being ploughed and the opinion of farmers towards the under taking. The crops grown were similar across the districts, but differed on quantities planted. Sorghum (Sekedo), maize (Longe V), and Cassava (Variety 2961) were grown widely.

3.2 Observation

In this method, we used our naked eyes to identify the various fields on a non-verbal form. We used our eyes to identify ploughed areas, different

FOCUS: OPM Permanent Secretary, Mr Pius Bigirimana

types of crops grown and the areas not yet planted.

3.3 Mapping

We used a pair of GPS handsets to take the geographical coordinates of the ploughed areas. These were then captured into a computer-based Geographical Information System (GIS). Using GIS software, the spatial location of these gardens was established and maps of these locations were produced.

Planning of the fieldwork (sampling procedure was done). At least one sub-county in every District was sampled. Mapping of all the gardens in the whole region would require a lot more resources, and time and this was limiting.

4.1.1 Observations

(i) Farmers especially women were organised into groups and were supported with ploughing virgin land for cultivation and crops were then planted. Block farming in the area was a huge success.

(ii) All these acres have been ploughed except the 50 acres of Nabilatuk which are yet to be ploughed. The delay in ploughing was caused by presence of tree trunks and rocks, leading to breakdown of the tractors, hence slow progress.

(iii) The soils are very fertile and most of the crops in the area are in very good physiological condition, with expected good yields. Main crops include; simsim, maize, sunflower, rice, green vegetables, beans and cassava, among others. (inter-cropping with locally available crops was done in many gardens).

(iv) Crops such as sorghum and maize that were planted in swampy areas did not perform well due to flooding. Appropriate swampy crops such as paddy rice need to be introduced.

4.1.2 Challenges

(i) The undertaking interested many farmers, and this increased demand for the scheme, including requests for more seeds for planting

(ii) Also, there was a request for more varieties of seeds to be introduced; including; paddy rice, simsim, beans and green vegetables.

(iii) The area is faced with hunger and weeding of the gardens was a problem because farmers had to go and look for work in order to buy some food.

(iv) Flooding affected some areas, thus destroying crops.

(v) Pest infestation was reported in some parts of the district.

4.2.1 Observations

(i) Individual vulnerable farmers were identified in various sub-

counties and each was helped to plough and plant an acre of land. Block farming was not practised.

(ii) Land was successfully opened for cultivation and the main crops planted were sorghum, maize and green gram. Cassava was majorly planted in Iriiri sub-county.

4.2.2 Challenges

(i) Some vulnerable farmers were unable to utilise the plots of land

MECHANISATION: Mapping exercise has helped boost agriculture production

even after it had been ploughed and planted. Crop management remained a problem to very poor and vulnerable farmers.

(ii) In some areas, farmers had to re-plant seeds several times before they would get some crops growing due to high temperatures, (the district received early unplanned rains, and experienced with dry spells during the planting season)

4.3 Kotido District

Kotido District was allocated 400 acres of land to be ploughed by the OPM and it was subdivided amongst six Sub counties. Below

are maps showing the mapped ploughed areas.

4.3.1 Observations

(i) All acres have been ploughed and planted, but parts of the district continue to experience high temperatures and low rainfalls.

4.3.2 Challenges

(i) Inadequate facilitation of the district officials (agriculture officers) to monitor the project activities as there is no vehicle for this activity.

(ii) Some seeds required by the farmers were not among the seeds supplied.

(iii) Farmers needed more varied crop types for intercropping but this was not available.

(iv) High temperatures and low rainfall continues to affect crop performance in some areas.

4.4 Kaabong District

Kaabong District was allocated 400 acres of land which were evenly allocated to the five sub-counties each getting 80 acres.

4.4.1 Observations

(i) All the acres were ploughed and planted, but there was some delay in planting due to late arrival of the planter.

(ii) Farmers were grouped and helped to open up land for agriculture, leading to the success of block farming in the district.

4.4.2 Challenges

(i) Late planting in some areas

(ii) Tractor hire scheme was not enough to cover the overall demand in the district.

$100m recovery bid on course

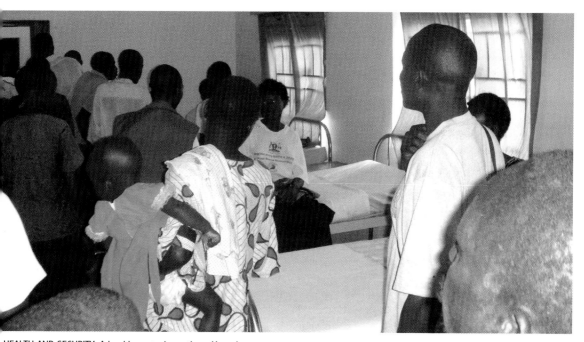

HEALTH AND SECURITY: A health centre in northern Uganda

Background

The Second Northern Uganda Social Action (NUSAF2) implementation is at the stage where the 55 district local governments in Acholi, Bukedi, Bunyoro, Elgon, Lango, Karamoja, Teso and West Nile are preparing community sub-projects for funding. Already districts have forwarded to the Office of the Prime Minister kick-start sub-projects for a committee of the Peace Recovery Development Plan (PRDP) working group to verify the generation, appraisal, approval and endorsement by the sub-county technical planning committees, district planning committees and district executive committees, respectively.

Mainstream

NUSAF2 is a Government of Uganda project that is financed by a loan of US $ 100 million from the World Bank and Pound 24 million from the Department for International Development (DFID) of the United Kingdom. It is a multi-community Project being implemented for five years (2009-2014). It is a successor to NUSAF1 which ended on March 31, 2009. It is mainstreamed into the central and local governments structures in the implementation.

The challenges of accountability, mismanagement and cases of corruption are being addressed through creation of Social Accountability Committees and the component of Transparency Accountability and Anti Corruption (TAAC) independently managed by the Inspectorate of Government.

PRDP Monitoring Committee

As the 4th PMC is chaired by the Right Honourable Prime Minister, participants who form the core of the actors to ensure PRDP succeeds, the Office of the Prime Minister wishes to affirm that implementation of NUSAF2 is on course.

In the coming weeks, the communities in northern Uganda will receive funds to implement their sub-projects after acquiring knowledge imparted during the district level sensitisation programmes, training of resource persons, training of trainers (ToTs), community facilitators and radio broadcasts. We hope in the 5th PMC we shall be reporting statistics of funded and implemented sub-projects.

Achievements

Sn Activities Conducted Input Output Outcome

1 District Level Sensitisation

a) Workshops
b) Radio Programmes
c) Stakeholders Meetings
d) Dissemination of educational materials

- Organise Broadcast Meetings
- Dissemination of materials
- 40 workshops
- 40 programmes
- 55 meetings
- 100 different documents given to more 55,000 participants
- Awareness of NUSAF2 created, boosted participation and created interest

2 Training of Resource Persons

a) Workshop
b) Practical EPRA processes

Organise
The training enabled core team, conversant in NUSAF2 processes to start work

3 Training of Trainers

a) Workshops
b) Community EPRA practical
c) Community sub-projects

- 40 workshops held
- 40 practical held
- 350 ToTs were trained
- 120 start-up sub-projects generated
- A core team to train community facilitators were trained

4 Training of Community Facilitators

a) Workshops
b) Community EPRA practical
c) Community Sub-projects

- 120 sub-project generated
- 40 workshops
- Four facilitators per sub-counties were trained

The training enabled a large team to

5 Sub-county Level Sensitisation

a) Workshops
b) Radio Broadcasts
c) Community meetings

- Organize in all sub-counties
- Conduct programmes targeting communities
- Workshops were organized in all the sub-counties

Radio programmes were organized to explain the role of sub-county leaders
The role of sub-county technical and political leaders were explained and awareness created

6 Awareness through Radio Broadcast

a) District Radio Broadcast
b) Regional Radio Broadcast
c) Radio Talk Shows

Radio programmes, radio talk shows, jingles and spots were broadcasted

- 60 talk shows,
- 60 radio programmes,
- 400 spots and jingles were broadcasted.

Public awareness of NUSAF2 was enhanced to spur participation and generate interest

7 Sector Collaboration & Participation

a) Sector Meetings
b) Joint Activities
c) Sector Strategies
d) Sector Norms & Standards

Explanation of sector norms and standards relevant to NUSAF2 implementation

- 10 meetings,
- 40 joint activities, Sector Norms and Standards studied in: health, education, infrastructure and agriculture

Sector collaboration and participation will enhance implementation of NUSAF2 and achievements captured

8 District Work Plans & Budgets

a) Implementation work plans
b) Sub-project budgets

- Make work plans based on indicative planning figures for districts
- All the 55 districts made their work plans and budgets

It is an orderly way to manage resource allocation based on the MoUs signed between Office of the Prime Minister and the districts

9 Generation of Community Sub-projects

a) Sub-project communities formation
b) Appraisal
c) Approval
d) Endorsement

- Generate sub-projects, appraise, approve and endorse for funding

Already 120 sub-projects are lined up for funding
Conduct field visits during the mission and conduct a stakeholders workshop
A successful mission was concluded and an Aide Memoire was written. The mission made several recommendations that will strengthen NUSAF2

Immediate future

The Office of the Prime Minister, in particular NUSAF2 Technical Support Team (TST) is working closely with the 55 districts to ensure that all kickstart sub-projects, more than 120 are funded in the second week of December 2010.

Once the maiden sub-projects are funded, the processes through which the generation, appraisal, approval and endorsement were conducted shall be replicated to enable many be funded in January 2011. It is certain that by February 2011 thousands of sub-projects will have been funded.

Police in the region have been trained on law and human rights issues

The Community

The Office of the Prime Minister wishes to reassure the community in northern Uganda to organise themselves into sub-project communities comprising members of households to benefit from the livelihoods investment programme.

The sub-county and district technical and political leaders should ensure proper targeting is done to enable the youth, women, disabled, ex-combatants and the most vulnerable to benefit.

For multi-community sub-projects focusing on public works programme like: roads, markets and water points among others, identification should be carefully done based on sub-county and district plans.

Similarly, for community infrastructure development like: community roads linking villages, education and health facilities among others should be carefully identified by the districts leaders based on priority in the work plans.

The Leaders

For better implementation of NUSAF2, the Office of the Prime Minister wishes to make a clarion call for political and technical leaders in the 55 districts, sectors and civil society to have concerted efforts to assist poor communities in northern Uganda access funds to improve their livelihoods and socio-economic infrastructures.

Leaders are particularly encouraged to mobilise, sensitise and make communities within their jurisdiction aware of the opportunities to reduce poverty and abject penury in northern Uganda. Leaders are urged to support the interventions under PRDP and in particular under NUSAF2 intervention.

The Public

The participation of the entire public is encouraged to pay attention to integrity, transparency, accountability to ensure that resources meant for the poor are used optimally during NUSAF2 implementation.

Due diligence and vigilance must be exercised by the public to keenly follow funds disbursed to the districts and ensure the funds reach the communities.

Any suspicion, alleged cases of corruption, misconduct and unclear processes of implementation should be reported to the mandated institutions like: the Inspectorate of Government, the Police and the Office of the Prime Minister for immediate action.

Directorate of Coordination and Monitoring

The contribution of Office of the Prime Minister to the overall economic development of Uganda is highlighted below.

Under Article 108A of the Constitution, Office of the Prime Minister is mandated to coordinate government policies across ministries. In order to coordinate effectively, the Office of the Prime Minister through the Government Annual Performance Report (GAPR) reports periodically on government's performance to cabinet and parliament. The report focuses on the performance of government across the sixteen sectors that constitute the annual planning and budgeting framework of all Ministries, Departments and Agencies (MDAs). Hence, the GAPR is a strategic report, providing performance and results information in key areas of government business, enabling Cabinet and Parliament to assess progress and target areas for reorganisation or increased investment.

Office of the Prime Minister under its coordination role coordinates Ministries, Departments and Agencies (MDAs) on cross cutting issues so as to enhance effective and efficient implementation of government policies and programmes in order to deliver good services to the people of Uganda.

Office of the Prime Minister coordinates the Presidential Investors Round Table (PIRT) which is a high level forum chaired by H.E the President and brings together a select group of 25 business leaders of whom 13 are local (foreign and local investors), and 12 are international to advise government on how to improve the investment climate. To date, the PIRT has recorded over 60 achievements some of which include; the creation of the ICT Ministry, the Business Processing Outsourcing Department in the Ministry of ICT as well as the implementation of government policies in Ministries, Departments and Agencies (MDAs). Other success stories include; lifting of the moratorium on new banks, establishment of the Agricultural Credit Facility of Uganda shillings 60 billion for commercial agriculture, creation of the Energy Equity Fund and the enactment of 7 prioritised commercial laws namely the Audit Act; the Copyright and Neighbouring Rights Act, the Mortgage Act, the Trade Secrets Act, the Hire Purchase Act, the Partnership Act and the Dual Citizenship Act.

Office of the Prime Minister coordinates the *barazas* which are a public forums where local leaders explain to the people how public funds they received were utilised. By this, sub-county local government leadership explains what resources they received; and what results are achieved in each and every sector. This tool puts checks on corruption and enhances the public's involvement in holding of government to account for service delivery.

Contribution of Office of the Prime Minister to sectors like Agriculture, Education, ICT, Urban Development, Infrastructure, Tourism among others include;

OPM through the Government Annual Performance Report (GAPR) makes assessment of each of the sixteen sectors that constitute the annual planning and budgeting framework of all Ministries, Departments and Agencies (MDAs). This enables the focus of the budget, and the decisions over allocations between sectors, to be informed by empirical data of past performance.

Through the Government Annual Performance Report (GAPR), which is a product of OPM, sectors are able to drive towards evidenced based policy making.

The GAPR also provided a strong set of sector-wide indicators and data that assisted in the finalisation of the National Development Plan (2010/11-2014/15). The five-year Plan was structured around sector and inter-sectoral initiatives that have a tangible contribution to the national priorities of enhancing agriculture, manufacturing, tourism, and other primary growth sectors.

OPM through the Government Annual Performance Report (GAPR) proposes measures to improve performance in subsequent financial year(s) for the sectors to improve on their performance.

Background

The Government of Uganda through Office of the Prime Minister designed the Luwero Rwenzori Development Programme (LRDP) as a special development recovery programme to address the effects of the national Resistance Movement (NRM) liberation struggle of 1981 - 1986 and the Allied Democratic Forces (ADF) insurgency of 1996 - 2003. The LRDP piloting phase is to be implemented for two financial years i.e. 2009/10 and 2010/11. Full scale implementation of the programme is expected to begin in FY 2011/12 for a period of five years in all the 40 districts. The total programme coist is estimated at Shs. 540 billion shillings. The piloting districts in 2009/10 FY were Mukono, Wakiso, Luwero, Nakasongola, Nakaseke, Mityana, Mubende, Kiboga, Kyenjojo, Kabarole, Kasese, Bundibugyo, Kiruhura, Kamwenge and Kibaale. In addition to the LRDP, the Luwero Triangle department is implementing the payment of one-off gratuity to civilian veterans that contributed to the liberation struggle and the fight against insurgency in different parts of the regions.

Programme Goals and Objectives

The goal of the programme is to redress the adverse socio-economic effects of the 1981-86 Liberation War and the ADF Insurgency of 1996-2003 and improve the wellbeing of the Population of Luwero and Rwenzori sub-regions.

The specific objectives are;

i)   To improve the economic wellbeing of 105 households per parish in 523 parishes by enabling them earn at least 20m per annum by 2015, To repair all road bottlenecks and improve the condition of 2,300kms district, 2900km community access and 30km urban roads to motorable state throughout the year by 2015,

ii) To increase the safe water coverage of the 11 districts below the national level coverage to 65% by 2015, To protect and sustainably manage the environment through use of environmentally friendly methods of production,

iii) To increase access to renewable energy to service delivery points and rural growth centres by 2015,

iv) To ensure that there is a government aided primary school and secondary school in all parishes and sub-counties, respectively,

v)   To improve the health service delivery to the communities of the region

vi) To promote peace, reconciliation and strengthen community based conflict mitigation and management within communities,

vii) To increase access and use of information and communications technology in the region, and

viii)To compensate civilian veterans who participated in the liberation struggle and the fight against ADF insurgency.

Pumping water out of a borehole in rural Uganda.

Northeastern Districts

| Abim | Amudat | Kaabong | Kotido | Moroto | Nakapiripirit | Napak |

The People: This area is mainly inhabited by the Karimojong and the Iteso. These people are mainly cattle keepers who rear short-horned cattle. They also carry out arable farming of food and cash crops. Cotton is the main cash crop produced here.

Tourism: Tourist attractions include wild game in the Kidepo Valley National Park and Pian-Upe Wildlife Reserve. The ostrich, the biggest non-flying bird is common in this region. Mt. Morungole is another attraction. Apok is a good camping site in the Kidepo Valley National Park.

How to get there: The area is accessible mainly by gravel roads. There is also access by air, but there are no scheduled regular flights to the region. There are good airstrips at Moroto, Kotido and Apok.

Sub-divisions: This region comprises Karamoja sub-region.

Top: Burchell's Zebra strolling past Apoka lodge. Left: Karimojong dancers in Kidepo Valley National Park in Kotido District. Right: Karimojong man with body decorations.

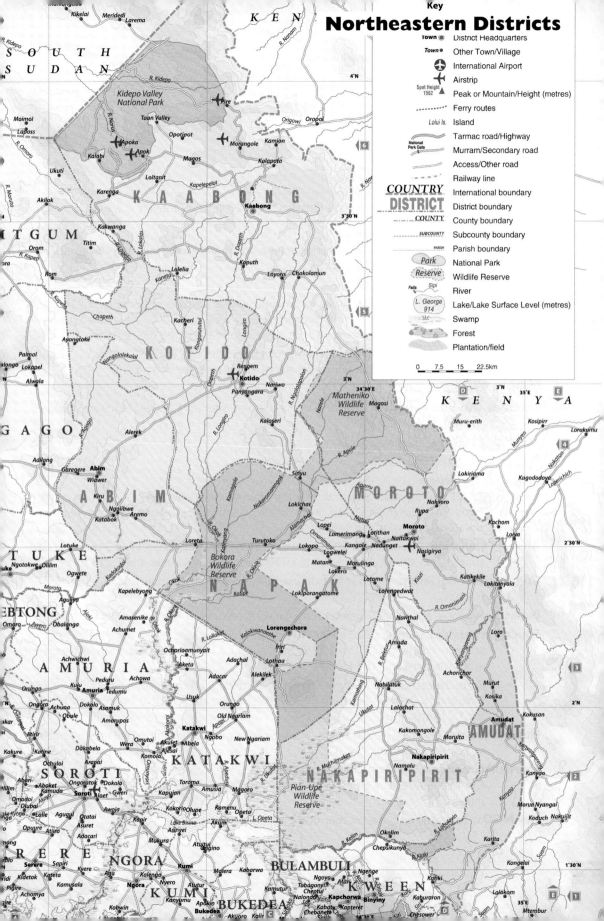

Key
Northeastern Districts

Town ⊚	District Headquarters
Town ●	Other Town/Village
✈	International Airport
✈	Airstrip
Spot Height 1562 ▲	Peak or Mountain/Height (metres)
- - - - -	Ferry routes
Lolui Is.	Island
	Tarmac road/Highway
	Murram/Secondary road
	Access/Other road
	Railway line
	International boundary
	District boundary
	County boundary
	Subcounty boundary
	Parish boundary
Park	National Park
Reserve	Wildlife Reserve
Sipi Falls	River
L. George 914	Lake/Lake Surface Level (metres)
	Swamp
	Forest
	Plantation/field

COUNTRY
DISTRICT
COUNTY
SUBCOUNTY
PARISH
National Park Gate

0   7.5   15   22.5km

Abim District

Abim District was carved out of Kotido District in July 2006. Until then, it was one of the two counties of Kotido District.

Location: It borders the districts of Kotido to the north and east, Napak to the south; and Agago and Otuke to the west.

Area: 2,361 sq.km

Climate, Relief and Vegetation: It lies at an approximate altitude of between 1,219m and 1,524m above sea level, with temperatures of well over 30°C. The rainfall regime is short and unreliable and thus Kotido has a semi-desert type of vegetation.

Population: Based on the 2009 population projections, there are: 53,500 people – 28,800 female and 24,700 male with a density of 22 persons per sq.km.

Major Towns: Abim Town Council

Counties and Sub-counties: Labwor County – Abim, Alerek, Lotukei, Morulem, Nakwae and Abim Town Council.

Main Language: Ng'akarimojong

People: Karimojong and Acholi

Economic Activities:
  (i)   Cattle rearing under pastoralism is the main economic activity.
  (ii) Food crops: Sorghum, maize, finger millet, pigeon peas, groundnuts, sunflower, sweet potatoes, cow peas and beans.

Animal Population: According to 2008 livestock census the district had 13,635 cattle; 37,229 goats; 8,381 sheep; 17,354 pigs, 61,330 chicken, 3,373 ducks and 2,213 turkeys.

Co-operative Societies: The district still uses the co-operative society services of Kotido District.

Banks: The people are still dependant on the banking services of Kotido District

Education Services: Primary schools: 48 – 40 government, 6 private, and 2 community. Primary school enrolment: 23,715 – 12,199 male and 11,516 female. Primary school teachers: 409 –306 male and 103 female.

  Secondary schools: 3 - (all government), Secondary school enrolment: 2,228 – 1,276 male and 952 female. Teachers: 88 – 72 male, 16 female. Available furniture is adequate for 1,216 students.

Health Services: 1 hospital (government – Abim Hospital); no health centre IV; 3 health centre III - (2 government and 1 NGO), and 7 health centre II - (6 government and 1 NGO).

Tourist Attractions: Morulem Gold Mining Fields are the main tourist attraction in Labwor County. There is a guide who translates and handles the encounters with the miners.

Key NGOs: The same as in the mother district, Kotido.

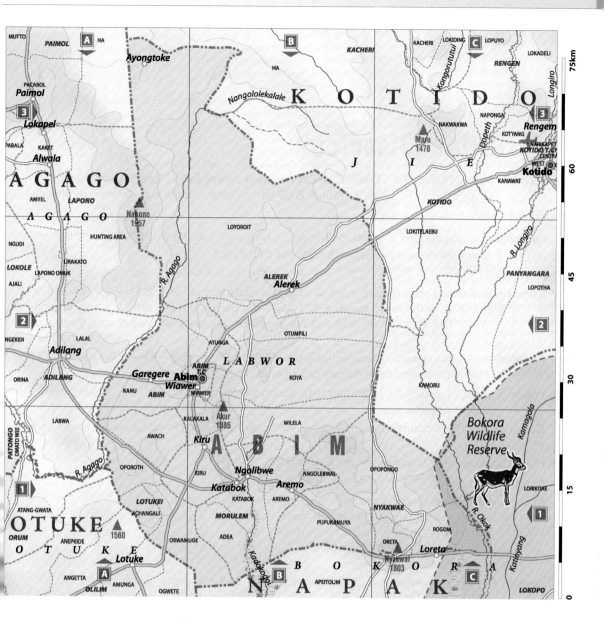

District Leaders:
District Chairperson
 – Mr Ochero, Jimbricky Norman
Ag CAO – Mr Bruno Mwayita
Deputy CAO – Vacant

Members of Parliament:
Labwor County – Mr Ayepa Michael
Woman MP – Ms Auma Juliana Modest

Amudat District

Formerly part of Nakapiripirit District, which was itself carved form Moroto District in 2001. Amudat existed as part of Nakapiripirit until 2009 when Pokot County was elevated to district status.

Location: Amudat borders Moroto to the north, Nakapiripirit to the west, Kween and Bukwo to the south, and the Republic of Kenya to the east.

Area: 1,617 sq km.

Climate, Relief and Vegetation: It lies at an approximate altitude of 1,356m – 1,524m above sea level, with rainfall totalling 400 – 600mm per annum and temperatures around 30°C. The area is semi-arid and the vegetation includes isolated thorny trees and shrubs.

Population: According to 2009 projections, there are 93,500 people – 41,700 female, 51,800 male with a population density of 57 persons per sq.km.

Major Towns: Nakapiripirit (administrative headquarters); Trading Centres – Namalu and Kokomongole.

Counties and Sub-counties: Upe County – Amudat, Amudat (Town Council), Karita and Loroo;

Main Language: Ng'akarimojong and Kiswahili.

People: Karamojong.

Economic Activities: Agriculture with emphasis on:
   (i)   Food crops: Sorghum, groundnuts, sunflower, sweet potatoes, cassava and bananas.
   (ii) Cash crops: Fruits and vegetables.
   (iii) Cattle rearing.

Animal Population: Amudat and Nakapiripirit have 674,746 cattle, 2,000 camels, 10,000 donkeys, 322pigs, 389,676 sheep, 547,365 goats, 104 rabbits and 314,308 chicken,15,653 ducks and 1,095 turkeys.

Co-operative Societies: Amudat, Nakapiripit, Napak and Moroto have 19 registered co-operative societies.

Industries: Brick making.

Education Services: Primary schools: 11 – 10 government and 1 community. Primary school enrolment: 5,132 –male and female not stated. Primary school teachers: 76, male and female not stated.

Secondary schools: 2 - (all government). Secondary school enrolment: 745 – 539 male and 206 female. Teachers: 29 – 25 male and 4 female.

No tertiary institutions.

Health Services: 1 hospital – (NGO- Amudat Hospital); no health centre (IV); no health centre (III) and 3 health centre II (all government).

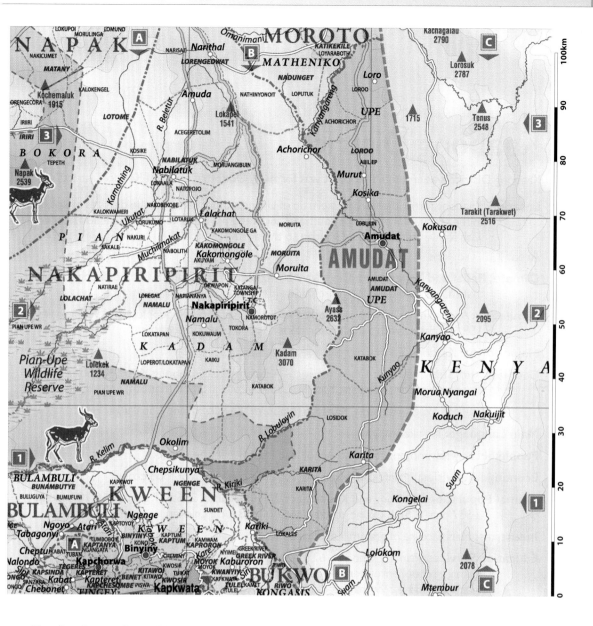

Tourist Attractions: There is a prison farm worth visiting. Kadam Mountain is the other attraction.

Key NGO: SNV Uganda.

District leaders:	Members of Parliament:
Chairperson – Mr Bwatum William K.	Upe County – Mr Lolem Micah Akasile
Ag Chief Administrative Officer (CAO)	Woman MP – Ms Nauwat Rosemary
– Kaziba M. Nandhala	
Deputy CAO – Vacant	

Kaabong District

Kaabong District was created in 2005. It was formerly Dodoth County of Kotido District.

Location: Kaabong forms the northeastern tip of Uganda. It borders with the districts of Kotido to the south, Moroto to the southeast and Kitgum District to the West. It also borders with Kenya to the East, and Sudan to the north.

Area: 7,219 sq. kms.

Climate, Relief and Vegetation: Dry savannah vegetation and is arid with undulating scenery that makes it suitable for game parks. Has high potential for minerals.

Population: According to 2009 projections, the district has 316,500 people – 157,900 females, 158,600 males with a population density of 43 persons per sq.km.

Major Towns: Kaabong Town Council

Counties and Sub-counties: Dodoth East – Kaabong East, Kaabong West, Kaabong Town Council, Kamion, Kalapata, Kathile, Lodiko, Lolelia, Sidok (Kapoth) and Loyoro

Dodoth West – Kapedo, Karenga (Napore), Kawalakol and Lobalangit.

Main Language: Ng'akarimojong.

People: Mainly Karimojong, but also Acholi and Iteso live in the district.

Economic Activities: Mainly cattle keeping and little cultivation of food crops.

Animal Population: Kaabong and Kotido have 280,090 cattle, 256,627 goats, 210,287 sheep, 2,537 pigs, 2,562, exotic chicken and174,868 local chicken.

Industries: Manufacture of grainmill products.

Education Services: Primary schools – 62 schools - 55 government, 5 community and 2 private. Primary school enrolment: 44,712 – 25,869 male and 18,843 female. Primary school teachers: 483 – 399 male and 84 female. Available furniture is adequate for 13,257 pupils.

Secondary schools: 2 schools - (all government). Secondary school enrolment: 1,871 – 1,219 male and 652 female. Teachers: 86– 74 male and 12 female.

Health Services: 1 hospital – (government – Kaabong Hospital); 1 health centre III – (government); and 24 health centre II – (20 government, 4 NGO).

Tourist Attractions (Developed and Potential): Kaabong Gold Mining Fields. The traditional method of gold extraction is worth watching and is the main tourist attraction in Kaabong District.

Hotel and Catering Industry: Apoka Rest Camp and the Uganda Wild Authority Hostel, found in the Kidepo Valley National Park are the most outstanding, designed to cater for the upmarket and budget visitors. Both facilities have a total capacity of 38 beds.

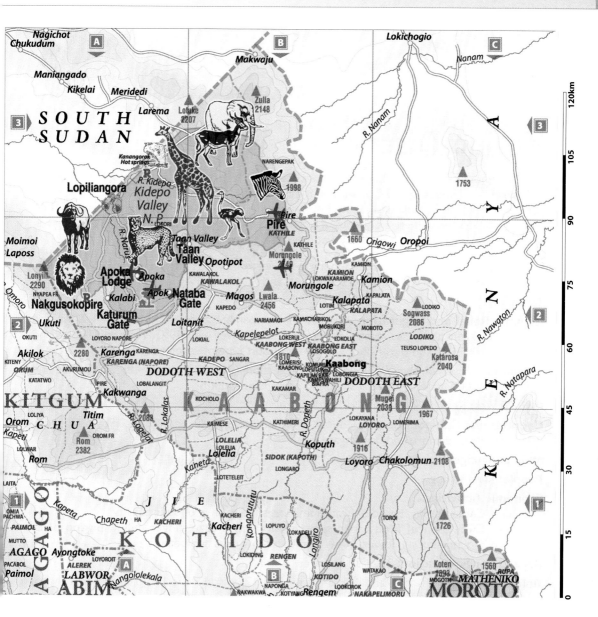

District Leaders:
District Chairperson
– Mr Lomonyang Joseph
Ag Chief Administrative Officer (CAO)
– Mr Fancis Andrew Oluka
Deputy CAO – Vacant

Members of Parliament:
Dodoth East County – Mr Lokeris Samson
Dodoth West County – Mr Simon Lokodo
District Woman MP – Ms Akello Rose Lilly

Kotido District

At independence in 1962, Karamoja consisted of the present-day Kotido, Moroto and Nakapiripirit. Under the 1974 provincial administration, the district was divided into North Karamoja, South Karamoja and Central Karamoja. In 1980, North Karamoja became Kotido District. In 2005 and 2006 two counties of Kotido namely; Dodoth and Labwor, were each given district status leaving only Jie County to constitute Kotido.

Location: It borders the districts of Kaboong to the north, Moroto to the east, Napak to the south, Abim to the west and the southwest, and Kitgum and Agago to the northwest.

Area: 3,701 sq.km.

Climate, Relief and Vegetation: It lies at an approximate altitude of between 1,219m and 1,524m above sea level, with temperatures of well over 30°C. The rainfall is low and unreliable and thus Kotido has a semi-desert type of vegetation.

Population: Based on the 2009 population projections: 188,200 people - 89,200 female and 99,000 males with a density of 50 persons per sq.km.

Main Towns: Kotido (administrative headquarters).

Counties and Sub-counties: Jie County – Kacheri, Rengen, Kotido, Kotido (Town Council), Nakapelimoru and Panyangara.

Main Language: Ng'akarimojong.

People: Karamojong.

Economic Activities:
(i)   Cattle rearing, based on transhumance is the main economic activity.
(ii) Cultivation of food crops such as sorghum, maize, finger millet, pigeon peas, groundnuts, sunflower, sweet potatoes, cow peas and beans.

Area under Forestation: 232,137 hectares.

Animal Population: Kotido and Kaabong have 384,122 cattle, 267,106 goats, 288,074 sheep, 1,002 pigs, 638 exotic chicken and 33,688 local chicken.

Co-operative Societies: Kotido and Kaabong have 41 registered primary societies with Karamoja Union at the district level.

Industries: Grain milling.

Banks: Stanbic Bank Uganda Ltd – 1.

Education Services: Primary schools: 26 – 21 government, 1 private and 4 community. Primary school enrolment: 16,530 pupils – 9,517 male and 7,013 female. Primary school teachers: 148 – 92 male, 56 female. Available furniture is adequate for 6,870 pupils.

Secondary Schools: 2 schools – 1 government and 1 community. Secondary schools enrolment: 1,295 –871 male and 424 female. Teachers: 28 – 25 male and 5 female. Available furniture is adequate for 1,326 students.

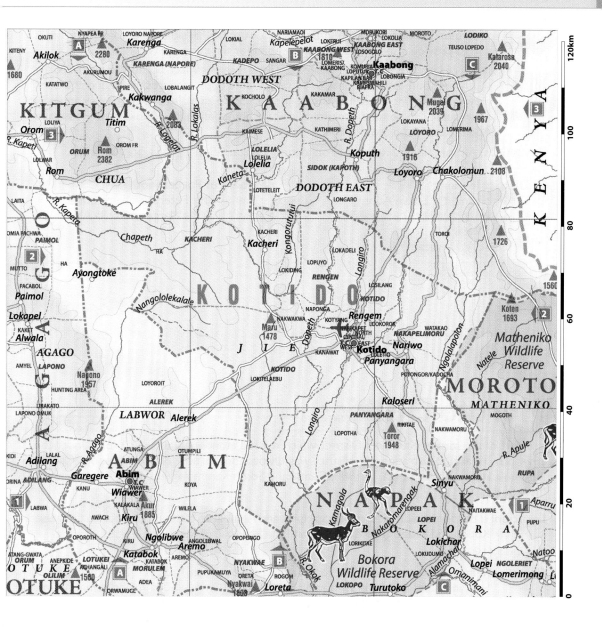

Health Services: 1 health centre IV – (government); 3 health centre III - (2 government – 1 NGO) and 5 health centre II (all government).

Transport & Communication: The district has a murram road network connecting all sub-counties to the district headquarters as well as to the neighbouring districts. There is also an airfield at Kotido which connects the district to Entebbe airport and the capital city. The Civil Aviation Authority provides H.F. radio communication. Transportation from the airfield to town can be provided by taxi. Mobile telephone and public payphone services are available in town.

Tourist Attractions: The Largest Village in East Africa: The village is located about half a kilometre from Kotido town, at Watakau Parish, Nakapirimur Sub-county. Comprising of as many as 10,000 grass-thatched homes and a population of 21,000 people, it is

said to be the largest village in East Africa. A rocky hill situated at the village site is said to provide a security observatory point for the community.

Mathenicko and Bokora Wild Reserves: These reserves which border the district to the south and southeast are home to ostriches, antelopes, leopards, lions, and cheaters. However, with increase in livestock, most of these animals have gone away and only a few game can be sited occasionally. For accomodation, the Apoka Rest House and Apoka Rest Camp are available.

Key NGOs: African Medical Research Foundation, Oxfam GB in Uganda, SNV Uganda.

District leaders:	**Members of Parliament:**
Chairperson – **Mr Lokwi Adome C.**	Jie County – **Mr Peter Abrahams Lokii**
Chief Administrative Officer (CAO)	Woman MP – **Ms Margaret Achila Aleper**
– **Mr Peter Okello**	
Deputy CAO – **Vacant**	

Moroto District

It is part of the former Karamoja District which existed at independence in 1962. Under the 1974 provincial administration, the district was divided into three – North Karamoja, Central Karamoja and South Karamoja. In 1980, Cental and South Karamoja were joined and renamed Moroto district.

Location: It borders the districts of Nakapiripirit and Amudat to the south, Napak to the west, Kotido and Kaabong to the north and the Republic of Kenya to the east.

Area: 4,419 sq. km.

Climate, Relief and Vegetation: It lies at an altitude of between 1,356m – 1,524m above sea level in a semi-arid zone with rainfall as low as 400mm – 600mm and temperatures over 30°C per annum. Vegetation includes isolated thorny trees and shrubs.

Population: According to 2009 projections, there are 101,600 people – 50,200 female, 51,400 male with a population density of 23 persons per sq.km.

Major Towns: Moroto (administrative headquarters); Trading Centre – Kangole.

Counties and Sub-counties: Matheniko County – Katikekile, Nadunget, Rupa and Tapac. Moroto Municipality – South Division, North Divison.

Main Language: Ng'akarimojong.

People: Karamojong.

Economic Activities: Mainly cattle keeping and some subsistence cultivation with emphasis on:
  (i) Food crops: Sorghum, maize, groundnuts, beans, sunflower, sweet potatoes and cassava.
  (ii) Vegetables: Cabbage.

Banks: Stanbic Bank Uganda Ltd –1.

Area under Forestation: 68,366 hectares.

Animal Population: Moroto and Napak have 352,867 cattle, 5,534 pigs, 307,028 sheep, 380,172 goats, 260,997 chicken,18,834 ducks and 3,075 turkeys.

Co-operative Societies: Moroto, Nakapiripit and Napak have 19 registered primary societies with Karamoja Union as the main one.

Education Services: Primary schools: 24 schools – 19 government, 3 private and 2 community. Primary school enrolment: 9,071 – 4,820 male and 4,251 female. Primary school teachers: 172 – 95 male and 77 female. Available furniture is adequate for 6,899 pupils.

Secondary schools: 4 schools – 1 government, 2 private and 1 community. Secondary school enrolment: 1,646 – 1,318 male and 328 female. Teachers: 107 – 96 male and 11 female. Available furniture is adequate for 1,358 students.

Health Services: 1 government District Hospital – Moroto Hospital with 115 beds, 3 health centre III (all NGO); and 6 health centre II (5 Government, 1 NGO).

Transport Network: Moroto Airfield – Has a 1,496m x 30m grass airstrip that is regularly maintained. The Civil Aviation Authority provides H.F. radio communication. The airfield is 5.1 km from Moroto town and transportation from the airfield by taxi can be arranged. The district has a poorly distributed murram road network which serves mainly the southern part of the district.

Tourist Attractions: Magosian Culture with many beautifully fashioned quartz tools bearing a resemblance to tools of the Stillbay Stone Age culture of Somaliland have been found in Moroto. Named after a local borehole, the small Stone Age tools are thought to date – between 7,000 – 5,000 BC. The Matheniko Game Reserve is also found in Moroto District and is a home for ostriches and a variety of antelopes.

Operational Radio and TV Stations: Radio Management Services.

Key NGO: SNV Uganda.

District leaders:	Members of Parliament:
Chairperson – Mr Aol Mark M.	Matheniko County – Mr Lokii John Baptist
Chief Administrative Officer (CAO)	Moroto Municipality
– Mr Stephen Ouma	– Mr Aleper Simon Peter
Town Clerk (Moroto Municipal Council)	Woman MP – Ms Iriama Margaret
– Mr Mackay Odeke Opolot	
Mayor (Moroto Municipal Council)	
– Mr Alex Lemu Longoria	

Nakapiripirit District

Formerly part of Moroto District, in 1974, Nakapiripirit existed as South Karamoja District, but was in 1980 merged with Central Karamoja to form Moroto District. In 2001 it was again carved out of Moroto District.

Location: It borders Moroto and Napak to the north, Katakwi and Kumi to the west, Bulambuli and Kween to the south and Amudat to the east.

Area: 4,201.3 sq km.

Climate, Relief and Vegetation: It lies at an approximate altitude of 1,356m – 1,524m above sea level, with low rainfall totaling 400 – 600mm per annum and temperatures around 30°C. The area is semi-arid and the vegetation includes isolated thorny trees and shrubs.

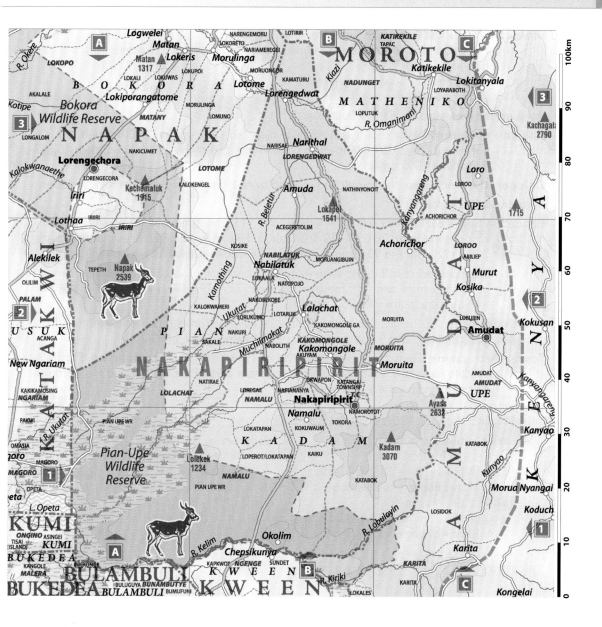

Population: According to 2009 projection, there are 133,100 people – 67,900 female, 65,200 male with a population density of 30 persons per sq.km.

Major Towns: Nakapiripirit (administrative headquarters); Trading Centres – Chepsikunya and Namalu.

Counties and Sub-counties: Cwekwii (Kadam) County – Kakomongole, Moruita, Nakapiripirit (Town Council), Namalu and Loregae. Pian County – Lorachat, Lorengedwat and Nabilatuk

Main Language: Ng'akarimojong.

People: Karamojong.

Economic Activities: Agriculture with emphasis on:
  (i)   Food crops: Sorghum, groundnuts, sunflower, sweet potatoes, cassava and bananas.
  (ii) Cash crops: Fruits and vegetables.
  (iii) Cattle rearing.

Area under Forestation: 45,855 hectares.

Animal Population: Nakapiripirit and Amudat have 674,746 cattle, 2,000 camels, 10,000 donkeys, 322 pigs, 389,676 sheep, 547,365 goats, 104 rabbits, 314,308 chicken, 15,653 ducks and 1,095 turkeys.

Co-operative Societies: Nakapiripit and Moroto have 19 registered co-operative societies.

Industries: Brick making.

Education Services: Primary schools – 44 schools - (43 government and 1 private). Primary school enrolment: 20,057 – 10,383 male and 9,674 female. Primary school teachers: 285 - 192 male and 93 female. Available furniture was not fully reported.

Secondary schools: 2 - (1 government and 1 community). Secondary school enrolment: 479 – 345 male and 134 female. Teachers: 33 – 29 male and 4 female. Available furniture is adequate for 392 students.

Health Services: No hospital; 2 health centre IV (all government); 3 health centre III (all government); and 9 health centre II (4 government and 5 NGO)

Tourist Attractions: There is a prison farm. Kadam Mountain is another attraction. Pian-Upe Wildlife Reseve: This is found in the southern part of the district and is a home to ostriches and a variety of antelopes.

Key NGO: SNV Uganda.

District leaders:
Chairperson – Mr John Lorot
Ag Chief Administrative Officer (CAO)
  – Mr Moses Bahemuka Kisembo
Deputy CAO – Vacant
Town Clerk (Nakapiripirit Town Council)
  – Mr Luke Abwangamoi

Members of Parliament:
Chekwii County (Kadam)
  – Mr Peter Aimat Lokeris
Pian County – Mr Achia Remigio
Woman MP – Ms Rose Iriama

Napak District

It is part of the former Karamoja District which existed at independence in 1962. Under the 1974 provincial administration, the district was divided into three – North Karamoja, Central Karamoja and South Karamoja. In 1980, Cental and South Karamoja were joined and renamed

Moroto district. Napak district was created when Bokora county of Moroto District was elevated to district status.

Location: It borders the districts of Nakapiripirit to the south, Katakwi to the southwest, Kotido to the north and the Republic of Kenya to the east.

Area: 8,441.3 sq. km.

Climate, Relief and Vegetation: It lies at an altitude of between 1,356m –1,524m above sea level in a semi-arid zone with rainfall as low as 400mm – 600mm and temperatures over 30°C per annum. Vegetation includes isolated thorny trees and shrubs.

Population: According to 2009 projections, there are 235,200 people – 119,600 female, 115,600 male.

Major Towns: Napak (administrative headquarters); Trading Centre – Kangole.

Counties and Sub-counties: Bokora County – Iriri, Lokopo, Lolengecora Lopei, Lotome, Matany, Napak (Town Council) and Ngoleriet

Main Language: Ng'akarimojong.

People: Karamojong.

Economic Activities: Mainly cattle keeping, while subsistence agriculture is done at a small scale. Emphasis is on:
  (i)   Food crops: Sorghum, maize, groundnuts, beans, sunflower, sweet potatoes and cassava.
  (ii) Vegetables: Cabbage.
  (iii) Cattle rearing.

Banks: Stanbic Bank Uganda Ltd –1.

Area under Forestation: 68,366 hectares.

Animal Population: Napak and Moroto have 352,867 cattle, 5,534 pigs, 307,028 sheep, 380,172 goats, 260,997 chicken,18,834 ducks and 3,075 turkeys.

Co-operative Societies: Moroto and Nakapiripit have 19 registered primary societies with Karamoja Union at the district level.

Education Services: Primary schools: 35 schools – 31 government, private 1 and 3 community. Primary school enrolment: 16,174 – 9,278 male and 6,896 female. Primary school teachers: 245 – 150 male and 95 female. Available furniture not fully reported.

Secondary schools: 3 Secondary school 2 government, 1 private and 1Techinical institution. Secondary school enrolment: 728 – 138 male and 590 female. Teachers: 80 – 68 male and 12 female.

Health Services: 1 hospital (NGO – Uganda Catholic Medical Bureau – St. Kizito Hospital, Matany with 244 beds); no health centre IV; 3 health centre III (2 government and 1 NGO), 3 health centres II (all government)

Transport Network: Moroto Airfield – Has a 1,496m x 30m grass airstrip that is regularly maintained. Mobile and telephone booths are available in town. The Civil Aviation Authority provides H.F. radio communication. The airfield is 5.1 km from Moroto town. Transportation from the airfield can be provided by taxi.

Tourist Attractions: Labwor and Nangeya hills and giant inselbergs, volcanic plugs that have remained after the erosion of the cones. The Bokora Wildlife Reserve which covers a bigger part of the district and the Matheniko Wildlfe Reserve which covers the northeastern part of the district are home to various wild animals. Matany has a busy hospital with Belgian doctors and a small market. There is a comfortable guest house.

Operational Radio and TV Stations: Radio Management Services.
Key NGO: SNV Uganda.

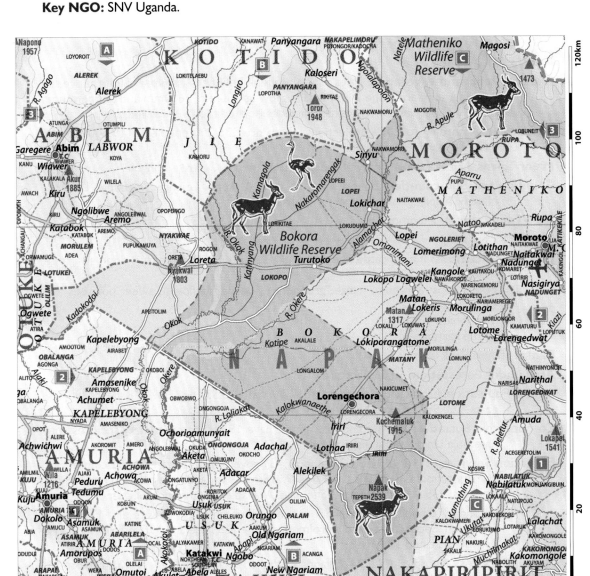

District leaders:
Chairperson – **Joseph Lomonyang**
Ag Chief Administrative Officer (CAO)
    – **Mr Joseph Lomongin**
Deputy Chief Administrative Officer
    (DCAO) – Vacant
Town Clerk (Moroto Municipal Council)
    – **Mr Jimmy Lorwor**

Members of Parliament:
Bokora County – **Mr Terence Naco Achila**
Woman MP – **Ms Namoe Stella Nyomera**

MINISTRY OF FINANCE

EXECUTIVE SUMMARY

In June both Annual headline inflation and core inflation remained relatively stable at 4.4% and 4.6% compared to 4.3% and 4.6% in May. URA collections amounted to Shs 436.86 billion against the month's target of Shs 531.42 billion resulting into a short fall of Shs 94.56 billion. Total non-tax revenue (NTR) collections amounted to Shs 4.18 billion against an estimate of Shs 4.30 billion. In June, the value of exports and imports amounted to US$ 128 million and US$ 378 million, down by 1.62% and 12.75%, respectively. In the foreign exchange market, the shilling depreciated by 4.4% from an average mid-rate of Shs of Shs 2,174.6/$ US in May to Shs 2257.44/$US in June 2010. The Central Bank Issued Government securities worth Shs 179.6 billion, with interest rates remaining relatively stable between 4.4% and 6.95% compared to May.

1. Real Sector

Inflation

Annual headline (all items) inflation remained relatively stable at 4.4% in June, compared to 4.3% in May 2010 as the decline in both food crop and utility prices was matched by increases in prices of other items including beverages, clothing and foot wear, rent, health and entertainment charges. The reduction in food crop inflation is largely a result of the increased supply of food items to the markets. Core inflation was at 4.6% during June 2010, which was the same level of increase registered for the month of May. Following a reduction in prices for diesel, paraffin and firewood in most centres, the energy, fuel and utilities inflation rate declined from 4.1% in May to 3.8% in June. Over the twelve month period, annual headline and core inflation averaged 9.5% and 7.8%, respectively.

2. Fiscal Sector

Overview and Cumulative Revenue Performance URA collections in June amounted to Shs 437 billion against the month's target of Shs 531 billion resulting into a shortfall of Shs 94.5 billion or 17.8%. There was an underperformance on collections on all the major tax categories – direct, indirect and international trade, which were 13.9%, 6.2% and 20.7% below their monthly target. Figure 3 shows collections and targets for tax revenues by major category in June 2010. Cumulatively, revenue collections during the financial year amounted to Shs 4,474 billion, which represents a growth of 14.8% over the previous financial year level and a shortfall of Shs. 268 billion or 6% as compared to the target.

i. Direct Domestic Taxes (DDT)

Direct domestic taxes amounted to Shs 199.9 billion, reflecting deficit collections amounting to Shs 36.61 billion or 15.48% against the monthly target. This performance is largely attributed to weaker performances by collections on PAYE and corporation tax, which more than offset the above target performance by withholding tax. Withholding tax collections were 25.6% above their monthly target, while PAYE and corporation taxes performed below their targets by 4.13% and 28.3% re-spectively. In addition, there were underperformances by collections on rental income tax and tax on bank interest.

The cumulative direct domestic tax collections for the financial year rose by 26.6% over the previous year's level to Shs 1,405.8 billion, and this represents surplus collections of 4.9% as compared to the target for the year.

ii. Indirect Domestic Taxes (IDT)

Indirect domestic tax collections fell short of projections for the month, as both excise and VAT collections underper-formed. Collections amounted to Shs 76.93 billion, which was Shs 5.15 billion or 6.28% below target. Excise duty collections amounted to Shs 25.6 billion against a projection of Shs 26.98 billion, which reflects a 94.9% monthly achieve-ment rate. With the exception of collections on soft drinks, sugar, bottled water and cement, there was an under-performance by duty collections on all the other goods. At the same time, collections on VAT fell short of projections by Shs 3.79 billion or 6.9%, as an over performance by VAT on beer, soft drinks and other goods was more than offset by short-falls totaling Shs 9.7 billion on spirits and VAT on Services.

On a cumulative basis, despite falling short by 1.2% on their target, indirect domestic tax collections during the financial year 2009/10 represent an increase of 23% as compared to the previous year.

iii. Taxes on International Trade (TIT)
Revenues accruing from taxes on international trade amounted to Shs 169.98 billion, which was Shs 44.42 billion or 20.7% below the monthly target. Trade taxes continued to be affected by the lower than projected import volumes. Collections on petroleum duty VAT on imports, and Import duty the three largest items in the sub category underperformed by 14%, 21.5% and 31%, respectively. However, on a cumulative basis, collections on international trade during the financial year 2009/10 rose by 3.65% over the previous year.

iv. Fees and Licenses
Revenues from fees and licenses for June 2010 amounted to Shs 8.93 billion, representing surplus collections of Shs 3 billion, or 51.3% against the target for the month. All the items within this sub category exceeded their monthly target. Cumulatively, collections from fees and licenses during the financial year were above target by 13.9%, and represent a growth of 31.25% over the previous year's level.

v. Non Tax Revenue
In some ministries and government departments, the function of collection of non-tax revenues has been transferred to URA. Subsequently, these revenues are collected and reported by URA. A total of Shs 4.18 billion was collected from non tax revenue sources against a target of Shs 4.30 billion, indicating a shortfall of Shs 0.12 billion. This was attributed to lower than expected collection from transport regulation fees and other unclassified sources of non tax revenues.

3. EXTERNAL SECTOR

The value of exports and imports during the month declined by 1.62% and 12.75% to US$ 128 million and US$ 378 million, respectively as compared to May 2010 (shown in Figure 5). An increase in both the volume and value of exports of coffee, live animals, gold, cobalt, iron and steel, and other precious metals was more than offset by a reduction in the value of exports of cotton, tea, cocoa beans, maize and vanilla.

i. Traditional Exports
The value of traditional exports in June amounted to US$

32.5 million, which was an 8% decline from the value recorded in May. Traditional exports accounted for 25.3% of total exports, with coffee contributing the largest share of 17.9% and amounting to US$ 23 million. While coffee export values registered a 26% increase during the month, the values of other traditional exports which include cotton, tea and tobacco recorded a decline.

ii. Non - Traditional Exports
The value of non-traditional exports, increased by US$ 0.2 million to US$ 96.2 million in June as compared to the may level. Fish and fish products constituted the biggest share of nontraditional exports during the month and amounted to US$ 9.3 million. During the month, there was a general improvement in the performance of most items in this category, notably cement, sugar, gold, fats and oils plus iron and steel, as compared to the previous month.

iii. Imports
The value of imports during the month amounted to US$ 378.1 million, which was a decline by US$ 55.3 million or 12.8% as compared to the level in May. This performance was largely attributed to a lower than projected growth in import demand during the month.

4. MONETARY SECTOR

i. Foreign Exchange Market
In the foreign exchange market, the Shilling depreciated by 3.8% against the US dollar. The monthly average inter bank mid rate rose from Shs 2,174/US$ in May to Shs 2,257/US$ in June. This depreciation represents the highest level so far since August 2009. The weakening of the shilling during the month was largely attributed to gross foreign exchange purchases by commercial banks resulting from strong corporate sector demand. The trends in the foreign exchange market for the Shilling against the US dollar during the period January 2008 to June 2010.

ii. Securities Market
During the month, the Central Bank issued government securities worth Shs 179.6 billion, which included three Treasury Bills and one Treasury Bond auction. The monthly average interest rate on the 91-day Treasury Bill was 4.4%, while the rate on the longest dated 364-day Treasury Bill was 6.95%. The movement in average monthly TB interest rates for the period June 2009 and June 2010.

Eastern Districts

The People: The inhabitants here include the Bagisu, the Bagwere, the Banyole, the Basoga, the Iteso, the Japadhola, the Kumam, the Samia and Sabiny.

These people are mainly cultivators but they also keep some cattle. The main cash crops produced in this area are cotton and coffee. This area also produces a lot of citrus fruits.

Tourism: There are numerous tourist attractions which include the source of the Nile and the Bujagali Falls both in Jinja District; the landscape and forests of Mt. Elgon National Park; the spectacular Sipi Falls at the foothills of Mt. Elgon, pre-historic rock paintings at Nyero in Kumi District and the magnificent Tororo Rock in Tororo District.

The Imbalu circumcision ceremony every even year, when the mass, public circumcision of Bagisu young males takes place is another interesting cultural festival that attracts tourists.

How to get there: This area is accessible by road and railway. Most of the districts are accessible by tarmac roads. There is a tarmac connection from Kampala to Jinja to Busia via Iganga. Other tarmac roads include the Jinja-Tororo Road, the Jinja-Soroti Road via Mbale and the Mbale-Kapchorwa Road via Sironko. The Jinja-Tororo railway line is functional while the Tororo-Kumi-Soroti line is under rehabilitation.

This region can also be accessed by air and there are good airstrips at Jinja, Soroti and Tororo, but there are no regular scheduled flights.

Sub-division: This sub region is sub-divided into sub-regions of Bugisu, Bukedi, Busoga, Sebei and Teso.

Left: The Owen falls dam bridge across the Nile in Jinja. Right: Storm gathers in Soroti District.

Eastern Districts

Amuria District

Up to 2005, Amuria District was a county of Katakwi District.

Location: Borders the districts of Napak to the north, Otuke to the northwest, Alebtong and Kaberamaido to the west, Soroti to the south, and Katakwi to the east.

Area: 2,576 sq.km.

Relief and Vegetation: Generally flat with dry savannah grasslands.

Population: According to 2009 projections; 310,700 people – 165,300 females, 145,400 males with a density of 120 persons per sq.km.

Major Towns: Amuria Town Council

Counties and Sub-counties: Amuria County: Abarilela, Asamuk, Kuju, Orungo, Wera, Morungatuny and Amuria Town Council; Kapelebyong County: Acowa, Kapelebyong and Obalanga.

Main Language: Ateso

People: Mainly Iteso, but Langi, Kumam, Karimojong, Acholi other Ugandans and non-Ugandans also live in the district.

Economic Activities: High economic potential in terms of apiary, crop and animal production.

Animal Population: Amuria has 171,375 cattle, 113,110 goats, 35,942 sheep, 41,318 pigs, 545,388 chicken, 5,703 ducks and 4,670 turkeys according to 2008 statistics.

Industries: Manufacture of textiles, grainmill products and bakery products.

Education Services: Primary schools: 101 – 100 government and 1 community. Primary school enrolment: 70,874 – 35,977 male and 34,897 female. Primary school teachers: 1,148 – 901 male and 247 female.

Secondary schools: 12 schools – (6 government, 5 community and 1 private) Secondary school enrolment: 4,360 students – 2,888 male and 1,472 female. Teachers: 98 – 59 male and 39 female. Available furniture is adequate for 2,913 students.

Health Services: 2 health centre IV - (government); 10 health centre III - (7government and 3 NGO); and 20 health centre II - (16 government and 4 NGO).

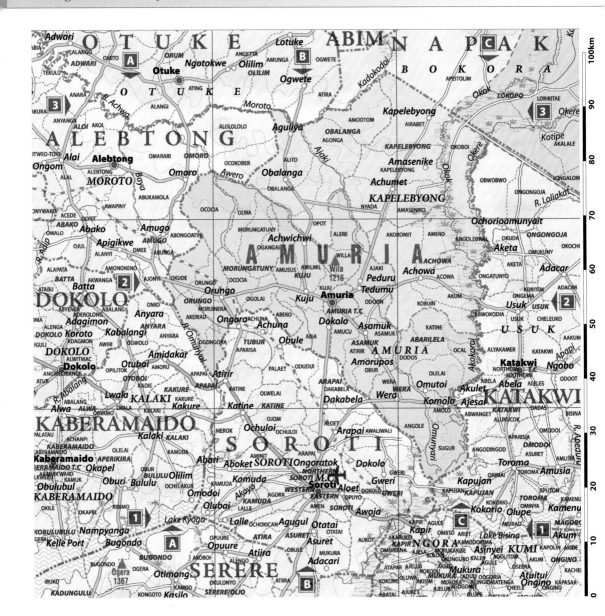

District leaders:
Chairperson – Mr Oluma John Francis
Ag Chief Administrative Officer (CAO)
   – Mr Alfred Malinga
Deputy CAO – Vacant

Members of Parliament:
Amuria County – Mr Musa Francis Ecweru
Kapelebyong County
   – Mr Eriaku Peter Emmanuel
Woman Representative – Ms Susan Amero

Budaka District

Budaka District was carved out of Pallisa District in 2005.

Location: Borders with the districts of Pallisa to the north, Mbale to the east, Butaleja to the south and Kibuku to the west.

Area: 826.88 sq. kms.

Climate, Relief and Vegetation: Generally flat and covered with savannah grasslands. Rainfall goes up to 1,164mm annually and temperatures up 29 C maximum and 16 C minimum.

Population: Based on the 2009 population projections there are 161,700 people – 84,200 female and 77,500 male , with a density of 195 persons per sq.km.

Major Towns: Budaka Town Council.

Counties and Sub-counties: Budaka County – Budaka (Town Council), Budaka, Kachomo, Kakule, Kaderuna, Lyama, Naboa, Nansanga; Iki-Iki County – Iki-iki, Kamonkoli, Kameruka, Katira, Muguti.

Main Language: Ateso and Lugwere

People: Bagwere, Banyole, Iteso, Basoga, Bagisu, Bakenyi, Baganda, Japadhola, other Ugandans and non Ugandans.

Economic Activities: Has a high economic potential in terms of apiary, crop and animal production.

Animal Population: 40,231 cattle, 51,942 goats, 3,987 sheep, 5,043 pigs, 172,627 chicken, 6,933 ducks and 8,940 turkeys.

Industries: Furniture, grainmill products, bakery products, metal products, textiles and wearing apparel, dairy products as well as sawmilling and furniture making.

Education Services: Primary schools: 68 – 52 government, 13 private and 3 community. Enrolment 57,741 pupils – 29,199 male and 28,542 female. Primary school teachers: 888 – 519 male and 369 female. Available furniture not fully reported.

Secondary Schools: 11 schools - 6 government, 5 private. Enrolment: 7,411 students, 3,913 male and 3,498 female. Secondary school teachers: 337 – 264 male and 73 female. Available furniture adequate for 5,665 students.

Health Services: 1 health centre IV (government); 10 health centre III (8 government and 2 NGO); and 3 health centre II (2 government and 1 NGO).

Tourist Attractions: Budaka Kakungulu Sites

District Leaders:
District Chairperson – Mr Mboizi Arthur
CAO – Mr Elias Byamungu
DCAO – Vacant

Members of Parliament:
Budaka County – Mr Mbugo Kezekia
Iki-Iki County
 – Mr Twa-Twa Mutwalante Jeremiah
Woman MP – Ms Kataike Sarah Ndoboli

Bududa District

Bududa District was in 2006 carved from Manafwa District which in 2005 had been carved out of Mbale District.

Location: Bududa District borders with Sironko to the north, the Republic of Kenya to the east, Manafwa District to the south and Mbale District to the west.

Area: 252 sq. kms.

Climate, Relief and Vegetation: Generally mountainous, because it is part of Mt. Elgon, with steep terrain. It experiences a montane type of climate that is characterised by heavy rains around April and October.

Population: Based on the 2009 population projection: 157,602 people - 79,388 female and 78,214 male with a density of 150 persons per sq.km.

Major Towns: Bududa Town Council

Counties and Sub-counties: Manjiya County – Bubiita, Bududa, Bududa (Town Council), Bukibokolo, Bukigai, Bulucheke, Bumayoka, Bumasheti, Bushiribo, Bushiyi, Buwali, Bukalasi, Bushika Nakatsi, Nalwanza and Nabweya.

Main Language: Lumasaba

People: The ethnic groups include Bagisu, Iteso, Banyole, Langi, Baganda, Basoga and Bagwere. The Bagisu are estimated to be 86% of the total population.

Economic Activities: Over 84% of households engage in subsistence arable farming. Animal rearing of mainly local Zebu cattle, sheep, piggery and poultry is also done.

Animal Population: Based on the 2008 statistics there are 50,809 cattle, 25,885 goats, 4,012 sheep, 21,386 pigs, 2,153 ducks and 6,061 turkeys.

Co-operative Societies: Bumati Growers, Bunamahe Co-op., Kitsatsa Co-op., Shilakano Co-op., Lulubi Co-op., Shireya Co-op., Tushi Growers Co-op, Kalitusi Co-op. And Busirirwa Growers Co-op.

Industries: Similar to those in the districts of Manafwa and Mbale.

Education Services: Primary schools; 120 – 95 government, 15 private and 10 community. Enrolment 57,087 students – 28,171 males and 28,916 females. Teachers: 983 – 636 males and 347 females. Available furniture adequate for 10,687 pupils.

Secondary schools: 6 schools - 3 government, 2 private, 1 community. Enrolment 3,498 students – 1,935 males and 1,563 females. Teachers: 142 – 122 males and 20 females. Available furniture adequate for 2,702 students.

Health Services: 1 hospital – Bududa Hospital (government); no health centre IV; 7 health centre III (all government); and 4 health centre II (2 Government and 2 NGO).

Banks: The district enjoys the banking services of the mother district.

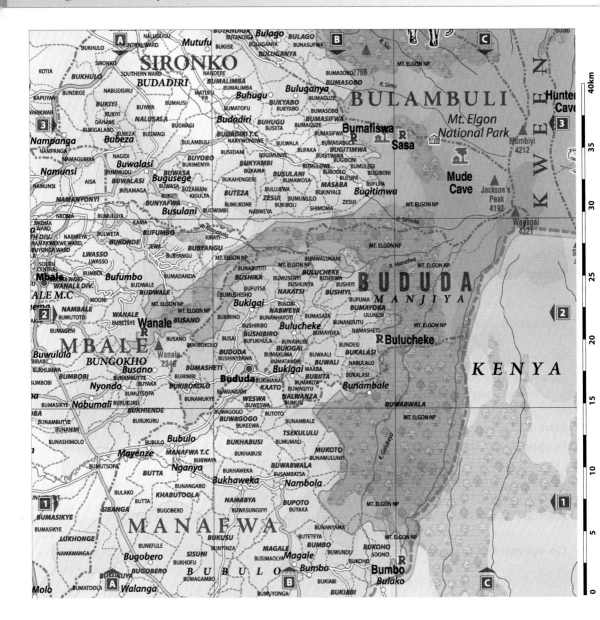

Transport Network: 175 kms of gazetted feeder-roads, 50 kms trunk roads and 250 km. of community roads, sub-post office and telecommunication services offered by Uganda Telecom Ltd, MTN and Airtel networks.

Tourist Attractions: Bulukyeke-Bukigai Hills: Found to the south of the Elgon ranges and with a moderate infrastructure dating to the colonial days, the hills have a historical aspect. They were used as a launching point for mountain climbing expeditions.

Additional information: The district suffered mudslides that claimed hundreds of human lives and livestock on 1st March 2010. Since then, there has been ongoing resettlement of people from the affected areas to Kiryandongo District in western Uganda. This created reduction of population in Bududa District and increase in population in Kirayandongo District.

District Leaders:
District Chairperson – Mr Nambeshe John B.
CAO – Mr Vital Kitui Oswan

Members of Parliament:
Manjiya County
   – Mr David Wakikona Wanendya
Woman MP – Ms Khainza Justine

Bugiri District

Bugiri District, which was originally a county of Iganga District, was created in 1997. Bugiri, Mayuge and present-day Iganga constituted Iganga District.

Location: Bugiri District is bordered by Iganga to the north and west, Mayuge District to the southwest, Tororo and Busia to the east, Namayingo to the southeast and Iganga to the west.

Area: 5,111 sq km.

Climate, Relief and Vegetation: The district lies on the extensive eastern plateau between 1000m and 1,800m above sea level. Rainfall is typical of lake shore patterns – evenly spread throughout the year and ranging between 1,250 – 2,200m. Away from the lake, the rainfall decreases. Temperatures are high with little fluctuation and the vegetation is tropical with savannah woodlands and grasslands.

Population: According to 2009 projections, there are 395,600 people – 186,400 males and 209,200 females with a density of 77 persons per sq.km.

Main Towns: Bugiri (administrative headquarters); Trading Centre – Naluwerere.

Counties and Sub-counties: Bukooli County – Bulesa, Buwunga, Muterere, Nankoma, Bulidha, Budhaya, Bugiri (Town Council), Buluguyi, Lwemba, Kapyanga, and Nabukalu.

Main Languages: Lusoga and Lusamia-Lugwe.

People: Basoga and Basamia.

Economic Activities: Agriculture with emphasis on:
  (i) Food crops: Maize, rice, finger millet, sorghum, bananas, sweet potatoes, beans, peas and cassava.
  (ii) Cash crops: Rice, cotton and coffee.
  (iii) Fishing on Lake Victoria.
  (iv) Animal grazing.

Area under Forestation: 26,131 hectares for Bugiri and Namayingo.

Animal Population: Bugiri and Namayingo have 118,427 cattle, 14 donkeys, 65,453 pigs, 14,280 sheep, 220,778 goats, 943,073 chicken, 74,332 ducks and 6,229 turkeys.

Co-operative Societies: Bugiri, Mayuge and Iganga have 255 registered co-operative societies.

Industries: Coffee processing, rice threshing, maize milling and jaggery production.

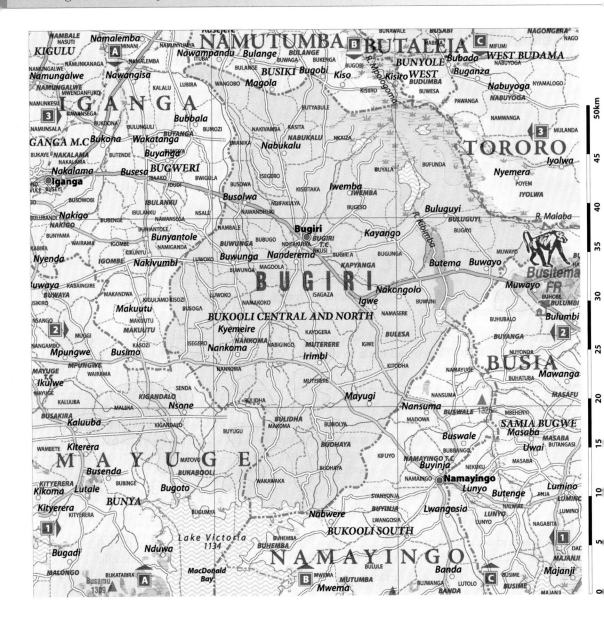

Education Services: Primary schools: 253 – 228 government, 7 private, and 18 community. Primary school enrolment: 116,633 pupils – 58,318 male and 58,315 female. Primary school teachers: 2,148 – 1,293 male and 855 female.

Secondary schools: 38 - 6 government, 24 private, 8 community. Secondary school enrolment: 12,006 – 7,375 male and 4,631 female. Teachers: 683 – 580 male and 103 female. Available furniture is adequate for 11,394 sudents.

Health Services: 1 hospital - Bugiri Hospital with 104 beds (government); 1 health centre IV (government); 7 health centre III (all government); and 31 health centre II (22 government and 9 NGO).

Transport Network: The district is linked with a tarmac road to Iganga and Tororo districts. It also has a well distributed network of feeder-roads, some of which are in poor condition.

Tourist Attractions: The lake and fishing activities at the Lugala Landing Site are a potential tourist attraction. Bird watching on Siiro Islands is another attraction. However, there is a need to improve accommodation facilities.

Additional Information: Land tenure customary. Areas around the lake are densely populated. Rice is produced mainly for the market while other food crops are basically for subsistence.

Key NGOs: Habitat for Humanity, Bukooli Bugiri Affiliate, Islamic Medical Association of Uganda, Uganda Red Cross Society, AIDS Free Generation Project, Caring for Orphans, Widows and the Elderly, Idudi Development Association, Mirembe Womens' Association, National Women Development, Tufungize Drama Group, Action for Community Development, Buwunga Development Association.

District leaders:	Members of Parliament:
Chairperson – Mr Baluboleire Malijhan	Bukooli County Central
Chief Administrative Officer (CAO)	– Mr Fred Douglas Mwanja Mukisa
– Mr Luke Lokwii Lokolomoi	Bukooli County North
Deputy Chief Administrative Officer	– Mr Stephen Bakka Mugabi
(DCAO) – Vacant	Bukooli South – Mr Peter Patrick Ochieng
Town Clerk (Bugiri Town Council)	Woman MP – Ms Justine Lumumba
– Mr Yakabu Kalibala	

Bukedea District

Bukedea District is one of the ten districts that were formed in July 2006. Until then, Bukedea was a county of Kumi District, then consisting of two other counties of Ngora and Kumi.

Location: Bukedea District borders with Mbale to the south, Budaka District to the southeast, Bulambuli and Sironko districts to the east, Katakwi to the north, Nakapiripirit districts to the northeast and Kumi District to the west.

Area: It covers a total area of 1,052 square kms.

Climate, Relief and Vegetation: Generally Bukedea District is a flat land with swamps/wetlands.

Population: Based on the 2009 population and housing census, there are160,900 people – 77,000 male and 83,900 female, with a density of 152 persons per sq.km.

Major Towns: Bukedea Town Council

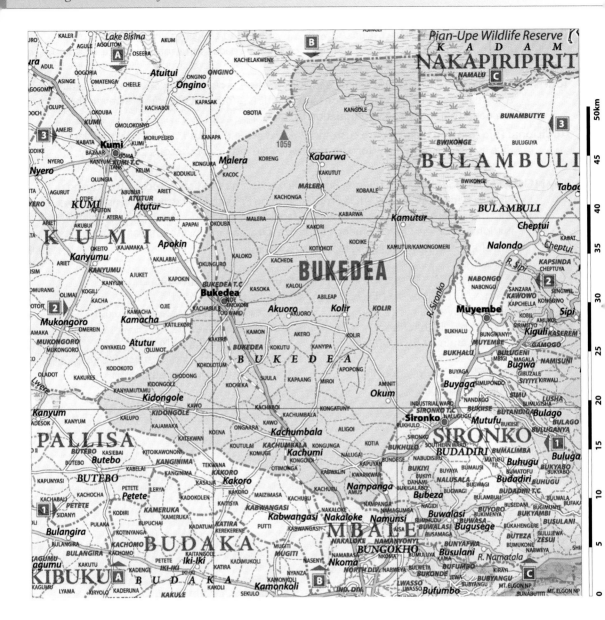

Counties and Sub-counties: Bukedea County – Bukedea, Kachumbala, Kidongole, Kolir and Malera and Bukedea Town Council.

Main Language: Ateso

People: The ethnic groupings include, Iteso, Bagisu, Banyole, Langi, Baganda, Basoga, Acholi Labwor and Bagwere. The Iteso constitute approximately 95% of the population.

Economic Activities: Over 84% of the households are engaged in agriculture, particularly subsistence farming. In addition to crop farming, there is animal rearing mainly of the local Zebu cattle, sheep, pigs and poultry.

Banks: The district enjoys the banking services of Kumi District.

Animal Population: 86,141cattle, 54,810 goats, 10,013 sheep, 23,264 pigs, 215,251 chicken, 4,400 ducks and 5,596 turkeys.

Co-operative Societies: The district enjoys the co-operative services of Kumi district.

Industries: Furniture making

Educational services: Primary schools: 86 – 81 government, 3 private and 2 community. Primary school enrolment: 51,605 – 25,813 female and 25,792 male. Primary school teachers: 804 – 482 female and 322 male. Available furniture was not fully reported.

Secondary schools 10.3 government, 3 private and 4 community. Enrolment: 4,175 students – 2,382 females and 1,793 males. Teachers: 180 - 145 females and 35 males. Available furniture is adequate for 3,278 students.

Health Services: No hospital; 1 health centre IV - (government); 5 health centre III - (all government) and 5 health centre II - (1 government, 2 private and 2 NGO).

Tourist Attractions: There are unique inselbergs, a variety of ecological features with rare bird species and beautiful flora and fauna.

Transport: The district has a road network of 213.2 km of gazetted feeder-roads, 80 km trunk roads and 350 km of community roads, railway line approximately 80 km stretches between Mbale and Soroti. There is a sub-post office and telecommunication services offered by Airtel, MTN and Uganda Telecom.

Operational Radio and TV Stations: Continental FM Station Ltd which used to serve the larger Kumi District is still serving Bukedea District.

Key NGOs: Though many of the NGOs indicated below used to serve the larger Kumi District, they have continued to extend these services to Bukedea. These are: Send a Cow Uganda, African Medical Research Foundation, Actionaid Uganda, Uganda Women's Effort to Save Orphans, Bukedea Women Strugglers Association, Church of Uganda Teso Diocese Planning and Development Offices, Faith Action, Kumi Human Rights Initiative and Self Governance, Kachumbala War Against Poverty Alleviation, Karev Youth and Orphans Link Initiative for Rural Development, Kumi Aids Support Organisation, Ongino Community Development Association, Uganda Women's Finance Trust, Save the Children Denmark, Vision Terudo.

District Leaders:	Members of Parliament:
District Chairperson	Bukedea County
– Mr Tukei William Wilberforce	– Mr Albert Charles Oduman Okello
Ag CAO – Mr Hosea Jonathan Mukoze	Woman MP – Ms Rose Akol Okullu
Deputy CAO – Vacant	

Left: The crowning of Teso king, Emorimor Augustine Osuban Lemukol in April 2000. Right: Ox-ploughing in Teso region.

Bukwo District

Bukwo District was carved out of Kapchorwa District in 2005. Before being made a district, this part of Kapchorwa District used to be known as Kongasis County.

Location: Bukwa District borders the districts of Kween to the west and northwest, Amudat to the north and the Republic of Kenya to the east and south.

Area: 527.87 sq. km.

Major Town: Bukwo (administrative headquarters)

Counties and Sub-counties: Kongasis County – Bukwa, Bukwo (Town Council), Chepskwata, Chesower, Kabei, Kamet, Kapterterwo, Kortek, Riwo, Suam Senendet and Tulel.

Main Language: Kupsabin

People: Sabiny

Population: According to population projection of 2009, the district has 63, 500 people – 31,400 male and 32,100 female with a density of 120 person per sq.km.

Economic Activities: Mainly agriculture of food crops and cash crops like cotton, coffee and wheat as well as fruits and vegetables.

Animal Population: 23,360 cattle, 23,312 goats, 2,137 sheep, 1,657 pigs, 94,993 chicken, 1,761 ducks and 126 turkeys according to 2008 statistics.

Industries: Manufacture of grainmill products, furniture, textile and wearing apparel.

Education Services: Primary schools: 64 – 25 government, 22 private and 17 community. Primary school enrolment: 30,290 pupils – 14,986 male and 15,304 female. Primary school teachers: 638 – 449 male and 189 female. Available furniture not fully reported.

Secondary schools: 9 schools - 4 government, 2 private and 3 community. Secondary school enrolment: 3,533 pupils – 1,765 male and 1,768 female. Teachers: 189 -152 male and 38 female. Available furniture is adequate for 1,470 students.

Health Services: No hospital; 1 health centre IV - (NGO); 3 health centre III - (all government); and 7 health centre II - (all government).

Tourist Attractions: Mount Elgon National Park was gazetted as an international ecological conservation area of unique vegetation species. The park is home to a number of endangered animal species, such as the buffaloes and cheetahs as well as a habitat to unique bird species. Mountain climbing trails are well developed. The Caldera found on top of the Elgon mountain ranges, together with Hot Springs, Crater Lake, the Swan Gorge within this Caldera and the scenic peaks constitute some of the tourist attractions of the Elgon Mountain. Another tourist attraction in the district is the Bukwa Fossil Site.

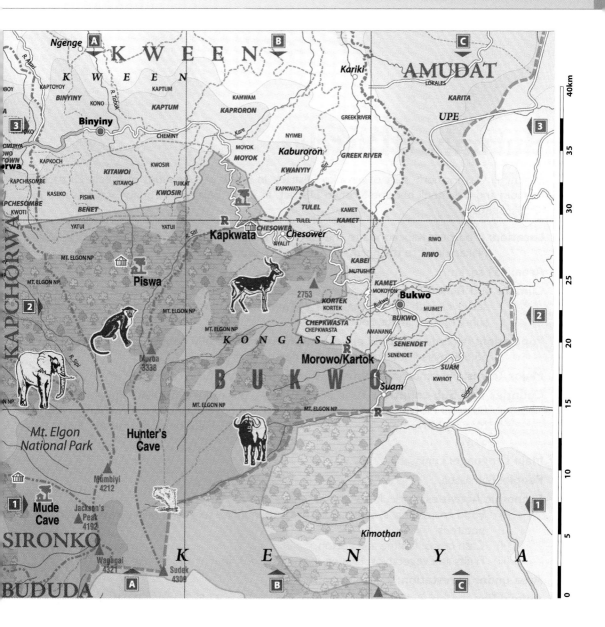

District Leaders:
District Chairperson
– Mr Manjara Wilson Salimo.
Chief Administrative Officer (CAO)
– Mr Seraphine Alia
Deputy Chief Administrative Officer
(DCAO) – Vacant

Members of Parliament:
Kongasis County – Mr Sabila Nelson
District Woman MP
– Ms Evelyn Chelangat Tete

Bulambuli District

Bulambuli was formerly part of Sironko District. In 2000, two counties of Mbale District – Budadiri and Bulambuli became Sironko District. In 2010, Bulambuli County was elevated to district status.

Location: It borders Kapchorwa to the east, Kween to the northeast, Bukedea to the west, Nakapiripirit to the north, Sironko to the south.

Area: 651 sq. km.

Climate and Relief: It lies at an approximate altitude of between 1,299m – 1,524m above sea level, with rainfall totalling 1,191mm per annum and low temperatures, within a sub-tropical climatic zone.

Population: According to 2009 projections, there are 113,800 people – 58,200 female and 55,600 male with a density of 174 persons per sq.km.

Major Towns: Muyembe (administrative headquarters) and Bulegeni.

Counties and Sub-counties: Bulamburi County – Buginyanya, Bukhalu, Bulago, Bulegeni, Bulegeni (Town Council), Buluganya, Bumasobo, Bunambutye, Bwikhonge, Lusha, Masira, Muyembe, Muyembe (Town Council), Nabbongo, Namisuni, Simu and Sisiyi.

Main Language: Lumasaba.

People: Bamasaba.

Economic Activities: Agriculture with emphasis on:
  (i) Food crops: Beans, sweet potatoes, groundnuts, sorghum, millet, cassava and irish potatoes.
  (ii) Cash crops: Coffee and cotton.
  (iii) Fruits and vegetables: Passion fruit, tomatoes, onions and cabbage.

Area under Forestation: 25,428 hectares.

Animal Population: Bulambuli and Sironko districts have 92,562 cattle, 250 donkeys, 32,733 pigs, 9,806 sheep, 79,141 goats, 8,496 ducks, 19,769 turkeys and 391,125 chicken.

Co-operative Societies: Bulambuli still depends on societies in Sironko, the mother district.

Industries: Manufacture of animal feeds, footwear, grain milling, manufacture of exhaust pipes, furniture and cotton ginning.

Education Services: Primary schools: 59 – 53 government, 4 private and 2 community. Enrolment: 381,544 pupils – 19,117 male and 19,427 female. Primary school teachers: 692 – 464 male and 228 female.

Secondary schools: 10 schools - 5 government, 3 private and 2 community. Secondary school enrolment: 3,908 students – 2,191 male and 1,717 female. Secondary school teachers: 174 – 151 male and 23 female.

Health Services: 1 health centre IV (Government); 8 health centre III (7 government, 1 NGO); and 3 health centre II (2 government, 1 NGO).

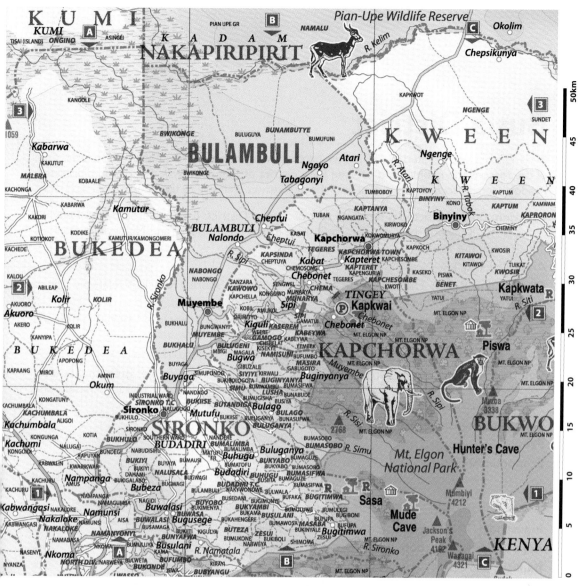

Tourist Attractions: Hiking and camping on Mountain Elgon.

Key NGOs: Send a Cow Uganda, Uganda Women's Effort to Save Orphans, Environmental Alert, Sironko Bee Farmers' Association, Buzibu Women's Group, National Association of Women Organisations in Uganda, Sironko Farmers' Association Ltd, Nadisi Women's Group, Sironko Yetana Project, Bundagala Women Group.

District leaders:

Chairperson
– Mr Wonanzofu Simon Peter.

Ag Chief Administrative Officer (CAO)
– Mr Simon Peter Kandole

Deputy Chief Administrative Officer
(DCAO) – Vacant

Members of Parliament:

Bulambuli County – Mr Mudimi Wamakuyu

Woman MP – Vacant

Busia District

Busia District was created in 1997 after protracted agitation by the people of the area. One of the reasons the people hard pressed for a district of their own was that the administrative headquarters in Tororo was distant and affected service delivery to the people.

Location: Busia District was formerly part of Tororo District. It is bordered by the Republic of Kenya to the east, Tororo District to the north, Bugiri and Namayingo Districts to the west.

Area: 759.4 sq. km

Climate and Relief: The district lies on the Lake Victoria shores. Rainfall is relatively high at the shores but declines as you move inland.

Population: According to 2009 projections, there are 268,500 people – 140,900 female and 127,600 male, with a density of 353 persons per sq.km.

Major Towns: Busia (administrative headquarters); Trading Centre – Majanji.

Counties and Sub-counties: Samia-Bugwe County – Bulumbi, Busime, Busitema, Buteba, Buyanga, Dabani, Sikuda, Buhehe, Lumino, Lunyo, Majanji, Masaba, Masafu and Masinya; Busia Municipality – Eastern Division and Western Division.

Main Languages: Lusamia-Lugwe.

People: Basamia.

Economic Activities:
  (i)   Food Crops: Millet, cassava, rice, sweet potatoes, simsim, sorghum, cow peas and bananas.
  (ii) Cash crops: Ginger, cotton and sunflower.

Industries: Oil milling, cotton ginning and flour milling.

Area under Forestation: 9,922 hectares.

Banks: Stanbic Bank Uganda Ltd –1, Crane Bank.

Education Services: Primary schools: 145 – 123 government, 19 private and 3 community. Primary school enrolment: 97,126 pupils – 48,256 male and 48,870 female. Primary school teachers: 1,644 – 1,039 male and 605 female. Available furniture not reported.

Secondary schools: 29 schools - 12 government, 15 private, 2 community. Secondary school enrolment: 14,750 students – 8,560 male and 6,190 female. Teachers: 667 – 531 males and 136 females. Tertiary institutions: 1 University (Busitema University).

Health Services: 1hospital (government); 2 health centre IV (1 government and 1 NGO); 7 health centre III (all government); and 14 Health Centre II (13 government and 1 NGO)

Animal Population: 26,787 cattle, 13 donkeys, 14,203 pigs, 2,908 sheep, 73,565 goats, 13,041 ducks, 3,777 turkeys and 391,312 chicken.

Co-operative Societies: Busia and Tororo have 255 registered co-operative societies.

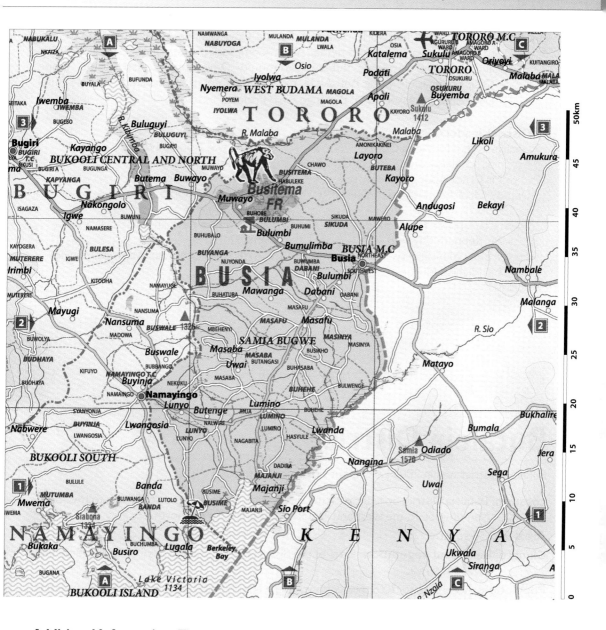

Additional Information: The most important resource in Busia is the fish from Lake Victoria. The location at the border with Kenya is also advantageous. The fishing industry employs a number of people in the district and a significant number engage in the booming cross-border trade. The growth of Busia town is largely attributed to the trade between Uganda and Kenya.

Land ownership in most of Busia District is customary. Agriculture is practised on a small scale and food production is basically for subsistence.

The population of Busia District is unevenly distributed. Areas near the south and along the border are more densely populated than those bordering Tororo in the north and Bugiri in the west.

Key NGOs: Africa 2000 Network – Uganda, Send a Cow Uganda, Uganda Women's Effort to Save Orphans, Environmental Alert, Compassion International, Human Rights and Paralegal Services, Nubian Community Development Association, Hope Case Foundation, Busia Anti-AIDS Youth and Womens' Association, Busime Rural Development Association, Buyengo CCP Project.

District leaders:	Members of Parliament:
Chairperson – Mr Adea Ouma	Samia-Bugwe County North
Ag Chief Administrative Officer (CAO)	– Ms Sarah Mwebaza
– Mr Grace Adong Choda	Samia-Bugwe County South
Deputy Chief Administrative Officer	– Mr Gabriel Opio
(DCAO) – Vacant	Busia Municipality
Town Clerk (Busia Municipal Council)	– Mr Taaka Kevinah Wanaha Wandera
– Mr Kenneth Ofwono	Woman MP
Mayor Busia Municipality	– Ms Rose Omusolo Wabwire Munyira
– Mr Micheal Mugeni	

Butaleja District

Butaleja District was in 2005 carved out of Tororo District.

Location: Butaleja District borders with the districts of Mbale to the east, Tororo to the south, Namutumba to the west and Kibuku and Budaka to the north.

Area: 515.58 sq. kms.

Climate, Relief and Vegetation: Parts of the districts are marshy with streams that flow into River Manafwa.

Population: According to 2009 projections, there are 195,800 people, 101,500 female and 94,300 males, with a density of 380 persons per sq.km.

Major Town: Busolwe Town Council

Counties and Sub-counties: Bunyole East County – Butaleja, Butaleja (Town Council), Himutu, Naweyo, Mazimasa and Kachonga; Bunyole West County – Budumba, Busaba, Busabi, Busolwe, Busolwe (Town Council), Nawanjofu,

Main Languages: Japhadhola, Lusamia-Lugwe, Ateso, Lugwere and Lunyoli

People: Japadhola, Iteso, Basamia, Bagwere, Banyole, Bagisu, Basoga, Baganda, Banyankore, Acholi and other Uganda and non-Ugandans.

Economic Activities: Commercial agriculture, food crop production, livestock farming,

Animal Population: Based on the 2008 statistics, there are 77,247 cattle, 71,609 goats, 9,732 sheep, 4,497 pigs, 251,946 chicken, 18,524 ducks and 10,397 turkeys.

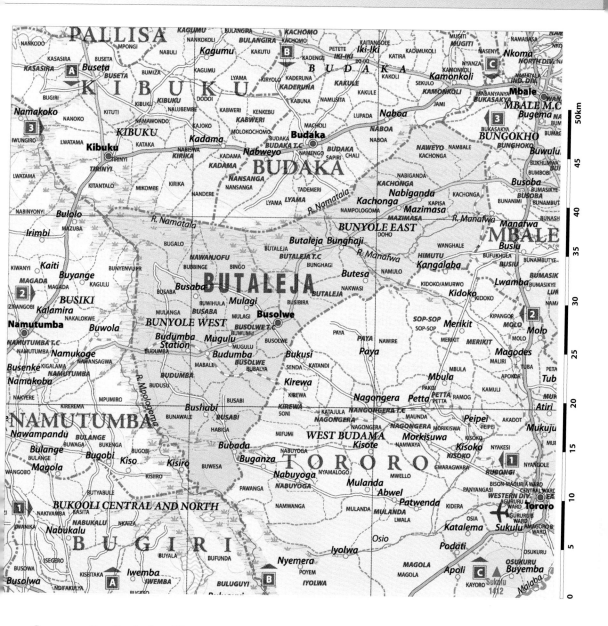

Co-operative Societies: The new district is still utilising the services of Tororo and Busia districts both of which have 255 registered primary societies with South Bukedi Co-operative Union at Tororo District level.

Industries: Manufacture of grainmill products, furniture, metal products, textiles and wearing apparel, prepared animal feeds and cotton ginning.

Education Services: Primary Schools: 113 – 89 government, 14 private and 10 community. Primary school enrolment: 75,402 pupils – 37,685 male and 37,717 female. Primary school teachers: 1,133 – 730 male and 403 female.

Secondary schools: 18 schools - 9 government, 7 private and 2 community. Secondary school enrolment: 6,038 students – 3,732 male and 2,306 female. Secondary school

teachers: 420 – 336 male and 84 female. Available furniture adequate for 4,694 students.

Banks: Stanbic Bank Uganda Ltd and Centenary Rural Development Bank are utilised by the people of both Butaleja and Tororo districts.

Health Services: 1 hospital - (government - Busolwe Hospital; no health centre IV; 9 Health centre III - (7 government, 1 NGO and 1 private); and 10 health centre II - (all government).

Transport Network: A railway line runs from Tororo through Nagongera, Budumba, Iganga, Jinja and Kampala with a station at Busolwe.

Tourist Attractions: The famous Tororo Rock which rises at 1,800 metres above sea level is a tourist attraction for Butaleja and Tororo District.

Nakwiga wetland and Osukuru bird sanctuary have been protected by local authorities and NEMA from degradation. They are also a seasonal home to rare migratory bird species. Potential exists for development of the two areas into big bird watching tourist destinations.

Key NGOs: The following NGOs carry out activities in both the districts of Tororo and Butaleja: Uganda Women's Effort to Save Orphans, Africa 2000 Network – Uganda, Send a Cow Uganda, Plan International, Family Planning Association of Uganda, World Vision Uganda, Community Vision, Tororo District Farmers' Association, Youth Training Advisory Mission, Mifumi Development Programme, Mulanda Women's Development Association, Nagonga Youth Development Project, Asinge Joint Youth Association, Osukuru Women's Network, Uganda Change Agent Association.

District Leaders:	**Members of Parliament:**
District Chairperson – Mr Muyonjo Joseph	Bunyole County
Ag CAO – Mr Mathias Ndifuna	– Mr Emmanuel Lumala Dombo
Deputy CAO – Vacant	District Woman MP
	– Ms Nebanda Cerina Arioru

Buyende District

Buyende was carved out of Kamuli District in 2009. Until then it was Budiope, one of the counties in Kamuli District.

Location: Buyende District borders the districts of Luuka and Kaliro to the east, Kamuli to the south, Kayunga to the west, Serere and Kaberamaido to the north (across Lake Kyoga), and Pallisa to the northeast.

Area: 1,878 sq.km.

Climate, Relief and Vegetation: It lies at an approximate altitude of between 914m and 1,101m above sea level with heavy rainfall and moderate temperatures. Vegetation consists of woodlands, thickets and bushes.

Population: According to 2009 population projections there are 235,600 people – 115,000 male and 120,600 female, with a density of 125 persons per sq.km.

Main Towns: Buyende (administrative headquarters); Trading Centres – Buyaga, Kibera, Bukungu.

Counties and Sub-counties: Budiope West County – Buyende, Buyende (Town Council), Kidera, and Nkondo; Budiope East County – Bugaya and Kagulu.

Main Language: Lusoga.

People: Basoga, Bakenyi, Iteso, Baruli, Banyoro, Banyara, Baganda, Basamia, Banyole, other Ugandans and non-Ugandans.

Economic Activities: Mainly agriculture with emphasis on:

  (i)   Food crops: Soya bean, maize, sorghum, cassava, sweet potatoes, finger millet, rice, groundnuts, simsim (sesame) and sunflower.
  (ii) Cash crops: Cotton, coffee and sugar cane.
  (iii) Vegetables: Tomatoes, onions and cabbage.

Banks: The district still depends on banks in Kamuli.

Area under Forestation: 27,909 hectares.

Animal Population: Buyende and Kamuli have 211,815 cattle, 219,194 goats, 6,540 sheep, 55,239 pigs, 724,489 chicken, 15,538 ducks and 2,421 turkeys.

Co-operative Societies: 155 registered primary societies with Busoga Union at the district level.

Industries: Manufacture of jaggery, brick making, maize milling, cotton ginning.

Education Services: Primary schools: 100 – 79 government, 18 private and 3 community. Primary school enrolment: 58,805 (male and female not reported). Primary school teachers: 2,793 – 1,782 male and 1,010 female.

Secondary school enrolment: 7,250 – 4,157 male and 3,093 female. Teachers: 717 – 606 male and 111 female. Enrolment in private and community secondary schools – private: 7,332 – 4,165 male and 3,167 female. Community: 1,270 – 680 male and 590 female. Tertiary institutions – 1 technical institution and 2 Teacher Training Colleges. Namasagali University.

Health Services: No hospital; 1 health centre IV (government); 4 health centre III (all government); and 13 health centre II (5 government and 8 NGO)

Operational Radio and TV Stations: Busoga People's Radio (Empanga)

Tourist Attractions: Lake Kyoga to the north of the district provides good sites for beach development. The lake is suitable for various tourism-related activities such as camping, excursions, canoeing, sport fishing and other tourism establishments.

Key NGOs: Africa 2000 Network – Uganda, Send a Cow Uganda, Integrated Rural Development Initiatives, Plan International, Environmental Alert, Traditional and Modern Health Practitioners, Kaliro Development Foundation, Uganda Red Cross, Buzaya Rural Savings Scheme, Family Keduabi World Peace, Citizens Link Development Project, AIDS Education Group for Youth, Sustainable Agricultural Farmers' Association, Twasakirala Aloe vera Growers' Association, Uganda Development Services, Buzaya Rural Savings Scheme.

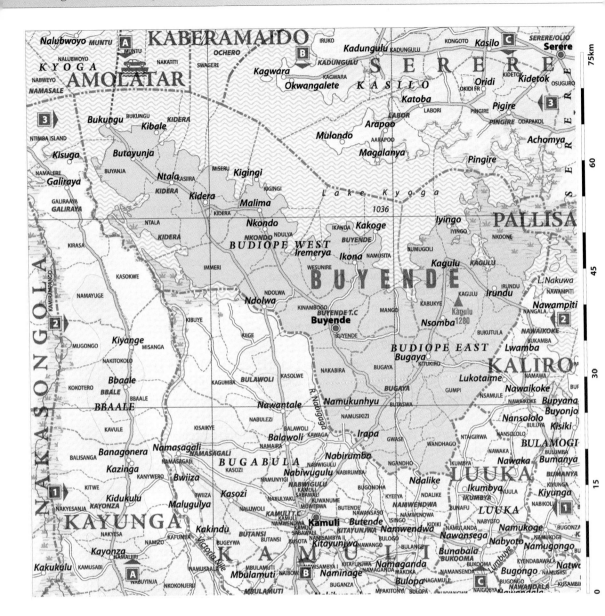

District leaders:
Chairperson – Mr Kanaku Michael
Ag Chief Administrative Officer (CAO)
  – Mr David Maleka Kyeyago
Deputy Chief Administrative Officer
  (DCAO) – Vacant
Town Clerk (Buyende Town Council)
  – Mr Richard Mugolo

Members of Parliament:
Budiope County East
  – Mr Balyejjusa Sulaiman Kirunda
Budiope County West
  – Mr Mubito John Bosco
Woman MP – Ms Barirye Veronica Kadogo

Iganga District

At independence in 1962, Iganga was part of Busoga District. In 1975 it gained district status and it became South Busoga District in the then Busoga Province. It was named Iganga in 1980.

Location: It borders the districts of Bugiri to the east, Namutumba to the northeast, Mayuge to the south, Luuka to the west and Kaliro to the north.

Area: 1,039 sq. km.

Climate, Relief and Vegetation: It lies at an altitude of about 1,070m and 1,161m above sea level with the annual rainfall ranging between 1,250mm and 2,200mm. Temperatures are always almost uniformly high at over 21°C. Vegetation here includes tropical rain forests.

Population: Based on population projections 2009, there are 442,200 people –233,400 female and 208,800 male, with a density of 425 persons per sq.km.

Main Towns: Iganga Town Council; Trading Centres – Busembatia and Busesa.

Counties and Sub-counties: Bugweri County – Busembatia (Town Council), Buyanga, Ibulanku, Makuutu, Namalemba, and Igombe; Kigulu County – Nabitende, Nambale, Namungalwe, Nawandala, Bulamagi, Nakalama, Nakigo and Nawanyingi; Iganga Municipality – Central Division and Northern Division.

Main Language: Lusoga.

People: Basoga. The district has attracted a cross-section of ethnic groups who have settled near the border for business purposes. Iganga town has a fast growing population and the potential of becoming a major commercial centre in eastern Uganda.

Economic Activities: Agriculture with particular emphasis on:
  (i)   Food crops: Finger millet, maize, sorghum, rice, bananas, sweet potatoes, irish potatoes, cassava, beans, simsim (sesame) and peas.
  (ii) Cash crops: Coffee, cotton and rice.
  (iii) Fruits and vegetables: Oranges, tomatoes and cabbage.
  (iv) Fishing is carried out on Lake Victoria.

Banks: Stanbic Bank Ltd 1, Crane Bank -1

Trade: Iganga town is a growing commercial hub. Its proximity to the border with Kenya has boosted trading activity.

Area under Forestation: 5,568 hectares for Iganga and Luuka.

Animal Population: Iganga and Luuka districts combined have 125,307 cattle, 169,915 goats, 5,064 sheep, 27,684 pigs, 904,493 chicken, 13,469 ducks and 6,550 turkeys.

Co-operative Societies: Iganga, Bugiri and Mayuge have 255 registered primary societies with Busoga Union at the district level for Iganga.

Industries: Processing of coffee, milling of rice, manufacture of jaggery and brick making.

Banks: Stanbic Bank Uganda Ltd –1, Bank of Baroda –1, Crane Bank.

Education Services: Primary Schools: 193 – 162 government, 28 private, 3 community. Primary school enrolment: 124,216 pupils – 60,497 male and 63,719 female. Primary school teachers: 2,373 – 1,213 male, 1,160 female. Available furniture not reported.

Secondary schools: 35 schools - 10 government, 3 private and 22 community. Secondary school enrolment: 18,855 stdents – 9,781 male and 9,074 female. Secondary school teachers: 828 – 668 male and 160 female. Available furniture is adequate for 17,406 students.

Tertiary institutions– 1 technical institution, 1 teacher training college, 1 Univeristy (Busoga University)

Health Services: 1 govt. hospital - Iganga Hospital with 117 beds and 1 private hospital – Uganda Catholic Medical Bureau, St. Francis Buluba with 164 beds; 2 health centre IV (all government); 11 health centre III (10 government and 1 NGO); and 32 health centre II (19 government and 13 NGO);

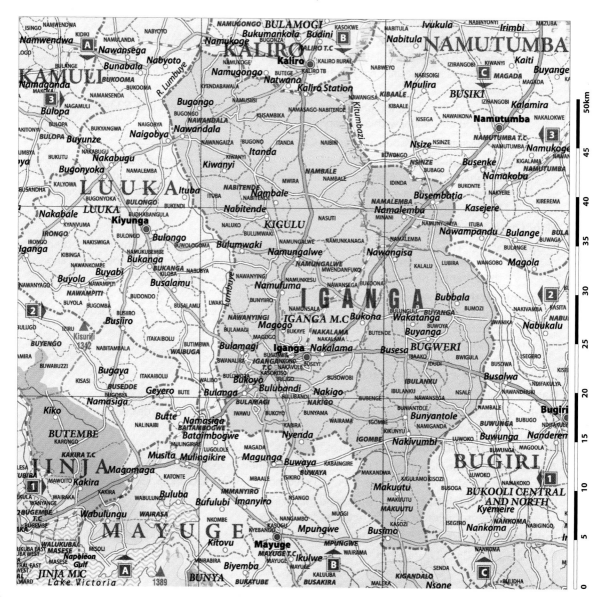

Transport Network: The district is accessible by road and rail. It has tarmacked roads from Iganga town to Mbale via Pallisa District, Tirinyi Road and Tororo Road. The road from Jinja to Iganga town is also tarmacked. The district is well connected with feeder-roads in the southern part that borders the lake.

There are plan for an airstrip is to be developed by local private investors. This will not only create jobs it will also increase the revenue of the district.

Tourist Attractions: Nenda Hill contains the shrine of the Bazungu (white people) and is a view point for the surrounding plains. Tweyambe Women's Handicraft Shop offers a variety of locally produced goods of reasonable quality. The district also has caves and forests which are tourist attractions. Lake Victoria is another attraction and fishing constitutes a major activity. Additional cultural shrines/sites consist of Bugweri cultural site, Kigulu Shrine and Bukowe shrines for the Ngobi and Menyha Clans, respectively.

Key NGOs: Africa 2000 Network – Uganda, Send a Cow Uganda, African Network for the Prevention and Protection Against Child Abuse and Neglect Uganda Chapter, Family Planning Association of Uganda, Uganda Women's Effort to Save Orphans, Foundation for Kigulu South Development Association, Musingi Rural Development Association, Ngangali Agali Wamu Women's Group, Uganda Biogas Development, Wider Opportunities for Women and Youth Association, Iganga District Farmers' Association, Tweyambe Women's Club, Bakuseka Majja Women's Farmers Development Association.

District leaders:
Chairperson – Mr Nkuutu Shaban
Chief Administrative Officer (CAO) – Mr Charles Nsubuga Kiberu
Deputy Chief Administrative Officer (DCAO) – Vacant
Acting Town Clerk (Iganga Municipal Council) – Mr Vincent Batwaula
Mayor Iganga Municipality – Mr Siraje Katono Mayaye

Members of Parliament:
Bugweri County – Mr Abdu Katuntu
Kigulu County North – Mr Edward Kafufu Baliddawa
Kigulu County South – Mr Milton Kalulu Muwuma
Iganga Municipality – Mr Mugema Peter
Woman MP – Ms Kabaale Kwagala Olivia

Jinja District

At Independence, Jinja was part of Busoga District. Under the 1974 provincial administration, Jinja became a district in Busoga Province.

Location: It borders the districts of Luuka and Kamulito the north, Buikwe to the southwest and west, Kayunga to the northwest and Mayuge to the East.

Area: 722.7 sq. km.

Climate, Relief and Vegetation: Most of the district stands at an approximate altitude of between 1,143m and 1,376m above sea level in an equatorial climatic belt, which extends 30 km – 40 km from Lake Victoria. It receives plenty of rainfall and has high temperatures throughout the year. Owing to the absence of a marked dry season, the vegetation is predominantly thick and lush.

Population: According to the 2009 population projections there are 454,900 people – 232,600 female and 222,300 male, with a density of 630 persons per sq.km.

Major Towns: Jinja (administrative headquarters); Trading Centres – Bugembe, Buwenge and Kakira.

Counties and Sub-counties: Kagoma County – Budondo, Butagaya, Buwenge, Buwenge (Town Council), Buyengo; Jinja Municipality – Walukuba/Masese, Jinja Central, and Kimaka/Mpumudde; Butembe County – Busedde, Bugembe (Town Council), Kakira (Town Council), and Mafubira.

Main Language: Lusoga.

People: Basoga.

Economic Activities: The rural areas of Jinja District are agricultural while a great deal of industrial activity takes place in Jinja Municipality.
  (i)   Food crops: Beans, cassava, maize, finger millet, bananas, sweet potatoes, soya bean, cow peas, pigeon peas, groundnuts, yams and sorghum.
  (ii) Cash crops: Coffee, cotton and sugar cane.
  (iii) Fishing is done on the River Nile and Lake Victoria.

Banks: Stanbic Bank Uganda Ltd –1, Orient Bank Ltd –1, Bank of Baroda – 1, Standard Chartered Bank Ltd –1, Crane Bank Ltd –1, DFCU Bank.

Area under Forestation: 3,994 hectares.

Animal Population: 40,247 cattle, 26,856 pigs, 1,691 sheep, 71,893 goats, 10,456 ducks, 2,463 turkeys and 524,159 chicken.

Co-operative Societies: 128 registered primary societies with Busoga Union at the district level.

Industries: Jinja is the largest commercial centre in eastern Uganda. As an industrial town it attracts a lot of trading in industrial products and there is demand for agricultural produce as raw materials for the industries, as well as food for the town dwellers. Jinja town is full of shops and markets (there are two main markets in the municipality alone). Businesses range from petty trading, groceries/supermarkets, large shops dealing in industrial hardware.

Wheat and maize milling, coffee processing, fish, tea, sugar cane, hides and skins, jaggery manufacture, animal feeds, soft drinks, bread and confectioneries, cigarettes, textiles and garments, electronics, saw milling, timber works, leather tanning, foam mattresses, paper, cardboard boxes, safety matches, printeries, steel and metal fabrication, tyres and tubes, ladders, knives and household utensils, hoes, charcoal stoves, baby napkins, laundry soap, sugar and molasses, carpentry and joinery and oil milling.

Education Services: Primary schools: 185 – 112 government, 57 private, 16 community. Primary school enrolment: 111,119 pupils – 53,933 male and 57,186 male. Primary school teachers: 2,660 – 1,309 male and 1,351 female. Available furniture not reported.

Secondary schools: 51 schools - 12 government, 37 private, 2 community. Secondary School enrolment: 32,286 students – 17,271 male and 15,051 female. Secondary school teachers: 1,604 – 1,143 male and 461 female. Available furniture is adequate for 27,005 students.

Tertiary institutions – 1 teacher training college, 1 vocational training institution, 1 business college.

Health Services: 3 hospitals (1 government - Jinja Regional Referral Hospital with 443 beds, 1 private – Kakira Hospital with 100 beds and 1 NGO – Buwenge Hospital); 6 health centre IV - (5 government and 1 NGO); 15 Health Centre III - (12 government and 3 NGO); and 45 health centre II - (36 government, 7 NGO and 2 private).

Tourist Attractions: Source of the River Nile, Speke Memorial more commonly known as the Source of the Nile Plaque marks the spot where the Nile begins its journey through Uganda, Sudan and finally Egypt.

Satya Narayan Temple contains shrines to Ambaji, Shankar Bhagwan, and Shitla Mata. The bronze bust of Mahatma Gandhi in the compound was unveiled by Indian Prime Minister Gujral accompanied by President Yoweri Museveni in 1997.

The Owen Falls Dam, now renamed Nalubaale, was built in 1954 and supplies electricity to Uganda and parts of Kenya, Tanzania and Rwanda. A new extension called Kiira Dam started generating additional hydro-electric power in 2000.

Nile Breweries tours are done on Tuesdays and Thursdays and include a free beer.

The Jinja Sailing Club offers short, reasonably priced boat cruises on Lake Victoria. White water rafting, an adrenaline pumping experience is provided by the Nile River Explorers, Adrift and Equator Rafts Uganda. Adrift also provides family float trips, river surfing, tandem kayaking, kayak school and fishing trips.

Bujagali Falls is a unique spot with 1 km of raging water, over seven falls. The Itanda falls are another spectacular sight 7.5 km to the north of the Owen Falls Dam.

There is plenty of budget and upmarket accomodation in Jinja.

The National Agricultural and trade show a yearly event that is organised in Jinja Municipality for farmers countrywide is an event worth visiting.

Transport Network: Steamers from Kisumu in Kenya and Mwanza in Tanzania, sail to the Jinja pier. The steamer service is managed by the Uganda Railways Corporation. Parts of Jinja District are linked by railway. The railway line runs through the district from Kampala to Iganga and offers cargo transportation services as it snakes through Jinja District while another railway line links Jinja to Kamuli.

The district has both tarmac and murram roads. It is linked to Kampala, Kamuli, Mayuge and Iganga districts by tarmac roads. There is a good network of murram feeder-roads linking various parts of the district. Jinja District has an airstrip that is presently not in use.

Jinja Airfield – The airfield is served by a 1,332m x 30m murram surface runway and is in good condition. Jinja Municipality runs the airfield. The Municipality also maintains the terminal building. The Civil Aviation Authority provides H.F. radio communication. The airfield is 2 km from Jinja town.

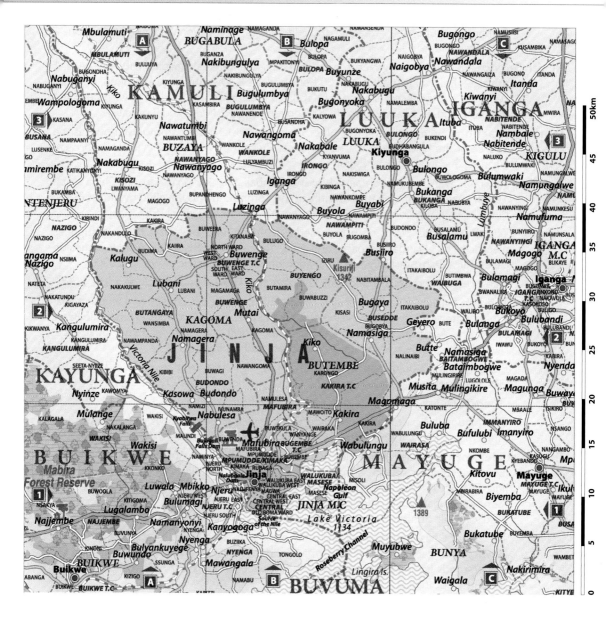

Additional Information: Jinja District basically produces agricultural commodities. Jinja was formerly the industrial capital of Uganda. Although it still has several industries, the political and economic turmoil of the 1970s and 80s saw the industrial sector collapse. As the Ugandan economy picked up, several investors have preferred to set up industries in Kampala.

One area of growth in Jinja seems to be the hotel industry. Hotels are springing up everywhere and the tourism industry is doing well. The Source of the Nile, the Bujagali Falls and Lake Victoria are important tourist attractions.

Many of the farmers living next to big sugar estates in Kakira have become sugar cane outgrowers who supply sugar cane to the Kakira Sugar Works.

Operational Radio and TV Stations: Radio Kiira Ltd, Nkabi Broadcasting Service, Radio Management Services (U) Ltd, Nkabi Broadcasting Ltd TV Station.

Key NGOs: African Network for the Prevention and Protection Against Child Abuse and Neglect Uganda Chapter, Aids Information Centre Butembe Development Agency, Uganda Red Cross Society, Uganda Change Agent Association, Uganda Church Women Development Centre, Arise Africa International, Action on AIDS and Development Foundation, Jinja District NGO Network, Jinja Child Development Centre, Busoga Trust Water and Sanitation Sector, Child Restoration Outreach.

District leade rs:	Members of Parliament:
Chairperson – Mr Gume Patrick	Jinja Municipality West
Chief Administrative Officer (CAO)	– Mr Balyeku Moses Grace
– Mr Ben Paul Otim Ogwette	Jinja Municipality East
Deputy Chief Administrative Officer	– Mr Nathan Igeme Nabeta
(DCAO) – Mr Francis Barabanawe	Kagoma County
Town Clerk (Jinja Municipal Council)	– Mr Fredercik Nkayi Mbagadhi
– Vacant	Butembe County – Mr Daudi Migereko
Town Clerk (Buwenge Town Council)	Woman MP – Ms Nabirye Agnes
– Mr Grace Kisembe	
Jinja Municipality – Mr Muhammed Kezaala	

Kaberamaido District

Formerly part of Soroti District until 2000 when it became a district. At independence in 1962 present-day Soroti, Kumi, Katakwi and Kaberamaido constituted Teso District.

Location: It borders the districts of Soroti to the east, Dokolo and Amolatar to the west, Buyende to the south, Amuria to the northeast and Alebtong to the north.

Area: 1,627.9 sq. km.

Climate and Relief: It lies at an approximate altitude of 1,036m – 1,127m above sea level, with rainfall totalling 1,000mm – 1,500mm per annum.

Population: According to 2009 projection, there are 172,400 people – 84,400 male and 88,000 female, with a density of 106 persons per sq.km.

Major Towns: Kaberamaido (administrative headquarters).

Counties and Sub-counties: Kaberamaido County – Alwa, Aperikira, Kaberamaido, Kaberamaido (Town Council), Kobulubulu, Ochero; Kalaki County – Anyara, Apapai, Bululu, Kakure, Kalaki and Otuboi.

Main Language: Ateso, Kumam and Kiswahili.

People: Itesot and Kumam.

Economic Activities: Agriculture with emphasis on:
- (i) Food crops: Finger millet, potatoes, soya bean, simsim and sunflower.
- (ii) Cash crops: Cotton.
- (iii) Fruits and vegetables: Tomatoes, vegetables and onions.
- (iv) Fishing on Lake Kyoga

Area under Forestation: 17,546 hectares.

Animal Population: 76,109 cattle, 31,607 pigs, 33,566 sheep, 97,516 goats and 367,924 chicken,13,146 ducks and 1,850 turkeys.

Co-operative Societies: Kaberamaido, Katakwi Amuria and Soroti have 155 registered co-operative societies.

Industries: Milling of flour and rice, cotton ginning and brick making.

Transport Network: A poor road network. Feeder-roads do not exist in some parts of the district, greatly hampering transport.

Education Services: Primary schools: 89 – 84 government and 5 community. Primary school enrolment: 60,584 pupils – 30,545 male and 30,039 female. Primary school teachers: 875 – 666 male and 209 female.

Secondary school enrolment: 4,805 – 3,215 male and 1,590 female. Secondary school teachers: 288 – 242 male and 46 female. Available furniture adequate for 4,034 students.

Health Services: 1 hospital (NGO); 1 health centre IV (government); 8 health centre III (7 government and 1 NGO); and 9 health centre II (6 government and 3 NGO);

Tourist Attractions: Lake Kyoga.

Key NGOs: African Medical Research Foundation, Abola Youth Group, Kalaki Livestock Women's Group, Uganda Red Cross Society, Youth with a Message of Health, Kalaki Rural Development Association, Livingstone Christian Development Association, Agency for Promoting Sustainable Development Initiatives, Uganda Seed Oil Producers and Processors Association, St. Karoli Catholic Women's Association.

District leaders:	Members of Parliament:
Chairperson – Mr Ejoku Albert A.	Kaberamaido County
Chief Administrative Officer (CAO)	– Mr Omoma Kenneth Olusegun
– Vacant	Kalaki County
Deputy Chief Administrative Officer (DCAO)	– Mr Ongalo Obote Clement Keneth
– Mr Mathias Akintore Muhuta	Woman MP – Ms Ekwau Ibi Florence

Kaliro District

Kaliro district was fomed in 2005. Until then it was Bulamogi County, in Kamuli District.

Location: It borders the districts of Buyende to the northeast, Luuka to the southwest, Iganga to the south, Namutumba to the east and Pallisa to the northeast.

Area: 871.74 sq. km.

Climate, Relief and Vegetation: Generally flat and covered with savannah grasslands.

Population: According to 2009 projections, there are 191,700 people, 98,500 female and 93,200 male, with a density of 220 persons per sq.km.

Major Towns: Kaliro Town Council.

Counties and Sub-Counties: Bulamogi County – Bumanya, Gadumire, Kaliro (Town Council), Namugongo, Namwiwa and Nawaikoke.

Main Language: Lusoga.

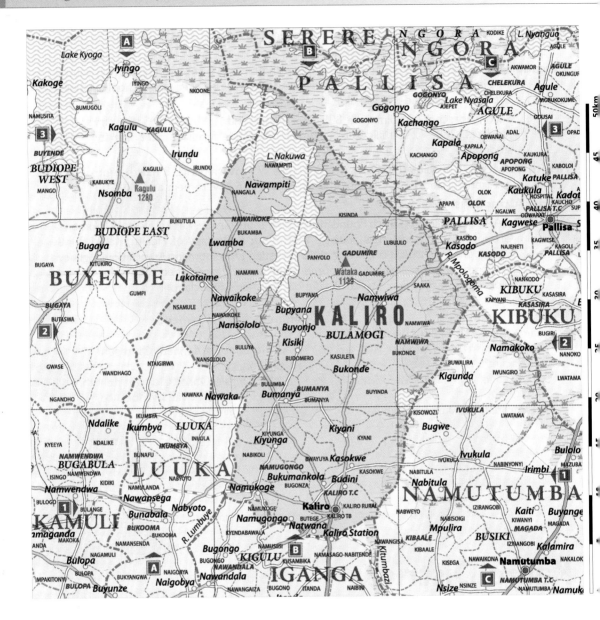

People: Basoga, Bakenyi, Iteso, Banyoro, Bagwere, Baganda, Banyole, Bagisu, Basamya, other Ugandans and non-Ugandans.

Economic Activities: Agriculture with emphasis on food crops, fisheries, forestry and apiary.

Animal Population: According to the 2008 livestock statistics, the district has 65,364 cattle, 56,090 goats, 2,144 sheep, 14,775 pigs, 188,942 chicken, 3,694 ducks and 2,298 turkeys.

Industries: Manufacture of grainmill products, textiles and wearing apparel, metal products and furniture.

Education Services: Primary schools: 234 – 171 government, 57 private and 16 community. Primary school enrolment: 60,067 pupils – 29,798 male and 30,269 female. Primary school teachers: 1,048 – 688 male and 360 female.

Secondary schools: 14 schools - 5 government, and 9 private. Secondary school enrolment: 8,195 students – 5,065 male and 3,130 female. Teachers: 380 – 312 male and 68 female. Available furniture is adequate for 5,684 students.

Tertiary institution – 1 teachers' college (National Teachers' College – Kaliro).

Health Services: - No hospital; 1 health centre IV - (government); 5 health centre III - (4 government and 1 NGO); and 10 health centre II - (4 government and 6 NGO);

Tourist Attractions: Bugonza Martyrs Shrine – Located at Namugongo 4 kilometres along the Kaliro-Kamuli road, the shrine was built in memory of one of the twenty-two catholic martyrs, St. Gonzaga Gonza, who was executed from this site which was also his birth place. The execution orders were given by Kabaka Mwanga in 1986. The shrine has a potential, if developed, to be included into the national religious pilgrimage circuit.

Wako Zibondo's Palace – Located within a kilometre's distance east of Kaliro town, the palace comprises of a residence with an impressive architectural design. Built in 1930, the palace was home to Ezekeri Tenywa Wako Zibondo IX, King (Isebantu) of Busoga from 15th March 1893 to 18th April 1952. Zibondo is the father of the late Kyabazinga, Wako Muloki. If renovated it could be one of the tourist attractions in the district.

Buguge Historical Site – Located 15 kilometres north of Kaliro town, in Saaka parish, Namwiwa Sub-county. The site is believed to have been the settlement of the first Lamogi (chief) from the Babito rulers of the Bito Dynasty of Bunyoro. Also at the site are two graves 100 metres apart and these are believed to be of the first Lamogi (Chief) and his escort Mukama from the Bito Dynasty of Bunyoro.

District Leaders:	Members of Parliament:
District Chairperson – Mr Ibanda Wickliffe	Bulamogi County – Mr Lubogo Kenneth
CAO – Mr Petero Gasumuni Gahafu	District Woman MP – Ms Nabugere Flavia
DCAO – Vacant	
Town Clerk (Kaliro Town Council)	
– Mr Stephen Kasadha	

Kamuli District

In the 1974 provincial administration, Kamuli was part of North Busoga Province. North Busoga Province became Kamuli District in 1980. At Independence, Busoga District comprised of the present day Bugiri, Iganga, Kamuli, Jinja and Mayuge districts.

Location: Kamuli District borders the districts of Luuka to the east, Jinja to the south, Kayunga to the west and Buyende to the north.

Area: 1554 sq.km.

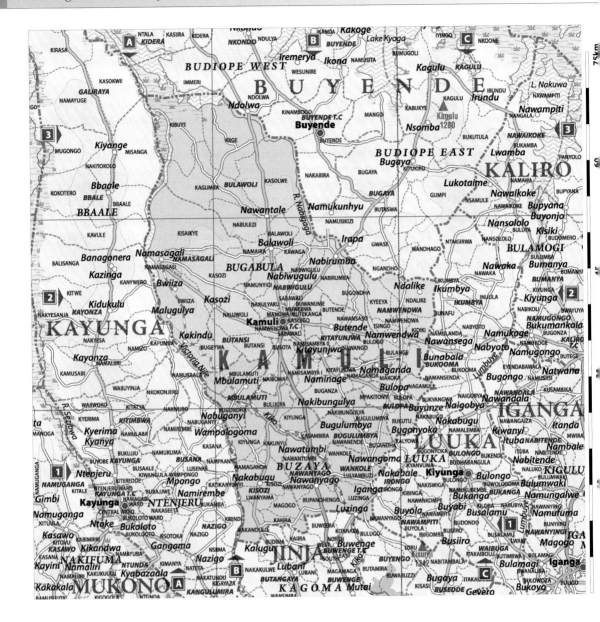

Climate, Relief and Vegetation: It lies at an approximate altitude of between 914m and 1,101m above sea level with heavy rainfall and moderate temperatures. Vegetation consists of woodlands, thickets and bushes.

Population: According to 2009 projections, there are 281,800 people – 135,400 male and 146,400 female with a density of 181 persons per sq.km.

Main Towns: Kamuli (administrative headquarters); Trading Centre – Kaliro.

Counties and Sub-counties: Bugabula County – Balawoli, Kamuli (Town Council), Nabwigulu, Namasagali, Bulopa, Kitayunjwa, Butansi, Namwendwa. Buzaaya County – Bugulumbya, Kisozi, Mbulamuti, Nawanyago and Wankole.

Main Language: Lusoga.

People: Basoga, Bakenyi, Iteso, Baruli, Banyoro, Banyara, Baganda, Basamia, Banyole, other Ugandans and non-Ugandans.

Economic Activities:

Mainly agriculture with emphasis on:
 (i) Food crops: Soya bean, maize, sorghum, cassava, sweet potatoes, finger millet, rice, groundnuts, simsim (sesame) and sunflower.
 (ii) Cash crops: Cotton, coffee and sugar cane.
 (iii) Vegetables: Tomatoes, onions and cabbage.

Banks: Stanbic Bank Uganda Ltd –1.

Area under Forestation: 27,909 hectares.

Animal Population: Buyende and Kamuli have 211,815 cattle, 219,194 goats, 6,540 sheep, 55,239 pigs, 724,489 chicken, 15,538 ducks and 2,421 turkeys.

Co-operative Societies: The district has 155 registered primary societies with Busoga Union at the district level.

Industries: Manufacture of jaggery, brick making, maize milling and cotton ginning.

Education Services: Primary schools: 266 – 249 government, 12 private and 5 community. Primary school enrolment: 127,824 – 62,433 male and 65,391 female. Primary school teachers: 2,339 – 1,368 male and 971 female. Available furniture was not fully reported.

 Secondary schools: 29 schools - 11 government, 14 private and 4 community. Secondary school enrolment: 19,649 students – 10,514 male and 9,135 female. Teachers: 773 – 624 males and 149 female. Available furniture is adequate for 17,851 students.

 Tertiary institutions – 1 technical institution and 2 teacher training colleges.

Health Services: 2 hospitals - (1 government and 1 NGO – Uganda Catholic Medical Bureau – Kamuli Mission Hospital with 153 beds); 2 health centre IV - (all government); 10 health centre III - (all government); and 35 health centre II - (18 government and 17 NGO).

Operational Radio and TV Stations: Busoga People's Radio (Empanga), CBS Radio, UBC Radio.

Tourist Attractions: Namasagali Pier on River Nile – situated on River Nile, about 25 kilometres west of Kamuli town. The pier was built during the colonial government era to transport cotton and coffee from rural areas of Busoga region to Jinja town for processing and export. The pier areas have since been abandoned due to the closure of the marine and railway services. Suitable for various tourism-related activities such as camping, excursions, canoeing and sport fishing.

 Kagulu Hills – Located 64 kilometres north of Kamuli town, the hills and caves are believed to be the home of the ancestral spirits of the Busoga Kings. The main Kagulu Hill is about 10,000 feet above sea level; camping on top of it is exciting to tourists and excursionists.

 Budhumbula Shrines/Palace – Located 2 kilometres from Kamuli along Kamuli-Jinja Road, the site comprises the residence of the first Kyabazinga (King) of Busoga, Sir William Wilberforce Kadhumbula Nadiope who died in 1976. Other features of the site are the graves of the various members of the royal family of the first king. The palace's main residence is a legacy of the British colonial government which was donated by the protectorate government in 1914. The significance of the site lies in its national heritage aspects and further developments could make the site a favourite site for picnics and overnight camping.

Key NGOs: Africa 2000 Network – Uganda, Send a Cow Uganda, Integrated Rural Development Initiatives, Plan International, Environmental Alert, Traditional and Modern Health Practitioners, Kaliro Development Foundation, Uganda Red Cross, Buzaya Rural Savings Scheme, Family Keduabi World Peace, Citizens Link Development Project, AIDS Education Group for Youth, Sustainable Agricultural Farmers' Association, Twasakirala Aloe Vera Growers' Association, Uganda Development Services, Buzaya Rural Savings Scheme.

District leaders:	Members of Parliament:

Chairperson – Mr Kaugu Kawoya M.A.
Chief Administrative Officer (CAO)
   – Ms Catherine Amal
Town Clerk (Kamuli Town Council)
   – Mr Richard Mugolo
	Bugabula County North
	   – Ms Allen Andrew
	Buzaaya County
	   – Mr Mugabi Muzaale Martin Kisule
	Bugabula County South
	   – Mr Asuman Kiyingi
	Woman MP – Ms Rebecca Kadaga Alitwala

Kapchorwa District

Kapchorwa District was in existence at independence in 1962. At that time, it was known as Sebei District. In 1980, it was renamed Kapchorwa. The district has reduced in size after new districts were carved out of it.

Location: Kapchorwa borders the districts of Sironko to the south, Bulambuli to the west and Kween to the east.

Area: 353 sq.kms.

Population: According to 2009 projection, there are 98,100 people – 47,500 male and 50,600 female with a denity of 277 persons per sq.km.

Major Towns: Kapchorwa (administrative headquarters).

Counties and Sub-counties: Tingey County – Sipi, Chema, Kabeywa, Kapchesombe, Kapchorwa (Town Council), Kapsinda, Kaptanya, Kapteret, Kawowo, Kaserem, Munarya, Tegeres and Gamogo.

Main Language: Kupsabin.

People: Sabiny.

Economic Activities: Mainly agriculture with emphasis on:
(i)   Food crops: Maize, beans, wheat, sunflower, groundnuts, yams, field peas, cassava, irish potatoes and millet.
(ii) Cash crops: Cotton, coffee and wheat.
(iii) Fruits and vegetables: Cabbage, tomatoes, passion fruit and onions.

Banks: Stanbic Bank Uganda Ltd –1.

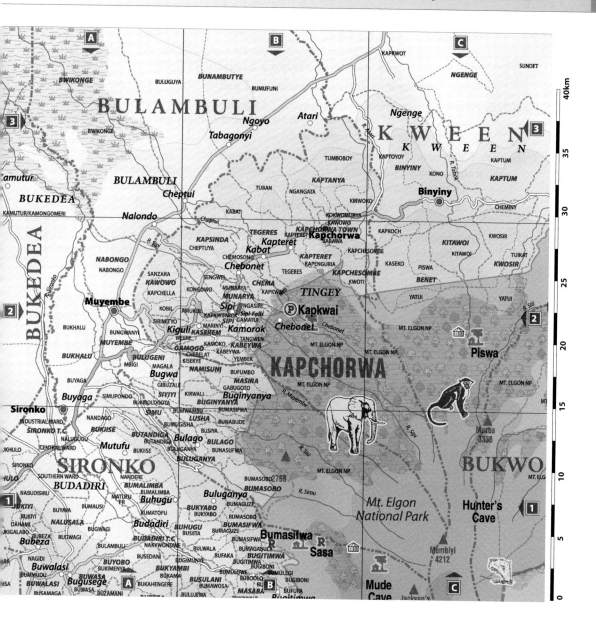

Area under Forestation: 62,596 hectares.

Animal Population: Kapchorwa and Kween districts have 95,564 cattle, 75,073 goats, 9,852 sheep, 8,070 pigs, 285,543 chicken, 2,898 ducks and 427 turkeys.

Co-operative Societies: Kapchorwa and Kween districts have 46 registered primary societies with Sebei Co-operative Union specialising in coffee at the district union.

Industries: Coffee processing saw milling and furniture making.

Education Services: Primary schools: 64 – 42 government, 20 private and 2 community. Primary school enrolment: 29,612 pupils – 14,602 male and 15,010 female. Primary school teachers: 765 - 430 male and 335 female. Available furniture is adequate for 22,054 pupils.

Secondary schools: 9 schools - 5 government, 1 private, 3 community. Secondary school enrolment: 6,472 students – 3,430 male and 3,042 female. Teachers: 282 - 217 male and 65 female. Available furniture is adequate for 5,417.

Tertiary institution: 1 Technical institution, 1 teacher training college.

Health Services: 1 government district hospital – Kapchorwa Hospital with a total of 100 beds. 1 health centre IV (government); 6 health centre III (all government); and 8 health centre II (5 government and 3 NGO);

Transport Network: The district has a poor road network. The rugged terrain impedes transportation. Currently there is one main road which connects Mbale and Sironko districts to Kapchorwa – the Sironko-Suam Road.

Tourist Attractions: The way of life of the Sabiny and Karimojong is worth seeing. The district has a beautiful, rugged landscape and its location is on the ranges of Mountain Elgon. The magnificent Sipi Falls and Mountain Elgon national park can be easily accessed from Kapchorwa. The Exploration Centre is another important tourist attraction. It is a facility designiged to train local communities and visitors on ecological aspects and sustainable use of the protected area.

Key NGOs: Actionaid Uganda, Family Planning Association of Uganda, Islamic Medical Association of Uganda, Kapchorwa Human Rights Initiative, Kapchorwa Rural Development Association, Reproduction, Educative and Community Health Programme, Sabiny Elders Association, Uganda Red Cross, Safeguard Integrated Development Foundation, The Youth Sports Organisation of Uganda.

District leaders:
District Chairperson – Mr Cheptoris Aam M.
Chief Administrative Officer (CAO) – Mr George Willia Omuge
Deputy Chief Administrative Officer (DCAO) – Vacant
Town Clerk (Kapchorwa Town Council) – Mr Alfred Mashandich

Members of Parliament:
Tingey County – Mr Chebrot Stephen Chemoiko
Woman MP – Ms Chemutai Phyllis

Katakwi District

Katakwi District was created in 1997. It was formerly part of Soroti District. The three sub-counties which comprise Katakwi (Kapelebyong, Amuria and Usuk) belonged to Soroti until then.

Location: It borders the districts of Napak to the northeast, Nakapiripirit to the east, Amuria to the west and Lake Bisina forms its border with Kumi and Ngora to the south.

Area: 2,477.13 sq. km.

Climate, Relief and Vegetation: The district is located on the northern plateau. It is characterised by extensive flat plains with grassland savannah and frequent shrub vegetation. There is a marked long, dry, season and rainfall is relatively low, ranging from 850mm – 1,500mm, with the northern parts receiving less rainfall.

Population: According to 2009 projections, there are 153,700 people – 79,300 female and 74,400 male with a density of 62 persons per sq.km.

Major Towns: Katakwi (administrative headquarters); Trading Centre - Achowa.

Counties and Sub-counties: Usuk County – Ongongoja, Katakwi, Katakwi (Town Council), Ngariam, Palam, and Usuk. Toroma County –Kapujan, Magoro, Omodoi, and Toroma,

Main Language: Ateso.

People: Mainly Iteso, but Karimojong also live in the district.

Economic Activities: Agriculture with emphasis on:
   (i)   Food crops: Finger millet, sorghum, groundnuts, cassava, cow peas, sweet potatoes, soya bean, simsim, maize and vegetables.
   (ii) Cash crop: Cotton.

Area under Forestation: 6,926 hectares.

Animal Population: Katakwi has 136,966 cattle, 104,932 goats, 25,511 sheep, 19,381 pigs, 286,229 chicken 4,902 ducks and 3,423 turkeys.

Co-operative Societies: Katakwi, Amuria and Soroti have 153 registered co-operative societies.

Industries: Flour milling, cotton ginning and woodwork.

Education Services: Primary schools: 75 schools - 70 government, 2 Private, 3 community. Primary school enrolment: 42,833 – 21,762 male and 21,071 female. Primary school teachers: 731 – 539 male and 192 female. Available furniture is adequate for 29,661 pupils.

Secondary schools: 12 schools – 5 government, 3 private and 4 community. Secondary school enrolment: 2,973 – 1,849 male and 1,124 female. Teachers: 214 – 182 male and 32 female. Available furniture is adequate for 2,095 students.

Health Services: 1 health centre IV – (government); 5 health centre III – (3 government and 2 NGO); and 12 health centre II – (10 government and 2 NGO).

Transport Network: The Katakwi District road network is all murram. But the roads are well distributed throughout the district thus linking all sub-counties. The roads are in a fair condition.

Tourist Attractions: Lakes Opeta and Bisina both found along the southern border of the district are famous for the variety of birds. Opeta and Bisina are Ramsar Sites, meaning that they are internationally recognised wetlands and are protected.

The variety of wild game which wanders between Pian-Upe and Bokora Wildlife Reserves of Karamoja are a great tourist attraction. Abila rocks used to be the home of a large concentration of primates. The rock tops provide a view of most of the district and Soroti town, 50 kilometres away.

Additional Information: Katakwi District has a low population. It was borne out of the need to take services closer to the people. Katakwi has virtually no industrial activities and is typically an agricultural district. There is some limited fishing on Lake Bisina and Lake Opeta. In some parts of the district water sources are non-existent. In addition, the district receives low rainfall and has long, dry, seasons. This does not favour cultivation of some crops.

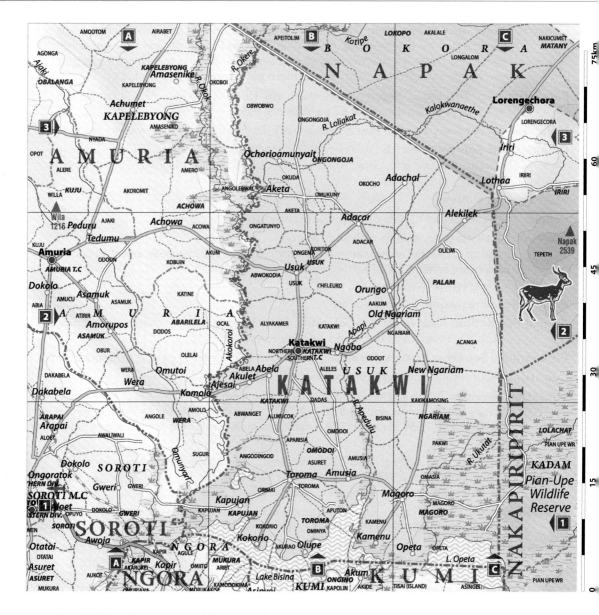

Key NGOs: African Medical Research Foundation Uganda, Actionaid Uganda Concern Uganda, Traditional and Modern Health Practitioners, Self-Help Development International, the Komolo Development Association.

District leaders:

Chairperson – Mr John Robert Ekongot
Chief Administrative Officer (CAO)
    – Mr Milton M. Kato
Deputy Chief Administrative Officer
    (DCAO) – Vacant
Acting Town Clerk (Katakwi Town
    Council) – Mr Richard Alioka

Members of Parliament:

Usuk County – Mr Oromait Michael
Toroma County
    – Mr Amodoi Cyrus Imalingat
Woman Representative
    – Ms Jessica Epel Alupo

Kibuku District

Kibuku District was carved out of Pallisa District in 2010.

Location: Borders with the districts of Pallisa to the north, Budaka to the east, Butaleja to the south and Namutumba to the west.

Area: 479 sq. kms.

Climate, Relief and Vegetation: Generally flat and covered with savannah grasslands. Rainfall goes up to 1,164mm annually and temperatures up 29 C maximum and 16 C minimum.

Population: Based on the 2009 population projections there are 160,200 people – 83,500 female and 76,700 male with a density of 334 persons per sq.km.

Major Towns: Budaka Town Council

Counties and Sub-counties: Kibuku County – Bulangira, Buseta, Kabweri, Kasasira, Kibuku, Kibuku (Town Council), Kadama, Tirinyi, Kagumu and Kirika.

Main Language: Lugwere

People: Bagwere, Banyole, Iteso, Basoga, Bagisu, Bakenyi, Baganda, Japadhola, other Ugandans and non Ugandans.

Economic Activities: A high economic potential in terms of apiary, crop and animal production.

Animal Population: Pallisa and Kibuku have 136,225 cattle, 149,003 goats, 20,488 sheep, 25,302 pigs, 440,035 chicken, 20,748 ducks and 27,928 turkeys.

Industries - Furniture, grainmill products, bakery products, metal products, textiles and wearing apparel, dairy products as well as sawmilling and plying of wood.

Education Services: Primary schools: 61 – 41 government, 16 private and 4 community. Enrolment: 47,703 pupils – 23,995 male and 23,708 female. Teachers: 718 - 445 male and 273 female. Available furniture not fully reported.

Secondary schools: 8 schools - 3 government, 4 private, 1 community, Enrolment: 5,349 students – 3,129 male and 2,220 female. Teachers: 234 – 200 male and 34 female. Available furniture is adequate for 3,627 students.

Health Services: No hospital; 1 health centre IV (government); 9 health centre III (8 government and 1 NGO); and 4 health centre II (3 government and 1 NGO).

Tourist Attractions: Budaka Kakungulu Sites

District Leaders:
District Chairperson
  – Mr Nakeba Muhamad
Ag CAO
  – Mr Ananias Kweyamba Ruhemba
DCAO – Vacant

Members of Parliament:
Kibuku County – Mr Saleh M. W. Kamba
Woman MP
  – Ms Sarah Mwebaza Wenene

Kumi District

Kumi District was originally part of former Teso District. In the 1974 provincial administration Teso District was divided into three districts: North Teso, Central Teso and South Teso. In 1980, South Teso District became Kumi.

Location: It borders the districts of Bukedea to the east, Budaka and Pallisa to the south, Ngora to the west and Katakwi to the north.

Area: 1,075 sq. km.

Climate and Relief: It lies at an approximate altitude of between 1,036m and 1,127m above sea level in a modified equatorial climatic zone with both heavy rainfall and high temperature.

Population: Based on the population projections 2009, there are 219,500 people – 106,100 male and 113,400 female, with a density of 204 persons per sq.km.

Major Town: Kumi (administrative headquarters).

Counties and Sub-counties: Kumi County – Atutur, Kanyum, Kumi, Kumi (Town Council), Mukongoro, Nyero, and Ongino;

People: Itesot.

Economic Activities: Mainly agriculture with emphasis on:
    (i)   Food crops: Finger millet, groundnuts, sweet potatoes, cassava, sorghum, rice, cow peas, soya beans, bananas, sunflower and onions.
    (ii)   Cash crops: Cotton.

Banks: Stanbic Bank Uganda Ltd – 1.

Area under Forestation: 8,177 hectares for Kumi and Ngora.

Animal Population: Kumi and Ngora districts have 220,055 cattle, 168,887 goats, 30,994 sheep, 67,650 pigs, 549,135 chicken 9,936 ducks and 20,360 turkeys according to 2008 statistics.

Co-operative Societies: 88 registered primary societies with Teso Union at the district level.

Education Services: Primary schools: 230 – 217 government, 5 private and 8 community. Primary school enrolment: 67,406 pupils – 33,684 male and 33,722 female. Primary school teachers: 1,017 – 648 male and 369 female. Available furniture was not reported.

Secondary schools: 11 schools - 5 government, 5 private and 1 community. Secondary school enrolment: 5,595 – 3,415 male and 2,180 female. Teachers: 257 – 211 male and 46 female. Available furniture is adequate for 4,661 students.

Tertiary institutions– 1 technical institution, 1 teacher training colleges and 1 university - Kumi University.

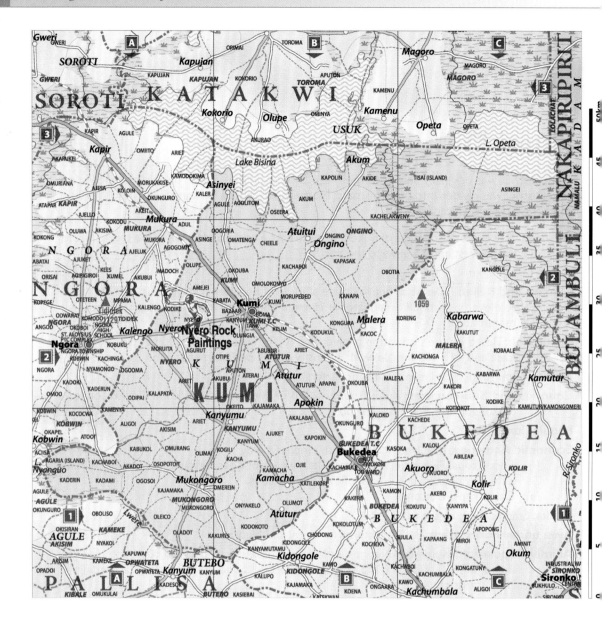

Health Services: 2 hospitals – (1 Government District Hospital- Atutur Hospital with 104 beds and 1 NGO); no health centre IV); 6 health centres III - (all government); and 7 health centres II - (4 Government and 3 NGO).

Tourist Attractions: Nyero Rock Paintings which consist of three painted caves close to each other (Nyero Site One, Nyero Site Two and Nyero Site Three). Paintings are in red and white pigmentation and are mainly of geometric shapes. They are believed to be 300 – 1000 years old and regarded as being among the best rock paintings in East Africa. The surrounding area is covered with smooth boulders, mainly occupied by sunbathing monkeys. Occassionally reptiles can be seen sunbathing on the rock mostly in the afternoon. Camping facilities are available at the Nyero Campsite at the base of Nyero Site One.

Lake Opeta:

Additional Information: The rolling plains of Kumi form part of the modified equatorial climate zone in northeastern Uganda which favours food crops like cassava, sweet potatoes, sorghum and finger millet.

The main activity in Kumi was cattle keeping, but as a result of the insurgency from 1987-1991, and cattle rustling, the cattle population was decimated. Many people have now turned to cultivation to make a living. Kumi is a sparsely populated district.

Operational Radio and TV Stations: Continental FM Station Ltd.

Key NGOs: Send a Cow Uganda, African Medical Research Foundation, Actionaid Uganda, Uganda Women's Effort to Save Orphans, Bukedea Women Strugglers Association, Church of Uganda Teso Diocese Planning and Development Offices, Faith Action, Kumi Human Rights Initiative and Self Governance, Kachumbala War Against Poverty Alleviation, Karev Youth and Orphans Link Initiative for Rural Development, Kumi Aids Support Organisation, Ongino Community Development Association, Uganda Women's Finance Trust, Save the Children Denmark, Vision Terudo.

District leaders:
Chairperson – Mr Ismael Orot
Chief Administrative Officer (CAO)
  – Mr Willy Bataringaya
Deputy Chief Administrative Officer
  (CAO) – Vacant
Town Clerk (Kumi Town Council)
  – Mr Francis Oluka

Members of Parliament:
Kumi County – Mr Patrick Oboi Amuriat
Woman MP
  – Ms Amongin Aporu Christine Hellen

Kween District

Kween was carved out of Kapchorwa District in 2010, when Kween County was elevated to district status.

Location: It borders the districts of Kapchorwa to the west, Bulambuli to the northeast, Sironko and Bududa to the southwest, Nakapiripit to the north and Bukwa to the east. Its southern tips border the Republic of Kenya and Mbale District.

Area: 828 sq.kms.

Population: According to 2009 projections, the district has 88,800 people – 43,500 male, 45,300 female with a density of 104 persons per sq.km

Major Towns: Binyiny (administrative headquarters); Trading Centre – Kaproron.

Counties and Sub-counties: Kween County – Benet, Binyiny, Binyiny (Town Council), Greek River, Kaproron, Kaptum, Ngenge, Kitawoi, Kwanyiy, Kwosir and Moyok.

Main Language: Kupsabin.

People: Sabiny.

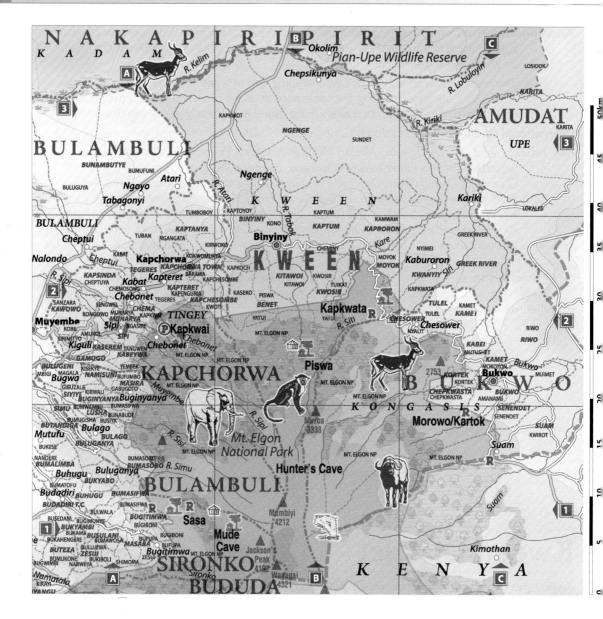

Economic Activities: Mainly agriculture with emphasis on:
- (i) Food crops: Maize, beans, wheat, sunflower, groundnuts, yams, field peas, cassava, irish potatoes and millet.
- (ii) Cash crops: Cotton, coffee and wheat.
- (iii) Fruits and vegetables: Cabbage, tomatoes, passion fruit and onions.

Banks: Still depends on banks in Kapchorwa District.

Area under Forestation: 62,596 hectares.

Animal Population: 41,968 cattle, 3,735 goats, 3,171 sheep, 497 pigs and 32,221 chicken.

Co-operative Societies: 46 registered primary societies with Sebei Co-operative Union specialising in coffee at the district union.

Industries: Coffee processing, saw milling and furniture making.

Education Services: Primary schools: 60 – 28 government, 29 private and 3 community. Primary school enrolment: 28,403 pupils – 14,047 male and 14,356 female. Primary school teachers: 636 – 413 male and 223 female. Available furniture is adequate for 17,691 pupils.

Secondary schools: 10 schools - 4 government, 2 private, and 4 community. Secondary school enrolment: 3,484 students – 1,755 male and 1,729 female. Teachers: 182 - 142 male and 40 female. Available furniture is adequate for 2,713 students.

Health Services: No hospital; 1 health centre IV; 4 health centre III (all government); and 10 health centre II (5 government and 5 NGO);

Transport Network: The district has a poor road network. There is a loose surface road which connects the district to her neighbours. The easiest access from Kampala is the Mbale-Sironko-Kapchorwa Road which is paved up to Kapchorwa.

Tourist Attractions: Same as Kapchorwa.

Key NGOs: Actionaid Uganda, Family Planning Association of Uganda, Islamic Medical Association of Uganda, Kapchorwa Human Rights Initiative, Kapchorwa Rural Development Association, Reproduction, Educative and Community Health Programme, Sabiny Elders Association, Uganda Red Cross, Safeguard Integrated Development Foundation, The Youth Sports Organisation of Uganda.

District leaders:	Members of Parliament:
District Chairperson	Kween County
– Mr Nangusho Lawrence Cherop	– Mr Chemaswet AbdiFadhil Kisos
Ag Chief Administrative Officer (CAO)	Woman MP – Ms Chekwei Lydia
– Mr Anthony Lukwago	
Deputy Chief Administrative Officer	
(DCAO) – Vacant	

Luuka District

Luuka District was a county of Iganga District until 2010 when it was elevated to district status.

Location: It borders the districts of Iganga and Kaliro to the east, Jinja and Mayuge to the south, Kamuli to the west and Buyende to the northeast.

Area: 650 sq. km.

Climate, Relief and Vegetation: It lies at an altitude of between 1,070m and 1,161m above sea level with the annual rainfall ranging between 1,250mm and 2,200mm. Temperatures are always almost uniformly high at over 21°C. Vegetation is tropical lush green.

Population: Based on population projections 2009, there are 230,600 people – 121,000 female and 109,600 male, with a density of 354 persons per sq.km.

Main Towns: Luuka Town Council; Trading Centres – Busembatia and Busesa.

Counties and Sub-counties: Luuka County – Bukanga, Bukooma, Bulongo, Ikumbya, Irongo, Nawampiti and Waibuga.

Main Language: Lusoga.

People: Basoga.

Economic Activities: Agriculture with particular emphasis on:
  (i)   Food crops: Finger millet, maize, sorghum, rice, bananas, sweet potatoes, irish potatoes, cassava, beans, simsim (sesame) and peas.
  (ii) Cash crops: Coffee, cotton and rice.
  (iii) Fruits and vegetables: Oranges, tomatoes and cabbage.
  (iv) Fishing on Lake Victoria.

Area under Forestation: 5,568 hectares for Luuka and Iganga.

Trade: Iganga town is a growing commercial centre. Its proximity to the border with Kenya has boosted business activity, although some of the business activities are illicit, for example, smuggling.

Animal Population: Luuka and Iganga districts combined have 125,307 cattle, 169,915 goats, 5,064 sheep, 27,684 pigs, 904,493 chicken, 13,469 ducks and 6,550 turkeys.

Co-operative Societies: Iganga, Bugiri and Mayuge have 255 registered primary societies with Busoga Union at the district level for Iganga.

Industries: Processing of coffee, milling of rice, the manufacture of jaggery and brick making.

Banks: Stanbic Bank Uganda Ltd –1, Bank of Baroda –1.

Education Services: Primary schools: 102 – 88 government, 12 private, 2 community. Primary school enrolment: 67,912 pupils – 32,470 male and 35,442 female. Primary school teachers: 1,057 – 705 male and 352 female.

Secondary schools: 14 schools - 5 government, 5 private, 4 community. Secondary school enrolment: 5,781. Secondary school teachers: 279 - 235 male, 44 female. Available furniture is adequate for 5,051 students.

Health Services: No Hospital; 1 health centre IV - (government); 5 Health Centre III - (all government); and 18 health centre II - (14 government and 4 NGO).

Transport Network: The district is accessible by road and rail. It has tarmacked roads from Iganga town to Kamuli, off the Jinja - Iganga main road. The district is well connected with feeder-roads.

Tourist Attractions: Nenda Hill, contains the shrine of the Bazungu (white people) and is a view point for the surrounding plains. Tweyambe Women's Handicraft Shop offers a variety of locally produced goods of reasonable quality. The district also has caves and forests which are tourist attractions. Lake Victoria is another attraction and fishing constitutes a major activity. Additional cultural shrines/sites consist of Bugweri cultural site, Kigulu Shrine and Bukowe shrines for the Ngobi and Menyha Clans, respectively.

Key NGOs: Africa 2000 Network – Uganda, Send a Cow Uganda, African Network for the Prevention and Protection Against Child Abuse and Neglect Uganda Chapter, Family Planning Association of Uganda, Uganda Women's Effort to Save Orphans, Foundation for Kigulu South Development Association, Musingi Rural Development Association, Ngangali Agali Wamu Women's Group, Uganda Biogas Development, Wider Opportunities for Women and Youth Association, Iganga District Farmers' Association, Tweyambe Women's Club, Bakuseka Majja Women's Farmers Development Association.

Additional information: The predominant land tenure system in the district is customary. Agriculture is still at subsistence level except for rice which is grown specifically for other markets in the country.

District leaders:	Members of Parliament:
Chairperson – Mr Samuel Kakyada	Luuka County – Mr Bagoole John B. Ngobi
Ag Chief Administrative Officer (CAO)	Woman MP
– Christopher Sande Kyomya	– Ms Kaabule Evelyn Naome Mpagi
Deputy Chief Administrative Officer	
(DCAO) – Vacant	

MINISTRY OF PUBLIC SERVICE

Plot 12, Nakasero Hill Road. P.O. BOX 7003 KAMPALA, TEL: (256) – 41- 251002/344986/250570, FAX: (256) – 41-255463/346879
E-mail: ps@publicservice.go.ug, Website: www.publicservice.go.ug

"Putting people first: The key to improving Public Service"

Prisca B. Mbaguta Sezi (Mrs)
State Minister

Henry Muganwa Kajura.
Hon 2nd DPM and Minister

Mr. Jimmy Rwamafa
Permanent Secretary

Mandate

To develop Human Resource Policies, systems and structures that provide for an effective and harmonised public service; supported by a well developed and motivated human resource that will deliver timely and cost effective public services affordable by the Government of Uganda and responsive to the needs of the people, especially the poor.

Our Mission

To attract, develop and retain a competent and motivated public service workforce that delivers timely, high quality and appropriate services to the people at the least cost to the nation.

FINANCE AND ADMINISTRATION DEPARTMENT

Mandate

The Department of Finance and Administration, exists to ensure that there is a conducive work environment for the staff to deliver optimum services to both internal and external clients through provision of support services in the areas of administration and establishment, management of financial resource and manpower development.

It also facilitates the efficient and effective utilisation of human, financial and material resources in the Ministry. In addition, the department facilitates the political leadership in the Ministry specified under Circular Standing Instruction No. 2 of 2000 and No. 4 of 2001 and the former leaders of Uganda as required under the Presidential Emoluments and Benefits Act (1998).

Through the Planning; Policy Analysis and Procurement Units, the Department also supports the Permanent Secretary to coordinate and analyse the cross cutting policy issues on human resource and procurement matters.

Key Activities

Manage the provision of accounting and financial services, salaries and wages, bookkeeping and expenditure, budget and project accounts.

Assist the Permanent Secretary with the preparation and production of the annual budget estimates.

Manage the provision of human resource services to the Ministry.

Manage the provision, maintenance and allocation of buildings, offices, registry, office equipment and stationary, transport and travel, cleaning and building security.

The Department is composed of six Units/ Sections

- The Planning and Policy Analysis Unit
- The Procurement and Disposal Unit
- The Accounts Section
- Finance and Administration
- Security and Open Registry Section
- Resource Centre and Library Section

DIRECTORATE OF HUMAN RESOURCE MANAGEMENT

Mandate

To develop, review and monitor implementation of human resource management policies, rules, regulations and systems for an efficient and effective public service.

- Human Resource Management Department
- The Human Resource Development Department
- Compensation Department

HUMAN RESOURCE MANAGEMENT DEPARTMENT

Mandate

The Department of Human Resource Management is mandated to develop, interpret and review Human Resource Policies for the Public Service. The Department is responsible for the management, reviewing and updating of the Terms and Conditions of Service as well as the Public Service Policies, Procedures and Regulations, with a view to promoting good governance, accountability and transparency in the delivery of services and the Poverty Eradication Action Plan goals.

Roles/Duties

To ensure development and operation of effective Human Resource Policies, rules and regulations for the Public Service.

- To plan for the operations of the Department.
- To supervise and give guidance to the staff of the Department in the performance of their duties.
- To initiate formulation and review of human resource management policies, rules and regulations for the public service.
- To monitor the implementation of human resource management policies in ministries, departments and local governments.
- To identify the training needs of staff and recommend appropriate training.
- To provide information for human resource management for the public service.
- To carry out performance assessment of staff of the department.

- Promote work and professional ethics by upholding and encouraging the highest standard of behaviour in order to promote a good image of the Public Service.
- To monitor and regulate the size of the Public Service and give reports.
- To authorise and monitor financial expenditure of the Department.
- To ensure effective management of the wage bill for the Public Service.
- Sensitising public officers on Terms and Conditions of service.
- Translating human resource management policies into operational procedures and guidelines.
- To regularly report on the performance of the Department in relation to the annual performance plan.

The department has four Divisions which do different assignments i.e:

Payroll management division

Human resource policies and procedures division

Integrated personnel and payroll systems division (IPPS)

Wage bill management division

HUMAN RESOURCE DEVELOPMENT DEPARTMENT

The Department of Human Resource Development is one of the three departments in the Directorate of Human Resource Management that was created in 1979.

The department has three Divisions

- Research, Policy and Systems Standards Division
- Capacity Enhancement Division
- Learning and Development Division

Mandate

The Department of Human Resource Development is mandated to:

- Develop and review staff training and development policies, standards and guidelines, as well as designing and coordinating the implementation of management development programmes in the Public Service;
- Ensure that the training and capacity building activities undertaken within the public service advance national goals and priorities;
- Manage the training and development function in the public service in a professional and systematic manner;
- Develop and implement a system in which training funds are targeted to training the right people in critical areas;
- Raise the performance levels of public officers by designing training that is demand-driven, cost effective, gender sensitive and pro-active; and

Coordinate human resource planning in the Public Service to ensure acquisition and maintenance of the right personnel with the right skills, knowledge and attitudes.

Key Functions

The Department of Human Resource Development is responsible for:

Undertaking research and making policy proposals on the management of training and staff development across the Public Service;

Monitoring the implementation of the training and staff development policies in the Public Service and offering the necessary technical guidance;

Identifying leadership and management development needs, designing and coordinating the implementation of appropriate programmes/plans;

Evaluating training programmes and institutions;

Compiling and analysing human resource planning data and information from ministries, departments and local governments and advising on the necessary human resource action;

Providing advice on matters of staff training and development;

Coordinating the scholarship programmes;

Development of schemes of service and competency profiling for all cadres in the public service;

Coordination of strategic training programmes;

Maintaining skills inventory in the Public Service;

Developing and maintaining human resource development training information system;

Forecasting and projecting Public Service human requirements; and

Coordinating of common cadre training in Public Service e.g. secretaries, personnel officers, etc.

Strategic Objectives

Operationalising the training policy for the Public Service to harmonise all human resource development activities in the Public Service;

Introducing a comprehensive and sustainable human resource development programme (i.e. Introducing Succession planning in line with good practice as a basis for developing prospective successors for key positions in public service;

Building human resource (HR) planning capacity;

Conducting periodic audits to determine public officers skills levels against their relevant skills and competency profiles;

Undertake comprehensive review of schemes of service; and

Develop and implement a change management strategy for the entire Public Service.

Key Outputs

Change management strategy for the Public Service;

Capacity enhancement plan for the Public service;

Succession plans;

Schemes of service for all cadres in the Public service;

Systematic, demand-driven and client-centred training in the public service;

Capacity of public officers enhanced; and

Performance enhanced;

COMPENSATION DEPARTMENT

Mandate

It is mandated to ensure a fair, equitable, transparent and prompt system of computation and payment of pension and other terminal benefits to the senior citizens/pensioners.

It manages the pensions scheme for the Traditional Public Service Teaching Service and Defence and the compensation to the former employees of the defunct East African Community (EAC)

Aim of the Department

The department aims at promptly and accurately paying pension and other terminal benefits

The Department pays the following terminal benefits:

Monthly pension,

Commuted pension gratuities

Contract gratuities

Death gratuities

Severance packages

Special compensation

Repatriation expenses

Paying in lieu of leave

The Major achievements of the Department

Computerisation of records which has quickened:

The process of records maintenance and retrieval computation and assessment and also eases information dissemination.

Changing from cash payments to paying through the banks. This is very convenient for the clients.

Compensation to the defunct E.A.C has been completed.

Published pension management information guide to enhance communication with clients.

The pension revalidation that started in 1999.

Sections of the Compensation Department

The department is divided into four sections namely Assessment, Accounts, Records, and Database Information Management.

The Assessment Section

In this section all documents are initially processed and captured onto the Database. The Unit scrutinises all submitted documents in the files of the beneficiaries and promptly works on them. These files are then forwarded to the auditors for auditing and approval.

The Accounts Section

This section is concerned with the payments of the beneficiaries after the Assessment Section finishes work. The Accounts Section studies the files, computes what is due to each individual file and pays the computed dues.

Database Information Management Section

Assisted by the Accounts section is the computer room where payrolls, NS2s, NS7, Pay slips etc. are all electronically generated. The computer sections develops, generates, designs and produces reports and programmes used for the assessing, computing and subsequently payment of dues to the beneficiaries.

This Unit in managed by a Francis Lubega-Systems Analyst/Programmer who does the designing, troubleshooting and partial programming and, last but not least, system administration & training above all.

To an extent also this division takes charge of the Information Centre commonly known as the Pension Computer Room

The Management Section

It is so called because it oversees and is responsible for what happens in the Pension's Department and all its sections/divisions.

DIRECTORATE OF EFFICIENCY AND QUALITY ASSURANCE

Mandate

The Directorate of Efficiency and Quality Assurance undertakes efficiency audit to enable the Public Service to address the shortfalls in performance levels and take corrective action. The directorate has three departments:

Public Service Inspection Department
Management Service Department
Records Information Management Department

PUBLIC SERVICE INSPECTION DEPARTMENT

Mandate

The Inspectorate Department is mandated to develop performance standards for the Public Service; to carry out inspection and monitor the performance of both the central ministries and local governments in order to ensure total compliance with the set standards, rules, regulations and procedures; and to offer technical guidance, where necessary, to facilitate improved service delivery at the least cost to the citizens of Uganda with the aim of realising the PEAP goals.

Key Objectives

To ensure compliance with set standards, rules and regulations, so as to enhance the efficiency and effectiveness of the Public Service as well as enforce discipline among public servants.

To improve customer responsiveness, accountability, transparency, efficiency and effectiveness in service delivery by public servants.

Functions

Monitoring and evaluating the implementation of Government policies and programmes that fall within the mandate and portfolio of the Ministry of Public Service, and producing periodic reports.

Planning and carrying out inspections to ensure proper implementation of Public Service rules and regulations, and providing appropriate implementation guidelines.

Identifying performance bottlenecks against set targets/objectives and advising on possible solutions. Reviewing and evaluating performance of Public Officers and identifying cases of excellent and/or poor performance with a view to recommending rewards and/or remedial actions.

Investigating and making appropriate recommendations on staff and public complaints.

Targets

Inspecting the ministries and districts with a view to identifying the human resource management problems of rectification

Conducting results oriented management (ROM) workshops for Judges and members of parliament.

Developing and/or reviewing Service Standards using information from the National Service Delivery Survey.

Continuing with the implementation of results oriented management in all ministries and districts up to departmental level.

Designing inspection guidelines in line with the principles of ROM and developing an inspection manual.

MANAGEMENT SERVICES DEPARTMENT

The Management Services Department is primarily a specialised internal consultancy to help improve the performance of government by giving technical advice. In addition, the department offers specialised consultancy to other institutions outside government.

Mandate

The Department is mandated to ensure that appropriate structures, and systems are developed and instituted in the Public Service in a harmonised manner for efficient and effective service delivery. This is done through the periodic review and development of organisational structures, systems and procedures in line with legislative and policy changes and support implementation of local government structures.

Activities:

Streamlining organisational structures of central ministries.

Restructuring secretaries of service commissions and other constitutional bodies

Completing the job evaluation exercise for central ministries and circulating the report to all stakeholders

Finalising the divestiture policy framework for implementation.

Reviewing the consultancy report on facilities and assets management. The reports and the assets inventory were handed over to the Ministry of Finance, Planning and Economic Development Treasury Inspectorate Department for implementation.

Targets of the Department

Implementing the recommendations of the restructuring report for the constitutional commission and bodies.

Commencing the restructuring exercise for local governments.

Implementing the divestiture policy framework.

Focus of the Department

Organisation development and design

Systems development (methods & procedures)

Setting performance standards

Job analysis & design (Job description & specification)

Job evaluation

Competence profiling

Method study

Business Analysis

Work measurement (Industrial Engineering)

Strategic planning

Management services provides view of problems outside of those directly involved

Provide specialist help in the form of methodology, consulting skills and analysis

Provide specialist help in the form of methodology, consulting skills and analysis

Professional integrity

RECORDS INFORMATION MANAGEMENT DEPARTMENT. (RIM)

Introduction

Records and information management (RIM) is one of the departments in the Directorate of Efficiency and Quality Assurance in the Ministry of Public Service. RIM relates with all central government ministries, departments, local governments, statutory bodies, research bodies and academic institutions in records management and organisation of departmental registries.

Mandate

The Department is mandated to establish and promote efficient, economic and effective records and information management systems in the Public Service. It also oversees the preservation of the documented heritage (archives) for Uganda's posterity.

The objective of the Department is to establish efficient records management systems in MDAs and LGs to provide accurate and up to date information in order to support government operations for accountability, transparency and good governance and facilitate informed decision making.

Specific objectives

To develop records management and archives administration regulations and procedures

To supervise and monitor registries in public organisations that generate and manage records

To provide access to archives

To facilitate the process of records as they move through stages of semi-current to archival repositories or disposal channels

To coordinate and bring professionalism to collection, management and preservation of records in the country

Roles and responsibilities

Setting policies and standards

Offering technical assistance in records management to MDAs and LGs

Establishing records management systems, procedures and practices and promulgating them

Preserving records (National Archives)

Ensuring regular, timely and systematic disposal of records.

THE DIRECTORATE OF RESEARCH AND DEVELOPMENT

The main role of the Directorate of Research and Development is to coordinate the work of the two Departments of Monitoring and Evaluation and Information, Education Communication and provide technical input. It also includes guidance and harmonisation of planning, budgeting and research functions in the Ministry.

The Directorate of Research and Development has two Departments:

a) Department of Monitoring and Evaluation (M&E)

b) Department of Information, Education Communication (IEC)

The main functions are:

To guide research and analysis and identify areas for improving Public Service performance and Public Service management.

To strategically monitor and evaluate the Public Service reform programme.

To oversee the development and implementation of a monitoring and evaluation framework for the PSRP

To oversee the development and execution of an IEC Strategy for the Reform Programme

To organise regular interactive sessions with Cabinet, Members of Sessional Committee on Public Service and Local Government and Chief Executives of MDAs and LGs

To liaise with development partners on funding for the PSRP and other issues related to PSRP implementation

To promote Public/Private sector partnerships throughout the Public Service.

To participate in the Public Sector Management meetings and reviews

To provide guidance in planning and budgeting for the reform programme.

MONITORING AND EVALUATION (M&E) DEPARTMENT

The main purpose of the M&E Department is to monitor progress and impact of the various interventions being implemented by MoPS; provide feedback to implementers and stakeholders; and facilitate timely appropriate interventions.

The core functions and activities include:

Organisation and coordination of progress review meetings of Task Managers, chaired by the PS/MoPS.

Organisation and coordination of quarterly stakeholders' consultative meetings which include development partners, and representatives from the PSM Sector Institutions (namely: OPM; PSC; MoLG; LGFC; NPA; Cabinet Secretariat);

Production of quarterly progress reports and dissemination to stakeholders;

Production of annual performance reports on PSRP implementation;

Organisation and coordination of joint annual reviews of the PSRP and an independent assessment of the PSRP by an external consultant prior to the review;

Data collection, analysis and reporting on indicators as per the agreed M&E framework;

Procurement of relevant consultancies and technical supervision of their work (The current ones are: Impact Assessment of PSRP; Management Information System (MIS) and Staff Survey); and

Identifying research areas for improving the performance and management of the public Service.

THE INFORMATION EDUCATION AND COMMUNICATIONS DEPARTMENT

Introduction

IEC is a package of planned interventions that is a combination of informational, educational, communications and motivational processes.

It utilises a myriad of technologies and techniques to ensure that the intended message is conveyed to the target audience in the most effective form at the right time, and to support innovative information and communication channels.

IEC largely depends on modern Information and Communications Technology (ICT), research, audio-visual technologies, behavioural sciences and analytics, materials development techniques, mass communication, printing technology, etc.

It aims at achieving measurable changes in attitudes and behaviours in specific audiences.

Mandate of the IEC Department

The Department of IEC is responsible for developing, producing, and disseminating messages to support specific public service initiatives in an integrated manner. Through research and other cognitive processes, the department continually strives to provide effective and efficient information and communication processes and channels. The department works to meet the increasing demand for IEC by implementing an IEC strategy, and

utilising various media according to the needs of the client. Without being specific to technology, the various information and communication media are categorised into two classes, namely: mass media and inter-personal media.

Objectives

The general objective of IEC Department is to raise the awareness of the public servants as a means to promote service delivery standards through the efforts of the people themselves and through full utilisation of available resources.

The specific objectives of the department are:

- To increase awareness of the public service on service delivery issues;
- To increase positive attitudes towards work and service delivery in general;
- To promote healthy behaviour;
- To promote participation of the citizenry in public service programmes by creating demand and accountability for services at all levels of service; and
- To innovate and popularise usage and access to new information and technology as a better means of serving the wider stakeholder audience;

The Functions and Responsibilities of the IEC Department are as follows:

- To develop and implement an integrated IEC strategy (with internal and external linkages) and put in place measures for implementing it;
- Liaise with MoPS Departments, providing IEC services to them;
- To execute specific assignments – conceptualise designs and messages for print jobs such as booklets, brochures, leaflets, posters, and newspaper briefs;
- Develop and implement modern information and communication channels for MoPS and between MoPS and the wider stakeholder audience;
- Prepare messages and special communications;
- Execute programme specific print jobs, preparation of annual report, booklets, guidelines, newsletters etc;
- Service the Media Unit of the Resource Centre and coordinate, with all media units of MoPS;

Brief producers and oversee production of sponsored TV/radio programmes & other AV inputs;

Brief the Research and Development Directorate regarding field level interpersonal communication activities; liaise for special campaigns using folk and interactive media;

Administrative arrangements including budgeting and accounting of funds, release of funds to media units, monitoring of utilisation, commissioning of impact studies and follow up;

Liaise with F&A for preparing media liaison and PR Plan and its execution; organisation of media Workshops in the central and local governments and organising feedback from media;

To implement the follow-up sessions with journalists (fellowship) for MoPS seeking to build up a core group of journalists specialising in public sector reform initiatives;

Coordinate the production and distribution of various print materials through the Resource Centre e.g. booklets, newsletters, flyers, FAQs briefs, etc.

General Strategies

Implementing IEC interventions in an effective manner at the ministry, district, national, and community levels;

Ensuring adequate supply of IEC materials to intended recipients and ensuring that the most efficient distribution systems are used;

Ensuring and mobilising the participation of community service organisations as partners;

Building institutional IEC capacities at various levels of interventions;

Developing and disseminating messages on the public service reform programme;

Using modern multi-media techniques to enhance learning and stimulate behaviour change ;

Emphasising communication in all levels of interventions;

Establishing and strengthening co-ordination and co-operation with related governmental organisations at all levels;

Conducting research on different disciplines of IEC to determine the gaps in Knowledge, Attitudes and Practices (KAP) among target audiences and gaps in KAP among service providers; and

Segmenting audiences and developing specific messages for specific audience groups.

Manafwa District

Formerly part of Mbale District, Manafwa District was formed in 2005.

Location: Manafwa District borders the districts of Bududa to the north, Mbale to the west, Tororo to the south and the Republic of Kenya to the east.

Area: 603 sq. km.

Climate, Relief and Vegetation: Low temperatures and rainfall of up to 1000mm and above annually. Vegetation includes bamboo forests.

Population: Based on the 2009 Uganda population projections, there are 325,600 people – 156,400 male and 169,200 female with a population density of 539 persons per sq.km.

Major Town: Manafwa Town Council.

Counties and Sub-counties: Bubulo County – Bugobero, Butiru, Buwagogo, Kaato, Sibanga, Bukusu, Bukusuya, Butta, Khabutoola, Sisuni, Tsekululu, Magale, Nalondo, Namabya, Weswa, Bukhofu, Bunabwana, Buwabwana, Bumwoni, Bumbo, Bupoto Lwakhakha (Town Council), Manafwa Town Council), Bukoho, Mukoto, Namboko, Bukiabi, Bukhabusi, Bukhaweka, and Bubutu,

Main Language: Lumasaba

People: Bagisu, Iteso, Acholi, Sabiny, Babukusu, Baganda, Basoga, Japadhola, Bagwere, other Ugandans and non-Ugandans

Economic Activities: Mainly agriculture with emphasis on food crops. Cash crops consist of coffee and cotton.

Animal Population: 76,602 cattle, 79,928 goats, 4,795 sheep, 38,905 pigs, 444,266 chicken, 7,405 ducks and 8,65 turkeys, basing on 2008 statistics.

Industries: Manufacture of grainmill products, textiles and wearing apparel, furniture and metal products.

Education Services: Primary schools: 165 – 142 government, 12 private and 11 community. Primary school enrolment: 106,885 pupils – 52,529 male and 54,356 female. Primary school teachers: 1,919 – 1,224 male and 695 female. Available furniture not reported.

Secondary schools: 29 schools - 14 government, 13 private and 2 community. Secondary school enrolment: 13,572 students – 6,782 male and 6,791 female. Secondary school teachers: 672 – 655 male, 106 female. Available furniture was not reported.

Health Services: 1 hospital (government); no health centre IV; 4 health centre III (all government); and 5 health centre II (3 government and 2 NGO).

Tourist Attractions (Developed and Potential): Mt. Elgon National Park – Mt. Elgon National Park; Bulegeni and Butandinga Cliffs/Ridges – these are found 50 kilometres southeast of Mbale town, overlooking the Lwakaka border post. Both sites are important for scenery, bird watching and camping.

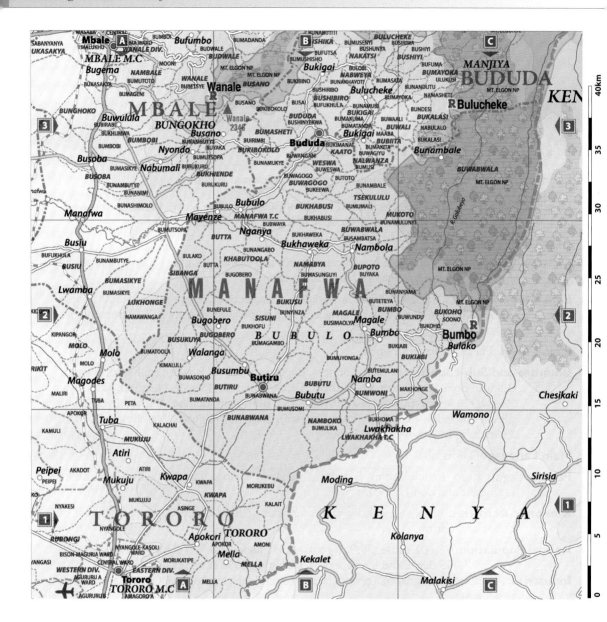

District Leaders
District Chairperson
– Mr Walimbwa Masolo Charles P.
CAO – Mr Juma Nkunyinyi Ssembajja

Members of Parliament
Bubulo County West
– Mr Kipoi Tonny Nsubuga
Bubulo County East – Mr Mulongo Simon
District Woman MP – Ms Sarah N. Kayagi
Netalisire

Mayuge District

Formerly part of Iganga District, Mayuge District was created in 2000 by elevating Bunya County, previously part of Iganga District, to district status. Present-day Iganga, Kamuli, Jinja and Mayuge Districts constituted Busoga District at independence in 1962.

Location: It borders Bugiri to the east, Buikwe, Buvuma and Jinja to the west, Iganga and Luuka to the north.

Area: 3,409.4 sq. km.

Climate, Relief and Vegetation: It lies at an approximate altitude of between 1,070m and 1,161m above sea level, with rainfall totalling 1,250mm and 2,200mm per annum. Temperatures are high at over 21°C. Vegetation is thick tropical rainforest.

Population: According to 2009 projections, there are 406,600 people – 211,500 female and 195,100 male, with a density of 119 persons per sq.km.

Major Towns: Mayuge (administrative headquarters); Trading Centre – Bunya.

Counties and Sub-counties: Bunya County – Buwaaya, Bukabooli, Bukatube, Busakira, Kigandalo, Kityerera, Jaguzi, Mpungwe, Malongo, Baitambogwe, Imanyiro, Mayuge (Town Council) and Wairasa.

Main Language: Lusoga.

People: Basoga.

Economic Activities: Agriculture with emphasis on fishing on Lake Victoria.
  (i)   Food crops: Finger millet, maize, rice, bananas and sweet potatoes.
  (ii) Cash crops: Coffee and cotton.
  (iii) Fruits and vegetables: Tomatoes, unions and cabbage.
  (iv) Cattle keeping.

Area under Forestation: 22,997 hectares.

Animal Population: 15,834 cattle, 4 donkeys, 6,000 pigs, 1,993 sheep, 32,248 goats, 9,217 rabbits and 132,645 chicken.

Co-operative Societies: Mayuge, Bugiri and Iganga have 255 registered co-operative societies.

Industries: Processing of coffee, brick making, milling of rice.

Education Services: Primary schools: 176 – 142 government, 30 private and 4 community. Primary school enrolment: 121,379 pupils – 59,675 male and 61704 female. Primary school teachers: 2,052 – 1,238 male and 814 female.
  Secondary schools: 27 schools - 6 government, 20 private and 1 community. Secondary school enrolment: 9,904 students – 5,564 male and 4,340 female. Teachers: 520 – 430 male and 90 female. Available furniture is adequate for 7,785 students.

Health Services: 1 hospital - (NGO); 2 health centre IV - (all government); 4 health centre III - (all government); and 22 health centre II (17 government and 5 NGO);

Tourist Attractions: Buluba Village The place Bishop Hannington, the first Bishop of the Diocese of Eastern Equatorial Africa was murdered.

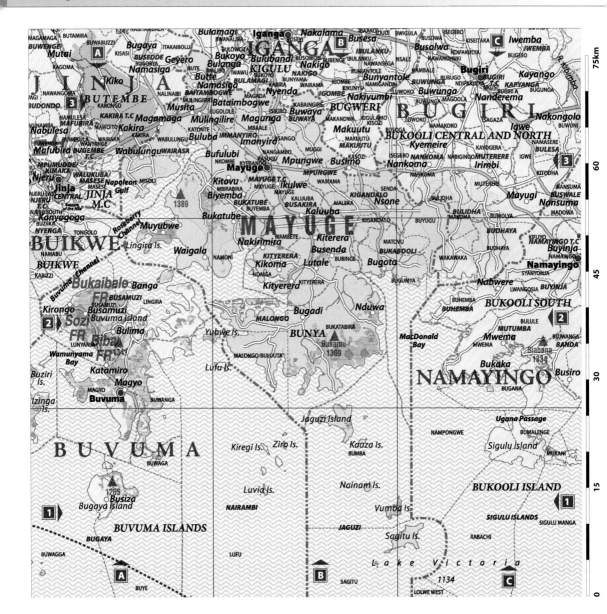

Key NGOs: Africa 2000 Network – Uganda, Send a Cow Uganda, Uganda Red Cross, Community Aid Scheme, Eastern Coffee Farmers' Association, Mpatesobola Disabled Persons Association, Sustainable Development Agency, Idudi Development Association, Kavule Development Association, Wabuluwgu PWDs Union, Yotaliga Integrated Development Group, Alikula Women's Organisation Group.

District leaders:	**Members of Parliament:**
Chairperson – Mr Omar Ductoor M.B.	Bunya County South – Mr Isabirye Iddi
Ag Chief Administrative Officer (CAO)	Bunya County East
– Ms Elizabeth Namanda	– Mr Waira Kyewalabye Majegere
Deputy Chief Administrative Officer	Bunya County West
(DCAO) – Vacant	– Mr Bagiire Vincent Waiswa .O.
	Woman MP – Ms Lukia Nakadama Isanga

Mbale District

Mbale and Sironko districts formerly constituted Bugisu District at independence in 1962. In 1980, Bugisu District was renamed Mbale. In recent years Mbale has been sub-divided to form other districts that are now its neighbours.

Location: It borders the districts of Sironko and Bukedea to the north, Bududa and Manafwa to the east, Tororo to the southeast and Budaka and Butaleja to the west and Pallisa in the northwest.

Area: 559.82 sq. km.

Climate, Relief and Vegetation: It lies at an altitude of between 1,299m and 4,321m above sea level with a sub-tropical type of climate. Temperatures are quite low and rainfall reaches up to 1,191mm per annum. Vegetation includes bamboo forests and some giant afro-alpine groundsels and lobelias on Mountain Elgon.

Population: According to 2009 projections, there are 397,400 people – 203,400 female, 194,000 male with a population density of 710 persons per sq.km.

Major Towns: Mbale (administrative headquarters); Trading Centre – Nakaloke.

Counties and Sub-counties: Bungokho County – Bufumbo, Bukonde, Nakaloke, Namanonyi, Wanale, Bubyangu, Budwale, Lwasso, Bukasakya, Bukhiende, Bumasikye, Bumbobi, Bungokho, Busano, Busiu, Busoba, Lukhonge, Nambale, and Nyondo; Mbale Municipality – Industrial Borough, Wanale Borough, and Northern Borough.

Main Language: Lumasaba.

People: Bamasaba (Bagisu).

Economic Activities: Mainly agriculture with emphasis on:
(i) Food crops: Beans, maize, groundnuts, sweet potatoes, cassava, bananas, soya bean, sorghum, yams and rice on a small scale.
(ii) Cash crops: Coffee and cotton.
(iii) Vegetables: Tomatoes, onions and cabbage.

Banks: Stanbic Bank Uganda Ltd –1, Centenary Rural Development Bank –1, Bank of Baroda –1, Standard Chartered Bank Uganda Ltd –1, Crane Bank -1.

Area under Forestation: 25,843 hectares.

Animal Population: According to 2008 statistics there are 63,826 cattle, 96,617 goats, 5,108 sheep; 23,315 pigs; 459,868 chicken, 13,100 ducks and 26,162 turkeys.

Co-operative Societies: Mbale and Sironko have 418 registered primary societies with Masaba Co-operative Union and Bugisu Union at the district level.

Industries: Processing of milk, coffee, skins; manufacture of exhaust pipes, garments, pharmaceuticals, furniture and cotton ginning.

Education Services: Primary schools: 185 – 131 government, 49 private and 5 community. Enrolment 121,079 pupils – 59,694 male and 61,385 female. Primary school teachers: 2,455 – 1,094 male and 1,361 female.

Secondary schools 50 schools: - 11 government, 34 private and 5 community. Secondary school enrolment: 31,343 students – 17,567 male and 13,776 female. Teachers: 1,652 – 1,290 males and 362 females. Tertiary institutions: 1 technical institution and 4 teacher training colleges, Health/Medical: School of Hygiene – Mbale, School of Clinical Officers, 1university (Islamic University in Uganda).

Health Services: 1 hospital (government– Regional Referral Hospital – Mbale Hospital with 332 beds); 2 health centre IV (all government); 12 health centre III (7 government and 5 NGO); and 8 health centre II (7 Government and 1 NGO).

Tourist Attractions: Commonweatlh War Graves Cemetery, Islamic University Mbale, Mount Elgon National park, the *Imbalu* cultural ceremony which takes place during even years.

Mountain Elgon National Park and the foothills of Mountain Elgon with Wagagai as the hightest peak, is the fourth highest mountain in East Africa. It is an extinct volcano. The foothills at the base of the mountain are known as "Masaba" by the local people and are an excellent hiking area. Flora includes the giant lobelia, giant heather and giant groundsel, wild flowers also abound. Mammals include the tree hyrax, the bush pig and buffalo, the blue monkey, baboons and the black and white colobus monkey.

The Caves of Mountain Elgon are most interesting and easily accessible.

The Sipi Falls which have been described as the most "romantic" in Africa. Accomodation is at Sipi Falls Rest Camp and Mountain Elgon Forest Cottages at Kapkwai.

Additional Information: The highland terrain hinders modernisation of agriculture. The district is densely populated and the land is fragmented. Land ownership is largely based on the customary tenure system. Owing to land shortage, agriculture is practised at subsistence level. Individual farms are too small to support high production for both other markets and local consumption. In 1993, Mbale became one of the first 13 pilot decentralised districts.

Operational Radio and TV Stations: Capital FM, Open Gate FM, BBC World Service FM, Radio France International, Buwalasi Hill FM, Radio Sanyu Ltd, Haustrs Ltd, Katinvuma Broadcasts, Ddembe FM Ltd, Uganda Broadcasting Corporation Radio, Christian Radio Network, Voice of Africa, Radio Maria Uganda Association, Christian Life Ministries, Tallcom Electron Broadcasts Ltd and UBC Television and radio, WBS TV.

Key NGOs: AIDS Information Centre, Africa 2000 Network Uganda, Uganda Project Implementation and Management Centre, Send a Cow Uganda, Integrated Rural Development Initiatives, Family Planning Association of Uganda, MS Uganda, Uganda Women's Effort to Save Orphans, Environmental Alert, UPDF Widows and Orphans Association, Uganda Small Scale Industries Association, Sironko Valley Integrated Projects, International Care and Relief, Bumityero Tubaana Women Group, Poverty Alleviation and Community Development Association, Child Restoration Outreach.

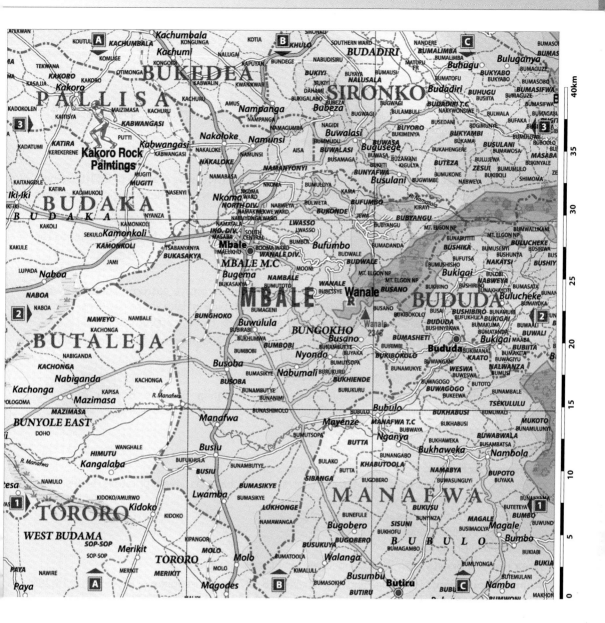

District leaders:
Chairperson
 – Mr Bernard Elly Masaba Mujasi
Chief Administrative Officer (CAO)
 – Mr Andrew Mawajje
Town Clerk (Mbale Municipal Council)
 – Mr Masaba Wonyema
Mayor Mbale Municipality
 – Mr Mutwalib Zandya

Members of Parliament:
Bunghoko County South
 – Mr Michael Werikhe Kafabusa
Bunghoko County North
 – Mr Yahaya Gudoi
Mbale Municipality
 – Mr Jack Wamanga Wamai
Woman MP
 – Ms Erinah Nagudi Rutangye Wangwa

Namayingo District

Namayingo District, which was formally part of Bugiri District, was created in 2010. Being a newly formed district, the information here about Namayingo is the same as Bugiri, the mother district.

Location: Namayingo District is bordered by Bugiri to the northwest, Mayuge District to the west, Busia District and the Republic of Kenya to the east.

Area: 611 sq km.

Climate, Relief and Vegetation: The district lies on the extensive eastern plateau between 1000m and 1,800m above sea level. Rainfall is typical of lake shore patterns – evenly spread throughout the year and ranging between 1,250 – 2,200m.

Population: Basing on the 2009 projections, there are 164,700 people – 79,200 males, 85,500 females, with a density of 269 persons per sq.km.

Main Towns: Namayingo (administrative headquarters).

Counties and Sub-counties: Bukooli South County – Banda, Buswale, Buyinja, Mutumba. Buhemba, Namayingo (Town Council). Bukooli Island – Sigulu Islands

Main Languages: Lusoga and Lusamia-Lugwe.

People: Basoga and Basamia.

Economic Activities: Agriculture with emphasis on:
(i)   Food crops: Maize, rice, finger millet, sorghum, bananas, sweet potatoes, beans, peas, coffee and cassava.
(ii) Cash crops: Rice, cotton and coffee.
(iii) Fishing on Lake Victoria.
(iv) Animal grazing.

Area under Forestation: 26,131 hectares for Namayingo and Bugiri.

Animal Population: Namayingo and Bugiri have 118,427 cattle, 14 donkeys, 65,453 pigs, 14,280 sheep, 220,778 goats, 943,073 chicken, 74,332 ducks and 6,229 turkeys.

Co-operative Societies: Namayingo, Bugiri, Mayuge and Iganga have 255 registered co-operative societies.

Industries: Coffee processing, rice threshing, maize milling and jaggery production.

Education Services: Primary schools: 79 schools – 63 government, 9 private and 7 community. Primary school pupils: 44,878 – 22,989 male and 21,889 female. Primary school teachers: 706 – 527 male, 179 female.

Secondary schools: 10 schools - 4 government, 5 private and 1 community. Secondary school enrolment: 2,842 students – 1,945 males and 897 females. Teachers: 136 - 111 male and 25 female.

Health Services: No hospital; 1 health centre IV (government); 4 health centre III (all government); and 22 health centre II (18 government and 4 NGO).

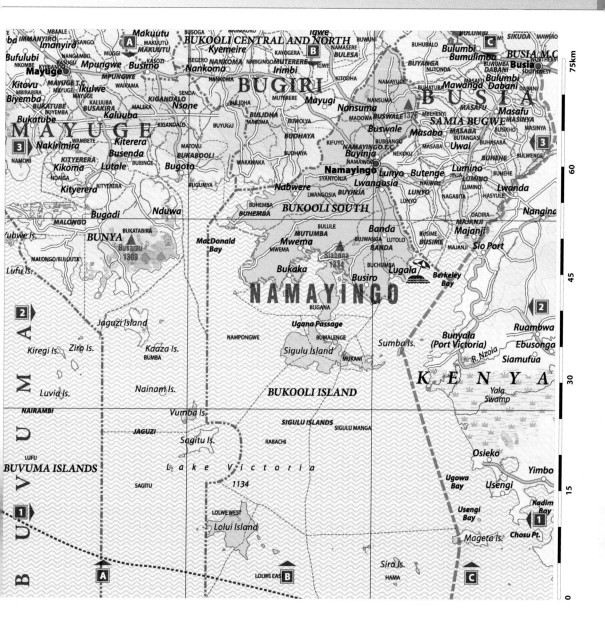

Transport Network: The district is linked with a tarmac road to Iganga and Tororo districts. There are feeder roads although many are in poor condition.

Tourist Attractions: The lake and fishing activities at the Lugala Landing Site are a potential tourist attraction. Bird watching on Siiro Islands is another attraction. However, the district lacks appropriate accommodation facilities for tourists.

Additional Information: Land tenure in the district is largely customary. Areas around the lake are densely populated. Rice is produced mainly for the market while other food crops are basically for subsistence.

Key NGOs: Habitat for Humanity, Bukooli Bugiri Affiliate, Islamic Medical Association of Uganda, Uganda Red Cross Society, AIDS Free Generation Project, Caring for Orphans, Widows and the Elderly, Idudi Development Association, Mirembe Womens' Association,

National Women Development, Tufungize Drama Group, Action for Community Development, Buwunga Development Association.

<table>
<tr><td>

District leaders:
Chairperson – Mr Obondo Waiswa
Ag Chief Administrative Officer (CAO)
– Mr Richard Mugolo
Deputy Chief Administrative Officer
(CAO) – Vacant

</td><td>

Members of Parliament:
Bukooli South County
– Mr Mayende Stephen Dede
Bukooli Island County – Mr Okeyoh Peter
Woman MP – Ms Makhoha Margaret

</td></tr>
</table>

Namutumba District

Namutumba District was Busiki County in Iganga District until July 2006 when the county was elevated to district status.

Location: Namutumba District borders the districts of Kibuku to the northeast, Kaliro to the northwest, Butaleja to the east, Bugiri to the south and Iganga to the southwest.

Area: 815 sq.km

Climate, Relief and Vegetation: It lies at an altitude of between 1,070m and 1,161m above sea level with the annual rainfall ranging between 1,250mm and 2,200mm. Temperatures are always almost uniformly high at over 21°C.

Population: Based on population projections for 2009, there are 198,200 people – 102,500 female and 95,700 male, with a density of 243 persons per sq.km.

Major Towns: Namutumba Town Council

Counties and Sub-counties: Busiki County – Bulange, Ivukula, Kibaale, Magada, Namutumba, Namutumba (Town Council), and Nsinze.

Main Language: Lusoga and Lugwere.

People: Basoga and Bagwere.

Economic Activities: Agriculture with emphasis on food crops such as finger millet, maize, sorghum, rice, bananas, sweet potatoes, Irish potatoes, cassava, beans and peas.

Animal Population: 76,704 cattle, 70,212 goats, 6,691 sheep, 12,287 pigs, 301,875 chicken, 7,995 ducks and 3,030 turkeys.

Co-operative Societies: The people are still enjoying the services of the Co-operative Societies of mother Iganga District.

Industries: Manufacture of food products, beverages, textiles, fabricated metal products and furniture making.

Banks: The banks in Iganga District are still being used.

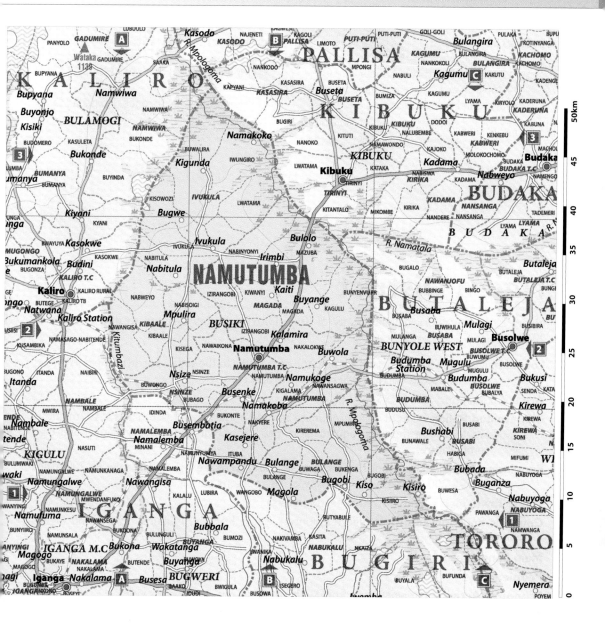

Education Services: Primary schools: 118 – 109 government, 8 private and 1 community. Enrolment: 71,955 pupils – 36,006 male and 35,949 female. Primary school teachers: 1,012 – 647 male and 365 female. Available furniture not reported.

Secondary schools: 15 schools - 7 government, 6 private and 2 community. Secondary school enrolment: 5,665 students – 3,263 male and 2,402 female. Teachers: 272 - 224 male and 48 female. Available furniture is adequate for 5,253 students.

Health Services: 1 health centre IV - (government); 10 health centre III - (9 government, 1 NGO); 19 health centre II - (17 government., 2 NGO).

Tourist Attractions: Namatalo Rocks and Namagero Rock/Shrine – These are sites where spiritual and cultural rituals by some clans in Busoga region are performed.

District Leaders:
District Chairperson – Mr Saire Michael
Ag Chief Administrative Officer (CAO)
   – Mr Edward Musoke Galabuzi
Deputy Chief Administrative Officer
   (CAO) – Vacant

Members of Parliament:
Busiki County
   – Mr Asupasa Isiko Wilson Mpongo
Woman MP
   – Ms Mutyabule Florence Tibafana

Ngora District

Ngora District was originally a county of Kumi District. It was elevated to district status in 2010.

Location: It borders the districts of Kumi to the east, Pallisa to the south, Soroti to the northwest, Katakwi to the north and Serere to the east.

Area: 722 sq. km.

Climate and Relief: It lies at an approximate altitude of between 1,036m and 1,127m above sea level in a modified equatorial climatic zone with both heavy rainfall and high temperature.

Population: Based on the population projections 2009, there are 135,400 people- 65,200 males and 70,200 females with a density of 187 persons per sq.km.

Major Town: Ngora (administrative headquarters).

Counties and Sub-counties: Ngora County – Kapir, Kobwin, Mukura, Ngora, and Ngora Town Council.

Main Languages: Ateso

People: Itesot.

Economic Activities: Mainly agriculture with emphasis on:
   (i)   Food crops: Finger millet, groundnuts, sweet potatoes, cassava, sorghum, rice, cow peas, soya bean, bananas, sunflower and onions.
   (ii) Cash crops: Cotton.

Banks: Still depends on Stanbic Bank Uganda Ltd in Kumi.

Area under Forestation: 8,177 hectares.

Animal Population: Ngora and Kumi districts have 220,055 cattle, 168,887 goats, 30,994 sheep, 67,650 pigs, 549,135 chicken 9,936 ducks and 20,360 turkeys according to 2008 statistics.

Co-operative Societies: Still depends on registered primary societies in Kumi with Teso Union as the main society.

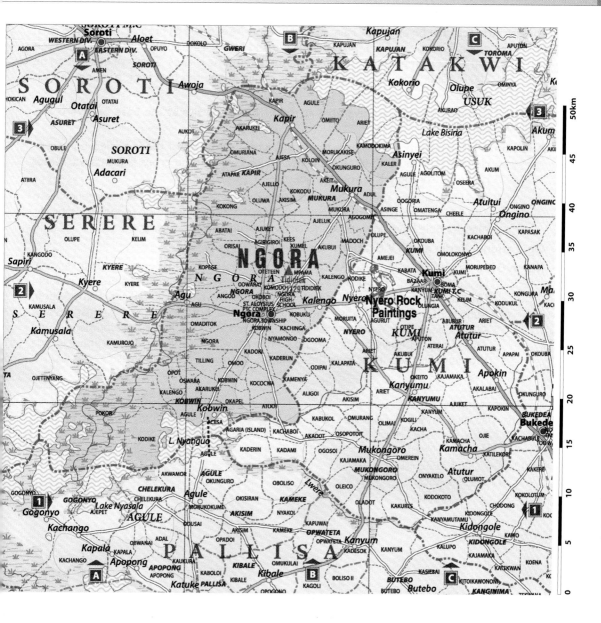

Education Services: Primary schools: 230 – 217 government, 5 private and 8 community. Primary school enrolment: 128,339 – 64,303 male and 64,036 female. Primary school teachers: 2,453 – 1,563 male and 890 female.

Secondary schools: 9 secondary schools; 4 government, 4 private, 1 community. Secondary school enrolment: 5,391– 3,304 males and 2,087 females. Teachers: 277 – 220 males, 57 females.

Tertiary institution – 1 technical institution and 3 teacher training colleges. 1 university - Kumi University.

Health Services: 1 hospital (NGO) Ngora Hospital with 180 beds; 1 health centre IV (government); 5 health centre III (all government); and 4 health centre II (3 government and 1 NGO).

Tourist Attractions: Nyero Rock Paintings which consist of three painted caves close to each other (Nyero Site One, Nyero Site Two and Nyero Site Three). Paintings are in red and white pigmentation and are mainly of geometric shapes. They are believed to be 300 – 1000 years old and regarded as being among the best rock paintings in East Africa.

Camping facilities are available at the Nyero Campsite at the base of Nyero Site One.

Additional Information: The rolling plains of Ngora form part of the modified equatorial climate zone in northeastern Uganda which favours food crops like cassava, sweet potatoes, sorghum and finger millet.

The main activity used to be cattle keeping, but as a result of the insurgency from 1987-1991 in the district and cattle rustling, the cattle population reduced drastically. Many people have now turned to crop growing to make a living.

Operational Radio and TV Stations: Continental FM Station Ltd.

Key NGOs: Send a Cow Uganda, African Medical Research Foundation, Actionaid Uganda, Uganda Women's Effort to Save Orphans, Bukedea Women Strugglers Association, Church of Uganda Teso Diocese Planning and Development Offices, Faith Action, Kumi Human Rights Initiative and Self Governance, Kachumbala War Against Poverty Alleviation, Karev Youth and Orphans Link Initiative for Rural Development, Kumi Aids Support Organisation, Ongino Community Development Association, Uganda Women's Finance Trust, Save the Children Denmark, Vision Terudo.

District leaders:
Chairperson – Mr Eumu Bernard
Chief Administrative Officer (CAO)
— Davis Dembe Beyaza
Deputy Chief Administrative Officer
(DCAO) – Vacant

Members of Parliament:
Ngora County – Mr Francis Epetait
Woman MP – Ms Amongin Jacquiline

Pallisa District

Formerly part of Tororo District, Pallisa District was created in 1991.

Location: The district borders the districts of Mbale, Bukedea to the east; Serere, Ngora and Kumi to the north, Kaliro to the west, Buyende to the northwest and Kibuku and Budaka to the south.

Area: 1,094.82 sq. km. (including Budaka)

Climate and Relief: It lies at an approximate altitude of between 1,097m – 1,219m above sea level with characteristics of a modified equatorial climate.

Population: Based on the population projection for 2009, there are 319,900 people 165,600 female and 154,300 male with a density of 292 persons per sq.km.

Major Towns: Pallisa (administrative headquarters); Trading Centre – Tirinyi.

Counties and Sub-counties: Butebo County – Butebo, Kabwangasi, Kakoro, Kangimina, Kibale, Opwateta, and Petete; Pallisa County – Kasodo, Pallisa (Town Council), Pallisa, Olok, Puti-Puti, and Kamuge. Agule County – Agule, Akisim, Apopong, Chelekura, Gogonyo and Kameke

Main Language: Ateso and Lugwere.

People: Iteso and Bagwere.

Economic Activities: Mainly agriculture with emphasis on:
(i) Food crops: Millet, rice, cassava, sorghum, sweet potatoes, groundnuts, beans, soya bean, bananas, cow peas, simsim (sesame) and maize.
(ii) Cash crop: Cotton.

Banks: Stanbic Bank Uganda Ltd –1.

Area under Forestation: 966 hectares.

Animal Population: Pallisa and Kibuku have 136,225 cattle, 149,003 goats, 20,488 sheep, 25,302 pigs, 440,035 chicken, 20,748 ducks and 27,928 turkeys.

Co-operative Societies: 86 primary societies. Some of these are for produce milling and marketing, livestock marketing and farming.

Education Services: Primary schools: 145 – 101 government and 40 private and 4 community. Enrolment: 100,843 pupils – 49,731 male and 51,112 female. Primary school teachers: 1,697 – 1,119 male and 578 female. Available furniture not fully reported.

Secondary schools: 25 schools - 10 government and 15 private. Enrolment: 10,533 students – 6,416 male and 4,117 female. Secondary school teachers: 580 - 465 male and 115 female. Available turniture is enough for only 8,908 students.

Health Services: 2 hospitals - (1 government and 1 NGO); 1 health centre IV - (government); 13 health centre III - (10 government and 3 NGO); and 9 health centre II (7 government and 2 NGO).

Industries: Manufacture of beverages, textiles, furniture, articles of straw plaiting materials and fabricated metal products.

Tourist Attractions: Kakoro Rock Paintings: There are two sites with red pantings, including some concetric circles on the south and west sides of a stone pillar at the southern end of the hill. On the underside of the rock ledge is a third example of rock art in white pigmentation, but the subject matter is unidentifiable.

The paintings are thought to be the work of hunters gatherers who lived in this region 2,000 years ago. There is a fairly spectacular ancient gong near the paintings that is balanced precariously at approximately 10m in the air and a rock slide nearby. Local children and animals moving to graze have wore out some of the rock paintings.

Key NGOs: Africa 2,000 Network – Uganda, Send a Cow Uganda, African Medical Research Foundation Uganda, Actionaid Uganda, Uganda Women's Effort to Save Orphans, Environmental Alert.

District leaders:
Chairperson – Mr Bantalib Isa Taligola
Chief Administrative Officer (CAO)
    – Mr Moses Bukenya Seguya
Deputy Chief Administrative Officer
    (DCAO) – Vacant
Town Clerk (Pallisa Town Council)
    – Mr Pius Epaju

Members of Parliament:
Agule County – Mr Ochwa David
Butebo County
    – Mr Mallinga Stephen Oscar
Pallisa County – Mr Opolot Jacob
    Richards
Woman MP – Ms Amoit Judith Mary

Cotton is the main cash crop of Pallisa district.

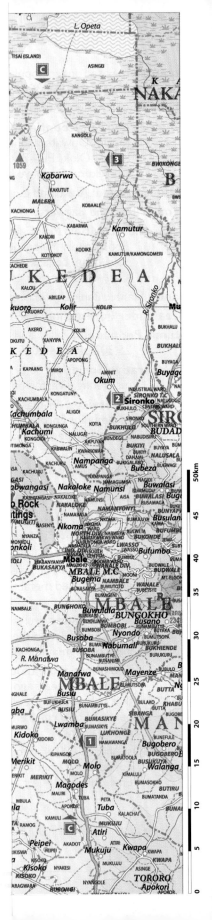

Serere District

Serere District was carved out of Soroti District in 2010.

Location: Serere borders the districts of Soroti to the north, Kaberamaido to the west, Ngora to the east, Katakwi to the north and Buyende and Pallisa to the south.

Area: 1964 sq. km.

Climate and Relief: It lies at an approximate altitude of 1,036m – 1,127m above sea level. Rainfall totals up to 1,000 – 1,500mm per annum with high temperatures.

Population: According to 2009 projections, there are 246,700 people – 125,900 female and 120,800 male with a density of 125 persons per sq.km.

Major Towns: Serere (administrative headquarters); Trading Centre – Kyere.

Counties and Sub-counties: Kasilo County – Bugondo, Kadungulu, Labor and Pingire; Serere County – Atiira, Kateta, Kyere, Serere/Olio and Serere (Town Council)

Main Languages: Ateso, Kumam and Kiswahili.

People: Iteso and Kumam.

Economic Activities: Mainly agriculture with emphasis on:
 (i) Food crops: Finger millet, sorghum, groundnuts, cassava, cowpeas, sweet potatoes, maize, soya bean, beans, simsim (sesame) and sunflower.
 (ii) Cash crop: Cotton.
 (iii) Fruits and vegetables: Tomatoes, onions and cabbage.

Banks: The district still depends on the banks in the mother district of Soroti.

Area under Forestation: 6,773 hectares.

Animal Population: Serere and Soroti have 271,634 cattle, 75,449 pigs, 53,010 sheep, 236,839 goats, 23,910 ducks, 19,677 turkeys and 808,290 chicken. Serere is more dependent on livestock than Soroti.

Co-operative Societies: Teso sub-region has 233 registered primary societies.

Industries: Bread baking and furniture making, milling of oil, rice and millet and cotton ginning.

Education Services: Primary schools: 106 – 85 government, 12 private and 9 community. Enrolment: 73,781 – 36,688 male and 37,093 female. Primary school teachers: 1,144 – 850 male and 294 female. Available furniture was not reported.

Secondary schools: 6 schools - 2 government, 3 private, 1 community. Secondary school enrolment: 4,583 students – 2,830 males and 1,753 females. Teachers: 98. Available furniture is adequate for 2,567 students.

Health Services: 2 health centre IV - (all government); 8 health centre III – (6 government, 2 NGO); and 9 health centre II - (7 government and 2 NGO).

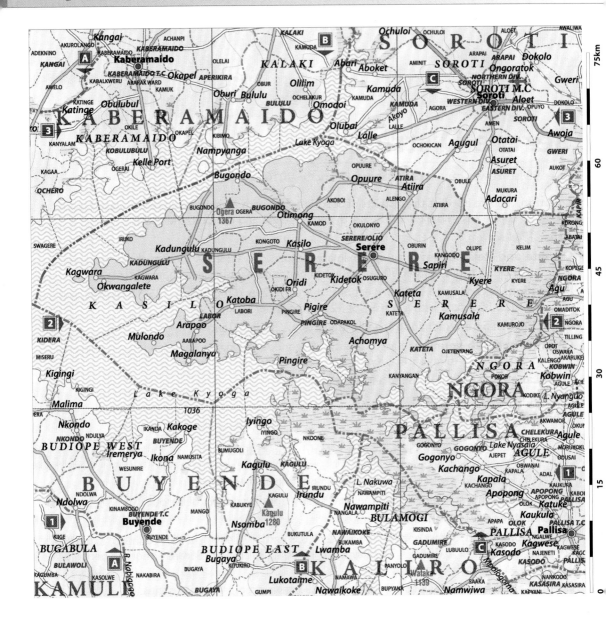

Transport Network: The district has a network of murram roads and a tarmacked highway to Lira and the other districts. The district also has water transport on Lake Kyoga. This connects the district to the districts of Kaberamaido, Buyende, Nakasongola, Kayunga, Amolatar and Apac.

Tourist Attractions: The Kyoga wetland is a habitat for many birds. Fishing and canoe rides take place on the lake.

Additional Information: The district has a fairly high population. The land tenure system is customary. The southern parts of the district are swampy, giving way to the open water of Lake Kyoga, which gives Serere a fishing culture.

Operational Radio Station: Voice of Teso Ltd, Kyoga Radio Ltd, Uganda Broadcasting Corporation Radio and Baptist International Mission (U), Uganda Broad Casting Corporation (UBC).

Key NGOs: AT Uganda Ltd, Uganda National Agro-input Dealers, Send a Cow Uganda, African Medical Research Foundation, World Vision Uganda, Uganda Women's Effort to Save Orphans, Action Against Child Abuse and Neglect, Komolo Development Association, Health NEED Uganda, Soroti Municipality Women's Association, Sober Uganda – Soroti Branch, Gweri Development Association.

District leaders:	Members of Parliament:
Chairperson – Mr Opit Joseph Okojo	Serere County – Mr Ochola Stephen
Ag Chief Administrative Officer (CAO)	Kasilo County – Mr Elijah Okupa
– Mr Ismail Ochengel	Woman MP – Ms Alice Alaso Asianut
Deputy Chief Administrative Officer	
(DCAO) – Vacant	

Sironko District

Formerly part of Mbale District. In 2000, two counties of Mbale District – Budadiri and Bulambi became Sironko District.

Location: It borders Kween to the east, Kumi to the west, Bulambuli to the north, Bududa and Mbale to the south.

Area: 445 sq. km.

Climate and Relief: It lies at an approximate altitude of between 1,299m – 1,524m above sea level, with rainfall totalling 1,191mm per annum and low temperatures, within a sub-tropical climatic zone.

Population: According to 2009 population projections - 217,600 people – 106,000 male and 111,600 female with a density of 488 persons per sq.km.

Major Towns: Sironko (administrative headquarters); Trading Centres – Mafuni, Nakaloke, Mutufu and Budadiri.

Counties and Sub-counties: Budadiri County – Budadiri (Town Council), Buhugu, Bukiise, Bukiyi, Bukyabo, Bunyafwa, Bukyambi, Bumalimba, Bumasifwa, Bugitimwa, Busulani, Butandiga, Buwalasi, Buyobo, Masaba, Buteza, Bukhulo, Buwasa, Nalusala, Sironko (Town Council) and Zesui.

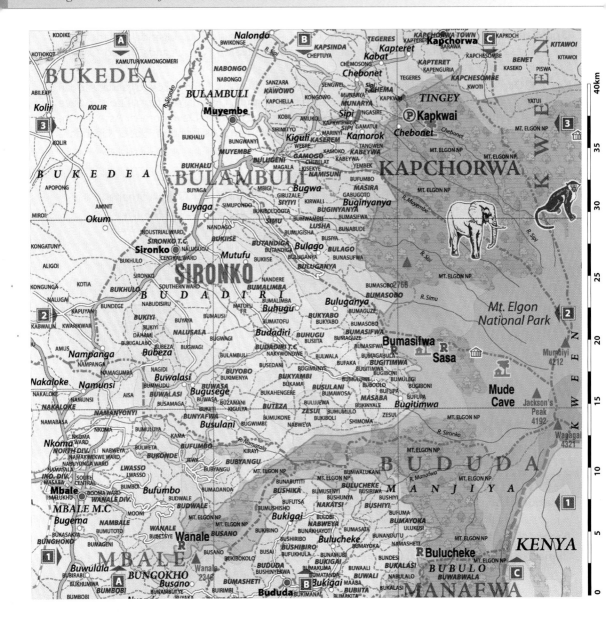

Main Language: Lumasaba (Lugisu).

People: Bamasaba (Bagisu).

Economic Activities: Agriculture with emphasis on:
- (i) Food crops: Beans, sweet potatoes, groundnuts, sorghum, millet, cassava and irish potatoes.
- (ii) Cash crops: Coffee and cotton.
- (iii) Fruits and vegetables: Passion fruit, tomatoes, onions and cabbage.

Area under Forestation: 25,428 hectares.

Animal Population: Bulambuli and Sironko districts have 92,562 cattle, 250 donkeys, 32,733 pigs, 9,806 sheep, 79,141 goats, 8,496 ducks, 19,769 turkeys and 391,125 chicken.

Co-operative Societies: Sironko and Mbale have 418 registered co-operative societies.

Industries: Manufacture of animal feeds, footwear, grain milling, exhaust pipes, furniture and cotton ginning.

Education Services: Primary schools: 121 – 110 government, 9 private and 2 community. Enrolment: 77,769 pupils – 38,892 male and 38,877 female. Primary school teachers: 1,305 – 696 male and 609 female. Available furniture not fully reported.

Secondary schools: 18 schools - 7 government, 5 private, 6 community. Secondary school enrolment: 7,994 – 4,348 male and 3,646 female. Teachers: 425 – 347 male and 78 female. Available furniture not fully reported.

Health Services: 2 health centre IV (with government); 13 health centre III (12 government and 1 NGO); and 10 health centre II (5 government and 5 NGO)

Tourist Attractions: Mountain Elgon

Key NGOs: Send a Cow Uganda, Uganda Women's Effort to Save Orphans, Environmental Alert, Sironko Bee Farmers' Association, Buzibu Women's Group, National Association of Women Organisations in Uganda, Sironko Farmers' Association Ltd, Nadisi Women's Group, Sironko Yetana Project, Bundagala Women Group.

District leaders:	Members of Parliament:
Chairperson	Budadiri County East
– Mr Nabende James Amulamu	– Mr Ssasaga Isias Johny
Chief Administrative Officer (CAO)	Budadiri County West
– Ms Marion Pamela Tukahurirwa	– Mr Nandala Nathan Mafabi
Deputy Chief Administrative Officer	Woman MP – Ms Wadada Femiar
(CAO) – Vacant	
Town Clerk – Mr Alex Majeme	

Soroti District

Formerly known as Teso District, it existed at independence in 1962 and consisted of present-day Kaberamaido, Katakwi, Soroti, Kumi and Katakwi districts. To ease administration, Teso District was in the 1970s divided into North Teso and South Teso, which in 1980, became Soroti and Kumi districts, respectively. The district has further reduced in size as new districts have been carved out of it. The last district to be carved out of Soroti was Serere in 2010, reducing the district to just one county.

Location: Soroti borders the districts of Kaberamaido to the west, Ngora and Katakwi to the east, Amuria to the north and Serere to the south.

Area: 1,411 sq. km.

Climate and Relief: It lies at an approximate altitude of 1,036m – 1,127m above sea level. Rainfall totals up to 1,000 – 1,500mm per annum with high temperatures.

Population: According to 2009 projections, there are 270,600 people – 138,000 female, 132,600 male, with a density of 191 persons per sq.km.

Major Towns: Soroti (administrative headquarters); Trading Centres – Serere and Kalaki.

Counties and Sub-counties: Soroti County – Arapai, Asuret, Gweri, Kamuda, Katine, Soroti, Tubur; Soroti Municipality – Western, Eastern, and Northern.

Main Languages: Ateso, Kumam and Kiswahili.

People: Iteso and Kumam.

Economic Activities: Mainly agriculture with emphasis on:
- (i)   Food crops: Finger millet, sorghum, groundnuts, cassava, cowpeas, sweet potatoes, maize, soya bean, bean, simsim (sesame) and sunflower.
- (ii) Cash crop: Cotton.
- (iii) Fruits and vegetables: Tomatoes, onions and cabbage.

Banks: Stanbic Bank Uganda Ltd –1, Centenary Rural Development Bank –1 Crane Bank.

Area under Forestation: 6,773 hectares.

Animal Population: Serere and Soroti have 271,634 cattle, 75,449 pigs, 53,010 sheep, 236,839 goats, 23,910 ducks, 19,677 turkeys and 808,290 chicken. Serere is more dependent on livestock than Soroti.

Co-operative Societies: Teso sub-region has 233 registered primary societies.

Industries: Bread baking and furniture making, milling of oil, flour and millet and cotton ginning.

Education Services: Primary schools: 123 – 88 government, 18 private and 17 community. Enrolment: 78,138 pupils – 38,353 male and 39,775 female. Primary school teachers: 1,443 – 865 male and 578 female. Available furniture was not reported.

Secondary schools: 32 schools - 8 government, 18 private and 6 community. Secondary school enrolment: 16,885 students – 10,995 male and 5,890 female. Teachers: 836 – 687 male and 149 female. Available furniture is adequate for 15,570 students.

Tertiary: 3 technical institutions and 2 teacher training colleges, and Soroti Aviation School.

Health Services: 1 hospital (government – Soroti Regional Referral Hospital with 195 beds); 1 health centre IV - (government); 10 health centre III - (9 government and 1 NGO); and 13 health centre II - (9 government and 4 NGO).

Transport Network: The district has a network of murram roads. A tarmac road runs through Soroti from the southeast to the northwest (from Kumi to Dokolo to Lira). The Soroti Lira stretch is under construction and nearing completion. Currently the Soroti-Lira stretch is being tarmacked and almost complete. Soroti is served by a railway line which runs from Mbale to Lira. Presently, the railway line is dormant.

Soroti Airfield – The runways and apron are tarmac and in good condition. The murram runway shoulders are regularly weeded and trimmed. Soroti Airfield terminal building is in good condition.

The air plane crash, fire and rescue equipment as well as personnel are kept in a state of readiness for emergencies. Soroti Airfield is the training base for the Soroti Flying School. The Civil Aviation Authority provides H.F. radio communication. The airfield is 2 km from Soroti town.

Tourist Attractions: Soroti Flying School was set up to train pilots in East Africa; Soroti Rock, a volcanic plug resembling the Tororo Rock.

The town's architecture reflects its multi-cultural history.

Central Soroti has a market place where the ingenuity of the local people at re-fashioning scrap metal to make cooking pots and other household items from the remains of cars and metal drums is amazing.

Additional Information: The district has a small population. The land tenure system is customary. There is evidence of a decline in water sources towards the northern parts of the district. There is fishing on Lake Kyoga. Agricultural production in Soroti District is carried out on a small scale.

Operational Radio Station: Voice of Teso Ltd, Kyoga Radio Ltd, Uganda Broadcasting Corporation Radio and Baptist International Mission (U). Uganda Broad Casting Corporation (UBC).

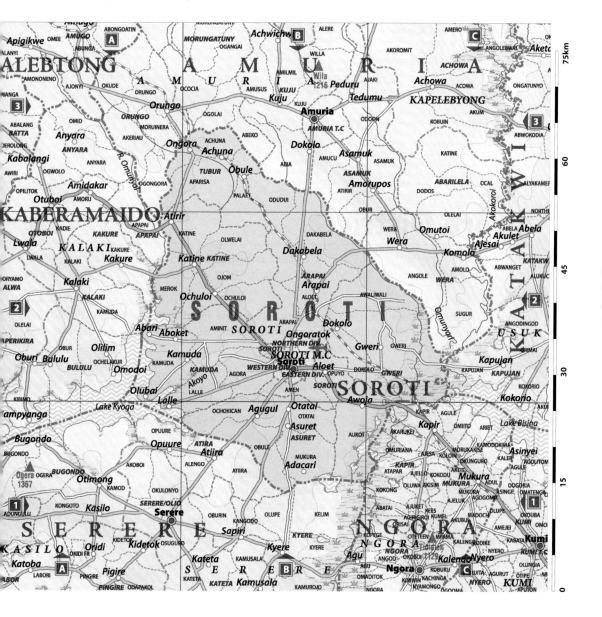

Key NGOs: AT Uganda Ltd, Uganda National Agro-input Dealers, Send a Cow Uganda, African Medical Research Foundation, World Vision Uganda, Uganda Women's Effort to Save Orphans, Action Against Child Abuse and Neglect, Komolo Development Association, Health NEED Uganda, Soroti Municipality Women's Association, Sober Uganda – Soroti Branch, Gweri Development Association.

District leaders:	Members of Parliament:
Chairperson – Mr Egunyu George Micheal	Soroti County – Mr Omolo Peter
Chief Administrative Officer (CAO)	Soroti Municipality
– Mr Charles Okello	– Mr Mukula George Michael
Deputy Chief Administrative Officer	Woman MP – Ms Osegge Angelline
(CAO) – Vacant	
Town Clerk (Soroti Municipal Council)	
– Mr Richard K. Monday	
Soroti Municipality	
– Mr Alfred Martin Aruo	

Tororo District

Tororo District is one of the districts that existed as Bukedi District at independence in 1962. It then included the present-day Pallisa and Busia districts. In 1980, Bukedi became Tororo District.

Location: Tororo borders the districts of Butaleja to the north and northwest, Mbale and Manafwa to the northeast, Busia to the south, Bugiri to the southwest and The Republic of Kenya on the east.

Area: 1,338.72 sq. km.

Climate and Relief: It lies at an approximate altitude of between 1,097m and 1,219m above sea level with moderate rainfall and high temperatures.

Population: According to the 2009 projection, there are 443,500 people – 229,500 female, 214,000 male with a density of 331 persons per sq.km.

Major Towns: Tororo (administrative headquarters); Trading Centre – Malaba.

Counties and Sub-counties: West Budama County – Kirewa, Petta, Kisoko, Nagongera, Nagongera (Town Council), Paya, Sopsop, Iyolwa, Magola, Mulanda, Nabuyoga, and Rubongi; Tororo County – Kwapa, Mella, Merikit, Molo, Mukuju, Osukuru and Malaba (Town Council); Tororo Municipality – Tororo Eastern, and Tororo Western.

Main Languages: Japadhola, Lusamia-Lugwe, Ateso, Lugwere and Lunyoli.

People: Japadhola, Iteso, Basamia, Bagwere and Banyoli.

Economic Activities: Mainly agriculture with emphasis on:
  (i)   Food crops: Finger millet, rice, maize, cassava, groundnuts, sweet potatoes, sorghum, beans, soya bean, cow peas, simsim, bananas and sunflower.
  (ii) Cash crop: Cotton.
  (iii) Vegetable: Onions.

Banks: Stanbic Bank Uganda Ltd –1, Centenary Rural Development Bank –1, Crane Bank

Area under Forestation: 3,106 hectares.

Animal Population: According to the 2008 livestock statistics, thre are 119,587 cattle, 154,058 goats, 13,086 sheep, and 45,256 pigs,591,552 chicken, 24,624 ducks and 33,535 turkeys.

Co-operative Societies: Tororo and Busia have 255 registered primary societies with South Bukedi Co-operative Union at the district level.

Trade: The location of the district at the border has encouraged trade between the people of Uganda and Kenya.

Industries: Manufacture of corrugated roofing sheets, cement, fertilisers and fungicides, laundry soap, jaggery, gunny bags, hessian cloth, cassava starch, oil milling and cotton ginning.

Education Services: Primary schools: 206 – 166 government, 30 private and10 community. Enrolment: 155,098 pupils – 77,363 male and 77,735 female. Primary school teachers: 2,445 – 1,406 male and 1,039 female. Available furniture adequate for 93,730 pupils.

Secondary schools: 43 schools - 17 government, 25 private, 1 community. Secondary school enrolment: 22,851 students - 13,106 male and 9,745 female. Teachers: 1,237 - 984 males and 253 female. Available furniture is adequate for 17,760 students.

Tertiary institutions: 6 technical institutions, 4 Primary teacher training colleges, 1 commercial college and 1 National Teacher's College

Health Services: 3 hospitals (1 government district hospital – Rubongi Hospital with 226 beds, and 2 NGO - Uganda Catholic Medical Bureau – St. Anthony's Hospital, Tororo and Benedictine Hospital with 110 beds); 3 HC IV (all government); 17 HC III (15 government, 1 NGO and 1 private); and 40 HC II (35 government, 3 NGO, and 2 private).

Tourist Attractions: Tororo Rock is a volcanic plug that rises to about 1,800m above sea level and can be seen from miles. It takes about an hour to climb the Tororo Rock.

Antiquities/Historical Sites: The district has a number of historical sites. Some of these sites are Nagiriga cultural site for Badama tribe in memory of the brutal tribal wars between Banyankore and Badama in the nineteenth century. The area was the burial site for Banyole killed during the battles. The site is near caves used as safe haven during the wars.

Transport Network: Tororo Airfield –The runway has a grass surface. The Civil Aviation Authority provides H.F. radio communication. The airfield is 26 km from Tororo town.

Operational Radio and TV Stations: Rock Mambo Radio Limited, Voice of Teso, Uganda Broadcasting Cooperation (UBC) Radio.

Additional Information: The district is accessible by both road and rail. Tororo is 217 km from Kampala, about four hours by bus. Tororo District is dry with sandy, rock soil and receives moderate rainfall. This climate is favourable for crops like millet and cassava which are widely grown.

Key NGOs: Uganda Women's Effort to Save Orphans, Africa 2000 Network – Uganda, Send a Cow Uganda, Plan International, Family Planning Association of Uganda, World Vision Uganda, Community Vision, Tororo District Farmers' Association, Youth Training Advisory Mission, Mifumi Development Programme, Mulanda Women's Development Association, Nagonga Youth Development Project, Asinge Joint Youth Association, Osukuru Women's Network, Uganda Change Agent Association.

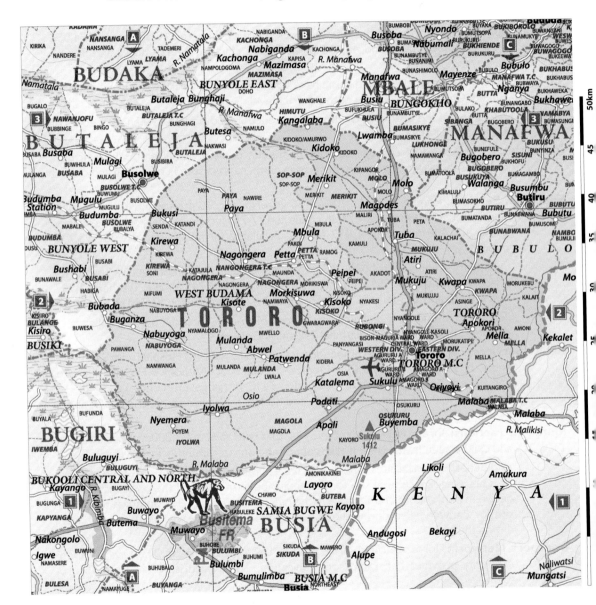

District leaders:
Chairperson – Mr Emmanuel Osuna
Chief Administrative Officer (CAO)
– Mr Felix Cuthbert Esoku
Town Clerk (Tororo Municipal Council)
– Mr Daniel Christopher Kawesi
Mayor Tororo Municipality
– Mr Geoffrey Emokol

Members of Parliament:
West Budama County North
– Mr Odoi Oywelowo Fox
West Budama County South
– Mr Oboth Marksons Jacob
Tororo Municipality – Mr Sanjay Tanna
Tororo County – Mr Geoffrey Ekanya
Woman MP – Ms Achieng Sarah Opendi

Tororo Rock rises dramatically against the plains.

MIFUMI

What does MIFUMI do?

MIFUMI	A women's rights agency
Domestic Violence	Supporting women access justice and security
21 Advice Centres	Providing counselling and support throughout Tor…
Bride Price	Leading the way on bride price reform
Women's Property Rights	Supporting greater economic security for women
Health	Quality health service at Mifumi Health Centre
Education	Quality education at Mifumi Primary School
Sure Start	Confidence building for girls through martial arts
Scholarships	Providing sponsorship to bright but needy childre…
Solar Lighting	Reducing environmental degradation in 4 villages
Polygamy	Seeking to address cultural issues that oppress wo…
Ethical Trading	Uplifting economic status of women
Legal Aid	Legal services and training practitioners
MIFUMI Network	Co-ordination of 20 partners in 5 districts

MIFUMI
Plot 1 Masaba Road,
P.O.Box 274 Tororo,Uganda
Email :mifumi@mifumi.org
Tel: +256 (0) 392 966 282
Mobile +256 (0) 752 581 122
www.mifumi.org

Central Districts

Bukomansimbi Buikwe Butambala Buvuma Gomba Kalangala Kalungu Kampala

Kayunga Kiboga Kyankwanzi Luweero Lyantonde Masaka Mityana Mpigi

Mubende Mukono Nakaseke Nakasongola Rakai Sembabule Wakiso

Central region stretches from lake Kyoga to lake Victoria. It borders Tanzania in the south.

The People: The region is inhabited by mainly Baganda. The other people include Banyoro in Mubende and Banyankore in Kiboga, Sembabule and Rakai, Baluli in Nakasongola and Banyala in Kayunga.

The people are mainly cultivators and coffee is the chief cash crop. Tea and sugar cane are other crops grown. Floriculture is gaining prominence. Cattle keeping is one of the chief economic activities in Sembabule, Rakai, Luweero Mubende, Nakaseke and Nakasongola districts.

Tourism: Tourist attractions include the numerous beaches around Lake Victoria, cultural sites such as the Kasubi Tombs, the Nagalabi Coronation site, King Kalema's Prison at Katereke and the Ssese Islands in Kalangala District. Other places of interest are Rubaga and Namirembe Cathedrals, the Bahai Temple (the largest in Africa) and the old Kampala and Kibuli Mosques. The Uganda Wildlife Educational Centre, Entebbe International Airport, Uganda Museum and Makerere University (the oldest university in East Africa) and to the list of attractions.

How to get there: All main access roads in Kampala and most parts of the district are tarmac. There is also accessibility by air through Entebbe International Airport and through airstrips at Kololo, Kajjansi and Nakasongola. A railway line connects Kampala to Jinja via Lugazi. The region is also accessible by water via Port Bell and Entebbe. There is a ferry connection between Bukakata in Masaka District and Bugoma on Bugala the main island of Kalangala District. The rest of the islands are connected by canoes and small boats.

Sub-divisions: This region does not have further sub-divisions. It comprises Buganda region.

A view of Kampala city in Kampala district (left). A traditional Kiganda dance performance; the Bagande people are spread in the cental districts of Uganda (middle). A woman harvesting coffee. Coffee is one of the major household earners in the central region (right).

Central Districts

Buikwe District

Buikwe was a county of Mukono District. It was elevated to district status in 2009.

Location: Buikwe District borders the districts of Jinja and Mayuge to the east, Kayunga to the north, Mukono to the west and Buvuma to the south.

Area: 1,449 sq. km.

Climate and Relief: It lies at an altitudinal range of 1,158m to 1,219m above sea level with high temperatures and heavy rainfall. For example, in the period April – June 1991, it received 470mm of rain in 44 rain days.

Population: According to 2009 projections, there are 389,100 people – 198,400 female and 190,700 males with a density of 26 persons per sq.km.

Major Towns: Buikwe (administrative headquarters), Njeru, Nkokonjeru and Lugazi; Trading Centre – Nyenga.

Counties and Sub-counties: Buikwe County – Njeru (Town Council), Nkokonjeru (Town Council), Lugazi (Town Council), Buikwe (Town Council), Nyenga, Wakisi, Kawolo, Najjembe, Buikwe, Najja, Ngogwe, Ssi.

Main Language: Luganda.

People: Baganda and Basoga.

Economic Activities: Mainly agriculture with emphasis on:
 (i) Food crops: Cassava, sweet potatoes, beans, maize, finger millet, groundnuts, soya bean, bananas, sorghum, simsim (sesame), cow peas, pigeon peas and yams.
 (ii) Cash crops: Cotton, coffee, sugar cane and tea.
 (iii) Fruits and vegetables: Tomatoes, onions, pineapples, vanilla, chillies, passion fruit and cabbage.
 (iv) Dairy farming.
 (v) Fishing on Lake Victoria.

Banks: Stanbic Bank Uganda Ltd – 2.

Area under Forestation: 107,980 hectares.

Animal Population: Buikwe, Mukono and Buvuma districts have 155,820 cattle, 61 donkeys, 181,846 pigs, 30,808 sheep, 206,704 goats, 1,551,702 chicken, 49,517 ducks and 5,558 turkeys, according to 2008 livestok census.

Co-operative Societies: Mukono, Buikwe, Buvuma and Kayunga have 267 registered primary societies with East Mengo Union at the district level.

Industries: Processing of coffee, tea, cocoa, sugar, manufacture of textiles, animal feeds, beer, boats, furniture, metal products and grain milling. Nytil, Lugazi Sugar Works and Nile Breweries are the biggest employers.

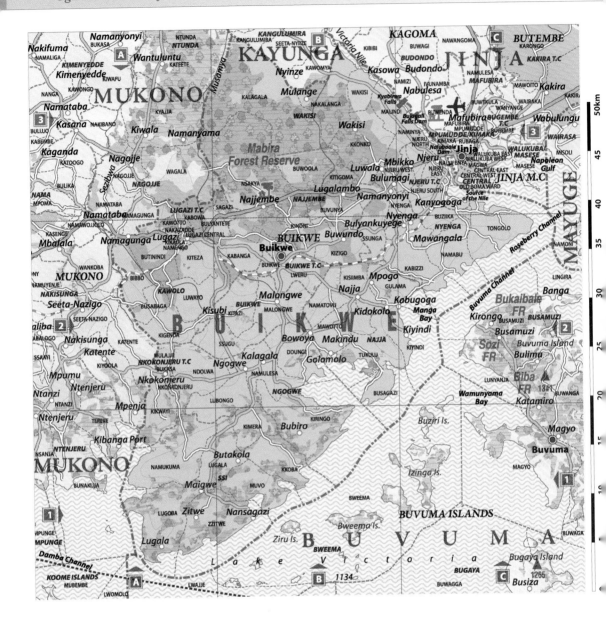

Education Services: Primary schools: 279– 169 government, 91 private and 19 community. Enrolment: 99,229 pupils – 48,553 male and 50,676 female. Primary School teachers: 2,316 – 1,169 male and 1,147 female. Available furniture is adequate for 72,960 pupils.

Secondary schools: 59 schools - 7 government, 47 private and 5 community. Secondary school enrolment: 18,447 – 8,960 male and 9,487 female. Teachers 1,130 - 873 male and 257 female. Available furniture is adequate for 16,434 students. Tertiary institutions: 1 university (Lugazi University).

Health Services: 4 hospitals (1 government - Kawolo Hospital with 100 beds, 3 NGO - Naggalama Hospital with 150 beds, Nkonkonjeru with 100 beds and St. Francis, Nyenga with 100 beds); 12 health centre III - (9 government, 3 NGO), 14 health centre II (8 government, 6 NGO).

Tourist Attractions: Mabira Forest Reserve's Najjembe village, a moist semi-deciduous forest famous for walking and cycling trails. The forest is home to approximately 100 species of large moths. It has extremely rich butterfly fauna. There are over 300 species of bird in the forest. Rare birds recorded in Mabira include the blue swallow, the papyrus gonolek and the nahan francolin, the tit hylia, the purple throated cuckoo, the grey apalis, the white bellied kingfisher and the blue crested flycatcher. Picnic facilities are available. The source of the Nile is shared by this district and Jinja.

Operational Radio Stations: Dynamic Broadcasting and Prayer Palace Ministries.

Key NGOs: Send a Cow Uganda, Uganda Women's Effort to Save Orphans, Integrated Rural Development Initiatives, African Network for the Prevention and Protection Against Child Abuse and Neglect Uganda Chapter, VEDCO, World Vision Uganda, Traditional and Modern Health Practitioners, Cape of Good Hope Orphan Care and Family Support Project, Literary AID Uganda, Uganda Environmental Education Foundation, Youth Alert Mukono, AIDS ACTION Uganda, Mukono Gatsby Club.

District leaders:	Members of Parliament:
Chairperson – Mr Kigongo Mathias	Buikwe County South
Chief Administrative Officer (CAO)	– Mr Bayigga Lulume Micheal
– Mr Sulaiman Kasozi	Buikwe County West – Mr Ssali Baker
Deputy Chief Administrative Officer	Buikwe County North
(DCAO) – Vacant	– Mr Onyango Kakoba
	Woman Representative
	– Ms Mpiima Dorothy Christine

Bukomansimbi District

Bukomansimbi District came into existence in 2010. Originally it was a county of Masaka District.

Location: Bukomansimbi District borders the districts of Sembabule to the west, Lwengo and Masaka to the south, Kalungu to the northeast and Gomba to the north.

Area: 599 sq. km.

Climate and Relief: It lies at an altitude of 1,219m – 1,524m above sea level. Temperatures are moderately high with rainfall throughout the year.

Population: According to 2009 projections, there are 146,700 people –75,400 female, 71,300 male with a density of 245 persons per sq.km.

Main Towns: Bukomansimbi (administrative headquarters); Kabasanda.

Counties and Sub-counties: Bukomansimbi County – Bigasa, Butenga, Kibinge, Kitanda and Bukomansimbi (Town Council);

Main Language: Luganda.

People: Baganda.

Economic Activities: Mainly agriculture with a bias to:
  (i)   Food crops: Sweet potatoes, bananas, beans, maize, cassava, groundnuts, soya bean, sorghum and finger millet.
  (ii) Cash crops: Coffee, cotton and maize.
  (iii) Fruits and vegetables: Pineapples, tomatoes, onions and cabbage.
  (iv) Cattle ranching.
  (v)   Fishing on Lake Victoria.

Banks: The district still depends on banks in Masaka, the mother district.

Area under Forestation: 21,990 hectares.

Animal Population: According to 2008 livestok census, Bukomansimbi, Masaka, Kalungu and Lwengo districts have 224,600 cattle, 236,148 pigs, 28,652 sheep, 244,706 goats, 1,108,363 chicken, 58,723 ducks and 16,223 turkeys.

Co-operative Societies: Masaka and Sembabule have 308 registered primary societies with Masaka Co-operative Union at the district level.

Industries: Manufacture of cassava starch, curry powder, garments, animal feeds, soft drinks, footwear, laundry soap, metalwork, furniture, jaggery, processing of tea, coffee, hand weaving and cotton ginning.

Education Services: Primary schools: 93 – 73 government, 19 private and 1 community. Enrolment: 45,968 pupils – 22,192 male and 23,776 female. Primary school teachers: 891 – 441 male and 450 female. Available furniture is adequate for 32,087 pupils.

Secondary schools: 15 schools - 5 government, 8 private and 2 community. Secondary school enrolment: 4,791 – 2,230 male and 2,561 female. Teachers: 248 - 205 male and 43 female.

Health Services: 1 health centre IV - (government), 4 health centre III - (2 government, 2 NGO), 7 health centre II - (4 government, 3 NGO).

Transport Network: The district has a well distributed feeder-road network which connects all counties and most sub-counties. The roads are in fairly good condition. Tarmac roads connect the district to Mbarara, Rakai and Mpigi. The feeder-roads link up with these main tarmac roads which facilitate transport to the neighbouring districts.

Tourist Attractions: The district does not have developed tourist attractions.

Additional Information: Some of the famous legendary Bachwezi settlements are found in Ntusi in this district. Bukomansimbi District is highly productive agriculturally. The farmers in the district grow crops with the intention of selling them, although crop production is basically subsistence. Most of the crops have a market in Kampala. Coffee farmers have benefited from the liberalisation of the coffee industry since, unlike in the past, they are promptly paid for the coffee.

Operational Radio and TV Stations: Central Broadcasting Service, Star Radio, Bwala Hill 88.0 FM, Radio West, Equator Radio, Buddu Broadcasting Services, Kalungu Foundation Ltd, Radio Maria Uganda Association, Christian Life Ministries, Uganda Broadcasting Corporation Radio, Christian Radio Network, Baptist International Mission (U) and Voice of Africa (MMC for ES and SA). UBC TV and WBS TV.

Key NGOs: Send a Cow Uganda, World Vision Uganda, Uganda Women's Effort to Save Orphans, Kitenga Development Foundation, Child Restoration Outreach.

District leaders:
Chairperson – Mr Huhammed Kamulegeya
Chief Administrative Officer (CAO)
    – Mr Solomon Ssonko
Deputy Chief Administrative Officer
    (CAO) – Vacant

Members of Parliament:
Bukomansimbi County
    – Mr Kiyingi Deogratius
Woman MP – Ms Namaganda Susan

Butambala District

Butambala district was part of Mpigi District. It existed as a county in Mpigi District until 2010 when it was elevated to district status.

Location: Butambala District borders the districts of Mityana to the north, Mpigi to the east and southeast, Kalungu to the southwest and Gomba to the west.

Area: 406 sq. km.

Climate and Relief: It lies at an approximate altitudinal range of between 1,182m – 1,341m above sea level. The district receives heavy and reliable rainfall and has relatively high temperatures. Butambala gets 1,513mm of rain per annum.

Population: According to 2009 projections, there are 93,700 people – 47,800 female, 45,900 male with a density of 230 persons per sq.km.

Major Towns: Gombe (administrative headquarters).

Counties and Sub-counties: Butambala County – Budde, Bulo, Kalamba, Kibibi, Ngando and Gombe Town Council).

Main Language: Luganda.

People: Mainly Baganda

Economic Activities: Mainly agriculture with a bias towards:
  (i)   Food crops: Sweet potatoes, beans, cassava, maize, bananas, groundnuts, sorghum, soya bean and Irish potatoes.
  (ii) Cash crops: Coffee and cotton.
  (iii) Fruits and vegetables: Tomatoes, onions and cabbage.
  (iv) Cattle keeping.

Banks: The district still depends on banks in the mother district, Mpigi.

Animal Population: According to 2008 statistcis, Butambala, Mpigi, and Gomba have 216,621 cattle, 108,082 pigs, 23,221 sheep, 102,828 goats, 600,950 chicken, 10,456 ducks and 1,143 turkeys.

Co-operative Societies: Mpigi and Wakiso have 341 registered primary societies with West Mengo Co-operative Union at the district level.

Industries: Manufacture of jaggery, footwear, furniture; printing, brick making, stone quarrying, processing of coffee, tea and bakeries.

Education Services: Primary schools: 86 – 67 government, 14 private and 5 community. Enrolment: 36,507 pupils: 18,050 male and 18,457 female. Primary School Teachers: 780 – 347 male and 433 female. Available furniture is adequate for 25,991 pupils.

Secondary schools: 28 - 6 government, 20 private and 2 community. Secondary school enrolment: 11,960 – 5,690 male and 6,270 female. Teachers: 620 - 463 male and 157 female. Available furniture is adequate for 11,050 students.

Tertiary institutions: 1 technical institution – Kabasanda Vocational Training Institute.

Health Services: 8 health centre III (5 government, 3 NGO), 8 health centre II (6 government, 2 NGO).

Tourist Attractions: The district has no tourist attractions

Operational TV and Radio Stations: Radio Simba, UBC TV, Dembe FM, WBS, NTV.

Key NGOs: Send a Cow Uganda, VEDCO, World Vision Uganda, Integrated Rural Development Initiatives, Concern Uganda, Omega Women's Group, Waggumbulizi Foundation, Kibibi Women's Association, Uganda Red Cross.

District leaders:	Members of Parliament:
Chairperson	Butambala County
– Mr Bavekuno Godfrey Mafumu	– Mr Kikulukunyu Faisal Ssali
Chief Administrative Officer (CAO)	Woman MP – Ms Nalubega Mariam
– Mr Joseph L. Byaruhanga	
Deputy Chief Administrative Officer	
(DCAO) – Vacant	

Buvuma District

At independence in 1962, Buvuma was part of Buganda. Following the abolition of kingdoms in 1967, it became part of one of the districts carved out of Buganda Kingdom and was named East Mengo. Under the 1974 provincial admininstation, East Mengo was renamed Kyagwe District and later, in 1980, became known as Mukono District with Buvuma forming the Island part of the district. Buvuma was elevated to district status in July 2010.

Location: Buvuma District borders the districts of Mayuge to the east, Buikwe to the north, Kalangala and Mukono to the west and United People's Republic of Tanzania to the south.

Area: 9,514 sq. km.

Climate and Relief: It lies at an altitudinal range of 1,158m to 1,219m above sea level with high temperatures and heavy rainfall. For example, in the period April – June 1991, it received 470mm of rain in 44 rain days.

Population: According to the 2009 projections, the district has 50,000 people – 22,100 female, 27,900 male, with a density of 5 persons per sq.km.

Major Towns: Buvuma (administrative headquarters).

Counties and Sub-counties: Buvuma Islands County – Bugaya, Busamuzi, Bwema, Nairamb and Buvuma (Town Council);

Main Language: Luganda.

People: Baganda and Basoga

Economic Activities: Mainly agriculture with emphasis on:
  (i) Food crops: Cassava, sweet potatoes, beans, maize, finger millet, groundnuts, soya bean, bananas, sorghum, simsim (sesame), cow peas, pigeon peas and yams.
  (ii) Fruits and vegetables: Tomatoes, onions, pineapples, vanilla, chillies, passion fruit and cabbage.
  (v) Fishing on Lake Victoria.

Banks: The districts depends on banks in Buikwe and Mukono districts.

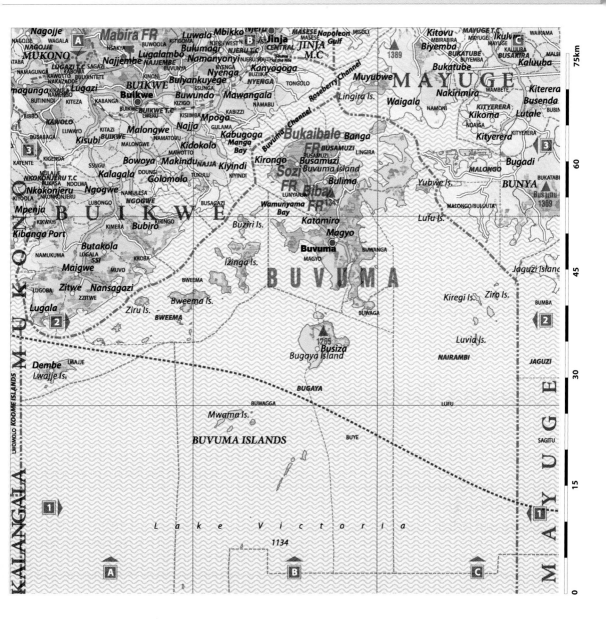

Animal Population: Buvuma, Mukono, Buikwe and districts have 155,820 cattle, 61 donkeys, 181,846 pigs, 30,808 sheep, 206,704 goats, 1,551,702 chicken, 49,517 ducks and 5,558 turkeys.

Co-operative Societies: The district depends on societies in Mukono and Buikwe districts.

Industries: Processing of coffee, building of boats, making of furniture.

Education Services: Primary schools: 20 – 12 government, 4 private, 4 community. Enrolment: 7,479 - 3,791 male and 3,688 female. Primary school teachers: 106 – 70 male and 36 female. Available furniture is adequate for 5,319 pupils.

Secondary schools: 2 schools - 1 government, 1 private. Secondary school enrolment: 206 students – 116 male and 90 female. Teachers 16 - 15 male and 1 female. Available furniture is adequate for 206 students.

Health Services: 1 health centre IV - (government), 1 health centre III - (government), 4 health centre II - (2 government, 2 NGO).

Tourist Attractions: Beaches and landing sites: The district is an archipelago in L. Victoria with great tourism potential, such as water sports and sport fishing.

Operational Radio Stations: Dynamic Broadcasting and Prayer Palace Ministries, CBS, Radio Simba.

District leaders:	Members of Parliament:
Chairperson – Mr Wasswa Adrian Dungu	Buvuma Island County
Chief Administrative Officer (CAO)	– Mr Migadde Robert Ndugwa
– Mr Paul Walakira	Woman Representative
Deputy Chief Administrative Officer	– Ms Egunyu Nantume Janepher
(CAO) – Vacant	

Gomba District

Gomba was a county in Mpigi District. It became a district in 2010.

Location: Gomba borders the districts of Mityana to the north, Mubende to the west and northwest, Butambala to the east, Kalungu, Bukomansibi and Sembabule to the south and Sembabule to the west.

Area: 1,679 sq. km.

Climate and Relief: It lies at an approximate altitudinal range of between 1,182m – 1,341m above sea level. The district receives heavy and reliable rainfall and has relatively high temperatures. Gomba gets 650 – 1000 mm of rain per annum.

Population: According to 2009 projections, there are 143,900 people – 71,900 female and 72,000 male with a density of 85 persons per sq.km.

Major Towns: Kanoni (administrative headquarters); Trading Centre – Gomba. Kabulasoke

Counties and Sub-counties: Gomba County – Kabulasoke, Kyegonza, Maddu, Mpenja, and Kanoni Town Council).

Main Language: Luganda.

People: Baganda.

Economic Activities: Mainly agriculture with a bias towards:
  (i)   Food crops: Sweet potatoes, beans, cassava, maize, bananas, groundnuts, sorghum, soya bean and Irish potatoes.
  (ii) Cash crops: Coffee and cotton.
  (iii) Fruits and vegetables: Tomatoes, onions and cabbage.
  (iv) Dairy farming.
  (v)   Fishing.

Banks: The district still relies on the banks in the mother district of Mpigi.

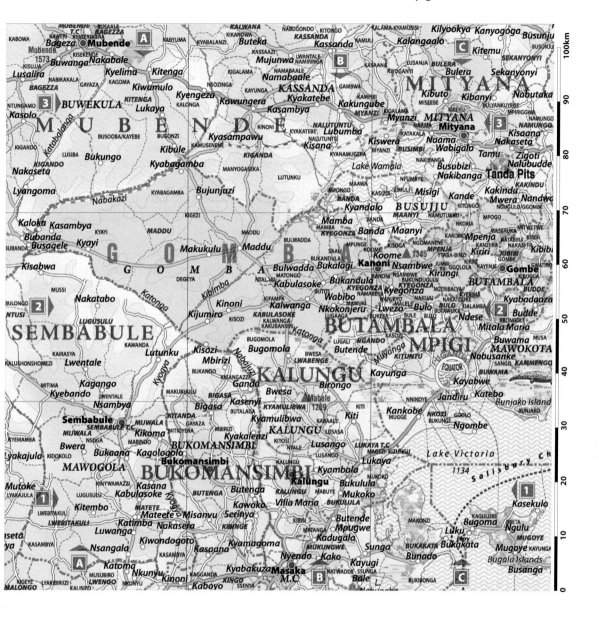

Animal Population: According to 2008 statistcis Gomba, Mpigi and Butambala have 216,621 cattle, 108,082 pigs, 23,221 sheep, 102,828 goats, 600,950 chicken, 10,456 ducks and 1,143 turkeys.

Co-operative Societies: Former Mpigi and Wakiso have 341 registered primary societies with West Mengo Co-operative Union at the district level.

Industries: Manufacture of jaggery, footwear, furniture, printing, brick making, stone quarrying, processing of coffee, tea and bakeries.

Education Services: Primary schools: 101 – 81 government, 16 private and 4 community. Enrolment: 48,660 pupils – 23,450 male and 25,210 female. Primary school teachers: 875 – 470 male and 405 female. Available furniture is adequate for 33,175 pupils.

Secondary schools: 21 schools - 6 government, 14 private and 1 community. Secondary school enrolment: 4,814 – 3,218 male and 2,496 female. Teachers: 308 - 259 male and 49 female. Available furniture is adequate for 4,332 students.

Tertiary institutions: 1 teacher training college – Kabulasoke PTC.

Health Services: 1 health centre IV (government), 4 health centre III (government), and 10 health centre II (government).

Tourist Attractions: The extreme western part of the district borders the Katonga Wildlife Reserve and game may be cited. However, the district does not have a share of the wildlife reserve.

The Katonga River, which links Lake Victoria and Lake George, are also in view.

Additional Information: The Equator crossing at 66 kms on the Kampala-Masaka Road, and part of Lake Victoria shores are in this district.

Operational TV Station: Uganda Broadcasting Corporation Television.

Key NGOs: Send a Cow Uganda, VEDCO, Integrated Rural Development Initiatives, Concern Uganda, Dutch Uganda Orphans Project, Gomba AIDS Support and Counselling Organisation, Omega Women's Group, Waggumbulizi Foundation, Uganda Red Cross.

District leaders:	Members of Parliament:
Chairperson – Mr Kyabangi Abdul	Gomba County
Chief Administrative Officer (CAO)	– Ms Rosemary Muyinda Najjemba
– Mr Esau Ekachelan	Woman MP
Deputy Chief Administrative Officer	– Ms Nakato Kyabangi Katusiime
(DCAO) – Vacant	

Kalangala District

Location: It borders the districts of Masaka and Rakai to the west; Mpigi, Mukono and Wakiso to the north; Buvuma to the east and the United People's Republic of Tanzania to the south. It is entirely surrounded by Lake Victoria and is made up of islands collectively referred to as Ssesse Islands. The district was formerly part of Masaka District.

Area: 12,878 sq.km.

Climate and Relief: It lies at an approximate altitude of between 1,189m and 1,219m above sea level, in the equatorial zone, with temperatures usually uniformly high and reliable rainfall averaging 2,193mm per annum.

Population: According to 2009 projections, there are 53,300 people – 21,600 female, and 31,700 male with a density of 4 persons per sq.km.

Major Town: Kalangala (administrative headquarters).

Counties and Sub-counties: Bujumba County – Bujumba, Kalangala (Town Council), Mugoye; Kyamuswa County – Bufumira, Bubeke, Kyamuswa and Mazinga.

Main Language: Luganda.

Economic Activities: Agriculture with emphasis on:
  (i)   Food crops: Cassava, sweet potatoes, bananas, maize, groundnuts, soya bean and sorghum.
  (ii) Cash crops: Sugar cane.
  (iii) Fruits and vegetables: Pineapples, onions, tomatoes and cabbage.
  (iv) Fishing.

Banks: Stanbic Bank Uganda Ltd –1.

Area under Forestation: 26,783 hectares.

Animal Population: The district has 5,814 cattle, 6,547 pigs, 5,762 goats, 58,088 chicken, 8,080 ducks and 157 turkeys.

Co-operative Societies: 10 registered primary societies.

Education Services: Primary schools: 27 – 23 government, 4 private. Enrolment: 4,652 – 2,446 male and 2,206 female. Primary school teachers: 145 - 77 male and 68 female. Available furniture is adequate for 4, 634 pupils.

Secondary Schools: 3 (all government). Secondary school enrolment: 528 - 291 male and 237 female. Teachers: 45 - 36 male and 9 female. Available furniture adequate for 565.

Tertiary institutions: The district has 1 technical institution.

Health Services: 2 health centre IV (all govement), 6 health centre III (all government), 3 health centre II (2 government, 1 NGO).

Tourist Attractions: An archipelago of 84 islands are found in Africa's largest fresh water lake, Lake Victoria. It is a bird watcher's and botanist's paradise and sport fishing. You can visit caves of bats, Speke's Fort (1862), pineapple and palm tree farms and fishing villages.

The islands are hilly and the uncultivated parts are still forested. The main island is Buggala which is about 34 km long. The main town is Kalangala, which is also the name of the district. A bus and taxis link the towns. The second largest island is Bukasa Island, Bubeke and Bufumira islands are also easy to visit.

Buggala Island has about 50 km of road on it. All around are wonderful views of Lake Victoria and other islands – some of which are forested, others are cultivated and others a mixture of both. Mutambala Beach, off the Kalangala – Luku Road is popular.

Bukasa has a wider range of wildlife and a small population. There are two beautiful beaches as well as a waterfalls.

There are many unihabited islands. One can arrange to visit the islands with one of the fishermen or with Andronica Lodge.

There is decent accomodation at Islands Club on Buggala Island, Ssesse Palm Beach Resort, Ssesse Islands Beach Hotel, Panorama Cottages/Camping Safari and Agnes' Guest House on Bukasa Island.

Camping can also be arranged.

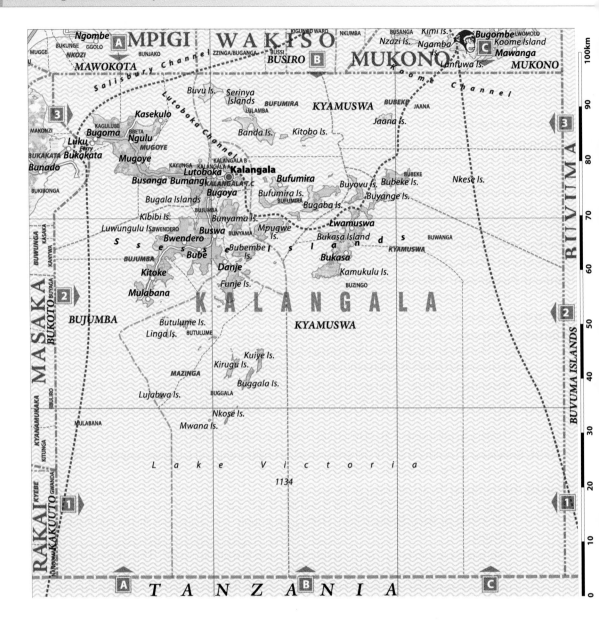

Additional Information: Water sports. There is also a high potential for ornithology. Huge and compact tropical forests thrill tourists. One can go on a trek to look at the apes and bats.

Key NGOs: Actionaid Uganda, National Association of Women Organisations in Uganda, KALANGANETT, Ssesse Islands Community Development Organisation, Bufumira Islands Development Association, Kalangala AIDS Care Education and Training, Bussumba Initiative for Adult Education and Development, AGALYAWAMU.

District leaders:
Chairperson – Mr Bageyente Lugoloobi W.
Ag Chief Administrative Officer (CAO)
 – Mr Fred Mukasa Kizito
Deputy(CAO) – Vacant
Town Clerk (Kalangala Town Council)
 – Mr Godfrey Semirembe

Members of Parliament:
Bujumba County – Mr Fred Badda
Kyamuswa County
 – Mr Lwanga Timothy Mutekanga
Woman MP
 – Ms Nanyondo Birungi Carolyn

Kalungu District

Kalungu District came into existence in 2010 when Kalungu County was elevated to district status. Before then it was one of the counties in Masaka District.

Location: Kalungu district borders the districts of Bukomansimbi to the west, Masaka to the south, Mpigi to the east, and Gomba and Butambala to the norh.

Area: 837 sq. km.

Climate and Relief: It lies at an altitude of 1,219m – 1,524m above sea level. Temperatures are moderately high with rainfall throughout the year.

Population: According to 2009 projections, there are 168,700 people – 86,900 female, and 81,800 male with a density of 201 persons per sq.km.

Main Towns: Kalungu (administrative headquarters); Trading Centre – Lukaya

Counties and Sub-counties: Kalungu County – Bukulula, Lwabenge, Kalungu, Kyamulibwa, Lukaya (Town Council), and Kalungu, (Town Council);

Main Language: Luganda.

People: Baganda.

Economic Activities: Mainly agriculture with a bias to:
  (i)   Food crops: Sweet potatoes, bananas, beans, maize, cassava, groundnuts, soya bean, sorghum and finger millet.
  (ii) Cash crops: Coffee, cotton and maize.
  (iii) Fruits and vegetables: Pineapples, tomatoes, onions and cabbage.
  (iv) Cattle ranching.
  (v)   Fishing on Lake Victoria.

Banks: Stanbic Bank Uganda Ltd-1, DFCU Bank –1, Centenary Rural Development Bank –1.

Area under Forestation: 21,990 hectares.

Animal Population: According to 2008 livestok census, Kalungu, Bukomansimbi, Masaka and Lwengo districts have 224,600 cattle, 236,148 pigs, 28,652 sheep, 244,706 goats, 1,108,363 chicken, 58,723 ducks and 16,223 turkeys.

Co-operative Societies: Kalungu, Lwengo, Bukomansimbi and Masaka have 308 registered primary societies with Masaka Co-operative Union at the district level.

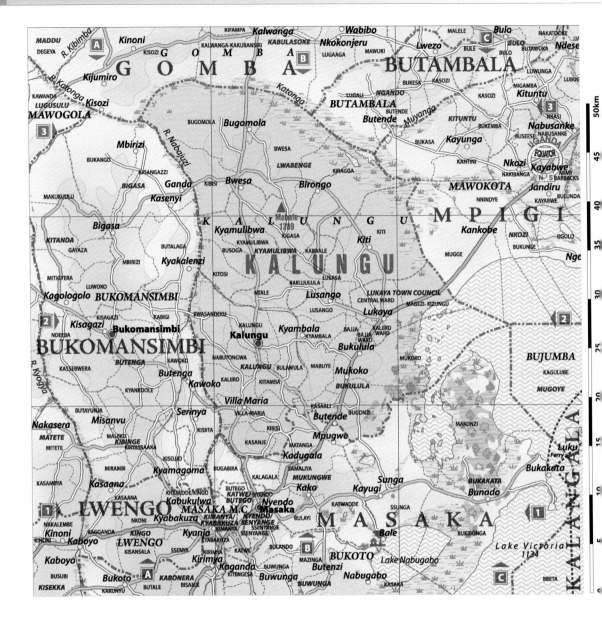

Industries: Manufacture of garments, animal feeds, soft drinks, footwear, laundry soap, metalwork, furniture, jaggery, processing of tea, coffee, hand weaving and cotton ginning.

Education Services: Primary schools: 98 – 88 government, 9 private and 1 community. Enrolment: 57,628 pupils – 27,585 male and 30,043 female. Primary school teachers: 1,160 – 522 male and 638 female. Available furniture is adequate for 45,932 pupils.

Secondary schools: 23 schools - 8 government, 13 private, and 2 community. Secondary school enrolment: 8,767 – 3,412 male and 5,355 female. Teachers: 466 male and female. Available furniture is adequate for 8,673 students.

Tertiary institution: 2 technical institutions, 1 teacher training college.

Health Services: 1 hospital (NGO - Villa Maria Hospital with 120 beds), 2 health centre IV - (1 government, 1 NGO), 4 health centre III - (all government), 9 health centre II (4 government, 4 NGO and 1 private).

Transport Network: The district has a well distributed feeder-road network which connects all sub-counties. The roads are in fairly good condition. A tarmac road traverses the southern part of the district connecting to Masaka and Mpigi. The feeder-roads link up with the other parts of the district to the main Mbarara-Masaka-Kampala (tarmac) Road.

Tourist Attractions: Kalungu district has no tourist attractions.

Operational Radio and TV Stations: Central Broadcasting Service, Star Radio, Bwala Hill 88.0 FM, Radio West, Equator Radio, Buddu Broadcasting Services, Kalungu Foundation Ltd, Radio Maria Uganda Association, Christian Life Ministries, Uganda Broadcasting Corporation Radio, Christian Radio Network, Baptist International Mission (U) and Voice of Africa (MMC for ES and SA). TV stations received are Uganda Broadcasting Corporation Television and WBS TV Limited.

Key NGOs: Send a Cow Uganda, World Vision Uganda, Uganda Women's Effort to Save Orphans, Kitenga Development Foundation, and Child Restoration Outreach.

District leaders:	Members of Parliament:
Chairperson – Mr Musoke Emmanuel	Kalungu County West
Ag Chief Administrative Officer (CAO)	– Mr Ssewungu Joseph Gonzaga
– Ms Lillian Nakamate	Kalungu County East
Deputy Chief Administrative Officer	– Mr Ssempijja Vincent Bamulangaki
(DCAO) – Vacant	Woman MP – Ms Kintu Florence
Deputy Chief Administrative Officer	
(CAO) – Mr Bbaale	
Town Clerk (Masaka Municipal Council)	
– Mr Lawrence Bagerize	
Town Clerk (Lukaya Town Council)	
– Mr Paul Walakira	

Kampala District

Location: It borders the District of Mukono to the east and is surrounded by Wakiso District for the rest of the parts. Kampala is the only urban district in the country. It is both a district and the capital city of Uganda. At Independence, it was part of Buganda Kingdom before becoming one of the districts in the Central Province in the 1970s.

Area: 197.0 sq. km.

Climate, Relief and Vegetation: Approximate altitude is between 1,189m and 1,402m above sea level in the equatorial climatic zone. Lake Victoria has a marked influence on its

climate. Temperatures and rainfall are usually high and the fringes of the district have dense deciduous, tropical, rainforests.

Population: According to 2009 projections, there are 1,510,200 people – 795,100 female and 715,100 male with a density of 7,666 persons per sq.km.

Major Towns: Kampala City (the national capital and district administrative headquarters); Trading Centres – Nakawa, Rubaga, Makindye and Kawempe.

Divisions: Kawempe, Nakawa, Makindye, Rubaga and Kampala Central.

Main Languages: Luganda, English, Swahili and other local languages.

People: Diverse.

Economic Activities: The city centre is mainly industrial while the suburbs are dominated by small scale industrial and agricultural production.
  (i)   Crops produced include sweet potatoes and bananas.
  (ii) Fishing is carried out on Lake Victoria.
  (iii) Poultry farming.

Banks: Stanbic Bank – 16, Development Finance Company of Uganda (DFCU) Bank – 4, Centenary Rural Development Bank – 3, National Bank of Commerce Ltd – 1, Orient Bank – 2, Barclays Bank Uganda Ltd – 2, Bank of Baroda – 2, Standard Chartered Bank Uganda Ltd – 3, Post Bank Uganda Ltd – 2, Crane Bank Ltd – 1, Cairo International Bank Ltd – 1, Diamond Trust Uganda Bank Ltd – 1, Citibank Uganda Ltd – 1 Equity Bank - ABC Capital bank, Kenya Commercial bank, Global bank, Uganda Housing Finance bank, Imperial bank, Tropical Africa bank, Stanford bank, United bank of Africa, ECO bank and East African Development bank, Bank of Uganda.

Area under Forestation: 52 hectares.

Animal Population: According to 2008 statistics, there are 31,614 cattle, 38,306 pigs, 8,790 sheep, 64,072 goats, and 1,053,031 chicken, 28,148 ducks and 5,675 turkeys.

Co-operative Societies: 298 registered primary societies with West Mengo Union at the district level.

Industries: Manufacture of jaggery, soya sauce, curry powder, sweets and confectionery, chicken and animal feeds, beer, whisky, brandy, dry gin, soft drinks, blankets and textiles, fish nets, cords and twine, footwear, foam mattresses, paper bags, stationery pads, toilet paper, paint, pharmaceuticals, soap, toothpaste, paraffin wax, safety matches, shoe polish, floor polish, candles, plastic ware, school chalk, lorry bodies, beds, charcoal stoves, window frames, kettles, brooms and brushes; safe gutters, bracelets, cider and banana wine, and nails. Processing of skins and hides, and sausages. Pineapples, milk and milk products, jam, oil milling, grain, maize and millet, welding and general engineering; printing and electrical machinery and apparatus; motor vehicle bodies and trailers, and bicycle manufacture.

Education Services: Primary schools: 636 schools – 87 government, 518 private, and 31 community. Enrolment: 217,038 – 105,241 male and 111,797 female. Primary school teachers: 8,098 – 3,564 male and 4,534 female. Available furniture adequate for 190,528 pupils.

Secondary schools: 142 schools – 18 government, 121 private, and 3 community. Secondary school enrolment: 89,534 students – 46,648 male and 42,886 female. Teachers: 4,644 – 3,204 male and 1,440 female. Available furniture is adequate for 78,939 students.

Post secondary institutions and universities: 3 teacher training colleges. Universities – Makerere University, Agha Khan University, Kampala University, Makerere University

Business School – Nakawa, Kyambogo University – Uganda Polytechnic Kyambogo, Kampala International University, Cavendish University, Ndejje University, Bugema University, Islamic University in Uganda, St Lawrence University, Mutesa I Royal University, Uganda Management Institute.

Health/Medical – 10 paramedical schools at Mulago. Vocational institutes – Nakawa Vocational Training Institute, Lugogo Vocational Training Institute, Uganda Wildlife Institute.

Health Services: 12 hospital; (4 government, 4 private,, 4 NGO), National Referral Hospitals – Mulago Hospital with 1,780 beds and Butabika Hospital with 850 beds, Luzira Hospital with 163 beds, Uganda Catholic Medical Bureau – Rubaga Hospital with 300 beds, St.Francis Nsambya Hospital with 361 beds, Uganda Protestant Medical Bureau – Mengo Hospital with 285 beds, Namungona Hospital with 20 beds, St.Stephen's Mpererwe with 56 beds, Kisekka Foundation Hospital. Uganda Muslim Medical Bureau – Old Kampala Hospital with 30 beds and Kibuli Hospital with 70 beds. 4 health centre IV (3 government, 1 NGO), 20 health centre III (11 government, 8 NGO, 1 private) several health centre II (12 government, 3 NGO, 22 private). Other hospitals – International Hospital Kampala, Kololo Hospital, Bugolobi Hospital, Mackenzie Valley, Makerere University. Hospitals belonging to other ministries – Mbuya Military Hospital and Murchisons Bay Hospital.

There are numerous other small clinics and health centres:

723 Private/NGO clinics.

Tourist Attractions: The Parliamentary Building where the Uganda Parliament sits, The National Theatre, for traditional music and dances, African Crafts Village next to the National Theatre with 36 small shops/kiosks, Nommo Gallery, Sheraton Gardens with craft shops and Tulifanya Gallery.

Kasubi Tombs on Nabulagala Hill, off the Kampala-Hoima Road, where the last four *Kabakas* (kings) of Buganda are buried, Namirembe Cathedral with the graves of Bishop Hannnington and the Cooks who founded Mengo Hospital, Bulange – the adminsitrative centre of Buganda Kingdom, Rubaga Cathedral with the remains of Joseph Kiwanuka – the first African Bishop.

The Kabaka's Lake and palace at Mengo, Nakasero Old Fort on Nakasero Hill, Uganda Museum at Kitante, the Bahai Temple on Kikaya Hill off Gayaza Road – the only temple of the Bahai faith to be found in Africa, Makerere University – the oldest university in East Africa and the Kibuli Mosque.

Nakasero Market is the largest fruit and vegetable market in the town centre. St. Balikuddembe Market near Nakivubo Stadium also sells food stuffs and fruits at prices much lower than Nakasero Market.

Accommodation: For accomodation, Kampala has a variety of hotels which include Sheraton Kampala Hotel, Kampala Serena, Imperial Royale, Grand Imperial Hotel, Speke Hotel, Speke Resort Munyonyo, Hotel Africana, and many other upmarket and budget hotels. There are Campsites such as the Backpackers Hostel and Campsite, Guest houses such as Namirembe Guest House, Apartments – Mosa Courts Apartments on Shimoni Road in Nakasero and many others.

Restaurants: Several eating places with both local and international dishes in the city centre and the suburbs. Kampala's restaurants serve different cuisine which include Belgian, Chinese, continental, Ethiopian, fast food, French, Italian, Indian, Lebanese, Thai and Ugandan food.

The local newspapers especially the *New Vision* and the *Daily Monitor* newspapers have updates of interesting places to visit.

Sports: Sports include canoeing at Munyonyo on Lake Victoria, tennis and cricket at Lugogo, rugby at Lugogo and Kyaddondo Rugby Clubs, golf, soccer, motor sports and many others.

Kampala Hash Harriers, a Monday evening jogging group with many tourists, expatriates and Ugandans. Contact either The Surgery on telephone 041-256003 or International Medical Centre, KPC building on Bombo Road, on telephone 041-341291.

Clubs and Associations: Alliance Francaise, American Recreation Association, Bridge Club, British Residents Association of Uganda, Caledonian Society, Food and Drink Association of Uganda, International Women's Organisation that meets at Uganda Museum, Irish Society in Uganda, Kampala Amateur Dramatics Society, Kampala Music School, Kampala Singers, Mountain Club of Uganda, Nature Uganda (which has nature walks every month) Uganda German Cultural Society, Uganda Bird Guides Club.

Internet and e-mail facilities are available in the city centre and the prices range from Shs 25 – 30 per minute. Internet connections in some places can be very slow. Mobile phone companies also offer mobile internet services at competitive prices.

Tourist Guide Books: There are a number of authoritative tourist guide books available on the market. They include Uganda at a Glance, Uganda Pocket Facts, Taste of Uganda – Recipes and Traditional Dishes, How to be a Ugandan, Peoples and Cultures of Uganda, Luganda-English Phrase Book. All these books are published by Tourguide Publications, an imprint of Fountain Publishers and are available in all good bookshops in town. Fountain Publishers can be contacted on telephone 031-263041/2 or 041-259163 and Tourguide Publications on 0312-264859 or at info@tourguide-uganda.co.ug.

Another book that contains useful information is Kampala A-Z, a guide to Kampala city. It has maps divided into three sections — the "MegaSuper-scale", the "Super-scale" and the "Standard-scale" sections. The "MegaSuper-scale" section covers the central and commercial part of Kampala city in most detail. The "Super-scale" section is less magnified and therefore covers a wider area of the city centre. The "Standard-scale" section which is least magnified, covers all of Kampala and also includes some of the bordering residential areas.

Other publications are Animals of Uganda, Dances of Uganda, Hills of Kampala, Welcome to Kampala, Tips on Ugandan Culture and the Tourguide Travel Map of Uganda.

You can also pay a visit to the Uganda Tourist Board offices on Plot 13/15, Kimathi Avenue, Impala House and contact telephone: 0414-342196/7.

Uganda Wildlife Authority on Kiira Road, Kampala, Contact Telephone: 0414-346287/8.

Operational TV and Radio Stations: Top Radio, Central Broadcasting Service, Power FM, BBC World Service, Voice of Africa, Radio Maria, Impact FM, Star Radio, Radio Sapientia, Radio France International, Butebo Radio, Uganda Broadcasting Corporation Radio, Capital Radio, Radio Simba, Sanyu FM, Radio West, East African Radio, Greater Africa Radio, Radio Two, Super Station INC Ltd, Christian Life Ministries, Radio One Ltd, Ddembe FM, Seventh Day Adventist, KFM, Uganda Episcopal Conference, Buddu Broadcasting, Touch FM Radio Ltd, Beat Radio FM Ltd, Africa FM Ltd, Christian Radio Network, FM Holdings, Ugand Media Women Association – MAMA FM, UNESCO Nabweru, UNESCO Nakaseke, S & J Promotions Ltd, Family Broadcasting Network, Makerere University and Kampala International University (KIU). TV stations are: Uganda Broadcasting Corporation TV, Lighthouse Television, Wavah Broadcasting Services, Multichoice Uganda, Pulse TV, East African TV, Christian Life Ministries (Top TV), Record TV Network, NBS and NTV.

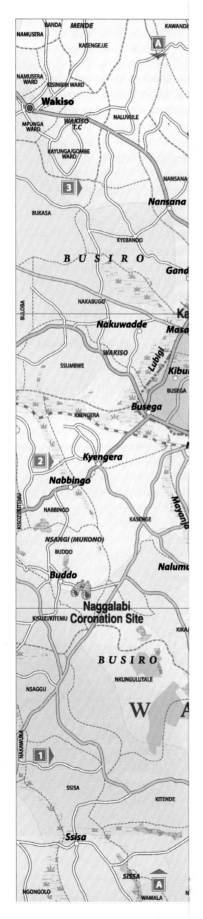

Key NGOs: AT Uganda Ltd, Africa 2000 Network, The Agricultural Council of Uganda, Uganda, National Farmers' Association, Send a Cow Uganda, AFXB Orphan Program Uganda, Integrated Rural Development Initiatives, Plan International, African Network for the Prevention and Protection Against Child Abuse and Neglect Uganda Chapter, Concern for the Girl Child, Community for Development Foundation Uganda, National Union of Disabled Persons in Uganda, National Organisation of Women with Disabilities in Uganda, Uganda Society for Disabled Children, Uganda Land Alliance, Environmental Alert, African Medical Research Foundation Uganda, Family Planning Association of Uganda, Traditional and Modern Health Practitioners, Transcultural Psychological Organisation, – Uganda National Health Users/Consumers Association, Alliance for African Assistance, Human Rights Network, International Aid Services, Concern Uganda, CARE International in Uganda, ded German Development Service, HORIZONT 3000, International Care and Relief Uganda, Oxfam GB in Uganda, PANOS Eastern Africa, SNV Uganda, Strømme Foundation, Uganda Development Trust, Uganda Joint Christian Council, Uganda Project Implementation and Management Centre, Voluntary for Development, VSO Uganda, Volunteer Efforts for Development Concerns, World Vision Uganda, Akina Mama Wa Afrika, Women and Children's Crisis Centre, The East African Sub-regional Support Initiative for the Advancement of Women, National Association of Women Organisations in Uganda, Uganda Women's Effort to Save Orphans, Straight Talk Foundation, Uganda Youth Forum, Compassion International, Hunger Project, Feed the Children, BUCADEF, Habitat

for Humanity, CDRN, Save the Children UK, Save the Children Denmark, Save the Children Norway, AfriCare, Christian Children's Fund, Uganda Red Cross Society, Aktion, Afrika Hilfe, Uganda Change Agents Association, Forum for Women in Democracy, Uganda Debt Network, and others.

District leaders:
Lord Mayor – Mr Erias Lukwago
Executive Director
  – Jennifer Semakula Musisi
Mayor Lubaga Municipality
  – Ms Joyce N Ssebuggwawo
Makindye Municipality – Mr Ian Clarke
Nakawa Municipality
  – Mr Ben Sebuliba Kalumba
Kawempe Municipality
  – Mr Mubarak Munyagwa
Central Municipality
  – Mr Godfrey Nyakana

Members of Parliament:
Central Division
  – Mr Muhammed Nsereko
Lubaga Division North
  –Mr Katongole Singh Marwaha P.
Lubaga Division South
  – Mr Ken Lukyamuzi John
Makindye Division East – Mr John Simbwa
Makindye Division West
  – Mr Kyanjo Hussein
Nakawa Division – Mr Fredrick Ruhindi
Kawempe Division North
  – Mr Abudulatif Ssengendo Ssebaggala
Kawempe Division South
  – Mr Richard Sebuliba Mutumba
Woman MP – Ms Nabilah Naggayi Sempala

Kampala Road.

THE PARLIAMENT
OF THE REPUBLIC OF UGANDA

Members of the 9th Parliament of Uganda pose for a group photo with H.E. President Yoweri K. Museveni, H.E. the Vice President Edward Ssekandi and His Lordship the chief Justice Benjamin Odoki.

The Parliament of Uganda derives its mandate and functions from the 1995 Constitution, the Laws of Uganda and its own Rules of Procedure.

The Constitution contains articles which provide for the establishment, composition and functions of the Parliament of Uganda and empowers Parliament "to make laws on any matter for the peace, order, development and good governance of Uganda", **Art.79(1)** and "to protect this Constitution and promote democratic governance in Uganda". **Art. 79(3)**

The term of Parliament is five years from the date of its first sitting after a general election. **Art 77(3)** The current Parliament (9th Parliament) started in May 2011 and ends in May 2016.

Functions of Parliament

The functions of the Parliament of Uganda are:

1. To pass laws for the good governance of Uganda.
2. To provide, by giving legislative sanctions taxation and acquisition of loans, the means of carrying out the work of Government.
3. To scrutinise Government policy and administration through the following:
   a. pre-legislative scrutiny of bills referred to the Parliamentary committees by Parliament
   b. scrutinising of the various objects of expenditure and the sums to be spent on each

c.   assuring transparency and accountability in the application of public funds

d.   monitoring the implementation of Government programmes and projects

4.   To debate matters of topical interest usually highlighted in the President's State of the Nation address.

5.   To vet the appointment of persons nominated by the President under the Constitution or any other enactment

Composition of the Ninth Parliament by Category

CATEGORY	MALE	FEMALE	NUMBER OF MP'S
Constituency (Directly Elected)	227	11	238
District Women Representatives	00	112	112
Uganda People's Defence Force Representatives	08	02	10
Workers' Representatives	03	02	05
Youth Representatives	03	02	05
Persons With Disabilities Representatives	03	02	05
Ex-officios	08	03	11
Total	252	134	386

Presidential appointees to cabinet for persons who do not have constituencies, automatically become Members of Parliament after swearing the oath of an MP. While they enjoy all the privileges and benefits of MP's they do not vote in Parliament, hence the term ex-officio.

Party Composition

National Resistance Movement Organisation (NRMO)..264
Forum for Democratic Change (FDC)..34
Democratic Party (DP) 12
Uganda People's Congress (UPC..10
Justice Forum (JEEMA) 01
Conservative Party (CP)..01
Independents 43
Total **365**

NB: Party Composition excludes the 10 UPDF Representatives.

Vital Contacts

Office of the Speaker
Tel: +256 (0) 414 377- 100/102
Fax: +256 (0) 414 231296

Office of the Deputy Speaker
Tel: +256 (0) 414 377- 110/112
Fax: +256 (0) 414 231295

Office of the Leader of Opposition
Tel: +256 (0) 414 377- 140/142
Fax: +256 (0) 414 348896

Clerk to Parliament
Tel: +256 (0) 414 377- 150/152
Fax: +256 (0) 414 346826

Public Relations Office
Tel: +256 (0) 414 377- 180/181
Fax: +256 (0) 414 250495

General line:
+256 (0) 414 377000

Reception North Wing:
+256 (0) 414 377478

Reception South Wing:
+256 (0) 414 377480

Reception Baumann House:
+256 (0) 414 377700

𝕶ampala 𝕮ity 𝕮ouncil

TELEPHONE CONTACTS

His Worship the Mayor
0414-230776
Deputy Mayor:
0414-231445
Speaker:
0414-233615
Town Clerk:
041 4-231446
Public Relations Office:
0414-231443
Hot Line:
0312-266913
Email:
mayorkcc.citycouncilofkampala.go.ug
townclerk@ citycouncilofkampala.ug
www. citycouncilofkampala.go.ug

DIRECTORS OF DEPARTMENTS

Director Works:
0414-258415
Director Finance:
0414-258416
Director Health:
0414-342434
Director Education:
'0414-258417
City Advocate:
0414-233236
Diretor Gender & Community Service
0414-345412

DIVISIONS

Central Division
Tel: Plot 86-88 William street,
Opposite Hotel Equatorial
Hotel car Park
Tel: 0312 110032/0312 106585
Lubaga Division
Kabakanjagala Rd near Lubiri
Gate
Tel. 0312 1 O687/041 4-690116

Nakawa Division:
Naguru Housing Estate, Adjacent
to Naguru Community Centre.
Kawempe Division:
Nabweru Road
Opposite Kabaka's Market -
Bwaise Tel 0392 -889796
Makindye Division:
Mubutu Road near Makindye,
Military barracks 0751-059210

Kampala City Council (KCC), is mandated by the Local Governments Act (Cap 243), to provide numerous services. It has two arms, one being administrative and the other being political. The political arm is the policy maker while the administrative arm is the policy implementer and technical advisor. Kampala City is made up of five (5) administrative divisions namely: Central, Kawempe, Makindye, Nakawa and Lubaga.

Our Shared Vision

A secure, economically vibrant, well managed, sustainable and environmentally pleasant city.

Mission

To provide quality, sustainable, customer oriented services effectively.
Services
The council is mandated with provision of services in the city that enable resi- and businesses operating in the city to function in as environment that supports development.

Specifically, the council is obliged to plan, implement and monitor the delivery of services that include but not limited to:

1. Preventive and curative health
2. Formal and non-formal education
3. Roads and infrastructure including drainage and street lighting
4. Gender mainstreaming
5. Youth and community development
6. Probation and social welfare
7. Extension services
8. Waste management
9. Environment management, etc

Kayunga District

Formerly part of Mukono District. In 2000, Ntenjeru and Bbaale counties of Mukono District became Kayunga District.

Location: It borders Jinja and Kamuli to the east, Luweero and Nakasongola to the west, Lira to the north, Mukono to the south.

Area: 1,703 sq. km.

Climate and Relief: It lies at an approximate altitude of between 1,158m and 1,219m above sea level, with high rainfall totalling 470mm per annum and high temperatures.

Population: According to 2009 projections, there are 331,500 people – 172,200 female, 159,300 male with a density of 195 persons per sq.km.

Major Towns: Kayunga (administrative headquarters); Trading Centres – Galiraya, Kayonza and Bbaale.

Counties and Sub-counties: Bbaale County – Bbaale, Galiraya, Kayonza, Kitimbwa; Ntenjeru County – Busaana, Kayunga, Kayunga (Town Council), Kangulumira and Nazigo.

Main Language: Luganda.

People: Diverse.

Economic Activities: Fishing on Lake Kyoga and along the Victoria Nile. Agriculture with emphasis on:
(i)   Food crops: Cassava, sweet potatoes, maize and finger millet.
(ii) Cash crops: Cotton and coffee.
(iii) Fruits and vegetables: Tomatoes, pineapples, vanilla, chillies and passion fruit.

Area under Forestation: 15,144 hectares.

Animal Population: The district has 88,814 cattle, 38,067 pigs, 7,707 sheep, 82,701 goats, 327,603 chicken, 14,327 ducks and 760 turkeys.

Co-operative Societies: Kayunga and Mukono have 267 registered co-operative societies.

Industries: Grain milling, furniture making, animal feeds.

Education Services: Primary schools: 199 schools – 155 government, 40 private and 4 community. Enrolment: 112,337pupils – 55,877 male and 56,460 female. Primary school teachers: 2,233 – 1,283 male and 950 female. Available furniture adequate for 81,397 pupils.

Secondary schools: 43 schools - 9 government, 29 private and 5 community schools. Secondary school enrolment: 17,457 students – 9,179 male and 8,278 female. Teachers: 938 - 734 male and 204 female. Available furniture adequate for 15,217 students.

Tertiary institution: 1 technical institute.

Health Services: 1 hospital (government – Kayunga Hospital, with 104 beds), 2 health centre IV (all government), 8 health centre III (all government), 12 health centre II (8 government, 4 NGO).

Tourist Attractions: The Victoria Nile and Lake Kyoga.

Key NGOs: Integrated Rural Development Initiatives, Action for Human Rights and Civil Awareness, Kayunga Child Development Centre, Kayunga Information Bureau, Peer AIDS and Counselling Organisation, Action for Human Rights and Civil Awareness.

District leaders:
Chairperson – Mr Dagada Stephen Watala
Chief Administrative Officer (CAO) – Mr Katehangwa Samuel
Deputy Chief Administrative Officer (CAO) – Ms Lucy Frances Amulen

Members of Parliament:
Bbaale County – Mr Sulaiman Kyebakoze Madada
Ntenjeru County North – Mr Lugoloobi Amos
Ntenjeru County South – Mr Nsanja Patrick K. Mabirizi
Woman MP – Ms Nantaba Idah Erios

Kayunga is famous for pineapple growing.

Kiboga District

It was formerly part of Mubende District.

Location: It borders the districts of Mubende and Mityana to the south, Kyankwanzi to the north and northwest and Nakaseke to the east.

Area: 1,587 sq. km.

Climate, Relief and Vegetation: The district has moderate rainfall and temperatures suitable for the growth of a number of crops.

Population: According to 2009 projections, there are 142,700 – 70,500 female and 72,200 male with a density of 90 persons per sq.km.

Major Towns: Kiboga (administrative headquarters); Trading Centres – Bukomera and Ntwetwe.

Counties and Sub-counties: Kiboga East – Dwaniro, Bukomero, Kibiga, Lwamata, Kapeke Muwanga, and Kiboga (Town Coucil).

Main Language: Luganda.

People: Baganda.

Economic Activities: Mainly agriculture with emphasis on:
- (i)   Food crops: Maize, beans, groundnuts, bananas, finger millet, soya beans, simsim (sesame), sweet potatoes and Irish potatoes.
- (ii) Cash crops: coffee, cotton and tea.
- (iii) Fruits and vegetables: Pineapples, tomatoes, onions, passion fruit and cabbage.
- (iv) Ranching.

Banks: Stanbic Bank Uganda Ltd –1, Centenary Bank.

Area under Forestation: 168,679 hectares.

Co-operative Societies: 51 cooperative societies.

Animal Population: Kiboga and Kyankwanzi have 365,154 cattle, 3 camels, 8 donkeys, 49,595 pigs, 26,270 sheep, 105,250 goats, 400 rabbits and 428,601 chicken, 4,582 ducks and 883 turkeys.

Health Services: 1 hospital (government – Kiboga Hospital with a total of 104 beds), 1 health centre IV (government), 8 health centre III (6 government, 1 private, 1 NGO), 18 health centre II (13 government, 5 NGO).

Education Services: Primary schools: 205 schools – 189 government, 9 private and 7 community. Enrolment: 74,530 – 16,899 male and 17,239 female. Primary school teachers: 885 – 506 male and 379 female. Secondary schools; 3 government, 8 private, 3 community.

Secondary school enrolment: 5,647 – 2,914 male and 2,733 female. Teachers: 270 male and female. Available furniture adequate for 4,573 students.

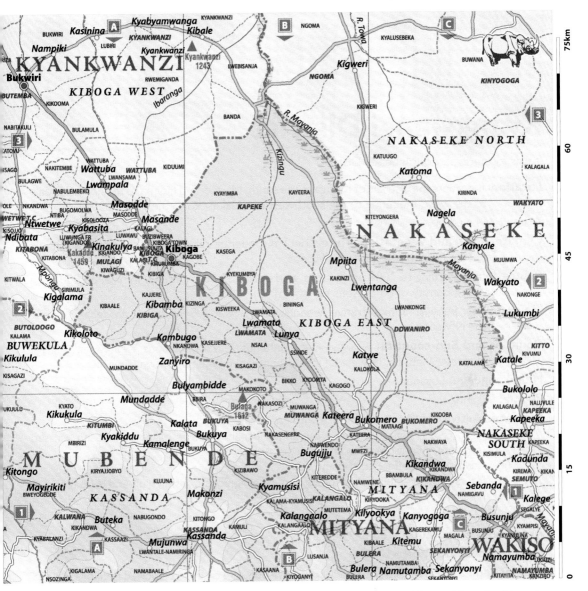

Key NGOs: African Medical Research Foundation Uganda, World Vision Uganda, Uganda Women's Effort to Save Orphans, Traditional and Modern Health Practitioners, Kiboga AIDS Awareness and Support Organisation, Kiboga Development Association, Kiboga Youth Drop-in Centre, Uganda Change Agent Association, Masodde Project CCF, Wattuba Youth Development Association.

District leaders:
Chairperson – Mr Yiga Israel
Chief Administrative Officer (CAO)
   – Ms Adongo Roseline Luhoni
Deputy CAO – Vacant
Town Clerk (Kiboga Town Council)
   – Mr John Gashenyi

Members of Parliament:
Kiboga County East
   – Mr Kabajo James Kyewalabye
Woman MP
   – Ms Ruth Sentamu Nankabirwa

Kyankwanzi District

It was formerly part of Mubende District.

Location: It borders the districts of Kiboga to the south, Masindi and Hoima to the north, Kibaale to the west, Mubende to the southwest and Nakaseke to the east.

Area: 2,444 sq. km.

Climate, Relief and Vegetation: The district has moderate rainfall and temperatures suitable for the growth of a number of crops.

Population: According to 2009 projections, there are 158,000 – 77,200 female, 80,800 male with a density of 65 persons per sq.km.

Major Towns: Bukwiri (administrative headquarters); Trading Centres – Kyabadeba, Masodde and Ntwetwe.

Counties and Sub-counties: Kiboga West – Butemba, Gayaza, Kitabona, Kyankwanzi, Mulagi, Nsambya, Wattuba, Ntwetwe (Town Council) and Butemba (Town Council).

Main Language: Luganda.

People: Baganda.

Economic Activities: Mainly agriculture with emphasis on:
  (i)   Food crops: Maize, beans, groundnuts, bananas, finger millet, soya bean, simsim (sesame), sweet potatoes and irish potatoes.
  (ii) Cash crops: Coffee, cotton and tea.
  (iii) Fruits and vegetables: Pineapples, tomatoes, onions, passion fruit and cabbage.
  (iv) Ranching.

Banks: Stanbic Bank Uganda Ltd –1.

Area under Forestation: 168,679 hectares.

Co-operative Societies: 51.

Animal Population: Kyankwanzi and Kiboga have 365,154 cattle, 3 camels, 8 donkeys, 49,595 pigs, 26,270 sheep, 105,250 goats, 400 rabbits and 428,601 chicken, 4,582 ducks and 883 turkeys.

Health Services: 1 health centre IV (government), 5 health centre III (all government), 5 health centre II (all government); Government District Hospital – Kiboga Hospital with a total of 104 beds.

Education Services: Primary schools: 205 – 189 government, 9 private and 7 community. Enrolment: 39,016 – 19,289 male and 19,727 female. Primary school teachers: 799 – 524 male, 275 female. 12 secondary schools; 6 government, 6 private. Secondary school enrolment: 2,758 male and 1,299 female. Teachers: 182 – 149 male and 33 female. Available furniture adequate for 1,940 students.

Key NGOs: African Medical Research Foundation Uganda, World Vision Uganda, Uganda Women's Effort to Save Orphans, Traditional and Modern Health Practitioners, Kiboga AIDS Awareness and Support Organisation, Kiboga Development Association, Kiboga

Youth Drop-in Centre, Uganda Change Agent Association, Masodde Project CCF, Wattuba Youth Development Association.

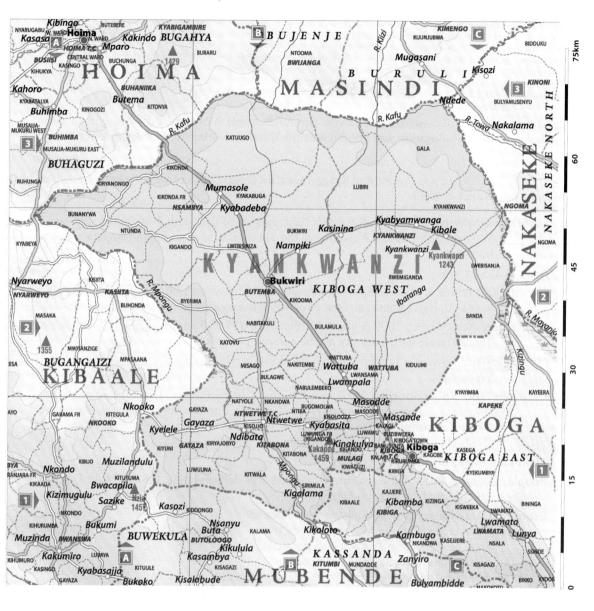

District leaders:
Chairperson
  – Mr Kinene Damulira Leopold
Chief Administrative Officer (CAO)
  – Mr Robert Mulondo
Deputy Chief Administrative Officer
  (DCAO) – Vacant

Members of Parliament:
Kiboga County West
  – Mr Ssemugaba Samuel
Woman MP – Ms Nankabirwa Ann Maria

Luweero District

At Independence, Luweero District was part of Buganda Kingdom. When kingdoms were abolished in 1967, Buganda was divided into the districts of Masaka, Mubende, West Mengo and East Mengo.

In 1974, East Mengo was divided into Kyaggwe and Bulemezi Districts, with the latter becoming Luweero District in 1980.

Location: Luweero borders the districts of Nakasongola to the north, Nakaseke to the west, Wakiso to the south, Mukono to the south and southeast then Kayunga to the northeast.

Area: 2,215 sq. km.

Climate and Relief: It lies at an approximate altitude of between 1,082m – 1,372m above sea level with high temperatures and rainfall of the modified equatorial climate type.

Population: According to 2009 projections, there are 399,900 people – 203,900 female and 196,000 male with a density of 180 persons per sq.km.

Major Towns: Luweero (administrative headquarters); Trading Centres – Bombo and Wobulenzi.

Counties and Sub-counties: Katikamu County – Butuntumula, Luweero, Makulubita, Nyimbwa, Katikamu, Luweero (Town Council), Bombo (Town Council), Wobulenzi (Town Council); Bamunanika County – Bamunanika, Kalagala, Kamira, Kikyusa, and Zirobwe.

Main Language: Luganda.

People: Baganda, Baruli, Nubians, Iteso, Banyankore, Banyarwanda, Basoga, Alur, Lugbara, other Ugandans and non-Ugandans.

Economic Activities: Mainly agriculture with a bias to:
(i) Food crops: Cassava, sweet potatoes, maize, groundnuts, beans, sorghum, bananas, soya bean, finger millet and Irish potatoes.
(ii) Cash crops: Cotton, coffee and cocoa.
(iii) Fruits and vegetables: Pineapples, tomatoes, onions and cabbage.

Area under Forestation: 237,450 hectares.

Animal Population: According to 2008 statistics, the district has 79,787 cattle, 68,527 goats, 13,275 sheep, 59,040 pigs, 464,943 chicken, 7,032 ducks and 1,398 turkeys.

Co-operative Societies: Luweero and Nakasongola have 191 registered primary societies with Buruli Union and East Mengo Growers Union at the district level.

Industries: Processing of coffee and milk, manufacturing of jaggery, furniture, *waragi* (local gin) and cotton ginning.

Banks: Stanbic Bank Uganda Ltd –1, DFCU Bank –1, Centenary Rural Development Bank –1.

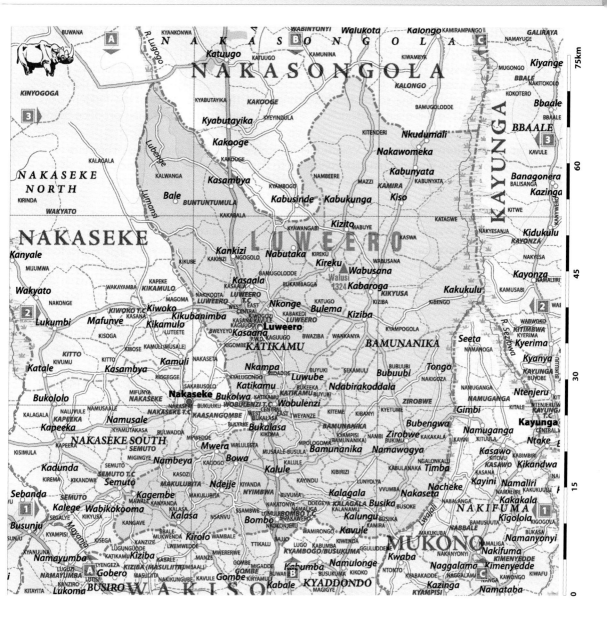

Education Services: Primary schools: 493 – 219 government, 150 private and 24 community. Enrolment: 153,101 pupils – 75,031 male and 78,070 female. Primary school teachers: 3,069 - 1,439 male and 1,630 female. Available furniture is adequate for 111,487.

Secondary schools: 71 schools - 18 government, 46 private and 7 community. Secondary school enrolment: 29,551 students – 14,533 male and 15,018 female. Teachers: 1,683 – 1,214 male, 469 female. Available furniture adequate for 26,084.

Tertiary institution: 2 teacher training colleges, 2 universities – Bugema University (1994), East African Christian University – Ndejje, College of Agriculture – Bukalasa.

Health Services: 3 hospitals (1 government, 1 military - Bombo Military Hospital and 1 NGO - Uganda Protestant Medical Bureau hospital – Kiwoko Hospital with 114 beds), 3

health centre IV (all government), 20 health centre III (13 government, 6 NGO, 1 private), 31 health centre II (15 government, 13 NGO, 3 private).

Transport Network: The district has an inadequate distribution of feeder-roads most of which are impassable during the rainy season. There is a main tarmac road linking Luweero to Kampala to the south and Nakasongola to the north. Most of the feeder-roads connect to this main road and this enables farmers to transport their produce to the markets.

Tourist Attractions: Walusi Hill: Walusi Hill is located about 25 kilometres from Luweero Town. The hill is of cultural significance to Baganda people. The shrines on the hill are used for cultural ceremonies such as traditional worship and offertory. Local spirits are believed to reside on the hill.

Bamunanika Palace: This is one of the King of Buganda's palaces and is located on the way to Walusi Hill and visitors to the hill can make a stop over here.

Additional Information: Luweero was devastated by a guerilla war 30 years ago. Agriculture and livestock rearing came to a halt. Today, that is all in the past. Agriculture is back to normal and livestock rearing is steadily picking up. Most of the peasants in the district produce for subsistence but sell the surplus. There are large scale farms in the district, as well as dairy farms.

The district has large tracts of unutilised land. Part of the central plateau is suitable for modern farming using tractors. Owing to the low population, the land is not heavily fragmented and is suitable for large scale farming.

Key NGOs: Send a Cow Uganda, Plan International, Concern for the Girl Child, African Medical Research Foundation, Family Planning Association of Uganda, VEDCO, World Vision Uganda, Environmental Alert, Traditional and Modern Health Practitioners, Community Development and Child Welfare Initiative, Promoting Moringa in Uganda, Uganda Society for Disabled Children, Association Francois-Xavier Bagnoud.

District leaders:	Members of Parliament:
Chairperson – Hajji Naduli Abdul	Katikamu County North
Chief Administrative Officer (CAO)	– Mr James Abraham Byandala
– Mr Nelson Kirenda	Katikamu County South
Deputy CAO – Vacant	– Mr Edward Khiddu Makubuya
Town Clerk (Luweero Town Council)	Bamunanika County
– Mr Muluta Mugaga	– Mr Muyingo John Chrysostom
Town Clerk (Bombo Town Council)	Woman MP
– Ms Halima Sebyala	– Ms Rebecca Nalwanga Lukwago
Town Clerk (Wobulenzi Town Council)	
– Mr Thomas Lutaaya	

THE REPUBLIC OF UGANDA

GOVERNMENT OF UGANDA
OFFICE OF THE PRIME MINISTER
LUWERO TRIANGLE

ACHIEVEMENTS UNDER LUWERO -RWENZORI DEVELOPMENT PROGRAMME 2009/10

Background

The Goverment of Uganda, through Office of the Prime Minister, designed the Luwero Rwenzori Development Programme (LRDP) as a special development recovery programme. During the FY 2009/10, the programme was piloted in the districts of Mukono, Wakiso, Luwero, Nakasongola, Nakaseke, Mityana, Mubende, Kiboga, Kyenjojo, Kabarole, Kasese, Bundibugyo, Kiruhura, Kamwenge and Kibaale.

In addition the programme is responsible for the payment of one-off gratuity to civilian veterans that contributed to the liberation struggle and the fight against insurgency in different parts of the regions.

Programme Goals and Objectives

The goal of the programme is to redress the adverse socio-economic effects of the liberation war and the ADF insurgency so as to improve the well-being of the population of Luwero and Rwenzori sub regions.

Hon. Nyombi Thembo MP
Minister of State Luwero Triangle

The specific objectives are;
i) To improve the economic wellbeing of 105 households per parish in 523 parishes by enabling them earn at least UGX 20 million per annum by 2015;

ii) To repair all road bottlenecks and improve the condition of 2,300 km district, 2900 km community access and 30 km urban roads to motorable state throughout the year by 2015;

iii) To increase the safe water coverage of the 11 districts below the national level coverage to 65% by 2015;

iv) To protect and sustainably manage the environment through use of environmentally friendly methods of production;

v) To increase access to renewable energy to service delivery points and rural growth centre's by 2015;

vi) To ensure that there is a government aided primary school and secondary school in all parishes and sub counties, respectively;

vii) To improve the health service delivery to the communities of the region;

viii) To promote peace, reconciliation and strengthen community based conflict mitigation and management within communities;

ix) To increase access and use of information and communications technology in the region and

x) To compensate civilian veterans who participated in the liberation struggle and the fight aganist ADF insurgency.

LRDP Programme Focus in 2009/10

The Programme has two components: (i) the Community Interventions (household income enhancement) and (ii) the Sector Interventions components that reinforce and support each other in improving the wellbeing of the population of the two sub regions. During 2009/10, the programme supported districts to implement sector interventions in education, health, water and sanitation, environment, energy and roads. In addition, the programme supported household income enhancement initiatives by providing grants to parishes through SACCOs; support to individual

Office of the Prime Minister, Postel Building, Yusuf Lule Road | **P. O. Box** 341, Kampala, Uganda
Tel: +256 414 344 839 | **Email:** lrdp.opm@gmail.com

microenterprises, support to commercialisation of agriculture, and provision of inputs and other materials for production especially to poor households that had challenges in increasing production.

Implementation Modalities

According to the LRDP design, implementation of the programme follows the government decentralised system where funds are channelled through the respective district local councils for implementation.
Government laws and procedures like the Local Government Act, Public Finance and Accountability Act, Public Procurement and Disposal of Public Assets Authority, Local Government Financial and Accounting Regulations, etc. are all applicable in implementation of the programme.

LRDP Achievements 2009/10

Community Interventions (Household Income Enhancement)

The LRDP supported a total of 3,135 households and 14 groups with various income generating projects.
Household Income Enhancement is a major component of the LRDP and during the 2009/10 FY, disbursements through districts to various households in the fifteen piloting districts were made.

The enterprises supported range from agricultural production, marketing and processing to transport, communication and small scale businesses as indicated in table below.

Enterprises Supported and Beneficiaries

	Type of enterprise	Quantity	Number of Beneficiary households / groups
1	Motorcycles (boda boda)	68	68
2	Heifers	305	250
3	Maize mills	4	4
4	Coffee seedlings	248,737	1,322
5	Banana Suckers	36,244	240
6	Hair salons and barber shops	17	17
7	Piglets and two boars	495	165
8	Pineapple Suckers	452,500	68
9	Chicken	6,480	102
10	Bee hives	330	30
11	Goats	1,264	257
12	Mixed commercial farmers	239	239
13	Small scale businesses (produce buying, retail shops, bakery, etc)	368	368
14	Carpentry	3	3
15	Metal fabrication unit	1	1
16	Brick making units	7	7
17	Incubators	2	2
18	Fishing gear, three sets of oxen and ploughs	2	5
19	Metric tonnes of maize seeds for commercialisation of agriculture	125	1
	Total		3,135 Households and 14 groups

Farming

The programme supported 2,673 household farming enteprises in areas of dairy farming, coffee growing, banana suckers, goat rearing, etc. For example over one hundred sixty five (165) households received 495 piglets from the programme. On average, each household received 2-4 piglets on the understanding that once they reproduced, a certain number of piglets is passed on other group members.
The piggery projects, due to the short gestation period of pigs, are having quik results for the beneficiaries with each piglets being sold at Shs. 60,000/=. More than 195 group members are expected to benefit within the next eight months thus increasing the multiplier effect of the programme. Sales from the piglet business are also enhancing the incomes of the beneficiaries in a relatively short period.

A piggery project for a beneficiary under parish grants in Mityana District

A heifer for one of the beneficiary of parish grants in Mityana District

Through micro loans received from SACCOs, a number of women groups have been supported to improve their incomes. With loans as little as Shs. 100,000 they have established fields of eggplants, tomatoes, cabbages, etc which have made a difference in their earning capabilities. For example, one beneficiary received Shs. 200,000 and invested in a ¾ acre egg-plants garden. Currently she harvests 2 bags of eggplants per week which is sold at Shs. 20,000 per bag. Given the current weekly earnings

projection, the beneficiary will earn Shs. 2,080,000 (52 weeks x 2 sacks x 20,000 per bag) for the next one year from an investment of only Shs. 200,000.

Members of Bukooko Women Action for Development (Kabalore District) in their tomatoes and egg plant gardens

Transport Sector

The programme supported 68 individuals to acquire loans through SACCOs for purchase of motor cycles for transport business, with the youth being the main beneficiaries. Transport business has been the most successful enterprise supported and most of the beneficiaries are already servicing their SACCO loans.

A youth waits for customers in Kamwenge District

Business Sector

The programme also supported 408 business enterprises-carpentry workshops, metal fabrication, salon and barber shop, bakeries, fishinggear, etc as wey of promoting household incomes.

A worker adds firewood in the oven of one of the small bakeries supported in Kamwenge District

SECTOR INTERVENTIONS

Under Sector Interventions, the LRDP supported various projects in areas of roads, water, health, energy, education, and environment.

I.Roads

The LRDP has earmarked improvement of the state of district and community roads as crucial in enabling communities to earn more from their enterprises. A total of **216.3 kilometres** of district and community roads have been rehabilitated.

District and Community roads rehabilitated by LRDP in 2009/10

	District	Roads
1	Bundibugyo	16 kms of Busaru Road
2	Kabalore	15.5 km Kicuucu – Lyamabwa; Kahondo, Kabagarana roads
		Kyabagajana – Kabagona Road
		5 kms Harugongo Kakundwa road
3	Kasese	1.5 km Of Mithimusanju – Kasanga Road
4	Kiboga	1 km along Kitumbi swamp
		39 km of Lubiri - Mpago – Nabweyo Road
		20 km Bakijulula – Muyenje – Masiriba Road

5	Luwero	9 kms Ndalike swamp Kibungo – Lwanyani Road
		15 km of community roads
6	Mubende	17 km of Kazigwe – Biwalume – Kyempazi road
		16 km Kiryanongo – Kasana Road
7	Nakaseke	21.8 km Towa – Rwesidizi Road
		3 km Biduku – Migyera Road
8	Kiruhura	12 km road opening and grading of Tangiriza, Kagaramira, Nkungu Road
		7.5 km opening and grading of Buyanga – Kiguma
		11 km Kikanja – Byabasita Kiguma Road
		3 km Kenwa - Kabimba Road
		3 km Buhembe Rweibugumya Road

The rehabilitation and opening of new community roads has had a tremendous improvement on the lives of the communities through better accessibility to previous hard--to-reach areas or reduced time and distance. In addition, the programme supported the construction of a foot bridge, and four small bridges in Kasese and Fort Portal districts.

A farmer transports bananas to the market along the graded Kicuucu – Lyamabwa Road in Kabarole District

The rehabilitation of Lubiri -Nabweyo - Mpango Road in Kiboga District has enabled taxis to move up to Mpango trading centre from the main road of Kyankwanzi-Butemba. Farmers easily transport their livestock products from Mpango and the nearby villages to Lubiri cattle loading market, thus enabling them to negotiate for higher prices. The opening of 3–kilometre Biduku – Migyera Road in Nakaseke has opened a link to Nakasongola District, reducing the distance by over five kilometres and greatly facilitating travel between the two areas.
The road spot improvement along Kitumbi Swamp along kabindula-Butologo road raised the road to avoid flooding during the wet season. As a result the does not flood, enabling motor vehicles to use the road throughout the year.

A 3 km hard core road spot along Kabindula – Butogolo Road in Kiboga District that was constructed with support from LRDP

The programme earmarked hard core road spots as priority during the piloting phase for projects that were not covered by the existing funding. The section of the Kabindula Butogolo Road repaired has enabled road users to cross the swamp throughout the year, something that was impossible during the rainy season.

II. Education

The LRDP programme is working towards improvement of education facilities at primary and secondary levels in the Luwero-Rwenzori regions. As a result, the LRDP has supported the construction of :

- Twenty two (22) staff houses in the district of Kasese, Nakaseke and Kiruhura;
- Twenty five (22) classrooms the district of Kabarole, Kasese and Luwero;
- Two (2) dormitory blocks in Mubende and Kasese;
- Forty three (43) toilet stances in the districts of Kasese, Mubende, Kiruhura and Bundibugyo; and
- One hundred (100) 3-seater desks procured in Mubende.

The construction of various educational facilities is crucial in improving performance and welfare of various institutions in the area. With support from LRDP, Butologo Seed Secondary School is constructing a girl's dormitory block.

A girl's dormitory block being constructed at Butologo Seed Sec. School, Mubende District

Once completed, the dormitory will offer decent accommodation to students but also enable girls to stay at school other than having to walk long distances to their homes which poses a danger to the girl child.

The programme is also supporting Lake Mburo Secondary School, in Kiruhura District with 16 units of staff houses with outside kitchen and toilets. The school had inadequate staff houses to accommodate the teachers.

One of the staff houses being constructed with LRDP support at Lake Mburo Secondary School, Kiruhura

A science kit supported by LRDP at Kiganda High School, Mubende

III.   Water and Sanitation

The LRDP supports districts to improve safe water coverage especially those that are below the national level of 65%. The programme is supplementing other government programmes in improving the situation. The programme supported the repairs of boreholes that provide safe water which sometimes breakdown and require regular servicing and repairs. The programme supported the rehabilitation of 46 boreholes, extension of a three-kilometre pipeline of

piped water to Naama trading centre in Mityana District, and constructed 57 animal watering points in Mubende, Nakaseke and Luwero districts.

A public water stand in Naama trading centre, Mityana District

With piped water connected, over 20 people have directly accessed water to their premises and 3 public water stands have been constructed for the community.

The community at Naama trading centre was relying on unprotected springs for water. However, with support from LRDP, the trading centre has been able to access clean water from the main Mityana water supply.

The rehabilitation of 46 boreholes in Luwero and Nakaseke districts has enabled communities to access safe water without having to travel long distances or resort to the use of unsafe sources like open ponds which may be contaminated. In addition, the repairs have alleviated the pressure on the few functioning boreholes.

A cattle watering point constructed with support from LRDP in Ngoma Sub-County, Nakaseke District

The programme has been able to support the construction of 57 watering points in the districts of Luwero, Nakaseke and Mubende. This has gone a long way in improving access to

water for animals by farmers which has been a challenge, especially during the dry season.

IV. Energy

The LRDP aims at improving the power connection to the national grid to a number of rural growth centres as a way of stimulating rural growth. The programme aims at supporting installation of step-down transformers and power lines to connect to various locations and institutions that have been unable to do so in an effort to improve not only service delivery but to support agro-processing and value addition.

- 1.3 km of power line to Nkimbiri TC, Kabarole District;
- 2.5 km power line Kibito TC, Buhesi SC, Kabarole District; and
- 2 km power line to Nyamango Polytechnic Institute, Kyenjojo District.

The extension of power has encouraged the establishment of business like hair salon and welding/metal fabrication

V. Health

The government aims at strengthening health delivery systems as a way of attaining MDGS in areas of health. However, a number of districts still face challenges in health infrastructure and a number of these are in Luwero Rwenzori regions. The LRDP was able to support the construction of specific infrastructural projects in the health sector as indicated below

Health Infrastructure Supported

	District	Intervention
1	Bundibugyo	1 health block at Bulyambwa Health Centre
2	Kasese	2 maternity wards, 1 staff house, and 7 block building at various health centres
3	Kyenjojo	1 maternity ward and 2 HC building at Kisojo and Kataraza
4	Luwero	1 health centre block at Lutuula HC II
5	Mityana	Fencing of Cardinal Wamala Health Centre, Kadde

A maternity ward being constructed with support from LRDP at Kisojo Health Centre III, Kyenjojo District

The programme has been able to support the construction of 9 health centre blocks, four maternity buildings and two staff houses at the various health centres within the region.

Inputs Procured and Distributed to the Poor

In an effort to support agricultural production for the poor as well as improve their welfare, the programme procured and distributed hand hoes, spray pumps, cement and iron sheets as indicated below.

Materials Procured and Distributed

S/n	Items	Quantities
1	Hand hoes	42,757
2	Spray pumps	900
3	Iron sheets	10,100
4	Cement (bags)	4,332
5	Hydra form machines	5

The hydra form machines are for use in constructing low cost houses for the very poor, civilian veterans and institutions.

Payment of a One-off Gratuity (*Akasimo*)

The Luwero Triangle portfolio is also responsible for managing compensation to third parties (payment of one-off gratuity). The *akasimo* payment is for those civilian veterans who participated alongside the combatants in the NRM liberation struggle and containing the ADF insurgency. During the last financial year, **3104 civilian veterans** were paid one off gratuity from twenty one districts.

Conclusion

The communities in the Luwero-Rwenzori regions have high expectation of the programme as we start full implementation in the 40 districts. The piloting phase has resulted in real tangible benefits to the households participating in the programme. The disbursement of parish grants through SACCOs is strengthening them and improving their relevance to their communities. The community and district roads rehabilitated have improved access to markets for farmers.

Lwengo District

Lwengo District came into existence in 2010 when parts of Masaka District were elevated to district status.

Location: Lwengo borders the districts of Lyantonde in the west, Rakai in the south, Sembabule and Bukomansimbi to the north and Masaka to the east.

Area: 1,025 sq. km.

Climate and Relief: It lies at an altitude of between 1,219m and 1,524m above sea level. Temperatures are moderately high with rainfall throughout the year.

Population: According to the 2009 projections, the district has 254,500 people – 131,900 female and 122,600 male with a density of 248 persons per sq.km.

Main Towns: Lwengo (administrative headquarters), Kyazanga, Kinoni.

Counties and Sub-counties: Lwengo County – Lwengo, Kyazanga, Malongo, Kingo, Ndagwe, Kisekka, Lwengo (Town Council), Kyazanga (Town Council);

Main Language: Luganda, Runyankore.

People: Baganda, Banyankore, Banyarwanda.

Economic Activities: Mainly agriculture with a bias to:
- (i) Food crops: Sweet potatoes, bananas, beans, maize, cassava, groundnuts, soya bean, sorghum and finger millet.
- (ii) Cash crops: Coffee, cotton and maize.
- (iii) Fruits and vegetables: Pineapples, tomatoes, onions and cabbage.
- (iv) Cattle ranching.
- (v) Fishing on Lake Victoria.

Banks: Stanbic Bank Uganda Ltd, DFCU Bank, Centenary Rural Development Bank.

Area under Forestation: 21,990 hectares.

Animal Population: According to 2008 livestok census, Lwengo, Kalungu, Bukomansimbi, and Masaka districts have 224,600 cattle, 236,148 pigs, 28,652 sheep, 244,706 goats, 1,108,363 chicken, 58,723 ducks and 16,223 turkeys.

Co-operative Societies: Lwengo, Bukomansimbi, Kalungu, Masaka and Sembabule have 308 registered primary societies with Masaka Co-operative Unionas the main society.

Industries: Manufacture of cassava starch, curry powder, garments, animal feeds, soft drinks, footwear, laundry soap, metalwork, furniture, jaggery, processing of tea, coffee, hand weaving and cotton ginning.

Education Services: Primary schools: 157 – 120 government, 31 private and 6 community. Enrolment: 80,743 pupils – 38,961 male and 41,782 female. Primary school teachers: 1,586 – 794 male and 792 female. Available furniture is adequate for 56,737 pupils.

Secondary schools: 15 schools - 5 government, 8 private and 2 community. Secondary school enrolment: 6,604 male and female. Teachers: 238 – 265 male and 63 female. Available furniture is adequate for 5,687 students.

Health Services: 3 health centre IV (all government), 4 health centre III (2 government, 2 NGO), and 14 health centre II (6 government, 8 NGO).

Transport Network: The district has a well distributed feeder-road network which connects all counties and most sub-counties. The roads are in fairly good condition. Tarmac

roads connect the district to Mbarara, Rakai and Mpigi. The feeder-roads link up with the main tarmac roads which facilitate transport to the neighbouring districts.

Operational Radio and TV Stations: Central Broadcasting Service, Star Radio, Bwala Hill 88.0 FM, Radio West, Equator Radio, Buddu Broadcasting Services, Kalungu Foundation Ltd, Radio Maria Uganda Association, Christian Life Ministries, Uganda Broadcasting Corporation Radio, Christian Radio Network, Baptist International Mission (U) and Voice of Africa (MMC for ES and SA). Uganda Broadcasting Corporation Television and WBS Limited.

Key NGOs: Send a Cow Uganda, World Vision Uganda, Uganda Women's Effort to Save Orphans, Kitenga Development Foundation, Child Restoration Outreach.

District leaders:	Members of Parliament:
Chairperson	Bukoto County West – Mr Aboud Kitatta
– Mr Mutabazi George	Bukoto County South
Chief Administrative Officer (CAO)	– Mr Mbabaali Muyanja
– Mr Samuel Ruhweza Kaija	Bukoto County Mid-West
Deputy Chief Administrative Officer	– Mr Isaac Sejjoba
(CAO) – Vacant	Woman MP
	– Ms Nakabira Gertrude Lubega

Lyantonde District

Formerly known as Kabula County in Rakai District, Lyantonde became a district in July 2006.

Location: Lyantonde District borders the districts of Masaka to the east, Rakai to the south, Kiruhura to west and Sembabule to the north.

Area: 888 sq.km

Counties/Sub-counties: Kabula County – Kasagama, Kaliiro, Kinuuka, Mpumudde, Lyantonde and Lyantonde Town Council.

Climate and Relief: Lyantonde district lies in the dry belt of the cattle corridor and is largely a pastoral area. Lyantonde and Kaliiro have hilly features while Mpumudde, Kinuuka and Kasagama are wide flat valleys. The soils are generally lithoid with stony and sometimes bare rocks.

Population: Based on the 2009 population and housing census, there are 74,100 people – 37,400 female and 36,700 male with a density of 83 persons per sq.km.

Major Town: Lyantonde Town Council

Main Language: Luganda and Lunyakole.

People: Baganda, Banyankole and Banyarwanda.

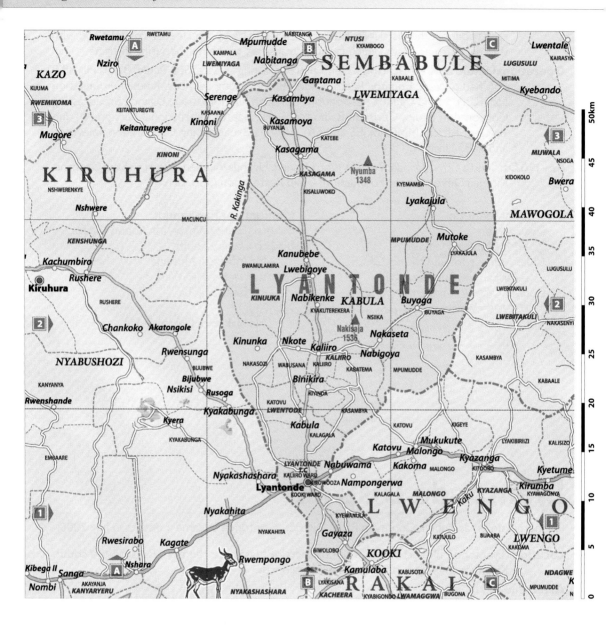

Economic Activities: A large sections (60%) of the population is engaged in livestock farming. The rest is engaged in crop farming. Some of the crops grown are potatoes, bananas, beans, groundnuts, maize, onions, coffee, millet and sorghum.

Animal Population: Lyantonde has 68,572 cattle, 58,642 goats, 5,590 sheep, 7,770 pigs, 73,588 chicken, 2,392 ducks and 259turkeys, according to 2008 statistics.

Banks: Stanbic Bank Uganda Ltd and other banks

Industries: Manufacture of food products, beverages, apparel dressing, dyeing of fur, fabricated metal products and furniture.

Education Services: 46 primary schools; 35 government aided primary schools, 10 private, and 1 community. Enrolment: 18,135 pupils – 9,057 males and 9,078 female. Teachers: 506 – 301 males and 205 female.

Secondary schools: 9 schools: 4 government, 3 private and 2 community. Enrolment: 2,381 students - 1,298 male and 1,083 female. Available furniture adequate for 1,970 students.

Health Services: 1 hospital (government), 6 health centre III (all government), 3 health centre II (all government).

Tourist Attractions: The Wold War Caves at Lyantonde are the main attraction in the district.

Key NGOs: The same as those in mother district, Rakai.

District Leaders:	Members of Parliament:
District Chairman – Muhangi Fred	Kabula County – Mr James Kakooza
CAO – Ms. Olive Hope Nakyanzi.	District Woman MP
Deputy CAO – Mr Samuel Ruhweza Kaja	– Ms Grace K. Namara
Town Clerk – Nayebare Fred K.	

Masaka District

Masaka District came into existence in 1967 after the abolition of Buganda Kingdom. It was one of the four districts carved out of Buganda Kingdom, the others being Mubende, East Mengo and West Mengo.

Location: Masaka borders the districts of Lwengo to the west; Rakai to the south; Mpigi and Butambala to the northeast; Kalangala to the east and Bukomansimbi and Kalungu to the north.

Area: 2,196 sq. km.

Climate and Relief: It lies at an altitude of 1,219m – 1,524m above sea level. Temperatures are moderately high with rainfall throughout the year.

Population: According to 2009 projections, there are 239,700 people – 123,700 female, 116,000 male with a density of 109 persons per sq.km.

Main Towns: Masaka (administrative headquarters); Trading Centres – Lukaya, Kinoni, Mateete and Mbirizi.

Counties and Sub-counties: Bukoto County – Bukakata, Buwunga, Mukungwe, Kabonera, Kyanamukaka and Kyesiga; Masaka Municipality – Katwe/Buttego, Kimanya/Kyabakuza, and Nyendo/Senyange.

Main Language: Luganda.

People: Baganda.

Economic Activities: Mainly agriculture with a bias to:
  (i)   Food crops: Sweet potatoes, bananas, beans, maize, cassava, groundnuts, soya bean, sorghum and finger millet.

(ii)   Cash crops: Coffee, cotton and maize.

(iii) Fruits and vegetables: Pineapples, tomatoes, onions and cabbage.

(iv) Cattle ranching.

(v)   Fishing on Lake Victoria.

Banks: Stanbic Bank Uganda Ltd-1, DFCU Bank –1, Centenary Rural Development Bank –1, Bank of Baroda-1, Standard Chartered Bank-1.

Area under Forestation: Masaka, Lwengo, Kalungu, and Bukomansimbi have 21,990 hectares.

Animal Population: According to 2008 livestok census, Masaka, Lwengo, Kalungu, and Bukomansimbi districts have 224,600 cattle, 236,148 pigs, 28,652 sheep, 244,706 goats, 1,108,363 chicken, 58,723 ducks and 16,223 turkeys.

Co-operative Societies: Masaka and Sembabule have 308 registered primary societies with Masaka Co-operative Union at the district level.

Industries: Manufacture of cassava starch, curry powder, garments, animal feeds, soft drinks, footwear, laundry soap, metalwork, furniture, jaggery, processing of tea, coffee, hand weaving and cotton ginning.

Education Services: Primary schools: 180 – 116 government, 58 private and 6 community. Enrolment: 68,121 pupils – 33, 379 male and 34,742 female. Primary school teachers: 1,757 – 817 male and 940 female. Available furniture is adequate for 59,030 pupils.

Secondary schools; 28 schools - 4 government, 21 private and 3 community. Secondary school enrolment: 16,894 students – 8,936 male and 7,958 female. Teachers: 970 – 728 male and 243 female. Available furniture is adequate for 14,328.

Tertiary institutions: 2 technical institutions, 2 teacher training colleges and Masaka Comprehensive Nursing, University – Mutesa 1 Loyal University.

Health Services: 2 hospitals (government – Masaka Hospital Regional Referral with 330 beds, NGO - Kitovu Hospital with 220 beds) 4 health centres IV - (3 government, 1 NGO), 6 health centre III (4 government, 2 NGO), and 13 health centre II - (9 government, 4 NGO).

Transport Network: The district has a well distributed feeder-road network which connects all sub-counties. The roads are in fairly good condition. Tarmac roads connect the district to Lyantonde, Rakai and Mpigi.

Tourist Attractions: Masaka was extensively damaged during the Tanzanian invasion of 1979 and much of the destruction has not been repaired. Leaving the town to the south is the road through Mutukula to Tanzania – the route through which the Tanzanian troops advanced to liberate Uganda from the rule of Idi Amin.

Lake Nabugabo is a small, oval lake and is located about 3 km from the western shores of Lake Victoria. It is a popular place to relax and watch birds, either along the shores of the lake, or from a fishing boat.

The Church of Uganda Guest House at Lake Nabugabo, was built in 1926 as a holiday resort and conference centre for the missionaries of the church.

Nabugabo sand beach, 1km from the Church of Uganda Guest House is lively and a nice place to swim. Camping is permitted but bring your own equipment.

Bukakata Landing Site is another site of interest to tourists visiting the area.

Some of the famous legendary Bachwezi settlements are found in Ntusi, here in Masaka.

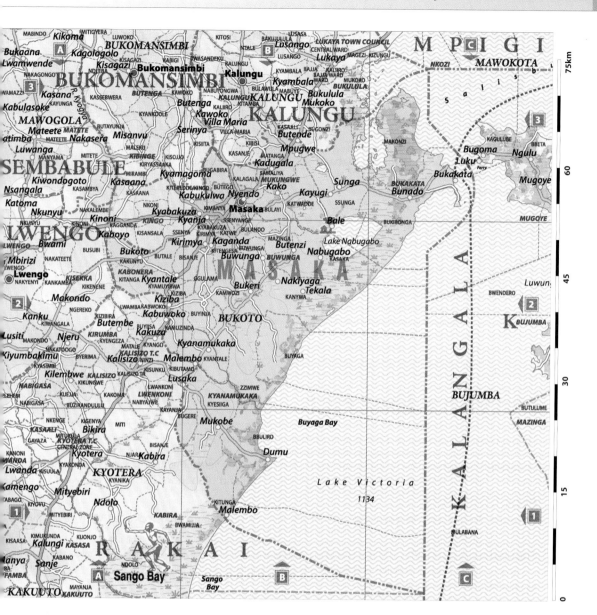

Additional Information: Masaka District is highly productive agriculturally. The farmers in the district grow crops with the intention of selling them, although crop production is basically subsistence. Most of the crops have a market in Kampala. The changes in the country have transformed farming in Masaka into a reasonably profitable enterprise. Large scale farms, fruit growing and cattle ranching are making steady progress. Coffee farmers have benefited from the liberalisation of the coffee industry since, unlike in the past, they are promptly paid for their coffee.

Operational Radio and TV Stations: Central Broadcasting Service, Star Radio, Bwala Hill 88.0 FM, Radio West, Equator Radio, Buddu Broadcasting Services, Kalungu Foundation Ltd, Radio Maria Uganda Association, Christian Life Ministries, Uganda Broadcasting Corporation Radio, Christian Radio Network, Baptist International Mission (U), Voice of Africa (MMC for ES and SA), UBC TV and WBS TV.

Key NGOs: Send a Cow Uganda, World Vision Uganda, Uganda Women's Effort to Save Orphans, Kitenga Development Foundation, Child Restoration Outreach.

District leaders:	Members of Parliament:
Chairperson – Mr Kalungi Joseph	Bukoto County East
Chief Administrative Officer (CAO)	– Ms Namayanja Florence
– Mr George Ntulume	Masaka Municipality – Mr Mpuuga Mathias
Deputy Chief Administrative Officer	Bukoto County Central
(CAO) – Mr Kisule Martin Mabandha	– Mr Edward Kiwanuka Ssekandi
Town Clerk (Masaka Municipal Council)	Woman MP
– Mr Lawrence Bagerize	– Ms Kase-Mubanda Freda Nanziri
Mayor (Masaka Municipality)	
– Mr Godfrey Kayemba	

Mityana District

Mityana District was up to 2005 a part of Mubende District.

Location: Borders with Kiboga to the north, Luweero District to the northeast, Wakiso District to the southeast, Mpigi District to the south and Mubende District to the west.

Area: 1,578 sq. kms.

Climate, Relief and Vegetation: Generally flat with undulating hills covered with savannah grasslands.

Population: According to 2009 projections, there are 291,500 people – 147,100 female, 144,400 male with a density of 184 persons per sq. km.

Major Town: Mityana Town Council

Counties and Sub-counties: Mityana County – Mityana Town Council, Bulera, Kikandwa, Sekanyonyi; Busujju County – Maanyi, Butayunja, Kakindu, Malangala and Busimbi.

Main Language: Luganda

People: Baganda, Banyarwanda, Banyoro, Banyankore, Bakiga, Bafumbira, Batooro, Basoga, Banyabindi, other Ugandans and non-Ugandans.

Economic Activities: Mainly agriculture with emphasis on food crops. Some of the cash crops are coffee and tea.

Animal Population: Basing on 2008 livestock statistics the district has 75,767 cattle, 51,029 goats, 18,000 sheep, 80,346 pigs, 364,398 chicken, 8,449 ducks and 1,786 turkeys.

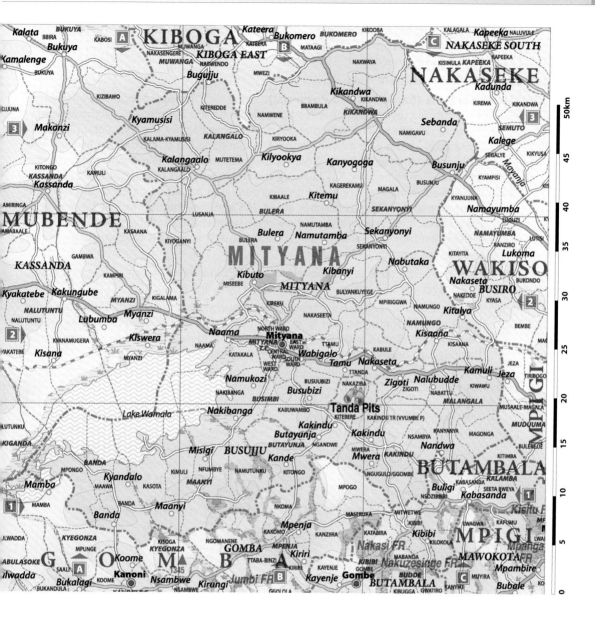

Industries: Manufacture of furniture, metal products, textiles and wearing apparel, grain mill products, dairy products, footwear, food products, bakery products, vegetable and animal oils and fats, printing and publishing, coffee processing, tea processing and sawmilling and planing of wood.

Education Services: Primary schools: 236– 157 government, 71 private and 8 community. Enrolment: 73,346 – 36,348 male and 36,998 female. Primary school teachers: 2,039 – 956 male and 1,083 female. Available furniture is adequate for 58,029.

Secondary schools: 39 schools - 11 governments, 24 private and 4 community. Secondary school enrolment: 14,446 students – 6,999 male and 7,447 female. Teachers: 839 - 636 male and 203 female. Available furniture adequate for 13,051 students.

Health Services: 1 hospital (government - Mityana Hospital with 100 beds), 3 health centre IV (2 government, 1 NGO), 12 health centre III; (8 government, 4 NGO), 29 health centre II (19 government, 10 NGO).

Operational Radio Station: Radio Skynet Ltd.

Tourist Attractions (Exploited and Potential): Tanda Pits: These are located 8 kilometres from Mityana town, 92 kilometres from Mubende and 3 kilometres off the Kampala-Mubende Highway. The legend about their existence goes that Walumbe ("Death") is the sister to the wife (Nambi) of the first Ganda to live on earth from heaven. The pits were created as Walumbe kept escaping from a brother (Kayikuzi) who had come to return him to heaven. Kayikuzi dug the pits in an effort to capture Walumbe who is believed to have disappeared underground and remained on earth to cause the death of people. The pits number about 266 and their bottom cannot be seen with naked eyes. It is believed they were more than that and some have been filled up to provide land for cultivation. Most striking about these pits is their similarity in size and precise equality in diameter.

Lake Wamala: Found in Busimbi sub-county. Culturally significant to Baganda ethnic group who link its origin to the existence of their first King.

Magongo Shrines: Located in Malangala sub-county, the shrines are believed to be the burial place of Kintu, the first King of the Baganda. The site comprises a tile-roofed house where Kintu's and other graves are found. Near the shrine is a forest where the kings are believed to disappear when they die.

District Leaders:	**Members of Parliament:**
District Chairperson – Ms Kyazike Debora	Busujju County
CAO – Ms. Grace Namukhula Watuwa	– Mr Vincent Makumbi Nyanzi
Deputy CAO – Mr Esau ekachelan	Mityana County North
	– Mr Kiwanda Godfrey Ssuubi
	Mityana County South
	– Mr Jerome Sozi Kaddumukasa
	District Woman MP
	– Ms Sylvia Namabidde Ssinabulya

Mpigi District

At independence in 1962, it was part of Buganda Kingdom. Following the abolition of kingdoms in 1967, Buganda was divided into four districts – East Mengo, West Mengo, Mubende and Masaka Districts.

Under the 1974 provincial administration, West Mengo became Mengo District, which in 1980 became Mpigi District. In 2000, Busiro and Kyadondo counties and Entebbe Municipality were separated from it to create Wakiso District.

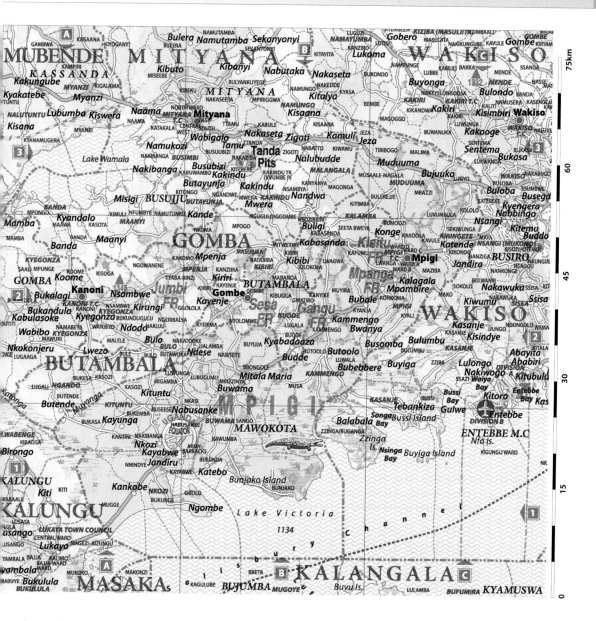

Location: It borders the Districts of Butambala to the west, Mityana to the northwest, Wakiso to the east, northeast and north, Kalangala to the south and Kalungu to the west.

Area: 1,526 sq. km.

Climate and Relief: It lies at an approximate altitudinal range of between 1,182m – 1,341m above sea level. The district receives heavy and reliable rainfall and has relatively high temperatures. Mpigi gets 1,513mm of rain per annum.

Population: According to 2009 projections, there are 202,700 people – 101,400 female and 101,300 male with a density of 133 persons per sq.km.

Major Towns: Mpigi (administrative headquarters); Trading Centre – Buwama.

Counties and Sub-counties: Mawokota County – Kamengo, Kiringente, Mpigi, Mpigi (Town Council), Mudduma, Buwama, Kituntu, and Nkozi.

Main Language: Luganda.

People: Baganda.

Economic Activities: Mainly agriculture with a bias towards:
   (i)   Food crops: Sweet potatoes, beans, cassava, maize, bananas, groundnuts, sorghum, soya bean and Irish potatoes.
   (ii) Cash crops: Coffee and cotton.
   (iii) Fruits and vegetables: Tomatoes, onions and cabbage.
   (iv) Dairy farming.
   (v)   Fishing.

Banks: Stanbic Bank Uganda Ltd – 4 and other banks.

Area under Forestation: Mpigi and Butambala have 71,950 hectares.

Animal Population: According to 2008 statistcis Mpigi, Gomba and Butambala have 216,621 cattle, 108,082 pigs, 23,221 sheep, 102,828 goats, 600,950 chicken, 10,456 ducks and 1,143 turkeys.

Co-operative Societies: Mpigi and Wakiso have 341 registered primary societies with West Mengo Co-operative Union at the district level.

Industries: Manufacture of jaggery, footwear, furniture, printing, brick making, stone quarrying, processing of coffee, tea and bakeries.

Education Services: Primary schools: 150 – 114 government, 30 private and 6 community. Enrolment: 66,945 pupils – 32,754 male and 34,191 female. Primary school teachers: 1,331 - 582 male and 749 female. Available furniture is adequate for 51,964 pupils.

Secondary schools: 40 schools - 6 government, 31 private, 3 community. Secondary school enrolment: 15,591 – 7,579 male and 8,012 female. Teachers: 1,018 – 739 male and 279 female. Available furniture is adequate for 12,391 students.

Tertiary: 1 technical institution, 1 national teacher's college – Nkozi, 1 university – Uganda Martyrs University Nkozi and Nsamizi Institute of Social work.

Health Services: 1 hospital (NGO - Nkozi Hospital with 90 beds), 1 health centre IV (government), 16 health centre III, (10 government, 6 NGO), and 10 health centre II, (government, 1 NGO).

Tourist Attractions: Mpanga Forest Reserve – It is about an hour's drive from the Kampala City. The main attractions are the mighty trees with their knotted roots. There are monkeys, birds and butterflies. Snakes can also be seen – some of them dangerous, so tour the forest with care and possibly with a guide. The forest provides five types of timber used in the making of drums. The royal drum makers are located in the nearby village of Mpambire.

Three trails have been marked; the Base line trail, the Butterfly loop and the 5 km Hornbill trail with exotic fungi, butterflies, birds and monkeys.

In the same area, along the Kampala-Masaka Highway, two large concrete circles on both sides of the road mark the Equator. Next to the Equator points are art and crafts shops and a restaurant.

The Katonga River, which links Lake Victoria and Lake George, can be seen.

Operational TV Station: Uganda Broadcasting Corporation - UBC TV and Radio.

Key NGOs: Send a Cow Uganda, VEDCO, World Vision Uganda, Integrated Rural Development Initiatives, African Network for the Prevention and Protection Against Child Abuse and Neglect Uganda Chapter, Concern Uganda, Nkozi AIDS Project, Elderly Welfare Mission, Dutch Uganda Orphans Project, Gomba AIDS Support and Counselling

Organisation, Omega Women's Group, Waggumbulizi Foundation, Kibibi Women's Association, Uganda Red Cross.

District leaders:
Chairperson – Mr Luwakanya John
Chief Administrative Officer (CAO)
  – Mr Solomon Musoke Kalibwanyi
Deputy CAO
  – Ms. Flida Kyendibaiza Naboye
Town Clerk (Mpigi Town Council)
  – Mr Sam Kayongo

Members of Parliament:
Mawokota County South
  – Mr Kiyingi Bbosa Kenneth Joseph
Mawokota County North
  – Mr Kyambadde Amelia Anne
Woman MP
  – Ms Nakawunde Sarah Temulanda

Mubende District

At independence in 1962 it was part of Buganda Kingdom. Following the abolition of kingdoms in 1967, it became one of the districts carved out of Buganda Kingdom.

Location: It borders the districts of Mityana to the east and southeast, Sembabule and Mpigi to the south, Kyenjojo to the southwest, Kibaale to the northwest and Kiboga to the north and norteast.

Area: 4,621 sq.kms.

Climate and Relief: It lies at an altitude of 1,372m – 1,448m above sea level with high temperatures and remarkably low rainfall.

Population: According to 2009 projections, there are 535,500 people – 270,200 female and 265,300 male with a density of 116 persons per sq.km.

Major Towns: Mubende (administrative headquarters).

Counties and Sub-counties: – Buwekula County – Butoloogo, Kitenga, Kiyuni, Madudu, and Mubende (Town Council); Kassanda County – Bukuya, Kassanda, Kalwana, Kitumbi Makokoto, Kiganda, Myanzi, Manyogaseka, Nalutuntu. Kasambya County – Bagezza, Kibalinga, Kasambya, Kigando, and Nabingoola.

Main Language: Luganda.

People: Baganda, Banyoro, Banyankore, Bakiga, Bafumbira, Banyarwanda, Bakhonzo, Batooro.

Economic Activities: Mainly agriculture with emphasis on:
(i) Food crops: Maize, beans, sweet potatoes, Irish potatoes, groundnuts, bananas, finger millet, simsim (sesame), soya bean and yams.
(ii) Cash crops: Coffee, cotton and tea.
(iii) Fruits and vegetables: Tomatoes, pineapples, passion fruit, onions and cabbage.
(iv) Cattle ranching and dairy farming.

Banks: Stanbic Bank Uganda Ltd –2, Centenary Rural Development Bank Ltd –1.

Area under Forestation: 124,157 hectares.

Animal Population: Basing on 2008 livestock statistics the district has 208,535 cattle, 139,400 goats, 31,094 sheep, 98,487 pigs, 536,342 chicken,12,525 ducks and 1,614 turkeys.

Co-operative Societies: 148 registered primary societies with Wamala Co-operative Union at the district level.

Industries: Processing of coffee and tea, bread baking, maize milling, brick making, printing and manufacture of jaggery.

Education Services: Primary schools: 316 – 220 government, 78 private and 18 community. Enrolment: 123,879 pupils – 61,751 male and 62, 128 female. Primary school teachers: 2,423 – 1,326 male and 1,097 female. Available furniture adequate for 81,557 pupils.

41 secondary schools; Secondary School enrolment: 14,040 – 7,894 male and 7,365 female. Teachers: 773 - 608 male and 165 female. Available furniture adequate for 12,163 students.

Tertiary institution: 1 Technical institutions, 2 teacher training colleges. 1 national Teacher's college – Mubende.

Health Services: 1 hospital (government - Mubende Hospital with 100 beds), 2 health centre IV (all government), 11 health centre II (9 government, 2, NGO), 32 health centre II (26 government, 6 NGO).

Operational Radio Station: Voice of Tooro, Buddu FM, CBS.

Tourist Attractions (Exploited and Potential): Nakayima Shrine A tree whose base has large root buttresses forming nooks and fissures located on Mubende Hill about 4 km out of town. The 213m hill with a flat table top where the ancient palace once stood, provides an excellent view of Mubende town and the surrounding area. The shrine is visited by people paying homage to the matriach Nakayima of the *Bachwezi*, a semi-god group that was believed to be immortal. Nakayima tree is said to have been planted by Ndahura, the first *Muchwezi* king. Excavations of the *Bachwezi*, like clay pots have been found here.

Muyinayina and Butorogo Rocks: The Muyinayina and Butorogo Rocks are found 20 kilometres from Mubende town in Kasambya sub-county. These rocks are said to have been a place where the Kings of Bunyoro used to play the Drafts (Mweso). The Drafts holes are dug in the rocks and are visible up to today. Although the rocks have no cultural significance, they are a popular camping site.

River Katabalanga: The river flows through areas close to Mubende Town Council. It is the place where legend says Isimbwa killed his brother Kayikuzi.

Key NGOs: Send a Cow Uganda, Family Planning Association of Uganda, Actionaid, Uganda Agali Wamu Members Group, Akwata Mpola Namago Women's Group, Balikyewunya Development Organisation, Barandiza Kimeze Youth Group, Kolping House Mityana Women's Group, Link Rural Based Organisation, Mityana Organisation of Disadvantaged Groups, Mubende Districts Farmers' Association, Kassanda Cornerstone Foundation, Butoloogo Rural Development Association.

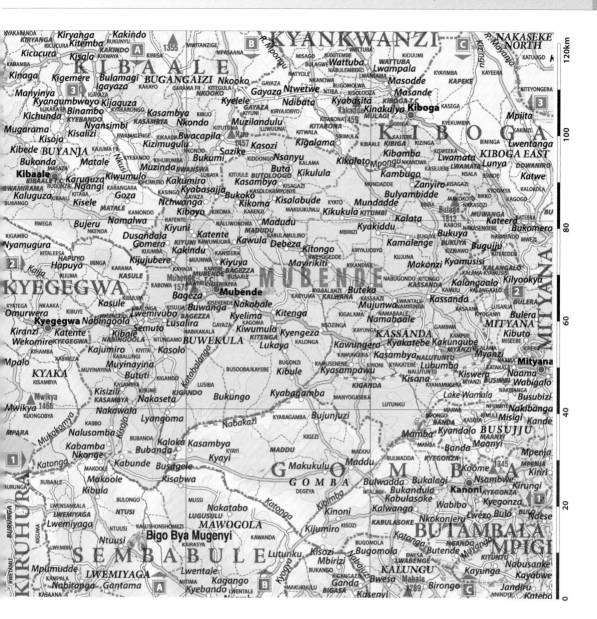

District leaders:

Chairperson – Mr Bazigatirawo K Francis

Chief Administrative Officer (CAO)
 – Mr Ocakara Nicholas

Deputy CAO – Vacant

Town Clerk (Mubende Town Council)
 – Mr Walusimbi Musoke

Town Clerk (Mityana Town Council)
 – Mr Edward Lwanga

Members of Parliament:

Buwekula County – Mr Anthony Ssemmuli

Kassanda County South
 – Mr Nyombi Thembo George William

Kassanda County North
 – Mr Lubega Godfrey

Kasambya County – Mr Mulindwa Patrick

District Woman MP
 – Ms Namugwanya Benny Bugembe

Mukono District

At independence in 1962, it was part of Buganda. Following the abolition of kingdoms in 1967, it became one of the districts carved out of Buganda Kingdom and was named East Mengo.

Under the 1974 provincial admininstation it was renamed Kyagwe District. In 1980, it became Mukono District.

Location: Mukono District borders the districts of Buikwe and Buvuma to the east, Kayunga to the north, Kampala, Luweero and Wakiso to the west and Kalangala to the south.

Area: 4,125 sq. km.

Climate and Relief: It lies at an altitudinal range of 1,158m to 1,219m above sea level with high temperatures and heavy rainfall. For example, in the period April – June 1991, it received 470mm of rain in 44 rain days.

Population: 498,500 people – 253,700 females and 244,800 male with a density of 120 persons per sq.km.

Major Towns: Mukono (administrative headquarters), Seeta; Trading Centres –Nakifuuma and Kyerima.

Counties and Sub-counties: Mukono County – Kyampisi, Nama, Kkoome Island, Nakisunga, Ntenjeru, Mpunge, Mpatta; Nakifuma County – Kasawo, Kimenyedde, Nabbale, Nagojje, Namuganga, and Ntunda; Mukono Municipality – Goma Division and Mukono Division.

Main Language: Luganda.

People: Baganda.

Economic Activities: Mainly agriculture with emphasis on:
(i) Food crops: Cassava, sweet potatoes, beans, maize, finger millet, groundnuts, soya bean, bananas, sorghum, simsim (sesame), cow peas, pigeon peas and yams.
(ii) Cash crops: Cotton, coffee, sugar cane and tea.
(iii) Fruits and vegetables: Tomatoes, onions, pineapples, vanilla, chillies, passion fruit and cabbage.
(iv) Dairy farming.
(v) Fishing on Lake Victoria.

Banks: Stanbic Bank Uganda Ltd – 2, Centenary, Crane Bank, others

Animal Population: Mukono, Buikwe and Buvuma districts have 155,820 cattle, 61 donkeys, 181,846 pigs, 30,808 sheep, 206,704 goats, 1,551,702 chicken, 49,517 ducks and 5,558.

Co-operative Societies: Mukono, Buikwe, Buvuma and Kayunga have 267 registered primary societies with East Mengo Union at the district level.

Industries: Processing of coffee, tea, cocoa, sugar, manufacture of textiles, animal feeds, beer, boats, furniture, metal products and grain milling. Nytil, Lugazi Sugar Works and Nile Breweries are the biggest employers.

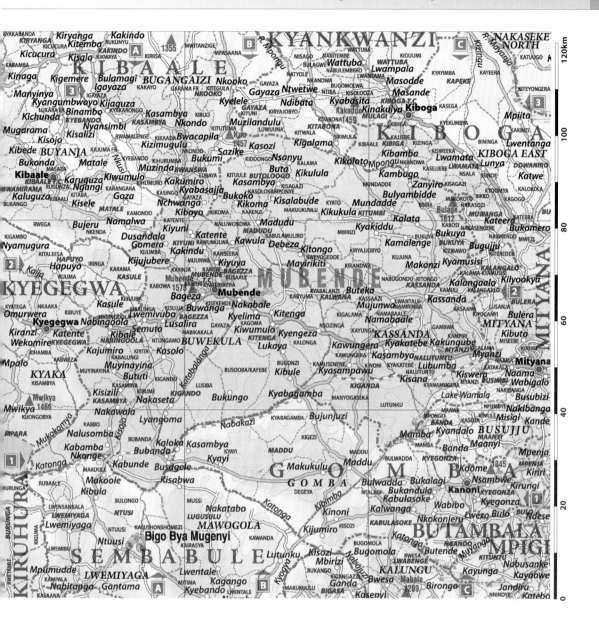

District leaders:

Chairperson – Mr Bazigatirawo K Francis
Chief Administrative Officer (CAO)
   – Mr Ocakara Nicholas
Deputy CAO – Vacant
Town Clerk (Mubende Town Council)
   – Mr Walusimbi Musoke
Town Clerk (Mityana Town Council)
   – Mr Edward Lwanga

Members of Parliament:

Buwekula County – Mr Anthony Ssemmuli
Kassanda County South
   – Mr Nyombi Thembo George William
Kassanda County North
   – Mr Lubega Godfrey
Kasambya County – Mr Mulindwa Patrick
District Woman MP
   – Ms Namugwanya Benny Bugembe

Mukono District

At independence in 1962, it was part of Buganda. Following the abolition of kingdoms in 1967, it became one of the districts carved out of Buganda Kingdom and was named East Mengo.

Under the 1974 provincial admininstation it was renamed Kyagwe District. In 1980, it became Mukono District.

Location: Mukono District borders the districts of Buikwe and Buvuma to the east, Kayunga to the north, Kampala, Luweero and Wakiso to the west and Kalangala to the south.

Area: 4,125 sq. km.

Climate and Relief: It lies at an altitudinal range of 1,158m to 1,219m above sea level with high temperatures and heavy rainfall. For example, in the period April – June 1991, it received 470mm of rain in 44 rain days.

Population: 498,500 people – 253,700 females and 244,800 male with a density of 120 persons per sq.km.

Major Towns: Mukono (administrative headquarters), Seeta; Trading Centres –Nakifuuma and Kyerima.

Counties and Sub-counties: Mukono County – Kyampisi, Nama, Kkoome Island, Nakisunga, Ntenjeru, Mpunge, Mpatta; Nakifuma County – Kasawo, Kimenyedde, Nabbale, Nagojje, Namuganga, and Ntunda; Mukono Municipality – Goma Division and Mukono Division.

Main Language: Luganda.

People: Baganda.

Economic Activities: Mainly agriculture with emphasis on:
  (i) Food crops: Cassava, sweet potatoes, beans, maize, finger millet, groundnuts, soya bean, bananas, sorghum, simsim (sesame), cow peas, pigeon peas and yams.
  (ii) Cash crops: Cotton, coffee, sugar cane and tea.
  (iii) Fruits and vegetables: Tomatoes, onions, pineapples, vanilla, chillies, passion fruit and cabbage.
  (iv) Dairy farming.
  (v) Fishing on Lake Victoria.

Banks: Stanbic Bank Uganda Ltd – 2, Centenary, Crane Bank, others

Animal Population: Mukono, Buikwe and Buvuma districts have 155,820 cattle, 61 donkeys, 181,846 pigs, 30,808 sheep, 206,704 goats, 1,551,702 chicken, 49,517 ducks and 5,558.

Co-operative Societies: Mukono, Buikwe, Buvuma and Kayunga have 267 registered primary societies with East Mengo Union at the district level.

Industries: Processing of coffee, tea, cocoa, sugar, manufacture of textiles, animal feeds, beer, boats, furniture, metal products and grain milling. Nytil, Lugazi Sugar Works and Nile Breweries are the biggest employers.

Education Services: Primary schools: 384– 226 government, 131 private, 27 community. Enrolment: 137,835 pupils – 67,779 male and 70,056 female. Primary school teachers: 3,618 – 1,594 male and 2,024 female. Available furniture is adequate for 109,088 pupils.

Secondary schools: 83 schools - 17 government, 62 private, 4 community. Secondary school enrolment: 41,551 – 20,023 male and 21,528 female. Teachers 2,345 – 1,664 male and 681 female. Available furniture is adequate for 33,235 students.

Tertiary institutions: Uganda Christian University Mukono.

Health Services: 1 hospital (NGO - Naggalama Hospital with 150 beds), 3 health centre IV (2 government, 1 NGO), 11 health centre III (all government), 21 health centre II (16 government, 5 NGO).

The picturesque Ssezibwa Falls in Mukono.

Tourist Attractions: Mabira Forest Reserve, Mabira Forest has a rich collection of birds, plants and insects and has an eco-lodge for the tourists who wish to stay longer. Mabira is a good springboard to other tourism hotspots such as Jinja.

Operational Radio Stations: Dynamic Broadcasting and Prayer Palace Ministries, CBS, Radio Simba.

Key NGOs: Send a Cow Uganda, Uganda Women's Effort to Save Orphans, Integrated Rural Development Initiatives, African Network for the Prevention and Protection Against Child Abuse and Neglect Uganda Chapter, VEDCO, World Vision Uganda, Traditional and Modern Health Practitioners, Cape of Good Hope Orphan Care and Family Support Project, Literary AID Uganda, Uganda Environmental Education Foundation, Youth Alert Mukono, AIDS ACTION Uganda, Mukono Gatsby Club.

District leaders:	Members of Parliament:
Chairperson	Mukono County North
– Mr Francis Mukoome Lukooya	– Mr Kibuule Ronald
Chief Administrative Officer (CAO)	Nakifuma County
– Mr George Eustance Gakwandi	– Mr Kafeero Ssekitoleko Robert
Deputy Chief Administrative Officer	Mukono County South
(DCAO) – Mr Francis Adap	– Mr Bakaluba Mukasa Peter
Ag. Town Clerk (Mukono Municipal	Mukono Municipality
Council) – Mr Alex N. Sseruwagi	– Ms Betty Bakireke Nambooze
Mayor Mukono Municipality	Woman Representative
– Mr Johnson S Muyanja	– Mr Kusasira Peace Kanyesigye Mubiru

Nakaseke District

Nakaseke was a county of Luweero District until 2005 when the county was elevated to district status.

Location: Nakaseke District borders the Districts of Masindi and Nakasongola to the north, Luweero to the east and southeast, Kyankwanzi and Kiboga in the west, and Wakiso and Mityana in the southwest.

Area: 3,475 sq. kms.

Climate: High temperatures and rainfall of the modified equatorial climate type.

Population: According to 2009 projections, there are 169,300 people – 84,900 female 84,400 male with a density of 48 persons per sq.km.

Major Town: Nakaseke Town Council

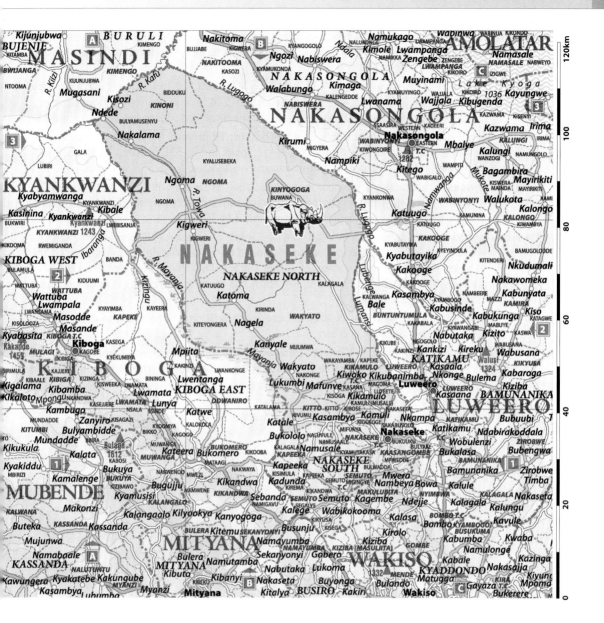

County and Sub-counties: Nakaseke South – Kapeeka, Nakaseke, Kaasangombe, Nakaseke (Town Council), and Semuto (Town Council). Nakaseke North – Kapeeka, Kikamulo, Ngoma, Semuto, Wakyato, Kinyogoga, Kinoni, Kitto, Nakaseke Butalangu (Town Council), Kiwoko (Town Council), Ngoma (Town Council),

Main Language: Luganda

People: Mainly Baganda, Banyankore, Baruli, Bakiga and Banyoro.

Economic Activities: Cultivation and cattle keeping.

Animal Population: The district has 160,737 cattle, 48,634 goats, 9,439 sheep, 29,706 pigs, 193,392 chicken, 1,995 ducks and 245 turkeys.

Industries: Manufacture of textiles and wearing apparel, furniture, grainmill products, metal products, beverages bakery products, food products, dairy products, coffee processing, sawmilling and tree planting.

Education Services: Primary Schools 138 – 114 government, 21 private and 3 community. Enrolment 57,258 pupils – 27,734 male and 29,524 female. Primary school teachers: 1,022 – 522 male and 500 female. Available furniture adequate for 38,394 pupils.

Secondary schools; 29 schools - 7 government, 19 private, 3 community. Secondary school enrolment: 6,949 students – 3,411 male and 3, 538 female. Teachers: 461 - 348 male and 113 female. Available furniture adequate for 5,586 students.

Health Services: 2 hospitals (1 government - Nakaseke Hospital with 104 beds, 1 NGO – Kiwoko Hospital), 1 health centre IV (government), 7 health centre III (6 government, 1 NGO), 10 health centre II (8 government, 2 NGO).

Tourist Atractions: Wakyato Local Wild Life Reserve: The reserve is part of the Lugogo wildlife corridor which connects to Masindi's Karuma Wildlife Reserve. Due to the large concentration of a variety of game, the local administration declared the area a local wildlife reserve. The administration has plans to develop game drives and a large zoo in the area.

Rivers Mayanja, Kafu and Lugogo: These rivers sustain a large wetland that is home to many types of game and birds.

Nabisojo Lake located in Wakyato Reserve area along the Luweero-Ngoma Road. The surrounding wetland is suitable for fish farming. If developed, the fish farming would add to the tourism attractions to Wakyato area.

District Leaders:	Members of Parliament:
District Chairperson	Nakaseke North County
– Mr Ignatius K. Koomu	– Ms Syda Namirembe Bbumba M.
Chief Administrative Officer (CAO)	Nakaseke South County
– Mr Ssenoga B.K. Emmanuel	– Mr Sempala Mbuga Edward William
Deputy Chief Administrative Officer	District Woman MP
(DCAO) – Vacant	– Ms Rose Nsereko Namayanja

Nakasongola District

Nakasongola District came into existence in 1997. It is made up of one county, Buruli, which was formerly part of Luweero District.

In the 1970s, during the Idi Amin regime, Nakasongola gained sub-district status. The commission of inquiry into the local government system in 1987 recognised that Nakasongola was too far away from the administrative centre of Luweero to be administered directly from there and hence suffered from relative neglect. This was the basis for the creation of Nakasongola District in 1997.

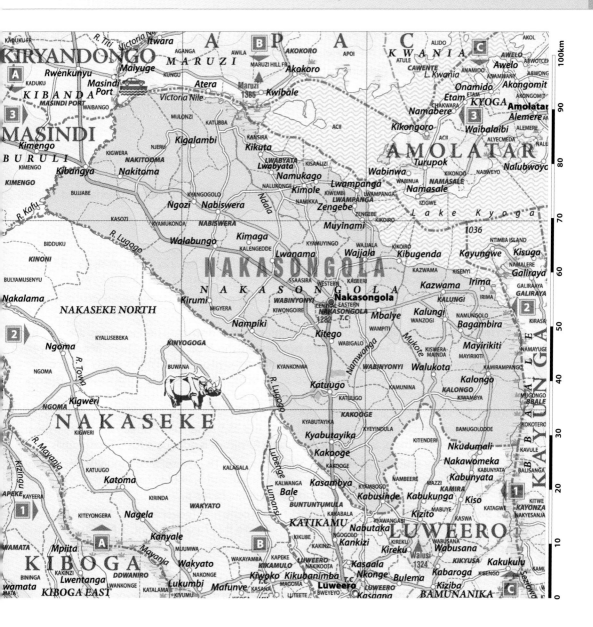

Location: Nakasongola District borders Apac and Amolatar to the north, Masindi and Kiryandongo to the northwest, Nakaseke to the west, Luweero to the south and Kayunga to the east.

Area: 3,510 sq. km.

Climate, Relief and Vegetation: Nakasongola lies on the central plateau at a height of between 1000m and 1400m above sea level. The area is characterised by undulating plains. Temperatures are high, reaching a maximum of between 30°C – 32°C. Rainfall ranges from 875mm – 1000mm per annum. In this region the dry season is long and may go up to 5 months. The district does not have great potential for tourism, although the undulating plains constitute good scenery. There are rocks and hills which are suitable for climbing.

Population: According to 2009 projections, there are 144,100 people – 71,700 female and 72,400 male with a density of 41 persons per sq.km.

Major Town: Nakasongola (administrative headquarters).

Counties and Sub-counties: Budyebo County – Lwampanga, Nabiswera, Rwabyata, and Nakitoma. Nakasongola County – Kakooge, Kalungi, Wabinyonyi, Nakasongola (Town Council), and Kalongo.

Main Languages: Luruli and Luganda.

People: Mainly Baruli, but Banyankore, Baganda and Banyarwanda also live in the district.

Economic Activities: Agriculture with emphasis on:
(i)   Food crops: Cassava, sweet potatoes, maize, beans, sorghum, bananas and finger millet.
(ii) Cash crops: Coffee and cotton.

Area under Forestation: 128,759 hectares.

Animal Population: According to 2008 statistics, the district has 222,185 cattle, 35,283 pigs, 6,839 sheep, 87,823 goats 287,834 chicken, 6,316 ducks and 550 turkeys.

Co-operative Societies: Nakasongola and Luweero have 191 registered co-operative societies.

Industries: There is a military industrial complex in the district. The industries are run by the Ministry of Defence and do not benefit the local people. There are, however, plans to convert the military industries to civilian use. This is likely to provide employment. There is also coffee processing, cotton ginning, milk cooling, jaggery and woodwork.

Education Services: Primary schools: 184 – 143 government, 39 private and 2 community. Enrolment: 50,854 pupils – 24,881 male and 25,973 female. Primary School teachers: 1,410 – 837 male, 573 female. Available furniture is adequate for 39,880 pupils.

Secondary schools; 28 schools - 5 government, 18 private, 5 community. Secondary school enrolment: 7,509 students – 4,167 male and 3,342 female. Teachers: 471 - 383 male and 88 female. Available furniture adequate for 6,202.

Health Services: 1 hospital (government), 1 health centre IV (government), 10 health centre III (9 government, 1 NGO), 19 health centre II (17 government, 2 NGO).

Transport Network: The district is connected by a tarmac road to Masindi and Luweero Districts. The feeder-road network, however, is inadequate. Travelling within the district is problematic and it affects transportation of agricultural produce within the district. Once the produce reaches the tarmac road however, it finds a ready market both in the neighbouring districts of Luweero and Masindi and as far away as Kampala.

Additional Information: Because the district lies on the central plateau, agricultural mechanisation is easy to undertake. There are large tracts of land that can be utilised for large scale farming. The district has various land tenure systems including customary, freehold and *mailoland*.

Key NGOs: African Medical Research Foundation Uganda, World Vision Uganda, Concern Uganda, VEDCO, Kazwama Disabled Association, Lwampanga Water Supply Project, Nakasongola District Change Agents Association, Uganda Society for Disabled Children, Nakasongola District Farmers' Association, Kyabataika Development Association, Nakasongola Boda-Boda Transport Saving and Credit Scheme.

District leaders:
Chairperson – Mr James Muruli Wandira
Ag Chief Administrative Officer (CAO)
  – Ms Joyce Loyce Nambooze
Deputy Chief Administrative Officer
  (DCAO) – Vacant
Town Clerk (Nakasongola Town Council)
  – Mr Martin Etyang

Members of Parliament:
Nakasongola County – Mr Peter Nyombi
Budyebo County
  – Mr Mukasa Muruli Wilson
Woman MP – Ms Komuhangi Margaret

Rakai District

Rakai District, created in 1980, was carved from Masaka District, which was established in 1967, when Buganda Kingdom was sub-divided into districts.

Location: Rakai borders the Districts of Lyantonde and Lwengo to the north; Masaka to the northeast; Isingiro and Kiruhura to the west; Kalangala to the east; and the United People's Republic of Tanzania to the south.

Area: 4,039 sq. km.

Climate and Relief: It lies in a modified equatorial climatic zone with high temperatures and heavy rainfall almost all the year round.

Population: Based on population projection 2009, there are 449,500 people; 218,100 male and 231,400 female with a density of 111 persons per sq. km.

Major Towns: Rakai (administrative headquarters); Trading Centres – Kyotera, Kalisizo and Kibanda.

Counties and Sub-counties: Kakuuto County – Kakuuto, Kasasa, Kibanda, Kifamba, Kyebe; Kooki County – Byakabanda, Rakai (Town Council), Kacheera, Ddwaniro, Kagamba(Buyamba), Kyalulangira, Lwamaggwa, Lwanda, Kiziba; Kyotera County – Kabira, Kalisizo, Lwankoni, Kasaali, Kirumba, Kyotera (Town Council), Kalisizo (Town Council), and Nabigasa.

Main Language: Luganda.

People: Baganda and Banyankore.

Economic Activities: Mainly agriculture with a bias towards:
  (i)   Food crops: Finger millet, maize, beans, bananas, sorghum, sweet potatoes, Irish potatoes, cassava and groundnuts.
  (ii) Cash crops: Coffee.
  (iii) Fruits and vegetables: Passion fruit, tomatoes, pineapples, onions and cabbage.
  (iv) Cattle keeping.

Banks: Stanbic Bank Uganda Ltd – 2, Centenary Rural Development Bank Ltd – 1.

Area under Forestation: 36,604 hectares.

Animal Population: Rakai has 279,594 cattle, 163,806 goats18,158 sheep, 102,870 pigs, 503,623 chicken, 15,399 ducks and 1,097 turkeys.

Industries: Coffee processing, furniture works, metal fabrication and carpentry.

Co-operative Societies: 140 registered primary societies.

Education Services: Primary schools: 269 – 232 government, 30 private and 7 community. Enrolment: 123,805 – 60,742 male and 63,063 female. Primary school teachers: 3,008 - 1,636 male and 1,372 female. Available furniture is adequate for 98,129 pupils.

Secondary schools; 47 schools - 21 government, 20 private and 6 community. Secondary school enrolment: 16,097 students – 7,624 male and 8,473 female. Teachers: 918 - 718 male and 200 female. Available furniture adequate for 13,822 students.

Tertiary institutions:1 Technical institution, 1 teacher training college.

Health Services: 2 hospitals (all government - Rakai Hospital and Kalisizo Hospital), 2 health centres IV (all government), 22 health centre III (all government), 61 health centre II (44 government, 17 NGO).

Tourist Attractions: The district is rich with tourist sites ranging from lakes and rivers, cultural/historical sites, scenery viewing, and landing sites. Lake Kijanebarola near the District Headquarters is joined to Lake Kachera, east of Rakai town, by River Rwizi. The lakes and rivers provide opportunity for the development of boat cruises, while the highlands, like Nakibanga Hill, next to the shores and river banks are ideal for development of hotels and game viewing from the nearby Lake Mburo National Park which is located in the adjacent district of Kiruhura.

Landing Sites: The Landing sites/beaches on the lakes are ideal for campsites. Kasensero Landing Site, at Masangana Forest Reserve, overlooking the point between Lake Victoria and River Kagera have been developed into an eco-tourism and picnic site.

Historical/Cultural Sites: Musambwa Island and Serinya tombs are some of the important cultural sites. In addition, Musambwa Island in Sango Bay, in Lake Victoria is famous for the variety of bird and snake species. It is a place of traditional worship for some people. Nature Uganda has developed it into an eco-tourism centre. Lukungu palace at Kasensero and Lukindu monuments are sites where the 2,827 victims of the 1994 Rwanda genocide were buried. Kasozi Church, near Rakai town is 105 years old and believed to be one of the oldest Catholic Churches in the country. Its old and unique architectural designs are the main attractions.

Serinya Shrines is a burial place for the Kings of Kooki; Lukoma airstrip was constructed by Idi Amin during his expansionist vision of annexing some parts of Tanzania.

Scenery Viewing: The small lake basins, river valleys and hills provide a unique landscape. Among such scenery is Simba Hill, believed to be where explorer, John Speke, stood and declared having discovered Lake Victoria; Katongero Site has a view of the meandering River Kagera; Nakakaikuru Stone in Lake Victoria and Nabunga Hills are believed to be linked to the mountain ranges in South Africa.

Additional Information: Rakai lies on a plateau in southern Uganda and it has rich soils that support agriculture. Both subsistence and commercial farming take place. Coffee, fruits, vegetables and bananas are grown on a large scale purposely for the market. There are no industries in this district.

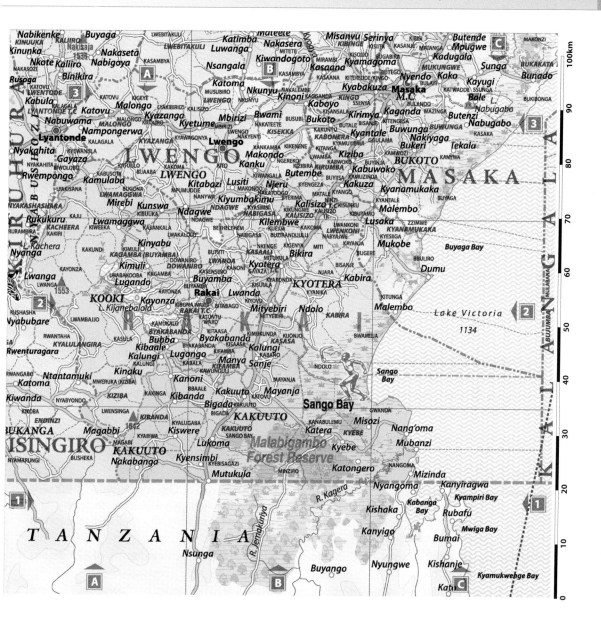

Key NGOs: Send a Cow Uganda, Integrated Rural Development Initiatives, African Network for the Prevention and Protection Against Child Abuse and Neglect Uganda Chapter, Concern Uganda, World Vision Uganda, International Care and Relief, Kakuuto Rural Development Foundation, Community Welfare Services, Rakai Tourism Development Association, Rural Development Services.

District leaders:
Chairperson – Mr Mugabi Robert Benon
Chief Administrative Officer (CAO)
 – Mr James B.K. Nkata
Deputy CAO – vacant
Town Clerk (Kyotera Town Council)
 – Mr Silvester Ntawuzi
Town Clerk (Kalisizo Town Council)
 – Mr Jude Kisirinya
Town Clerk (Rakai Town Council)
 – Mr Benon Iga

Members of Parliament:
Kooki County – Mr Mandera Amos
Kyotera County – Mr Kyeyune Harun
Kakuuto County – Mr Mathias Kasamba
Woman Representative
 – Ms Maria Emily Lubega Mutagamba

Sembabule District

Sembabule District came into existence in 1997. It consists of Mawogola and Lwemiyaga counties which were formerly part of Masaka District.

Location: The district borders Gomba and Mubende to the north, Kiruhura and Lyantonde to the west, Lwengo to the south and Bukomansimbi to the east.

Area: 2,319.2 sq. km.

Climate and Relief: The area lies on the low, western, plateau of Uganda between 1,200m – 1,500m above sea level. Temparatures are relatively high and rainfall declines in the district, ranging between 625mm – 875mm. There is a long, dry spell that sometimes goes beyond 5 months.

Population: 202,700 people – 103,000 female and 99,700 male with a density of 87 persons per sq.km.

Major Towns: Sembabule (administrative headquarters); Trading Centres – Mawogola, Mateete and Lwemiyaga.

Counties and Sub-counties: Lwemiyaga County – Lwemiyaga, Ntusi; Mawogola County – Lwebitakuli, Lugusulu, Mijwala, and Sembabule (Town Council), Mateete (Town Council).

Main Languages: Luganda and Runyankore.

People: Baganda and Banyankore.

Economic Activities: Agriculture with emphasis on:
  (i)   Food crops: Sweet potatoes, bananas, beans, maize, cassava, groundnuts, soya bean, sorghum and finger millet.
  (ii) Cash crops: Coffee and cotton.
  (iii) Cattle herding and ranching.
  (iv) Fishing in wetlands.

Area under Forestation: 15,848 hectares.

Animal Population: The district has 177,473 cattle, 35,399 pigs, 14,219 sheep, 113,204 goats, 194,462 chicken, 10,011 ducks and 2,528 turkeys.

Co-operative Societies: Sembabaule and Masaka have 308 registered co-operative societies.

Industries: Metal works, furniture, jaggery processing, coffee processing, cotton ginning.

Education Services: Primary schools: 221 – 193 government, 26 private, 2 community. Enrolment: 78,678 pupils – 37,788 male and 40,890 female. Primary school teachers: 1,685 – 937 male and 748 female. Available furniture is adequate for 57,132 pupils.

Secondary schools: 22 schools - 6 government, 14 private, and 2 community. Secondary school enrolment: 6,009 students – 3,050 male and 2,959 female. Teachers: 385 – 310 male and 75 female. Available furniture is adequate for 3,811 students.

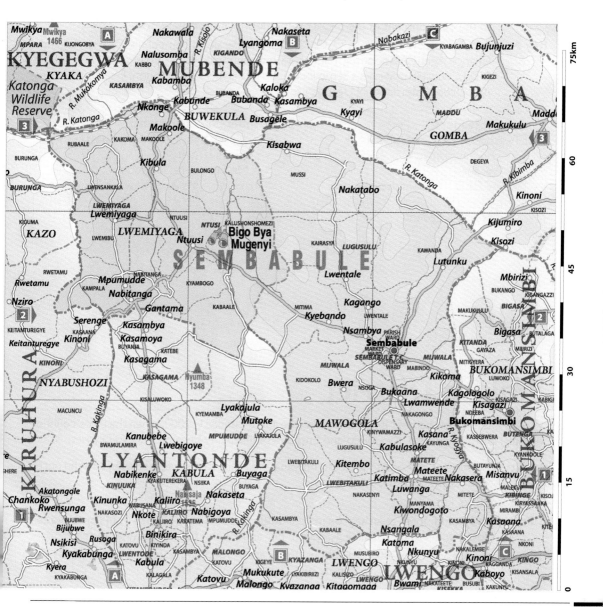

Health Services: 2 health centre IV (all government), 7 health centre III (4 government, 3 NGO) 15 health centre II (all government). More complicated cases are referred to Masaka Referral Hospital.

Tourist Attractions: Bigo Earth Works in the Bwera region appears to have been a significant late Iron Age settlement. Excavations at the sight have yielded iron blades (most probably used for harvesting grain), pottery with simple decorations, cattle dung and post-holes for fencing. During colonial times the site was called Bigo Bya Mugyenyi. Ntusi Archaelogical settlement is the site of both cattle herders and cultivators. Excavations have yielded pottery, cattle bones and odd items such as ivory carvings, ostrich egg shell beads, glass beads and copper items.

Additional Information: Sembabule District receives low rainfall and has long, dry, spells. This greatly affects agriculture, but cattle keeping is not seriously affected. Some cattle are reared on ranches. This forms the pillar of Sembabule's economy since cattle are in demand for meat in the towns of Masaka, Rakai and Kampala. The biggest hindrance to the development of the district is the poor transport network.

Key NGOs: Send a Cow Uganda, CO-CARE Uganda, Paralegal Sembabule District, Uganda Change Agent Association, Minnesota International Health Volunteers, Sembabule AIDS Counselling Services Sembabule District Farmers' Association, Financial Services Association International Uganda Ltd.

District leaders:	Members of Parliament:
Chairperson – Dr Muhumuza Elly	Mawogola County – Mr Sam Kutesa
Chief Administrative Officer (CAO)	Lwemiyaga County
– Vacant	– Mr Theodore Sekikubo
Deputy CAO – Ms. Sarah Nakarungi	Woman MP – Ms Anifa Kawoya Bangirana
Town Clerk (Sembabule Town Council)	
– Ms Jane Kiggundu	

Wakiso District

Wakiso was formerly part of Mpigi District. It came into existance in 2000, when the three counties of Mpigi District – Busiro, Kyadondo and Entebbe Municipality became Wakiso District.

Location: It borders Mukono to the east, Mityana and Mpigi to the west, Luweero to the north and Kalangala to the south.

Area: 2,808 sq. km.

Climate and Relief: It lies at an approximate altitude of between 1,182m – 1,341m above sea level, with rainfall totalling 1,513mm per annum and has high temperatures.

Population: According to 2009 projections, there are 1,186,900 people – 619,400 males and 567,500 females with a density of 422 persons per sq.km.

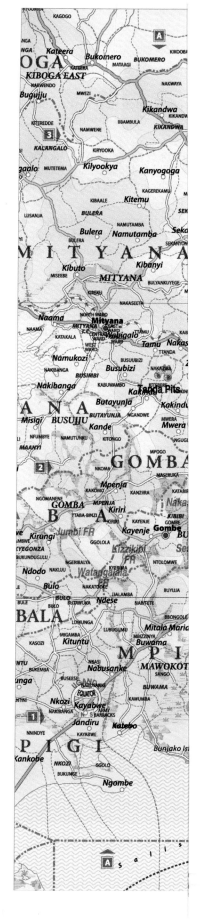

Major Towns: Entebbe, Wakiso (administrative headquarters); Trading Centres – Matugga and Kakiri.

Counties and Sub-counties: Busiro County – Nsangi (Mukono), Wakiso, Wakiso (Town Council), Kakiri (Town Council), Kakiri, Kiziba (Masulita), Namayumba, Kasanje, Katabi, Ssisa and Mende; Kyaddondo County – Kira, Nangabo, Gombe, Kyambogo (Busukuma), Nabweru, Makindye, Nansana (Town Council) and Kira (Town Council); Entebbe Municipality – Division A and Division B.

Main Language: Luganda.

People: Mainly Baganda.

Economic Activities: Fishing on Lake Victoria, trade in animal and poultry feeds and agriculture with emphasis on:
(i) Food crops: Sweet potatoes, beans, cassava, groundnuts, irish potatoes and soya bean.
(ii) Cash crops: Coffee and cotton.
(iii) Fruits and vegetables: Tomatoes, onions and cabbage.

Area under Forestation: 38,028 hectares.

Animal Population: The district has 114,769 cattle, 9 camels, 18 donkeys, 199,962 pigs, 27,542 sheep, 132,964 goats, 2,783,509 chicken, 33,350 ducks and 4,852 turkeys.

Co-operative Societies: Wakiso and Mpigi have 341 registered co-operative societies.

Industries: Roofings, tiles, brick making and furniture making.

Education Services: Primary schools: 767 – 262 government, 462 private and 43 community. Enrolment: 241,390 pupils – 118,216 male and 123,174 female. Primary school teachers: 8,516 – 3,707 male and 4,809 female. Available furniture adequate for 200,224 pupils.

Secondary schools: 195 - 22 government, 163 private and 10 community. Secondary school enrolment: 93,001 students – 43,825

male and 49,176 female. Teachers: 5,616 – 3,922 male and 1,694 female. Available furniture is adequate for 86,584 students.

Tertiary institutions: 1 teacher training college, 2 technical institutes, 1 meteorological school, fisheries training institute (Vocational Institute), and 1 univeristy – Nkumba University.

Health Services: 4 hospitals (2 government - Entebbe Grade A Hospital with 12 beds, Entebbe Grade B Hospital with 149 beds; 2 NGO - Kisubi Hospital and Mildmay Hospital.), 5 health centre IV (all government), 32 health centre III (17 government, 15 NGO), 57 health centre II (36 government, 21 NGO).

Tourist Attractions: The Kabaka's trail encompasses the most important sites of Buganda. Traditional dance, music and craft-making activities are demonstrated as well as story telling. The sites include Naggalabi Buddo Coronation site where *kings of Buganda* have been enthroned for the past 700 years.

Do not miss the cannon in the square in front of Entebbe Club, captured from the Germans during World War 1. Entebbe was the administrative centre of the colonial government and capital of the Uganda Protectorate. Entebbe has a lot of colonial architecture, like the Ministry of Agriculture building which still has the inscription, '1927'.

The Botanical Gardens are a popular picnic and swimming spot. The Johnny Weismuller "Tarzan" films were shot here. Different plant species from all over the world can be found here and lots of different smells and noises can be experienced.

There are a couple of hotels and lodges one can stay in including the Entebbe Backpackers Tourist Campsite and Hostel, the Imperial Botanical Beach Hotel and the Windsor Lake Victoria Hotel.

Uganda Wildlife Education Centre with an information centre, gift shop and kiosks – A pair of the rare shoebill stork lives here.

Ngamba Island with tropical rain forests is a chimpanzee sanctuary and wildlife conservation trust.

Bulago Island is an upmarket sailing and water sport resort on Lake Victoria.

Sport fishing also takes place on Lake Victoria and there are fishing tours. Lake Victoria is home to the gigantic Nile Perch.

Ngamba Island is sanctuary for chimpanzees.

Kigungu Landing Site contains a memorial plaque where the first Catholic Missionaries in Uganda landed.

Kasenyi Fishing Village showcases both traditional and modern fishing techniques.

Entebbe International Airport is well known for the 90 minutes raid by Israel to rescue Jewish passengers held hostage in 1976.

The Namugongo Martyrs Shrine is located about 12 km out of Kampala off Jinja Road. This is the site where 37 Christian converts were burnt to death on the orders of Kabaka Mwanga on the 3rd of June 1886. On the visit of Pope Paul VI to Uganda in 1969, the martyrs were canonised and since then the shrine has became an important site for Uganda Christians and tourists. There are two churches built at the site, one for the Roman Catholics and the other for the Anglicans. The 3rd of June is a public holiday in rememberance of the Uganda Martyrs.

Key NGOs: Send a Cow, VEDCO, Uganda Women's Effort to Save Orphans, Integrated Rural Development Initiatives, African Network for the Prevention and Protection Against Child Abuse and Neglect Uganda Chapter, Voluntary Action for Development, Environmental Alert, Agency for Integrated Rural Development, Children and Life Mission, Community Action for Development, Hunger Free World Uganda, The Hunger Project Uganda, Voluntary Action for Development, Compassionate Outreach to East Africa Mission Uganda, Uganda Red Cross.

District leaders:	Members of Parliament:
Chairperson – Mr Bwanika Mathias L.	Busiro County North
Chief Administrative Officer (CAO)	– Mr Gilbert Balibaseka Bukenya
– Mr Mukwaya Joseph	Busiro County South
Deputy Chief Administrative Officer	– Mr Balikudembe Mutebi Joseph
(DCAO) – Ms. Yusuf Senteza	Busiro County East
Town Clerk (Wakiso Town Council)	– Mr Segona Lubega Medard
– Mr Authman Sebaduka	Kyaddondo County North
Town Clerk (Entebbe Municipal Council)	– Mr Robert Sebunya Kasule
– Mr Joseph Kimbowa	Kyaddondo County South
Mayor (Entebbe Municipality)	– Mr Issa Kikungwe
– Mr Vincent Kayanja Gonza	Kyaddondo County East
	– Mr Ssemujju Brahim Nganda
	Entebbe Municipality
	– Mr Muhamed Kawuma
	Woman MP
	– Ms Rosemary Nansubuga Seninde

Southwestern Districts

Buhweju	Bushenyi	Ibanda	Isingiro	Kabale	Kanungu	Kiruhura	Kisoro
Mbarara	Mitooma	Ntungamo	Rubiriizi	Rukungiri	Sheema		

The People: The main inhabitants are the Banyankore, the Bakiga, the Bahororo, the Banyarwanda, the Bafumbira, the Banyaruguru and the Batwa (pygmies).

The main cash crops produced include tobacco, tea and coffee. Cattle keeping is a major economic activity and the indigenous Ankore long-horned, exotic and cross-bred cattle are reared for beef and dairy products.

Tourism: Tourist attractions in the region include the mountain gorillas in Bwindi Impenetrable Forest and Mgahinga; wild game in the Lake Mburo and Queen Elizabeth National Parks and the Kyambura Game Reserve; Lake Bunyonyi in Kabale; the volcanic landscape of Kisoro; Kabale and Bushenyi districts and the Kitagata and Mineera Hot Springs, which are believed to have healing powers. There are tourist lodges and camping resorts in all the national parks.

How to get there: This area is accessible mainly by tarmac roads which include: the Kampala-Mbarara-Bushenyi Road, the Mbarara-Kabale-Katuna Road, the Mbarara-Ibanda Road and the Ntungamo-Rukungiri Road. The rest of the roads in the area are gravel. This region can also be accessed by air and there are airstrips at Mbarara, Kisoro and Kayonza in Kanungu. However, there are no regular scheduled flights.

Sub divisions: The Ministry of Local Government subdivided the region into two main sub-regions namely Kigezi and Ankore.

Ankore long-horned cattle in Bushenyi district (left). A woman carrying a banch of bananas, it is one of the food crops in the southwestern region (middle) and mountain gorillas of Bwindi impenetrable forest and Mgahinga National park (right)

Southwestern Districts

Buhweju District

At Independence, Buhweju was part of Ankore Kingdom. It became a county in West Ankore district, which was renamed Bushenyi District in 1980. Buhweju was elevated to district status in 2010.

Location: Buhweju borders the districts of Mbarara to the east, Rubirizi to the west, Bushenyi and Sheema to the south, and Ibanda and Kamwenge to the north.

Area: Approximately 803 sq. km.

Climate, Relief and Vegetation: It experiences high amounts of rainfall. The district experiences an average temperature as high as 25°C. Vegetation includes a multitude of short grasses, bushes and thickets.

Population: Accordng to the 2009 population projections the district has 93,700 – 48,000 female and 45,700 male with a density of 116 persons per sq.km.

Major Towns: Nsiika (administrative headquarters)

Counties and Sub-counties: Buhweju County – Engaju, Bihanga, Bitsya, Burere, Karungu, Nyakishana, Rwengwe and Nsiika (Town Council);

Main Language: Runyankore.

People: Banyankore.

Economic Activities: Agriculture with emphasis on:
- (i) Food crops: Maize, bananas, millet, rice, simsim, cowpeas, sorghum, sweet potatoes, cassava, bananas, soya bean and beans.
- (ii) Cash crops: Ginger, cotton, sunflower, coffee and tea.
- (iii) Fruits, vegetables, citrus and other fruit varieties: Tomatoes, cabbage, onions and pineapples.
- (vi) Dairy farming.

Animal Population: Buhweju, Bushenyi, Mitooma, Rubirizi and Sheema have 207,184 cattle, 57,467 pigs, 79,757 sheep, 376,561 goats 364,568 chicken, 19,971 ducks and 2,343 turkeys.

Co-operative Societies: The district still depends on societies registered in the former Bushenyi, the mother district. Banyankore Kweterana Co-operative Union remains the umbrella union specialising mainly in coffee, ranching and distribution of agricultural chemicals.

Industries: Processing of coffee and tea, weaving and knitting industries, gold mining, brick and furniture making.

Banks: The district still depends on banks from Bushenyi, the mother district.

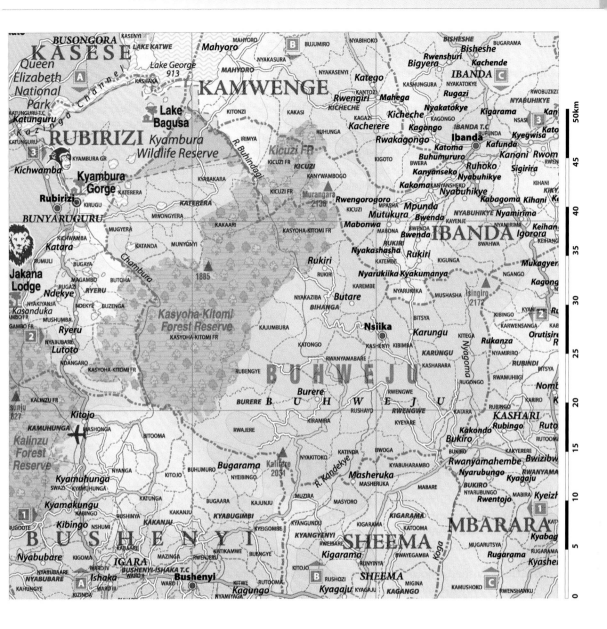

Education Services: Primary schools: 73 schools – 53 government, 15 private and 5 community. Enrolment 24,055 – 11,696 male and 12,359 female. Primary school teachers: 522 – 386 male, 136 female. Available furniture is adequate for only 15,969 pupils.

Secondary schools: 4 schools - 3 government and 1 private. Secondary school enrolment: 1,684 – 907 male and 777 female. Teachers: 83 – 70 male, and 13 female. Available furniture is adequate for 1,181 students.

Health Services: I health centre IV (government); 5 health centre III, (4 government and 1 NGO) and 7 health centre II (6 government and 1 NGO).

Transport Network: The district has a poor network of feeder-roads owing to its mountainous terrain. Some parts of the district are inaccessible and it gets worse during the rainy

season. The district is linked to Mbarara and Bushenyi districts by a murram road. Public transport to the district is problematic and is mainly by pick-up trucks.

Tourist Attractions: There are no tourist attractions, however, its hilly terrain provides the opportunity for climbing and sightseeing.

Key NGOs: The district stiil depends on NGOs registered and based in the mother district. They include Family Planning Association of Uganda, VSO Uganda, Uganda Women's Effort to Save Orphans (UWESO), National Adult Education Association, Nyanga Kwetungura Group, Bushenyi Disabled Persons Association, Ebenezer Women's Group, Bushenyi Bee Keepers' Association, Bushenyi Banana and Plantain Farmers' Association, Bushenyi Women in Development, and Trust for Community Empowerment.

District leaders:	Members of Parliament:
Chairperson – Mr Keereere Sebastian	Buhweju County
Chief Administrative Officer (CAO)	– Mr Biraaro Ephraim Ganshanga
– Ms. Edith Mutabaazi	Woman MP – Ms Arinaitwe Kariisa Joy
Deputy Chief Administrative Officer	
(DCAO) – Vacant	

Bushenyi District

At Independence, Bushenyi was part of Ankore Kingdom. After the kingdoms were abolished in 1967, Ankore became a district. Under the 1974 provincial administration, Ankore was divided into east and west Ankore. In 1980 west Ankore was renamed Bushenyi District. In 2010, the district was subdivided into five districts.

Location: Bushenyi borders the districts of Mitooma to the west, Kibingo (Sheema) to the southeast and to the east, Nsiika to the northeast and Rubirizi to the north.

Area: Approximately 943 sq. km.

Climate, Relief and Vegetation: It experiences high amounts of rainfall due to the altitude of most parts of the district, for example Buhweju. Average temperatures are high at 25°C while vegetation includes a multitude of short grasses, bushes in lowlands and thickets.

Population: Accordng to the 2009 population projections, the district has 232,200 – 120,100 female and 112,100 male with a population density of 246 pesons per sq.km.

Major Towns: Bushenyi-Ishaka (administrative headquarters); Trading Centres – Rwentuuha, Kyabugimbi and Kashenyi.

Counties and Sub-counties: Igara County – Mitooma, Bumbaire, Ibaare, Kyabugimbi, Kyeizooba, Nyabubare, Kakanju, Kyamuhunga, Ruhumuro. Bushenyi-Ishaka Municipality – Central Division, Ishaka Division, and Nyakabirirzi Division.

Main Language: Runyankore.

People: Banyankore.

Economic Activities: Agriculture with emphasis on:
  (i)   Food crops: Maize, bananas, millet, rice, simsim, cowpeas, sorghum, sweet potatoes, cassava, bananas, soya bean and beans.
  (ii) Cash crops: Ginger, cotton, sunflower, coffee and tea.
  (iii) Fruits, vegetables, citrus and other fruit varieties: Tomatoes, cabbage, onions and pineapples.
  (vi) Dairy farming.

Area under Forestation: 89,439 hectares.

Animal Population: Bushenyi, Buhweju, Mitooma, Rubirizi and Sheema have 207,184 cattle, 57,467 pigs, 79,757 sheep, 376,561 goats 364,568 chicken, 19,971 ducks and 2,343 turkeys.

Co-operative Societies: Bushenyi district (inclusive of Mitooma, Rubirizi, Buhweju and Sheema districts) have 258 registered primary societies with Banyankore Kweterana Co-operative Union as the umbrella district union specialising mainly in coffee, ranching and distribution of agricultural chemicals.

Industries: Processing of coffee, tea and bee honey, weaving and knitting industries, mining of gold and clay, metal fabrication brick and furniture making.

Banks: Stanbic Bank Uganda Ltd – 1 Centenary Rural Development Bank (Ishaka) –1.

Education Services: Primary schools: 196 schools – 151 government, 42 private and 3 community. Enrolment 64,838 – 31,723 male and 33,115 female. Primary school teachers: 1,741 – 800 male and 941 female. Available furniture is for 47,998 pupils.

Secondary Schools: - 27 government, 15 Private and 2 community.

Secondary School enrolment: 14,202 – 5,984 male and 8,218 female. Teachers: 951 – 717 male, and 234 female. Available furniture is adequate for 12,701students.

Tertiary institution: 2 technical institutions, 1 teacher training college and 1 university Kampala International University (Western campus)

Health Services: 4 hospitals (3 NGO - Comboni Hospital with 100 beds, Ishaka Hospital Seventh Day Adventist with 80 beds and 1 private Kampala International University Hospital; 8 health centre III (5 government, 2 private, and 1 NGO) and 4 health centre II (1 government, 2 private and 1 NGO),

Transport Network: The district has a network of feeder-roads in the area which are in a relatively good state compared to the other Southwestern districts. All sub-counties are linked by feeder-roads. The district is linked to the neighbouring districts of Kibingo (Sheema) and Rubirizi by the Kasese-Mbarara-Kampala tarmac road.

Tourist Attractions: Lake Katunga, a volcanic crater lake to the east of Bushenyi town is a potential tourist attraction.

Key NGOs: Family Planning Association of Uganda, VSO Uganda, Uganda Women's Effort to Save Orphans, Hand In Hand Group, National Adult Education Association, Nyanga Kwetungura Group, Bushenyi Disabled Persons Association, Ebenezer Women's Group, Bushenyi Bee Keepers' Association, Bushenyi Banana and Plantain Farmers' Association, Bushenyi Women in Development, Trust for Community Empowerment, Keizooba Community Based Health.

District leaders:

Chairperson – Mr Bashaasha Willis

Chief Administrative Officer (CAO)
 – Mr Danson Yiga Mukasa

Town Clerk (Bushenyi-Ishaka Municipal
 Council) – Mr Francis Byabagambi

Mayor Bushenyi-Ishaka Municipality
 – Mr Jackson Kamugasha

Members of Parliament:

Igara County West – Mr Magyezi Raphael

Igara County East
 – Mr Mawanda Michael Maranga

Bushenyi-Ishaka Municipality
 – Mr Basajjabalaba Nasser

Woman MP
 – Ms Mary Busin180 Busingye Karooro Okurut

Ibanda District

Ibanda District was up to 2005 a county of Mbarara District.

Location: Ibanda District borders the districts of Kiruhuura to the east, Kamwenge to the north and the west, Mbarara to the south and Nsiika (Buhweju) to the southwest.

Area: 966 sq. km.

Climate, Relief and Vegetation: The district is hilly with rivers which flow through the deep valleys and drain into the northern part of the area.

Population: According to the 2009 population projections the district has 232,400 people – 119,000 females and 113,400 male with a population density of 240 persons per sq.km.

Major Town: Ibanda Town (administrative headquarters), Ishongororo and Rushango; Trading Centres: Igorora, Nyabuhikye, Rwenkooba, Bisheshe.

Counties and Sub-counties: Ibanda County – Bisheshe, Ishongororo, Kashangura, Kihangara, Kikyenkye, Kijongo, Nsasi, Nyabuhikye, Nyamarembe, Rukiri, Kicuzi, Ishongororo (Town Council), Ibanda (Town Council) and Rushango (Town Council)

Main Language: Runyankore

People: Mainly Banyankore and Batagwenda.

Economic Activities: The district has a big potential in terms of mining, lumbering, crop and animal production.

Banks: Stanbic Bank Uganda Ltd – 1 Centenary Bank- 1.

Animal Population: As of 2008, there were 55,126 cattle, 89,704 goats, 13,997 sheep, 12,164 pigs, 144,301 chickens, 6,851 ducks and 153 turkeys.

Co-operative Societies: Primary schools: These are still linked to mother district, Mbarara, where most of the co-operative societies are registered with Banyankore Kweterana.

Industries: Manufacture of textiles and wearing apparel, grainmill products, furniture, metal products, footwear, beverages, bakery products, dairy products, coffee processing, sawmilling and plying of wood.

Education Services: 235 – 130 government, 77 private and 28 community. Enrolment: 68,326 pupils – 33,736 male and 34,590 female. Primary school teachers: 1,888 – 1,190 male and 698 female. Available furniture is adequate for 49,203 pupils.

Secondary Schools: 33 schools - 10 government, 16 private and 7 community. Secondary school enrolment: 10,734 – 5,511 male and 5,223 female. Teachers: 623 – 494 male and 129 female. Available furniture is adequate for 10,433.

Health Services: As of December 2006 - 1 hospital – (NGO - Ibanda Hospital (commonly referred to as Kagongo) with 152 beds; 2 health centre IV - (all government); 6 health centre III - (5 government and 1 NGO); and 26 health centre II - (25 government and 1 NGO)

Tourist Attractions: The Galt Memorial monument in Ibanda is a conical arrangement of stones to commemorate the untimely demise at the age of 33 years of Harry St.George Galt, the Sub-Commissioner of the Western Province, who was speared to death on 19th May 1903.

District Leaders:
District Chairperson
  – Mr Melchiades Kazwengye
Chief Administrative Officer (CAO)
  – Abert Mutungire Matsiko
Deputy Chief Administrative Officer
  (DCAO) – Vacant
Town Clerk (Ibanda Town Council)
  – Mr Kafura Kibanyendera

Members of Parliament:
Ibanda North
  – Mr Kyooma Xavier Akampurira
Ibanda South – Mr John Byabagambi
District Woman MP
  – Ms Margaret N. Kiboijana

Isingiro District

Location: Isingiro District borders the districts of Rakai to the east, Kiruhura and Mbarara to the north, Ntungamo to the west and the Republic of Tanzania to the south.

Area: 2657.18 sq. kms.

Climate, Relief and Vegetation: Hilly terrain. Vegetation is a combination of bush and short grass which is suitable for animal rearing. Rainfall is about 957mm annually.

Population: According to the 2009 population projections, the district has 378,600 people – 195,600 female and 183,000 males with a density of 142 persons per sq.km.

Major Town: Kabingo Town Council also the district administration HQs

Counties and Sub-Counties: Bukanga County – Rugaaga, Ngarama, Endinzi, Kashumba, Mbaare and Rushasha; Isingiro County – Nyakitunda, Nyamuyanja, Kabuyanda, Kikagate, Kabingo, Bireere, Masha, Ruborogota, Kabuyanda (Town Council), Isingiro (Town Council) and Kaberebere (Town Council).

Main Language: Runyankore

People: Mainly Banyankore and Bakiga. Others include Baganda, Bafumbira, Banyarwanda and Bahororo.

Economic Activities: A high potential in terms of mining, highly active in crop and animal production.

Banks: DFCU Bank – 1, Centenary Bank

Animal Population: As of 2008, there were 180,345 cattle, 19 donkeys, 7,552 pigs, 30,298 sheeep, 221,491 goats, 203,564 chickens, 13,905 ducks and1,370 turkeys.

Education Services: Primary schools: 316 – 199 government, 81 private and 36 community. Enrolment: 102,057 pupils – 50,228 male and 51,829 female. Primary school teachers: 2,458 – 1,510 male, 948 female.
Secondary schools: 36 - 13 government, 14 private and 9 community. Secondary school enrolment: 9,675 students – 4,657 male and 5,018 female. Teachers: 588 – 471 male and 117 female.
Tertiary institutions: 1 techical school and 1 primary teachers college.

Health Services: 3 health centre IV (all Government); 14 health centre III (7 government and 7 NGO); and 35 health centre II (32 government and 3 NGO).

Tourist Attractions (Exploited and Potential): Lake Nakivale: Located about 40 kilometres southeast of Mbarara town, the sandy beaches and the expansive open grounds around the lake could in future be exploited for tourism. The land around the lake has been a refugee settlement for many years. Nsongezi cave, a stone-age site has tourism potential too.

District Leaders:	Members of Parliament:

District Leaders:
District Chairperson
  – Mr Ignatius Byaruhanga
Chief Administrative Officer
  – Mr John Nyakahuma
Deputy Chief Administrative Officer
  – Vacant

Members of Parliament:
Bukanga County – Mr Matovu Gregory
Isingiro County North
  – Mr Bright Kanyontore Rwamirama
Isingiro County South
  – Mr Alex Bakunda Byarugaba
District Woman MP
  – Ms Grace Isingoma Byarugaba

Kabale District

At Independence, Kabale was part of Kigezi District. Present-day Kabale, Kanungu, Rukungiri and Kisoro districts constituted Kigezi. In 1974, Kigezi District was divided into North and South Kigezi, with the former becoming Kabale District.

Location: Kabale District borders the districts of Kisoro to the west, Rukungiri to the north, Kanungu to the northwest, Ntungamo to the northeast, and the Republic of Rwanda to the south and southeast.

Area: 1,729.6 sq. km.

Climate, Relief and Vegetation: It lies at an approximate altitude of between 1,219m – 2,347m above sea level. It has an average temperature of 17.5°C which sometimes drops to 10°C at night. Rainfall averages 1,000mm – 1,480mm per annum and vegetation includes bamboo forests and afro-alpine shrubs. Man's intense activity in the district is however, steadily changing this type of vegetation.

Population: According to 2009 projections, there are 477,500 people – 255,600 female and 221,900 male with a density of 275 persons per sq.km.

Major Town: Kabale (administrative headquarters), Katuna, Hamurwa and Muhanga.

Counties and Sub-counties: Ndorwa County – Buhara, Butanda, Kaharo, Kyanamira, Maziba, Kamuganguzi, Kitumba, Rubaya and Katuna (Town Council); Rubanda County – Bubare, Ruhija, Hamurwa, Bufundi, Ikumba, Muko, Nyamweeru and Hamurwa (Town Council); Rukiga County – Bukinda, Kamwezi, Kashambya, Rwamucucu, and Muhanga (Town Council); Kabale Municipality – Kabale Central, Kabale Northern, Kabale Southern divisions.

Main Language: Rukiga

People: Bakiga and Banyarwanda.

Economic Activities: Agriculture with emphasis on:
(i)   Food crops: Sweet potatoes, irish potatoes, sorghum, beans, pigeon peas, wheat and bananas on a small scale.
(ii)   Cash crops: Fruits and vegetables: Main vegetables – Tomatoes, cabbage, carrots, grapes and apples
(iii)   Fishing on Lake Bunyonyi.

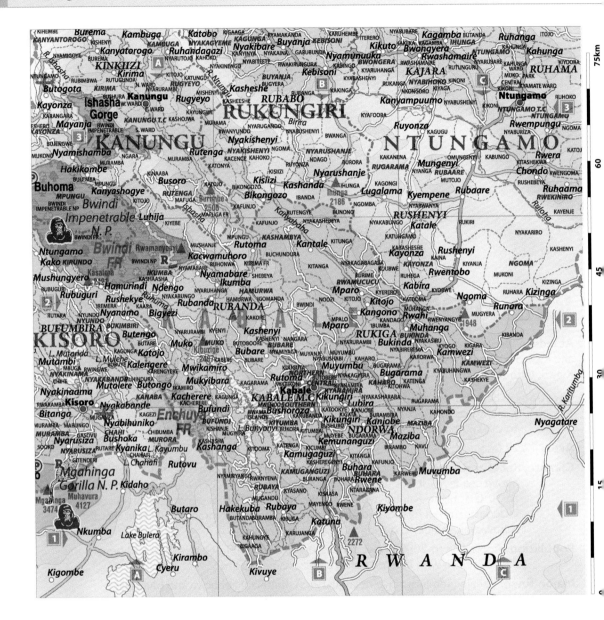

Banks: Stanbic Bank Uganda Ltd – 1, Centenary Rural Development Ltd – 1, National Bank of Commerce – 1.

Area under Forestation: 12,62 hectares.

Animal Population: As of 2008 there were 98,552 cattle, 5 donkeys, 22,255 pigs, 83,060 sheep, 201,597 goats and 218,800 chicken, 5,726 ducks and 865 turkeys.

Co-operative Societies: 226 registered primary societies with Kigezi Union and Kigezi Vegetable Growers at the district level.

Industries: Manufacture of wine, furniture, footwear, processing of coffee, grain, pit sawing, printing, brick making, metal fabrication; mining of wolfram and tin and stone quarrying.

Education Services: Primary schools: 353 – 323 government, 23 private and 7 community. Enrolment: 153,850 pupils – 74,520 male and 79,330 female. Primary school teachers: 4,037 – 2,687 male and 1,350 female.

Secondary schools: 69 schools: 34 government, 22 Private and 13 community. Secondary School enrolment: 26,918 – 14,093 male and 12,825 female. Teachers: 1,661 – 1,329 male and 332 female.

Tertiary institutions: 2 technical institutions, 2 teacher training colleges, national teacher's college – Kabale, Uganda College of Commerce Kabale. Universities: Kigezi International University, Kabale University and Bishop Barham University College.

Health Services: 1 hospital (government) Regional Referral Hospital – Kabale Hospital with 212 beds; 6 health centre IV (all government); 16 health centre III (12 government, 4 NGO); and 61 health centre II (51 government, 10 NGO).

Transport Network: Transport in the district is greatly hindered by the hilly terrain. Some areas are hardly accessible by road, while most of the available feeder-roads become impassable during the rainy season. The district is linked by tarmac to Mbarara and to Rwanda.

Tourist Attractions: Kabale is found in the southwestern pocket of Uganda, an area characterised by great diversity of topography, landscape and vegetation. Sir. Winston Churchill described it as, "The Switzerland of Africa."

The landscape of Kabale town is an amazing scenery of steep slopes.

There is an information office about Bwindi Impenetrable and Mgahinga Gorilla National Parks in Kabale. They also sell tourist maps, postcards and handicrafts.

Lake Bunyonyi: One of the top three deepest lakes in the world is worth a visit while in Kabale. Bunyonyi means 'many small birds' and the lake supports a vibrant bird life. Lake Bunyonyi is like a tin and is deep right from the edge. Bunyonyi Overland Camp, Karibuni Beach Campsite, Old Lodge, Crater Bay Cottages and Far Out Camp are on the shores of Lake Bunyonyi. Bushara Island Camp has fully furnished tents and is an eco-tourism campsite.

One can engage in motor boat riding, canoeing and fishing on the lake.

On Lake Bunyonyi is the Bwama Island, sometimes called Itambira Island. Jasper's Campsite is on this island.

White Horse Inn on Makanga Hill is the best accomodation facility in Kabale District. It has cottages with steep shingle roofs connected to walkways. There is a wonderful log fire to warm up guests at night, a tennis court and a pool table. It is set in wonderful gardens and the golf course is on your left before you enter the colonial gem. White Horse Inn also has camping facilities.

Other accomodation facilities include Holiday Inn, Hope Inn, Victoria Inn, Highland, Moritz Guest House, Skyblue Julieta and Skyline Hotel.

The newly opened Kabale University is found in Kikungiri on Gatuna Road that leads to Rwanda.

Additional Information: Kabale District's main activity is agriculture – subsistence and commercial. Kabale is overpopulated and the land is heavily fragmented. This limits agricultural output.

Irish potatoes and peas are a common delicacy among the Bakiga in Kabale. Presently, apple growing is producing promising results. Pyrethrum growing also takes place in some parts of the district although it is done on a small scale.

Kabale District has no industries, apart from the manufacturing of wine and coffee processing which employ only a small number of people. The mining of wolfram, tin and stone quarrying have not been fully exploited.

Operational Radio Stations: Voice of Kigezi, 89.3FM, Radio West, 94.3FM, Uganda Broadcasting Corporation Radio and The Roots (U) Ltd.

Key NGOs: Africa 2000 Network – Uganda, African Medical Research Foundation Uganda, World Vision Uganda, AfriCare, Compassion International, CARE International in Uganda.

District leaders:	Members of Parliament:
Chairperson – Mr Patrick K. Besigye	Kabale Municipality
Chief Administrative Officer (CAO)	– Mr Baryayanga Andrew Aja
– Mr Joseph Mukasa Maira	Rukiga County – Mr Sabiiti Jack
Deputy CAO – Vacant	Ndorwa County East
Town Clerk (Kabale Municipal Council)	– Mr Wilfred Nuwagaba
– Mr Johnson Baryantuma	Ndorwa County West – Mr David Bahati
Mayor Kabale Municipality	Rubanda County East
– Mr Pius Ruhemurana	– Mr Musasizi Henry Ariganyira
	Rubanda County West
	– Mr Henry Banyenzaki
	Woman MP – Ms Ninsiima Ronah Rita

Kanungu District

Formerly part of Rukungiri District. Although granted district status in the year 2000, it did not operate as a district until 2001.

Location: It borders Rukungiri to the east, the Democratic Republic of Congo to the west and Kabale and Kisoro disticts in the south. Present-day Kabale, Kisoro, Rukungiri and Kanungu districts were previously known as Kigezi District at independence in 1962.

Area: 1,328 sq. km.

Climate and Relief: It has got savanna and equatorial types of climate, with heavy rainfall totalling 118mm per annum.

Population: According to 2009 projections, there are 232,500 people – 120,600 female and 111,900 male, with a density of 175 persons per sq.km.

Major Towns: Kanungu (administrative headquarters); Trading Centre – Kambuga.

Counties and Sub-counties: Kinkiizi County – Kambuga, Kirima, Rugyeyo, Rutenga, Kayonza, Kihiihi, Kanyantorogo, Nyamirama, Mpungu, Kanungu (Town Council), and Kihiihi (Town Council).

Main Languages: Runyankore, Rukiga and Ruhororo.

People: Banyankore, Bakiga and Bahororo.

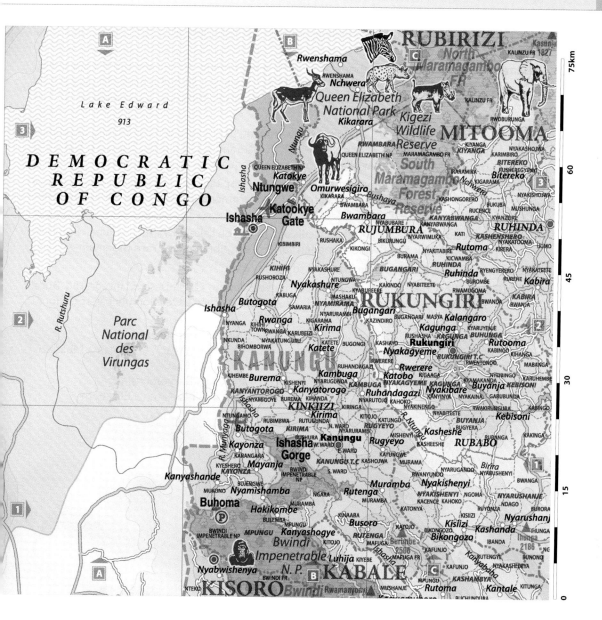

Economic Activities: Agriculture with emphasis on:

   (i)   Food crops: Beans, groundnuts, cassava, soya bean, sorghum, simsim and cow peas.

   (ii) Cash crops: Coffee and tobacco.

   (iii) Fruits and vegetables: Pineapples, tomatoes, onions and cabbage.

   (iv) Fishing on Lake Edward

Area under Forestation: 35,145 hectares.

Animal Population: 31,120 cattle, 22,900 pigs, 12,849 sheep, 105,498 goats, 196,564 chicken, 8,701 ducks and 427 turkeys.

Co-operative Societies: Kanungu and Rukungiri have 101 registered co-operative societies.

Industries: Grain milling, furniture making, woodwork, bakeries, silkworm rearing on a small scale.

Education Services: Primary schools: 187 -142 government, 40 private and 5 community. Primary school enrolment 67,455 – 33,088 male and 34,367 female. Primary school teachers: 1,537 – 1,040 male, 497 female. Available furniture is adequate for 50,124 pupils.

Secondary Schools: 27 schools: 14 government, 9 private and 4 community. Secondary school enrolment: 9,226 students – 4,813 male and 4,413 female. Teachers: 501 - 412 male and 89 female. Available furniture is adequate for 6,351 students.

Health Services: 1 hospital (government - Kambuga Hospital with 114 beds); 1 health centre IV (government); 10 health centre III (9 government, 1 NGO); and 34 health centre II (13 government, 2 NGO).

Tourist Attractions: The Kanungu church cult site, fishing on Lake Edward, the Queen Elizabeth National Park and Bwindi Impenetrable Forest, home of the rare mountain gorillas.

Operational Radio Stations: Kinkizi FM Ltd, Radio West.

Key NGOs: The Child Family Community Development Organisation, Integrated Rural Development Initiatives, Bugongi – Rukukuru Women's Development Association.

District leaders:
Chairperson – Ms Kasya Josephine Charlotte
Chief Administrative Officer (CAO) – Vacant
Dputy Chief Administrative Officer (DCAO) – Mr Swaib Balaba
Town Clerk (Kanungu Town Council) – Mr Christopher Ahimbisibwe

Members of Parliament:
Kinkizi County West – Mr Amama Mbabazi
Kinkizi County East – Mr Chris Baryomunsi
Woman MP – Ms Karungi Elizabeth

Kiruhura District

Location: Kiruhura District borders the districts of Lyantonde, Rakai and Sembabule to the east; Isingiro to the south, Ibanda to the northwest, Mbarara to the west; Kamwenge, Kyegegwa and Mubende to the north.

Area: 4,607. sq.km.

Climate, Relief and Vegetation: The district is generally flat with undulating hills covered with savannah grasslands. It is a cattle corridor.

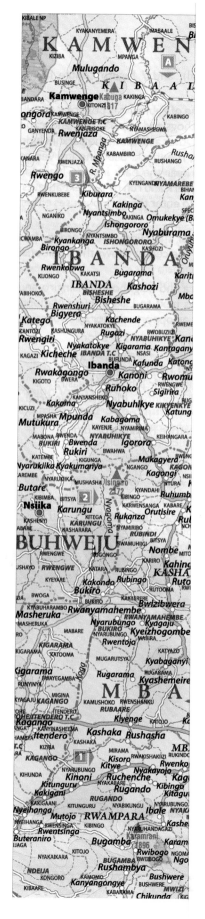

Population: According to 2009 projections, there are 265,500 people - 132,100 female and 133,400 male with a population density of 56 persons per sq.km.

Major Towns: Kiruhura (Administrative HQs), Sanga and Kazo.

Counties and Sub-counties: Kazo County – Buremba, Burunga, Engari, Kanoni, Kazo, Nkungu Rwemikoma, and Kazo (Town Council). Nyabushozi County – Sanga, Kanyaryeru, Nyakashashara, Kinoni, Kenshunga, Kashongi and Kikaatsi, Kitura, (Kiruhuura Town Council), and Sanga (Town Council).

Main Language: Runyankore.

People: Banyankore, Bakiga, Bahororo, Baganda, Banyarwanda, Bafumbira, Batooro, Banyoro, Batagwenda, other Ugandans and non-Ugandans.

Economic Activities: Cattle keeping, banana growing and apiary.

Banks: Stanbic Bank Uganda Ltd – 1

Animal Population: As of 2008, there were 342,315 cattle, 188,686 goats, 28,017 sheep, 3,967 pigs, 142,459 chicken, 4,719 ducks and 235 turkeys.

Industries: Manufacture of textiles and wearing apparel, furniture, grainmill products, metal products, bakery products, footwear, processing of dairy products, printing and publishing.

Education Services: Primary Schools: 285 – 140 government, 112 private and 33 community. Enrolment: 72,237 – 35,891 male and 36,346 female. Primary school teachers: 1,851 – 1,129 male and 722 female. Available furniture is adquate for 44,261 pupils.

Secondary schools: 21 schools - 9 government, 11 Private and 1 community. Secondary school enrolment: 6,875 – 3,708 male and 3,167 female. Teachers: 409 – 331 male and 78 female. Available furniture is adequate for 15,727 students.

Transport: The rugged terrain is a major obstacle to the expansion of the road network in the district. There are a limited number of feeder-roads. The district is connected to Kabale by a newly constracted tarmac road, thus connecting the district to the country's network of main trunk roads. It has an airstrip which facilitates air transport. Kisoro Airfield – The 1496m x 30m runway is grass and in good condition. The airfield is equipped for air plane crashes, fires and rescue services. The Civil Aviation Authority provides H.F. radio communication. The airfield is 5.1 km from Kisoro town. Transportation from the airfield to town can be provided by taxi.

Tourist Attractions: The major tourist attraction in this area is the Mgahinga Gorilla National Park. This is the smallest National Park in Uganda covering just 36 sq km and was established in 1991. It makes up the northeastern part of the Virunga Volcano range which extends into the Democratic Republic of Congo and Rwanda. Between 1960 and the early 80s, poaching affected the Gorilla population by 50 percent. Gorilla tracking permits are obtained from the Uganda Wildlife Authority offices in Kampala or via the website.

Other animals found in Mgahinga include elephants, buffaloes, giant forest hogs, the rare golden monkey and the rare blue monkey.

The Mgahinga Gorilla National Park office is in Kisoro.

The summit of Mountain Muhavura is the highest point of the park at 4, 127m and has a crater lake. The vegetation in the park includes montane, alpine and sub-alpine flora at each of the different levels up the volcano varying with altitude.

Mountain Sabyinyo offers the opportunity of straddling Uganda, Rwanda and the Democratic Republic of Congo simultaneously.

The Mgahinga Mountain climb includes a pleasant walk through bamboo forest, known locally as *rugano*, before the gradient increases up the summit.

The Garama Cave is enormous – over 340m in length and 14m deep. This was where the Batwa (pygmies) warriors used to live during their long-running conflict with their neighbours, the Bantu, almost 100 years ago.

Camping is at the Mountain Mgahinga Rest Camp, set in dramatic scenery in the shadow of the Virunga Volcanoes, it is a good base from which to see the gorillas, or to climb Mountain Muhavura and Mountain Mgahinga. Another campsite is the Amajambere Iwacu Community Camp ground (bandas and campsite) which are near the park headquarters.

Additional Information: Kisoro is one of the districts in Uganda with high agricultural production, although agriculture is carried out on a small scale. Farmers sell some of their produce to middle-men who sell them in urban areas as far as Kampala. But the inadequate road network, with virtually no roads in some parts, denies many farmers access to markets for their crops. The hilly district faces the problem of land shortage as the population is dense and the land is heavily fragmented.

Key NGOs: Africa 2000 Network, Uganda, African Medical Research Foundation Uganda, Adra Uganda, AfriCare Uganda, Kisoro District Farmers' Association, Uganda Red Cross, Uganda Change Agent Association, Microcare, Good Samaritan Community Development Programme, Nyakabingo Women's Health Group.

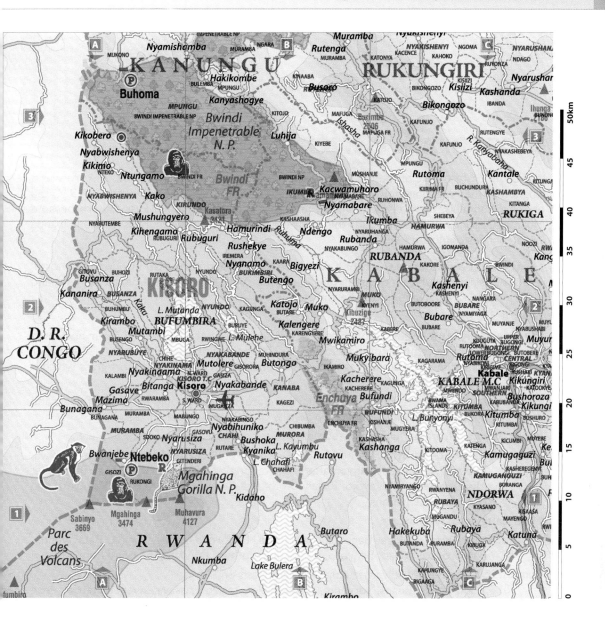

District leaders:
Chairperson – Mr Bazanye Milton M.
Chief Administrative Officer (CAO)
   – Mr David Lubuuka
Ag.Deputy Chief Administrative Officer
   (Ag.DCAO) – Rita
Town Clerk (Kisoro Town Council)
   – Mr Isaiah Tumwesigye

Members of Parliament:
Bufumbira County South
   – Mr Tress Bucyanayandi
Bufumbira County East
   – Mr Kwizera Eddie wa Gahungu
Bufumbira County North
   – Mr Kamara John Nizeyimana
Woman Representative
   – Ms Nyirabashitsi Sarah Mateke

Mbarara District

It was the eastern part of the old Ankore District. At independence in 1962, Ankore was a kingdom. When the kingdom was abolished in 1967, it became Ankore District. In 1974, the provincial administration divided Ankore into East and West Ankole. East Ankore became Mbarara District in 1980. Until 2005 the newly created districts of Kiruhura, Isingiro and Ibanda were counties of Mbarara District.

Location: It borders the districts of Kiruhura to the east and northeast, Ibanda to the north, Isingiro to the southeast, Ntungamoto the south Kibingo (Sheema) to the west and Nsiika (Buhweju) to the northwest.

Area: 1,778 sq. km.

Climate, Relief and Vegetation: It lies at an altitude of between 1290 m – 1,524m above sea level with temperatures averaging 25-27°C and rainfall reaching up to 1,200mm per annum in some areas. Vegetation is a combination of bush and short grass which is good for animal rearing.

Population: According to 2009 projections, there are 410,500 people – 210,200 female and 200,300 male with a population density of 230 persons per sq.km.

Major Towns: Mbarara Municipality (administrative headquarters).

Counties and Sub-counties: Kashari County – Biharwe, Bubaare, Kakiika, Kashare, Rubaya, Rubindi, Bukiro, Rwanyamahembe, Kagongi; Rwampara County – Bugamba, Mwizi, Ndeija, Nyakayojo, Rugando Mbarara Municipality – Kakoba, Kamukuzi and Nyamitanga Divisions.

Main Language: Runyankore.

People: Banyankore, Bakiga, Baganda, Bafumbira, Bahororo, Banyarwanda, Batagwenda, Batooro, Bakhonzo, Banyoro, Acholi, Iteso other Ugandans and non-Ugandans.

Economic Activities: Mainly agriculture with emphasis on:
- (i) Food crops: Beans, sorghum, finger millet, maize, cassava, sweet potatoes, Irish potatoes, groundnuts, bananas and peas.
- (ii) Cash crop: Coffee.
- (iii) Fruits and vegetables: Passion fruit, tomatoes, onions and cabbage.
- (iv) Ranching and dairy farming.

Banks: Bank of Uganda, Stanbic Bank Uganda Ltd – 1, Barclays Ltd –1, Centenary Rural Development Bank –1, Bank of Baroda –1, Standard Chartered Bank Uganda Ltd –1, Crane Bank -1, Fina Bank 1, DFCU Bank 1.

Area under Forestation: 23,985 hectares.

Animal Population: 149,992 cattle, 176,464 goats, 22,588 sheep, 12,243 pigs, 239,470 chicken, 5,966 ducks and 711 turkeys.

Co-operative Societies: 319 registered primary societies with Banyankore Kweteerana Co-operative Union at the district level.

Industries: Manufacture of animal feeds and footwear, leather tanning, making of furniture, laundry soap, jaggery, metal fabrication, agricultural machinery repairing industries, milk processing, coffee processing, grain milling,.

Education Services: Primary schools: 318 – 226 government, 77 private and 15 community. Enrolment: 109,947 – 52,448 male and 54,499 female. Primary school teachers: 3,206 – 1,658 male, 1,548 female.

Secondary schools: 36 schools - 18 government, 15 private and 3 community. Secondary school enrolment: 25,645 – 15,239 male and 10,406 female. Teachers: 1,572 – 1,199 male, 373 female.

Tertiary institutions: 5 technical institutions, 1 primary teachers college, 2 universities - Mbarara University of Science and Technology and Bishop Stuart University.

Health Services: As of December 2006, there were: 4 Hospitals (2 Govt. – Mbarara Hospital with 250 beds is the Regional Referral Hospital, Mbarara University Teaching Hospital has 246 beds, and 2 NGO). 3 government health centre IV (2 government 1 NGOs); 18 health centre III (17 government and 1 NGO), 27 health centre II (24 government and 3 NGO);

Transport Network: Mbarara Airfield – The runway length and width are 1,371m x 30m. Its surface is murram and in good condition and so is the terminal building. The Civil Aviation Authority provides H.F. radio communication. The airfield is 12.5 km from Mbarara town. A number of modern hotels offer reasonable accommodation with bed and breakfast. Transportation from the airfield to town can be provided by taxi.

Telephone services are offered by all mobile phone networks. Public payphones are also available in town.

Tourist Attractions: Mbarara is a lively town which receives many visitors and is a cross-road for travellers heading towards the Queen Elizabeth National Park, Lake Mburo, the Rwenzori Mountains, Mgahinga and Bwindi Impenetrable National Parks in the southwest.

Nkonkonjeru Tombs a burial site of the last two *abagabe* (kings) of Ankore; *Omugabe* (king) Kahaya II and *Omugabe* Gasyonga II and other Ankore royals.

Igongo Cultural Centre: A centre for cultural education is also a tourist attraction.

Hotels include Lake View Regency Hotel, Africa Guest House, Agip Motel & Campsite, Andrews Inn, Canan, Church of Uganda Hostel, Hotel Classic, Entry View Guest House, Kikome Rest House, Mbiringi Hotel, Memory Lodge, New Safari Hotel, Oxford Inn, Pelican Hotel, Riheka Guest House, Rwizi Arch Hotel, and the University Inn and Camping Area. Continental and Ugandan cuisine served in various hotels and restaurants within Mbarara town.

Operational Radio and TV Stations: Capital Radio, Radio Maria, Life Radio, Greater Afrikan Radio, Voice of Tooro, Uganda Broadcasting Corporation Radio, Radio West, Christian Life Ministries, Baptist International Mission (U) and Voice of Africa, UBC TV and WBS TV.

Key NGOs: Integrated Rural Development Initiatives, Family Planning Association of Uganda, Aids Information Centre, Uganda Women's Effort to Save Orphans, Traditional and Modern Health Practitioners, ACORD, Agency for Integrated Development Training Services, Conservation Effort Community Development, Foundation for AIDS Orphaned Children, Kakiika Women's Group, Uganda, Resources Management Foundation, Mbarara District Women's Development Association, Isingiro Family Promotion and Improvement Association.

District leaders:
Chairperson – Mr Tumusiime Deusdedit
Chief Administrative Officer (CAO)
   – Mr Wilson Tibugyenda
Deputy Chief Administrative Officer
   (DCAO)
   – Vacant
Mayor Mbarara Municipality
   – Mr Wilson Tumwine

Members of Parliament:
Mbarara Municipality
   – Mr Bitekyerezo Kab Medard
Rwampara County
   – Mr Mujuni Vicent Kyamadidi
Kashari County – Mr Yaguma Wilberforce
Woman MP – Ms Emma Boona

Mitooma District

At Independence, Mitooma was part of Ankore Kingdom. It later became a County in West Ankore District, which was renamed Bushenyi District in 1980. Mitooma was elevated to district status in 2010.

Location: Mitooma borders the districts of Bushenyi and Sheema to the east, Rukungiri to the west, Ntungamo to the south and Rubirizi to the north.

Area: Approximately 4,292.6 sq. km.

Climate, Relief and Vegetation: It experiences high amounts of rainfall. Average temperatures are as high as 25°C. Vegetation includes a multitude of short grasses, bushes in lowlands and thickets.

Population: According to 2009 projections, there are 181,600 – 96,600 female and 85,000 male with a density of 333 persons per sq.km.

Major Towns: Mitooma (administrative headquarters), and Kashenshero.

Counties and Sub-counties: Ruhinda County – Bitereko, Kabira, Kanyabwanga, Kashenshero, Katenga, Kiyanga, Mayanga, Mitooma, Mutara, Rurehe, Mitooma (Town Council) and Kashenshero (Town Council).

Main Language: Runyankore.

People: Banyankore.

Economic Activities: Agriculture with emphasis on:
  (i)   Food crops: Maize, bananas, millet, rice, simsim, cowpeas, sorghum, sweet potatoes, cassava, bananas, soya bean and beans.
  (ii)   Cash crops: Ginger, cotton, sunflower, coffee and tea.
  (iii) Fruits, vegetables, citrus and other fruit varieties: Tomatoes, cabbage, onions and pineapples.
  (vi) Dairy farming.

Animal Population: Mitooma, Buhweju, Bushenyi, Rubirizi and Sheema have 207,184 cattle, 57,467 pigs, 79,757 sheep, 376,561 goats 364,568 chicken, 19,971 ducks and 2,343 turkeys.

Co-operative Societies: The district still depends on societies registered in the former Bushenyi (the mother district). Banyankore Kweterana Co-operative Union remains the umbrella union specialising mainly in coffee, ranching and distribution of agricultural chemicals.

Industries: Processing of coffee, metal fabrication, weaving and knitting industries.

Banks: The district still depends on banks in the mother district.

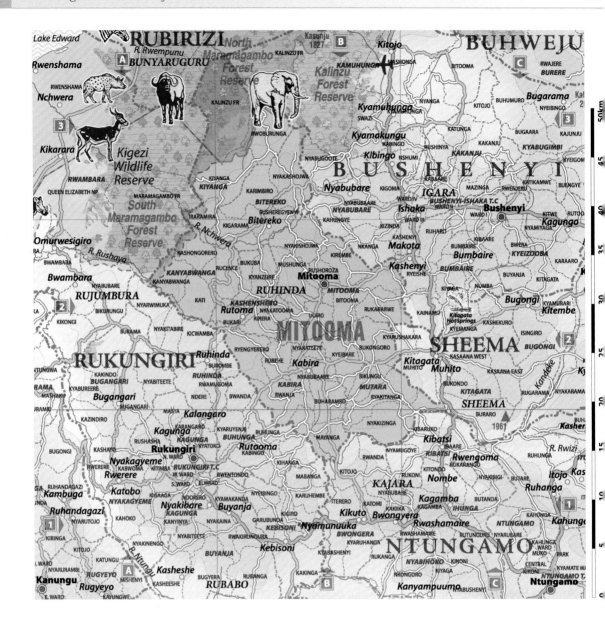

Education Services: Primary schools: 150 – 108 government, 36 private and 6 community. Enrolment 55,410 – 27,082 male and 28,328 female. Primary school teachers: 1,282 – 695 male, and 587 female. Available furniture is adequate for 37,966 pupils.

Secondary schools: 16 schools - 10 government, 5 private and 1 community. Secondary school enrolment: 7,467 – 3,327 male and 4,140 female. Teachers: 377 – 304 male, 73 female. Available furniture is adequate for 6,854 students.

Tertiary institutions: 1 technical institution.

Health Services: 1 health centre IV (government); 6 health centre III (4 government, 2 NGO); and 11 health centre II (8 government, 3 NGO).

Transport Network: The district has a good network of feeder-roads in most areas except those overlooking the rift valley. All counties are linked by feeder-roads although many of

the roads are usable only in the dry season. The district is linked to the neighbouring districts by murram road.

Tourist Attractions: The rift valley escarpment in the northern part of the district is a great potential.

Key NGOs: Family Planning Association of Uganda, VSO Uganda, Uganda Women's Effort to Save Orphans, Hand In Hand Group, National Adult Education Association, Nyanga Kwetungura Group, Bushenyi Disabled Persons Association, Ebenezer Women's Group, Bushenyi Bee Keepers' Association, Bushenyi Banana and Plantain Farmers' Association, Bushenyi Women in Development, Trust for Community Empowerment, Kyeizooba Community Based Health.

District leaders:	Members of Parliament:
Chairperson – Mr Karyeija Johnson B.	Ruhinda County – Mr Kahinda Otafiire
Ag Chief Administrative Officer (CAO) – Ms. Asiimwe Alice Rushere	Woman MP – Ms Kamateeka Jovah
Deputy Chief Administrative Officer (DCAO) – Vacant	

Ntungamo District

Ntungamo District was created in 1993, when parts of Mbarara and Bushenyi Districts were grouped together to from a district. The district had its size increased when Itojo sub-county, which was formerly part of Mbarara district, was added.

Location: It borders the districts of Isingiro to the east, Mbarara to the northeast, Mitooma and Sheema (Kibingo) to the north, Rukungiri to the northwest, Kabale to the southwest and the Republic of Rwanda to the south.

Area: 2,189.0 sq. km.

Climate, Relief and Vegetation: Ntungamo District lies between 1290m – 1,524m above sea level with temperatures averaging 25°C – 27°C and rainfall reaching up to 1,200mm per annum in some areas. The vegetation is a combination of bush and short grass.

Population: According to 2009 projections, there are 438,900 people – 229,500 female and 209,400 male with a density of 213 persons per sq.km.

Major Towns: Ntungamo (administrative headquarters); Trading Centres – Rwashamaire and Rubaare.

Counties and Sub-counties: Kajara County – Bwongyera, Ihunga, Kibatsi, Nyabihoko; Ruhaama County – Ntungamo, Ruhaama, Rukoni East, Rukoni West, Rweikiniro, Nyakyera, Itojo; Rushenyi County – Kayonza, Ngoma, Rubaare and Rugarama; Ntungamo Municipality – Eastern Division, Central Division and Western Division.

Main Languages: Runyankore, Runyarwanda and Rukiga.

People: Banyankore, Bahororo, Banyarwanda, Bakiga.

Economic Activities: Mainly agriculture with emphasis on:
- (i) Food crops: Beans, finger millet, cassava, sweet potatoes, groundnuts, bananas and peas.
- (ii) Cash crops: Coffee.
- (iii) Cattle rearing.

Banks: Stanbic Bank Uganda Ltd –1.

Area under Forestation: 2,555 hectares.

Co-operative Societies: 144 primary co-operative societies with Banyankore Kweterana Growers Co-operative Union as the umbrella district union specialising in coffee production.

Animal Population: According to 2008 statistics, the district has 229,004 cattle, 50 donkeys, 8,899 pigs, 41,556 sheep, 273,284 goats, 184,760 chicken, 8,814 ducks and 457 turkeys.

Industries: Coffee processing, brick making, milk cooling plants and silkworm rearing on a small scale in Kajara and Ruhaama.

Education Services: Primary schools: 354 – 250 government, 97 private and 7 community. Enrolment: 123,223 – 60,245 male and 62,978 female. Primary school teachers: 3124 –1,848 male and 1,276 female.

Secondary Schools: 30 - 4 government, 25 private and1 community. Secondary school enrolment: 18,307 – 9,846 male and 8,461 female. Teachers: 998 – 801 male and 197 female.

Tertiary institutions: 1 teacher training college, 1 technical institution and many small private commercial schools.

Health Services: 1 hospital (government - Itojo Hospital with 100 beds); 3 health centre IV (all government); 10 health centre III (all government); and 22 health centre II (19 government, 2 NGO and 1 private).

Transport Network: The district has a good feeder-road network which links all the counties and towns in the district. The tarmac road cuts across the district connecting Mbarara, Kabale and Rukungiri districts.

Tourist Attractions: The legendary Lake Nyabihoko offers boating, fishing and swimming as well as a chance to see a variety of birds. Lake Nyabihoko was the site of the first Commonwealth Scout Jamboree. The rare Karegyeya Rock and the general terrain of the district are attractive to touists.

Operational Radio Station: Radio Ankore, Radio West, Radio Rukungiri, Voice of Kigezi.

Additional Information: The district has a water problem. There are limited numbers of water sources.

Key NGOs: African Medical Research Foundation Uganda, VSO Uganda, Rushoka Women's Group, Rushoka Orphan Education Scheme, Ntungamo District NGOs/CBOs Forum, Kiyenje Dairy Co-operative Heifer Project, Ntungamo District Farmers' Association, Kabeezi Youth Farmers' Group, Ntungamo Rural and Urban Foundation, Rwoho Rural Development Associates, Western Micro-finance Union.

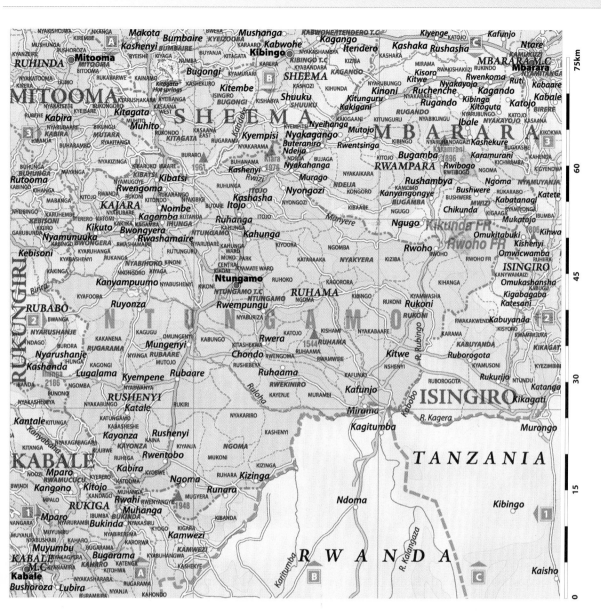

District leaders:
Chairperson – Mr Denis S.T.K. Singahache
Chief Administrative Officer (CAO)
  – Mr Chrizestom Kayise
Deputy Chief Administrative Officer
  (CAO) – Vacant
Ag. Town Clerk (Ntungamo Municipal
  Council) – Mr A. T. Abireebe
Mayor Ntungamo Municipality
  – Mr Jacob Kafuleeka

Members of Parliament:
Kajara County – Mr Stephen N. Tashobya
Rushenyi County
  – Mr Mwesigwa Rukutana
Ruhama County
  – Ms Janet Kataaha Museveni
Ntungamo Municipality
  – Mr Musinguzi Yona
Woman MP – Ms Kabasharira Naome

Kyambogo  University

P. O. BOX 1 KYAMBOGO
Tel: 041 -286237 /285001 Fax: 041 -220464
Email: arkyu@kyambogo.ac.ug, website: www. Kyambogo.ac.ug

Office of the Vice Chancellor

Kyambogo University, one of the five public universities in Uganda is the 2nd largest having been established after the merger of Uganda Polytechnic Kyambogo, Institute of Teacher Education Kyambogo and Uganda National Institute of Special Education.

These Institutions have now been fully integrated into the university which has now got six faculties, namely:

- Faculty of Engineering
- Faculty of Arts and Social Sciences
- Faculty of Vocational Studies
- Faculty of Special Needs Education and Rehabilitation
- Faculty of Science
- Faculty of Education

And two schools namely:
- School of Management and Entrepreneurship
- School of Post Graduate Studies

Kyambogo University now offers a multiplicity of courses ranging from certificate to masters degree programmes for a whole range of academic scholars. Kyambogo University is a unique university that focuses on producing graduates who are resilient, practical and who quickly add value to their chosen vocation/place of work.

It seeks to produce quality graduates with a positive attitude, and hands on experience (practical orientation) and with the ability to adopt to the demands and needs of a dynamic society.

The University has adopted an integrated approach to the provision of high quality university experience through embracing its vision: "To be a Centre of Academic and Professional Excellence"

Kyambogo University has the Council as the highest policy making body which is assisted by top Management headed by the Vice Chancellor, currently (Prof. Omolo).

At the academic level, it is headed by the Senate whose mandate covers quality and standards of academic provision.

At the financial level, the Finance Management Committee sets and agrees on financial concerns both at Council level and at management level.

Thus all this reinforces its motto of providing "Knowledge and Skills for Service".

Rubiriizi District

At Independence, Rubirizi was part of Ankore Kingdom. It later became a county called Bunyaruguru in West Ankore District which was renamed Bushenyi District in 1980. Bunyaruguru was elevated to district status in 2010.

Location: Rubirizi borders the districts of Nsiika (Buhweju) to the east, Rukungiri to the southwest, Mitooma and Bushenyi to the south, Kasese to the north, Kamwenge in the northeast and the Democratic Republic of Congo to the west.

Area: Approximately 1,327 sq. km.

Climate, Relief and Vegetation: It experiences high amounts of rainfall. Average temperatures are as high as 25°C while vegetation includes short grasses, bushes thickets and forests in some parts.

Population: According to 2009 projections, there are 115,000 – 59,800 female and 55,200 male with a density of 86 people per sq.km.

Major Towns: Rubirizi (administrative headquarters); Trading Centres – Katerera.

Counties and Sub-counties: Bunyaruguru County – Rutoto, Magambo, Katunguru, Kichwamba, Ryeru and Rubirizi (Town Council). Katerera County: Kirugu, Katanda, Kyabakara, Katerera, Katerera (Town Council) .

Main Language: Runyankore.

People: Banyankore.

Economic Activities: Agriculture with emphasis on:
- (i) Food crops: Maize, bananas, millet, rice, simsim, cowpeas, sorghum, sweet potatoes, cassava, bananas, soya bean and beans.
- (ii) Cash crops: Ginger, cotton, sunflower, coffee and tea.
- (iii) Fruits, vegetables, citrus and other fruit varieties: Tomatoes, cabbage, onions and pineapples.
- (vi) Dairy farming.

Area under Forestation: 89,439 hectares.

Animal Population: Rubirizi, Buhweju, Bushenyi, Mitooma and Sheema have 207,184 cattle, 57,467 pigs, 79,757 sheep, 376,561 goats 364,568 chicken, 19,971 ducks and 2,343 turkeys.

Co-operative Societies: The district still depends on societies registered in the former Bushenyi (the mother district). Banyankore Kweterana Co-operative Union remains the umbrella union specialising mainly in coffee, ranching and distribution of agricultural chemicals.

Industries: Processing of coffee and tea, curing tobacco, weaving and knitting industries, brick and furniture making.

Banks: The district still depends on banks in the mother district.

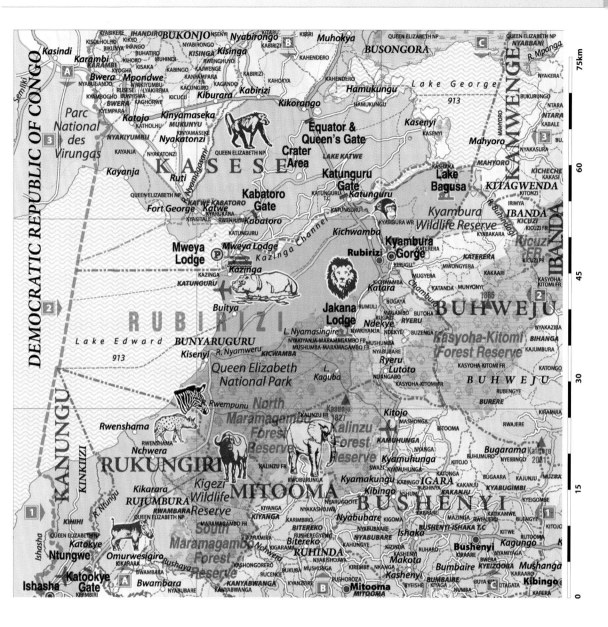

Education Services: Primary schools: 69 – 56 government, 11 private and 2 community. Enrolment 27,206 – 13,522 male and 13,684 female. Primary school teachers: 573 – 383 male, 190 female. Available furniture is adequate for 18,422 pupils.

Secondary schools: 8 schools – 3 government, 3 private and 2 community. Secondary School enrolment: 3,303 – 1,764 male and 1,629 female. Teachers: 154 – 128 male, 26 female. Available furniture is adequate for 2,166 students.

Health Services: 1 health centre IV (government); 4 dispensaries III (all NGO); 9 health centre II (6 government and 3 NGO).

Transport Network: The district has a poor network of feeder-roads. The two counties are linked by feeder-roads, most of which are impassable during the rainy season. The district is linked to Bushenyi and Kasese districts by a good tarmac road.

Tourist Attractions: The district shares part of Queen Elizabeth National Park with Kasese District. There are many scenic crater lakes in the district and the beautiful Rift Valley escarpment.

Kalinzu Forest Reserve is situated 10 km northwest of Ishaka on the main Mbarara-Kasese Road. There are guided forest walks in Kalinzu.

The palm trail is a 5 km trail which takes two hours to complete – it is dotted with the flame tree and dragon tree.

The valley trail is a three-and-a-half kilometre-walk, taking two hours with a wonderful view overlooking the Rift Valley. The trek includes a ridge walk and gives visitors the chance to see a *"Viagra"* tree, Mutragyne rubrostipuleta.

The waterfall trail is an 11km trail over hilly terrain taking four or five hours.

Kasyoha Kitomi Forest overlooks the Albetine Rift Valley and supports a large bio-diversity of forest, flora and fauna.

Key NGOs: Family Planning Association of Uganda, VSO Uganda, Uganda Women's Effort to Save Orphans, Hand In Hand Group, National Adult Education Association, Nyanga Kwetungura Group, Bushenyi Disabled Persons Association, Ebenezer Women's Group, Bushenyi Bee Keepers' Association, Bushenyi Banana and Plantain Farmers' Association, Bushenyi Women in Development, Trust for Community Empowerment.

District leaders:	Members of Parliament:
Chairperson – Mr Kisembo David	Bunyaruguru County
Chief Administrative Officer (CAO)	– Mr Tindamanyire Gaudioso Kabondo
– Mr Fredrick Kwihiira Rwabuhoro	Katerera County – Mr Katoto Hatwib
Deputy Chief Administrative Officer	Woman MP
(DCAO) – Vacant	– Ms Mbabazi Betty Ahimbisibwe

Rukungiri District

Rukungiri District was formerly part of Kigezi District. In 1974, under the provincial administration, Kigezi was divided into South Kigezi and North Kigezi. In 1980, South Kigezi was renamed Kabale while North Kigezi became Rukungiri.

Location: Rukungiri borders the districts of Bushenyi and Ntungamo to the east, Kabale to the south, Kasese to the north and Kanungu to the west.

Area: 1,527 sq. km.

Climate and Relief: The district has characteristics of both the savannah and modified equatorial climatic zones. Rainfall is heavy. For example, in the period between April and June 1991, it received 118mm in 8 rain days.

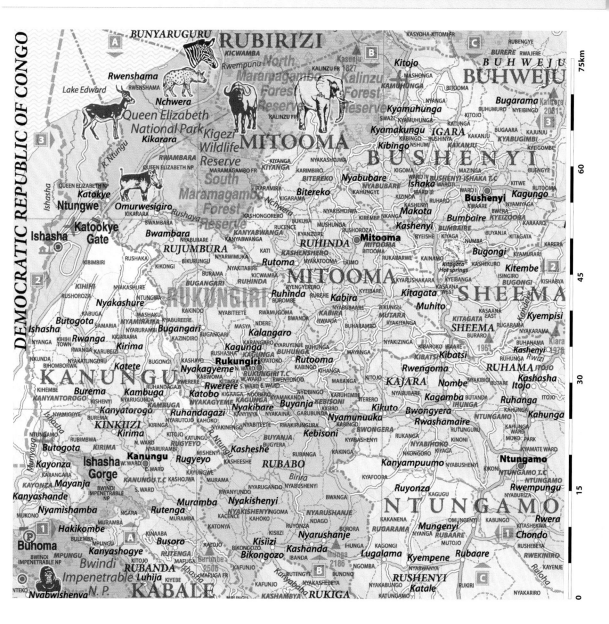

Population: According to 2009 projections, there are 301,100 people – 158,200 female, 142,900 male with a density of 197 persons per sq.km.

Major Towns: Rukungiri (administrative headquarters); Trading Centres – Bwambara, Buyanja and Kagunga.

Counties and Sub-counties: Rubabo County – Buyanja, Kebisoni, Nyakishenyi, Nyarushanje; Rujumbura County – Bugangari, Buhunga, Bwambara, Kagunga, Nyakagyeme, Ruhinda; Rukungiri Municipality - Eastern Division, Southern Division,

Main Languages: Ruhororo, Runyankore and Rukiga.

People: Bahororo, Banyankore and Bakiga.

Economic Activities: Mainly agriculture with emphasis on:
  (i)   Food crops: Beans, sweet potatoes, maize, sorghum, cassava, soya bean, groundnuts, bananas, sunflower, simsim and cowpeas.
  (ii) Cash crops: Coffee and tobacco.
  (iii) Fruits and vegetables: Pineapples, tomatoes, onions and cabbage.
  (iv) Dairy farming.
  (v)   Fishing on Lake Edward.

Banks: Stanbic Bank Uganda Ltd – 2, Cetenary Rural Developmnt Bank, Crane Bank.

Area under Forestation: 26,050 hectares.

Co-operative Societies: Rukungiri and Kanungu have 101 registered co-operative societies.

Animal Population: 60,061 cattle, 20 donkeys, 25,176 pigs, 19,262 sheep, 134,757 goats, 138,100 chicken, 5,858 ducks and 515 turkeys.

Industries: Grain milling, bakeries, furniture and woodwork, processing of coffee, tobacco and silkworm rearing on a small scale.

Education Services: Primary schools: 203 – 173 government, 26 private and 3 community and 1 not reported. Enrolment: 86,465 – 42,102 male and 44,363 female. Primary school teachers: 2,125 – 1,301 male and 894 female.

  37 Secondary Schools: 23 government, 10 private, 4 community. Secondary School Enrolment: 16,274 male and female. Enrolment in Private and Community secondary schools. Private: 1,684 – 882 male and 802 female. Community: 144 – 56 male and 88 female. Teachers: 845 male and female and 1 not stated.

  Tertiary institutions: 2 Technical Institutions and 2 Teacher Training Colleges.

Health Services: 2 hospitals (all NGO) - Uganda Catholic Medical Bureau – Nyakibale Hospital with 165 beds, Uganda Protestant Medical Bureau – Kisiizi Hospital with 200 beds, 3 health centre IV (all government), 17 health centre III (9 government, 8 NGO), 38 health centre II (23 government, 15 NGO). Private/NGO – 9 dispensaries, 28 clinics.

Transport Network: The district has a network of murram roads. The district is connected to the neighbouring districts of Kabale and Mbarara by tarmac roads. The network of feeder-roads is well distributed, connecting all parts of the district.

Tourist Attractions: Rukungiri District lies in the Western Rift Valley. It is endowed with attractive physical features.

  The Kigezi Wildlife Reserve and the 27m Kisiizi Falls near the village of Kisiizi, which is about 30 km from Kabale.

Additional Information: Because of its close proximity to the border with the Democratic Republic of Congo, the district has the advantage of benefiting from cross-border trade. One of the important crossing points in this trade is the Ishasha border town. Rukungiri enjoys high agricultural productivity. The district is self-sufficient in food. Most people produce at subsistence level but sell the surplus.

Operational Radio Station: Radio Rukungiri and Maendeleo Company Limited.

Key NGOs: African Medical Research Foundation Uganda, Wildlife Clubs of Uganda, Twimukye Group, Rubabo Community Initiative to Promote Health, Rukungiri Functional Literacy Resource Centre.

District leaders:
Chairperson – Mr Byabakama Charles
Chief Administrative Officer (CAO)
 – Mr Owen Muhenda Rujumba
Town Clerk (Rukungiri Municipal Council)
 – Mr Aggrey Muramira
Mayor Rukungiri Municipality
 – Mr Charles Makuru

Members of Parliament:
Rubabo County
 – Ms Mary Paula K. Turyahikayo
Rujumbura County
 – Mr Jim Katugugu Muhwezi
Rukungiri Municipality
 – Mr Mugume Roland
Woman MP
 – Ms Sezi prisca Bessy Mbaguta

Sheema District

At Independence, Sheema (Kibingo) was part of Ankore Kingdom. It was one of the counties in West Ankore District which was renamed Bushenyi District in 1980. Sheema was elevated to district status in July 2010.

Location: Sheema District borders the districts of Mbarara to the east, Bushenyi and Mitooma to the west, Ntungamo to the south and Nsiika (Buhweju) to the north.

Area: Approximately 700 sq. km.

Climate, Relief and Vegetation: It experiences high amounts of rainfall. Average temperatures are as high as 25°C. Vegetation includes a multitude of short grasses, bushes in lowlands and thickets.

Population: According to 2009 projections, there are 203,500 – 106,100 female and 97,400 male with a density of 290 persons per sq.km.

Major Towns: Kabwohe-Itendero; Trading Centre – Masheruka.

Counties and Sub-counties: Sheema County – Kagango, Kasaana, Kigarama, Kyangyenyi, Bugongi, Kitagata, Masheruka, Shuuku, Bugongi (Town Council), Kabwohe-Itendero (Town Council), and Kibingo (Town Council).

Main Language: Runyankore.

People: Banyankore.

Economic Activities: Agriculture with emphasis on:
(i) Food crops: Maize, bananas, millet, rice, simsim, cowpeas, sorghum, sweet potatoes, cassava, bananas, soya bean and beans.
(ii) Cash crops: Ginger, cotton, sunflower, coffee and tea.
(iii) Fruits, vegetables, citrus and other fruit varieties: Tomatoes, cabbage, onions and pineapples.
(vi) Dairy farming.

Animal Population: Sheema, Buhweju, Bushenyi, Mitooma, and Rubirizi have 207,184 cattle, 57,467 pigs, 79,757 sheep, 376,561 goats 364,568 chicken, 19,971 ducks and 2,343 turkeys.

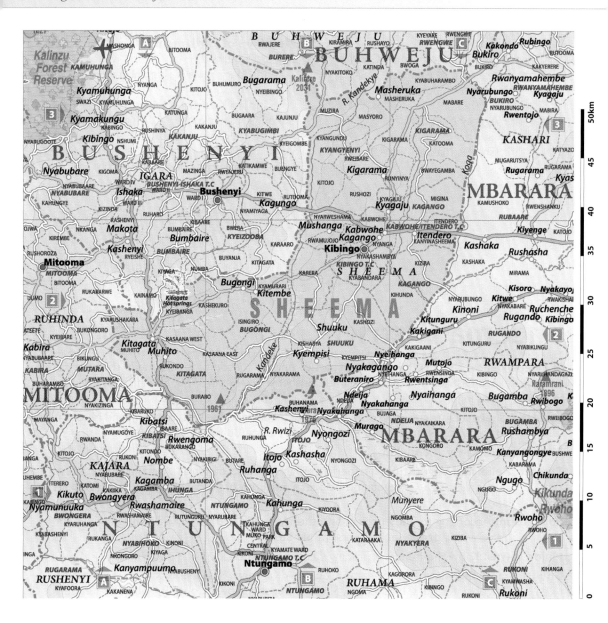

Co-operative Societies: The district still depends on societies registered in the former Bushenyi (the mother district.) Banyankore Kweterana Co-operative Union remains the umbrella union specialising mainly in coffee, ranching and distribution of agricultural chemicals.

Industries: Processing of coffee and tea, curing tobacco, weaving and knitting industries, mining of gold and limestone, brick and furniture making.

Banks: Stanbic Bank Uganda Ltd –1.

Education Services: Primary schools: 175 – 127 government, 46 private and 2 community. Enrolment 59,188 – 29,066 male and 30,122 female. Primary school teachers: 1,619 – 797 male and 822 female. Available furniture is adequate for 46,348 pupils.

Secondary schools: 20 schools – 10 government, 8 private and 2 community. Secondary school enrolment: 14,152 – 6,987 male and 7,165 female. Teachers: 820 – 620 male and 200 female. Available furniture is adequate for 9,647 students.

Tertiary institution: 1 university – Nganwa University.

Health Services: 1 Hospital – (government - Kitagata Government Hospital with 106 beds); 1 health centre IV (government) 3 health centre III (2 Government and 1 NGO) , 23 health centre II (20 government, 2 private and 1 NGO).

Transport Network: The district has a network of feeder-roads in the area which are in a relatively good state compared to the other southwestern districts. All sub-counties are linked by feeder-roads. The district is linked to Mbarara and Bushenyi districts by a good tarmac road.

Tourist Attractions:

Kitagata Hot-Springs is worth a visit. These sulphur rich springs are used by the local people suffering from rheumatism and arthritis.

Modern tea plantations and farming systems are an addition to the natural beauty of the district.

Key NGOs: Family Planning Association of Uganda, VSO Uganda, Uganda Women's Effort to Save Orphans, Hand In Hand Group, National Adult Education Association, Nyanga Kwetungura Group, Bushenyi Disabled Persons Association, Ebenezer Women's Group, Bushenyi Bee Keepers' Association, Bushenyi Banana and Plantain Farmers' Association, Bushenyi Women in Development, Trust for Community Empowerment.

District leaders:	Members of Parliament:
Chairperson – Mr Mugisha Pastor	Sheema County South
Ag Chief Administrative Officer (CAO)	– Mr Katwiremu Yorokamu Bategana
– Mr Kuruhiira Godfrey Metuseera	Sheema County North
Chief Administrative Officer (CAO)	– Mr Elioda Tumwesigye
– Vacant	Woman MP – Ms Nyakikongoro Roemary

Left: Ankole maidens with their traditional milk pots. Right: Herding the long-horned Ankole cattle.

Western Districts

Buliisa   Bundibugyo   Hoima   Kabarole   Kamwenge   Kasese   Kibaale   Kiryandongo
Kyegegwa   Kyenjojo   Masindi   Ntoroko

The People: The inhabitants are the Banyoro, the Batooro, the Bamba, the Bakonzo, the Batagwenda and the Bakiga.

Economic activities: The main cash crops produced are coffee, tea and tobacco. People in this area also keep long-horned cattle.

The pygmiod people known as the Bambuti, relatives of Batwa also dwell in this area.

Tourism: Tourist attractions include wild game in Queen Elizabeth, Semliki, and Murchison Falls National Parks; as well as in the Game Reserves of Karuma, Bugungu, and Katonga. Chimpanzees are found in Kibale Forest Reserve, while the Queen Elizabeth National Park has many animals including the Uganda Kob, elephants, lions, buffaloes and many others. Other attractions include, Mt. Rwenzori and stalagmites and stalactites locally known as "*Amabeere ga Nyinamwiru,*" (Nyinamwiru's breasts) found in caves near Fort Portal. There are also the Sempaya Hot Springs in Bundibugyo and the luxuriant rain forests of Budongo and Kibale.

How to get there: The region is accessed mainly by road. There is the Kampala-Masindi Road, the Kampala-Mbarara-Kasese-Fort Portal Road and the Fort Portal-Kyenjojo Road all of which are tarmac. The Kampala-Mubende-Kyenjojo Road is near completion and the Kampala-Hoima Road is under construction. The rest of the roads in the area are gravel. There is also accessibility by air; there are airstrips at Masindi, Kasese, and Fort Portal, although there are no regular scheduled flights. The Kampala-Kasese railway is currently out of service.

Subdivision: The region is subdivided into three subregions namely Rwenzori, Tooro, and Bunyoro.

"Caught in a shower . . ." a young chimpanzee in Kibale forest seems to ponder the way forward (left). Mount Speke and its glaciers (Middle). It is the second highest peak of the Rwenzori Mountain range which stretches through Kasese, Kabarole and Bundibugyo districts. Part of the oil exploration infrastructure in Hoima. (right)

Western Districts

Buliisa District

Buliisa District is one of the ten districts that were formed in July 2006. Until then Buliisa was a county in Masindi District then consisting of other counties of Bujenje, Buruli and Kibanda.

Location: Buliisa district borders the districts of Nwoya to the north, Kiryandongo to the northeast, Masindi to the east and south, Hoima to the southwest and the Democratic Republic of Congo, separated by Lake Albert, to the west.

Area: 2,027 sq.km

Climate, Relief and Vegetation: It lies at an altitude of between 621m – 1,158m above sea level in a savannah climatic zone, with temperatures averaging over 25°C and rainfall 100mm – 1,000mm per annum. Vegetation is punctuated by short grass and shrubs.

Population: Based on 2009 population projections, there are 73,700 people – 38,200 female and 35,500 male with a density of 36 persons per sq.km.

Major Town: Buliisa Town Council (district administration HQs); *Trading Centres:* Biiso, Buliisa, Buliisa (Town Council), Butiaba, Kigwera, Kihungya, and Ngwedo.

Counties and Sub-Counties: Buliisa County – Biiso and Buliisa.

Main Language: Rugungu and Runyoro

People: Banyoro and other tribes

Economic Activities: Mainly agriculture with emphasis on:

(i) Food crops: Maize, finger millet, beans, cassava, simsim (sesame), groundnuts, sorghum, peas, Irish potatoes, sweet potatoes and bananas.
(ii) Cash crops: Tobacco, coffee and cotton.
(iii) Vegetables: Tomatoes and cabbage.
(iv) Fishing

Animal Population: Based on the 2008 statistics there are 34,801 cattle, 43,326 goats, 3,884 sheep, 849 pigs 99,932 chicken, 8,542 ducks and 115 turkeys.

Co-operative Societies: The same as in mother district, Masindi.

Industries: Manufacture of food products, beverages and other transport equipment.

Banks: The people are using the services of the banks in the mother district, Masindi.

Education Services: Primary schools: 34 schools – 30 government, 2 private and 2 community. Enrolment: 22,247 pupils – 11,582 male and 10,665 female. Primary school teachers: 307 – 228 male and 79 female. Available furniture is adequate for 11,244 pupils.

Secondary schools: 5 schools - 2 government and 3 private. Secondary School Enrolment: 2,153 students - 1,427 male and 726 female. Teachers: 90 – 81 male and 9 female. Available furniture is adequate for 1,005 pupils.

Health Services: 1 health centre IV (government), 1 health centre II (government), and 6 health centre II (5 government, 1 NGO).

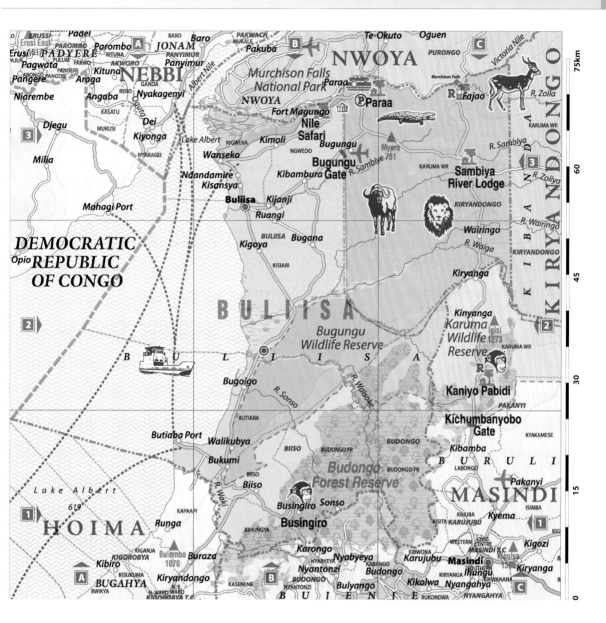

Tourist Attractions: Butyaba Port is located on Lake Albert on the Western Rift Valley, below Biiso escarpment and Bugungu Wildlife Reserve. The services and other activities of the Port were at their peak during the days of the East African Community. One of the ruins at the site is an abandoned ship estimated to have had a capacity of 300 people. The families of the former workers still occupy some of the workers houses. With such a housing infrastructure from the East African Community, the Port has a potential for tourism investment.

Budongo Forest-Busingiro and Kaniyo Pabidi Eco-Tourism Centre: Located close to Budongo Forest Reserve, the econ-tourism centre offers forest/nature and primate walks and bird watching in Budongo Forest Reserve. The "royal mile", a road stretch constructed by one of the Kings of Bunyoro is another attraction. In addition Kaniyo Pabidi centre is wel! known for easy chimpanzee viewing.

Wanseko Communtity Campsite: Located on Lake Albert, the site offers expansive camping grounds, a sandy beach for bird watching and canoeing.

Buliisa Escarpment and Hot Springs: Found in the western rift valley in the Lake Albert basin, the area offers a good opportunity for viewing the effects and features of faulting as well as the western rift valley. The salty waters of the hot springs have provided opportunities for the communities to make salt farms from which they harvest and treat the salt using traditional methods. The beaches of Buliisa are ideal for development of water sports.

Key NGOs: Same as in mother district, Masindi. Conservation and Promotion Association, Youth Effort against STDs/AIDS, Uganda Society for Disabled Children, Masindi District Farmers' Association, Uganda Fisheries and Fish Conservation Association, Vision for Rural Development Initiatives, Poverty Alleviation Credit Trust, Participatory Rural Development Organisation, Masindi Small Scale Industries Association, Nutrifarm Services Uganda, Budongo Forests Community Development Association, Masindi Seed and Grain Growers Association, Action for Children, Masindi.

District Leaders:	**Members of Parliament:**
District Chairperson	Buliisa County
– Mr Lukumu J.N.W. Fred	– Mr Stephen Biraahwa Mukitare
Ag Chief Administrative Officer (CAO)	Adyeeri
– Mr Leonard Micheal Nandala	District Woman MP
Deputy Chief Administrative Officer	– Ms Beatrice Mpairwe
(DCAO) – Vacant	

Bundibugyo District

At independence in 1962, Bundibugyo was part of Tooro Kingdom. When the kingdoms were abolished in 1967, Tooro Kingdom attained district status. In 1974, Semliki District was carved out of Tooro District and in 1980 it was renamed Bundibugyo. In 2009, it was divided to give way to a new district of Ntoroko.

Location: It borders the districts of Kabarole to the east, Kasese to the south, Lake Albert to the north and the Democratic Republic of Congo to the west. It is the extreme western part of the former district of Tooro.

Area: 851 sq. km.

Climate and Relief: It lies at an approximate altitude of between 619m and 3,556m above sea level. Lies in the savanna zone with moderately high rainfall and temperatures.

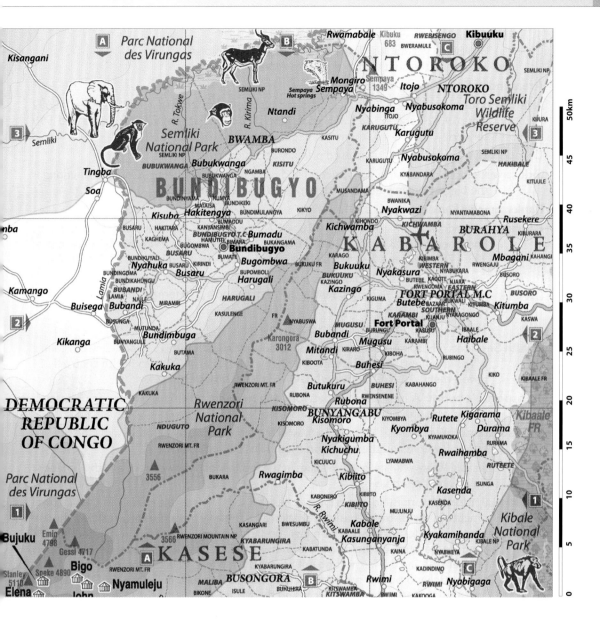

Population: According to 2009 projections, there are 220,800 people – 116,800 female, 104,000 male with a density of 259 persons per sq.km.

Major Towns: Bundibugyo (administrative headquarters); Trading Centres – Budadi, Busoro and Nyahuka.

Counties and Sub-counties: Bwamba County – Budandi, Bubukwanga, Busaru, Bundibugyo (Town Council), Nyahuka (Town Council), Kirumya, Kisubba, and Mirambi; Bughendera County – Harugali, Kasitu, Ndugutu, Bukonzo, Ntotoro, Sindila and Ngamba.

People: Bamba and Batooro.

Economic Activities: Agriculture with a bias towards:
  (i)   Food crops: Maize, cassava, beans, sweet and Irish potatoes, soya bean, yams, groundnuts and bananas.

(ii) Cash crop: Cocoa, vanilla and palm oil.

(iii) Fruits and vegetables: Tomatoes, cabbages and onions.

(iv) Fishing on the southern end of Lake Albert.

Area under Forestation: 74,084 hectares.

Animal Population: As of 2008 Bundibugyo and Ntoroko districts had 163,913 cattle, 14,692 pigs, 14,824 sheep, 131,765 goats and 312,931 chicken, 27,645 ducks and 519 turkeys.

Co-operative Societies: 51 registered primary societies.

Industries: Cocoa processing, construction and carpentry, brick making. Cocoa fermenting is the biggest single industry and it involves about 52 people.

Banks: Stanbic Bank Uganda Ltd – 1.

Education Services: Primary schools: 110 – 97 government, 9 private and 4 community. Enrolment 54,513 pupils – 28,872 male and 25,641 female. Primary school teachers: 985 – 782 male and 203 female. Available furniture is adequate for 37,748 pupils.

Secondary schools: 13 schools - 5 government, 7 private and 1 community. Secondary school enrolment: 4,268 students – 2,718 male and 1,550 female. Teachers: 213 - 193 male and 20 female.

Tertiary institution: 1 teacher training college.

Health Services: 1 hospital (government) - Bundibugyo Hospital with 153 beds. 2 health centre IV (government), 4 health centre III, (3 government, 1 NGO), 15 health centre II (14 government, 1 NGO). Private/NGO – 2 dispensaries, 6 clinics.

Transport Network: A murram road network that meanders over rugged terrain. Transport to and within the district is a big problem.

Tourist Attractions: Semliki National Park which contains Sempaya Hot Springs, the Semliki Forest Reserve and the Rwenzori Mountains National Park.

Semliki Valley Wildlife Reserve, hikes at the foothills of the Rwenzoris and the Amabere Caves and Waterfalls.

Additional Information: Bundibugyo District has rich soils and reliable rainfall. But agricultural practice in the district is basically small scale. The hilly terrain greatly restricts the use of machines for large scale farming. The farmers face difficulties in marketing their produce because of the poor road network. During the rainy season transport is problematic and the farmers do not access the market. There is some trade between the district and border areas of the Democratic Republic of Congo. But the densely forested borderline in some places and the absence of roads frustrates possible large scale trade. There are virtually no industries in Bundibugyo apart from small ones like cocoa processing, which are not widespread and employ only a few people.

Key NGOs: Actionaid Uganda, World Vision Uganda, Abanya Rwenzori Mountaineering Association, Uganda Red Cross, North Rwenzori Rural Community Agriculture and Conservation Link, Self Care Bundibugyo, National Association of Women Organisations in Uganda, Baghendera Farmers' Organisation for Organic Farming, Bundibugyo Association of Women Living with AIDS, Green Dove Puppeter for Adolescent Awareness, Thukolendeke Disabled Group, Mataisa Womens Group, Community Hygiene and Sanitation Promoters Association.

Hoima District

Hoima was originally part of former Bunyoro District. At Independence, Bunyoro was a kingdom and Hoima was an entity within the kingdom. When Ugandan kingdoms were abolished in 1967, Bunyoro became a district.

In 1974 Bunyoro was divided into North Bunyoro and South Bunyoro, with the latter becoming Hoima District in 1980 and the former Masindi District.

Location: Hoima District borders Kibaale to the south, Masindi and Kyankwanzi to the east, Buliisa to the northeast, Ntoroko and the Democratic Republic of Congo to the west and northwest.

Area: 5,639 sq. km.

Climate, Relief and Vegetation: It lies at an approximate altitude of between 621m and 1,158m above sea level. Annual rainfall ranges between 700mm – 1,000mm with high temperatures. Vegetation includes short savannah grass and isolated bushes.

Population: According to the 2009 population projections the district has 466,700 people –233,900 female, 232,800 male with a density of 82 persons per sq.km.

Major Towns: Hoima (administrative headquarters); Trading Centres – Kigorobya and Kyangwali.

Counties and Sub-counties: Bugahya County – Buhanika, Buseruka, Busiisi, Kigorobya, Kigorobya(Town Council), Kitoba, Kyabigambire; Buhaguzi County – Bugambe, Buhimba, Kabwoya, Kiziranfumbi, and Kyangwali. Hoima Municipality – Bujumbura Division, Mparo division, Busiisi division and Kahoora division.

Main Language: Runyoro.

People: Banyoro.

Economic Activities: Agriculture with a bias to:
  (i)   Food crops: Sweet potatoes, bananas, maize, cassava, beans, soya bean, rice, finger millet, sorghum, cow peas and pigeon peas, groundnuts, simsim, yams, and Irish potatoes.

(ii) Cash Crops: Cotton, tea and coffee.

(iii) Fruits and vegetables: Tomatoes, cabbage, onions and pineapples.

(iv) Fishing carried out on Lake Albert.

Banks: Stanbic Bank Uganda Ltd –1, Centenary Rural Development Bank –1, Crane Bank.

Area under Forestation: 160,511 hectares.

Animal Population: 109,998 cattle, 104,669 pigs, 25,593 sheep, 187,128 goats, 942,843 chicken, 26,898 ducks and 2,677 turkeys.

Co-operative Societies: 147 registered primary societies with Kitara Growers Union at the district level.

Industries: Processing of tea, cotton and coffee, manufacturing of jaggery, furniture, woodwork and brick making. The largest single factory is woodwork with 345 people.

Education Services: Primary schools: 223 – 165 government, 48 private and 10 community. Enrolment: 105,835 – 54,997 male and 50,838 female. Primary school teachers: 2,112 – 1,139 male and 973 female. Available furniture is adequate for 76,869 pupils.

Secondary schools: 35 schools - 11 government, 20 private and 4 community. Secondary school enrolment: 18,511 pupils – 9,659 male and 8,852 female. Teachers: 914 - 722 male and 192 female. Available furniture is adequate for 14,789 students.

Health Services: 1 hospital (government - Hoima Regional Referral Hospital with 139 beds, 1 health centre IV (government), and 21 health centre III (19 government, 2 NGO), 27 health centre II (19 government, 8 NGO).

Tourist Attractions: Kataisha Port is located about 3 km along the Butiaba road which leads north towards Lake Albert. The fort was established in 1894, by Colonel Colville when he was trying to subdue *Omukama* Kabalega.

The Mparo Tombs are the burial places of two most influential Bunyoro Kings of modern times. In keeping with his wishes Kabalega's tomb has a thatched roof supported by a circular stone wall. Inside, his tomb is covered with cow hide and is surrounded by a collection of the king's traditional personal belongings. Sir. Tito Winyi's tomb is similar. The site is surrounded by bark-cloth trees and a reed fence. Outside the compound is a memorial stone for Kabalega and Emin Pasha's first meeting. However, the tombs attract few visitors and there is need for more publicity.

Functional Radio and TV Stations: Kisembo Electronics Engineers Ltd, Madison Baptist Church, Ababaigara Company, UBC TV and radio.

Additional Information: One limiting factor to agriculture is the low rainfall that the district receives. Annual rainfall ranges between 700mm –1,000m.

The palace and headquarters of Bunyoro – Kitara Kingdom are in Hoima. Land ownership varies between *mailoland*, freehold and customary systems. Water is a big problem in areas that are far from the lake and rivers.

Operational Radio Station: Hoima Radio.

Key NGOs: Africa 2000 Network – Uganda, Family Planning Association of Uganda, MS Uganda, World Vision Uganda, Uganda Women's Effort to Save Orphans, Environmental Alert, Traditional and Modern Health Practitioners (THETA), Hoima District Change Agent Association, Hoima District Farmers' Association, Uganda Red Cross Society, Uganda Society for Disabled Children, Kidea Co-operative Savings and Credit Society Limited, Kinogou Integrated Rural Development Organisation, Mirembe Multi-Purpose.

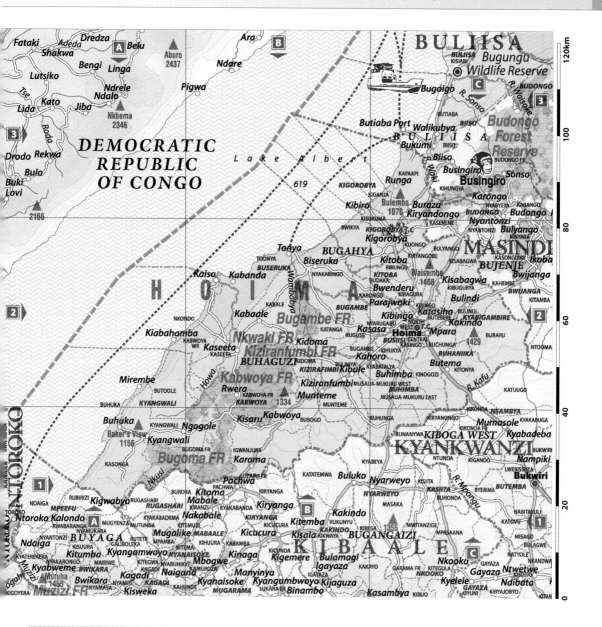

District leaders:

Chairperson – Mr Tinkamanyire George

Acting Chief Administrative Officer
– Mr Walter Iriama

Deputy CAO – Ms. Lillian Nakamate

Ag Town Clerk (Hoima Municipal Council)
– Mr Amir Nsamo

Town Clerk (Kigorobya Town Council)
– Mr Fred Tinka

Mayor Hoima Municipality
– Mr Grace Mugasa

Members of Parliament:

Bugahya County
– Mr Kiiza, Rwebembera James

Buhaguzi County
– Mr Bigirwa Julius Junjura

Hoima Municipality
– Mr Kajura Henry Muganwa

Woman MP – Ms Kaahwa Tophace Byagira

TULLOW UGANDA

SOCIAL ENTERPRISE PROGRAMMES BENEFITING COMMUNITIES WITHIN THE ALBERTINE GRABEN

Tullow Uganda's policy is to conduct her business operations to the best industry standards and to behave in a socially compatible way, with the goal conforming ethically and with integrity in the communities where we work, and to respect cultural, national and religious diversity.

Tullow Uganda is committed to high standards of environment, health and safety across her business with the ambition to preserve biodiversity and promote sustainable development by protecting people, minimising harm to the environment and reducing disruption to our neighbouring communities.

As a responsible operator and good neighbour, Tullow Uganda works directly with the communities adjacent to her operations, addressing their most pressing needs to improve quality of life as well as enabling long-term social empowerment.

Tullow Uganda's social enterprise programmes currently cover two districts in the Albertine Graben region – Hoima and Buliisa. It is a comprehensive community - driven initiative covering infrastructure, health, education and environment.

Each element of the programme targets key issues facing the communities thereby fostering trust, promoting good stakeholder relations and facilitating the necessary approvals for our operations. These projects are developed in line with District Development Plans, after consultation with the local communities in the areas of operation.

As our oil and gas projects develop, and as our long-term commitment to Uganda takes hold, we have enhanced our approach to stakeholder engagement especially within the Albertine Graben region. The aim is to ensure that oil and gas resources generate new opportunities for long-term economic development, creating shared prosperity.

A summary of some of the social enterprise programme achievements to date:

Infrastructure - Building and investing in access roads combined with upgrading existing rural roads has reduced transport costs, resulting in faster delivery of products thereby enhancing market access for fishermen and farmers. Overall, the improvement in infrastructure (and social services) has started to enhance the livelihoods of people through economic opportunities that have been created.

Health and Welfare - 5,900 expectant mothers have accessed maternal health care including immunization, malaria treatment and family planning services through the Kyehoro Health Centre, built by Tullow Uganda and to date, 170 babies have been born at the health centre.

"To stay in business for the long term, we must demonstrate that we are part of society, making a unique and valuable contribution to economic and social development through responsible operations. To this end, we focus on social enterprise programmes that make a real and sustainable difference in the communities where we operate."

Jimmy Kiberu, Head of Corporate Affairs

Kyehoro Health Centre now a level 2 clinic

Reaching over 4423 people in both districts, there is better HIV/AIDS voluntary counselling and testing services through the 402 community peer educators and health staff that have been trained so that HIV/AIDS, malaria prevention and family planning awareness programmes remain sustainable in the long term. Over 30,000 people now have improved access to clean and safe water; hygiene and sanitation through the provision of community boreholes and rain water harvesting tanks.

Sustainable livelihoods - We are working to create and support a diversified economy in the Lake Albert region as part of our objective to create shared prosperity in Uganda. For several years, now we have worked with local farmers to establish a beekeeping and honey production cooperative as well as a vegetable gardening programme.

More recently we have started to work with farmers' groups on a community agro-enterprise development programme in both Hoima and Buliisa districts. So far, more than 80 farmer groups in Hoima and Buliisa have been identified and are receiving support through the whole process from identification of produce, production, business planning, micro finance and market analysis up to the point of signing contracts with identified buyers.

Education - An incredible 10,103 text books were provided to primary schools in both districts. Tullow Uganda has also supported capacity building for teachers, government officials and school management committees, and carried out construction and/or refurbishment of 3 classroom blocks.

"Over 30,000 people now have improved access to clean and safe water; hygiene and sanitation through the provision of community boreholes and rain water harvesting tanks. "

Nkondo Primary School refurbished by Tullow

Investing in the improvement of primary school education and infrastructure at community level is also essential to building the foundation of an educated workforce that is able to participate and benefit from the economic opportunities that oil industry development will bring in the long term.

Tullow Uganda is cognizant of the reciprocal benefits which investment in education and skills training can confer to its own long-term business interests. Improved education provides opportunities to the younger generation and this, in turn, enables Tullow Uganda and other investors to cost-effectively recruit locally trained personnel.

Environment – We believe that conservation is a key partnership for both wealth generation for the communities and preservation of the natural resources of Uganda, man and the beast for today and for generations to come.

35,000 tree seedlings were provided to Chimpanzee Sanctuary and Wildlife Conservation trust to support natural forest restoration, and conservation programmes. 50 Tullow Uganda staff participated in planting 550 trees to support initiatives of a greener Hoima town. Additionally, 105,000 tree seedlings have been planted in both districts over time to promote the sustainable use of natural resources. Local women have been trained to construct energy saving stoves and briquettes as a quick start activity addressing fuel wood scarcity.

In addition, Tullow has also given support in other areas and aspects in other parts of the country. Tullow was among the first companies to donate to the victims of the Bududa landslide in March, Tullow also recently joined efforts with Katelema Cheshire Home (KCH), a home for disabled children, by donating a concert and helping to raise more funds coming close to 40million Uganda shillings.

" We believe that conservation is a key partnership for both wealth generation for the communities and preservation of the natural resources of Uganda, man and the beast for today and for generations to come."

Enterprise developement through natural resource development

The above are just a number of social enterprise programmes being undertaken and Tullow Uganda believes that the significant oil and gas resources being developed will have a major transformative effect on the overall Ugandan economy, and in turn, on human development. Social investment projects from health through to safe water, hygiene and sanitation at a community level in the Albertine Graben region, makes good business sense as they reduce the spread of common contagious diseases and improve the overall health of both the community and business. This definitely reduces health care costs for the labour force, their beneficiaries, and for Tullow Uganda.

Moving towards the future, Tullow Uganda's main social enterprise programmes'theme will be, **'developing entrepreneurs'**. We realize that health, education and environment programmes are the primary prerequisites for building entrepreneurs and an entrepreneurial environment, so many of our initial social sector investments will continue. In addition however, we will work to create a skilled workforce and a diversified local economy. This will be achieved by supporting agro-enterprises and other small/medium enterprises (SMEs) that enable people in the albertine Graben to create or obtain employment. Corporate Social Responsibility will focus on developing community skills, capacity and community incomes to yield more sustainable benefits. In addition to community projects, we will also help to build capacity for the oil and gas industry and support local content initiatives in Uganda. Tullow Uganda constantly strives to be a force for transforming people's lives in the Albertine Graben region.

" We realise that health, education and environment programmes are the primary prerequisites for building entrepreneurs and an entrepreneurial environment. "

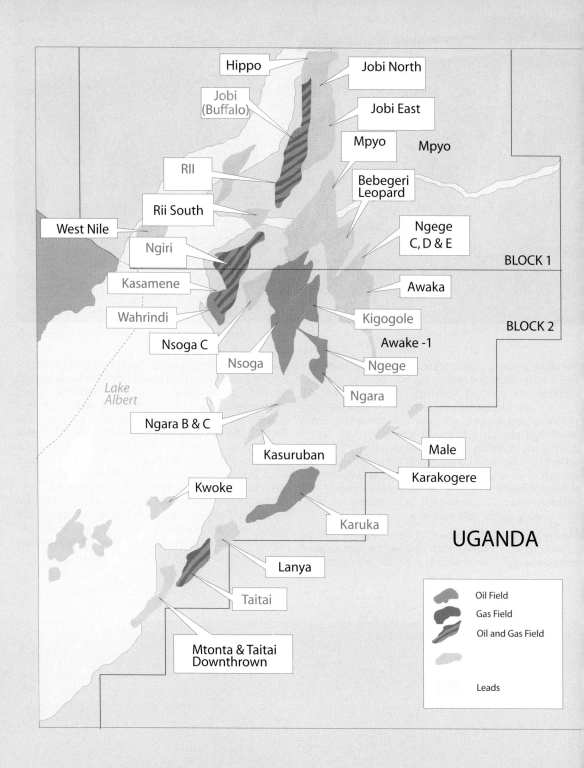

Hippo

Jobi North

Jobi (Buffalo)

Jobi East

Mpyo

Mpyo

RII

Bebegeri
Leopard

Rii South

Ngege
C, D & E

West Nile

Ngiri

BLOCK 1

Kasamene

Awaka

Wahrindi

Kigogole

BLOCK 2

Nsoga C

Awake -1

Nsoga

Ngege

Ngara

Ngara B & C

Kasuruban

Male

Karakogere

Kwoke

Karuka

Lake
Albert

UGANDA

Lanya

Taitai

Mtonta & Taitai
Downthrown

Oil Field

Gas Field

Oil and Gas Field

Leads

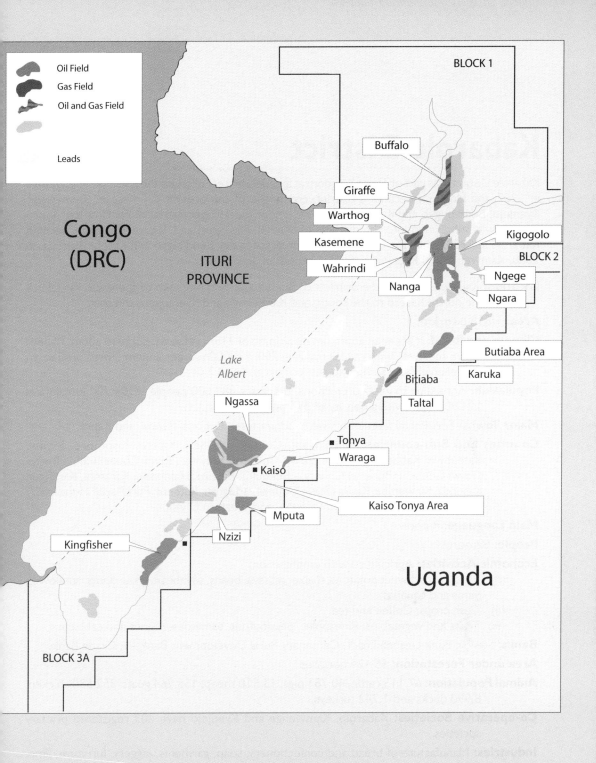

BLOCK 1

Oil Field
Gas Field
Oil and Gas Field

Leads

Congo
(DRC)

ITURI
PROVINCE

Buffalo

Giraffe

Warthog

Kasemene

Wahrindi

Nanga

Kigogolo

BLOCK 2

Ngege

Ngara

Butiaba Area

Karuka

Lake
Albert

Bitiaba

Taltal

Ngassa

Tonya

Waraga

Kaiso

Kaiso Tonya Area

Mputa

Nzizi

Kingfisher

Uganda

BLOCK 3A

Kabarole District

Kabarole District was part of Tooro Kingdom at independence. Following the abolition of kingdoms in 1967, the kingdom became a district, composed of the present-day Kasese, Kamwenge, Kyenjojo, Bundibugyo and Kabarole districts. Under the 1974 provincial administration, Tooro District was subdivided into the districts of Semliki, Rwenzori and Tooro. The latter became Kabarole in 1980, while the other two are the present-day Bundibigyo and Kasese districts. In 2000, Kamwenge and Kyenjojo were carved out of Kabarole.

Location: Kabarole borders the districts of Bundibugyo and Ntoroko to the west, Kibaale to the north, Kasese to the south, and Kamwenge and Kyenjojo to the east.

Area: 1,818.6 sq. km.

Climate and Relief: It lies at an approximate altitude of 915m at Lake George to about 3,556m above sea level, with rainfall totalling 750m – l000mm per annum. Fort Portal town has relatively low temperatures, not exceeding 19°C.

Population: According to 2009 projections, there are 389,600 people – 194,700 female and 194,900 male with a density of 214 persons per sq.km.

Major Towns: Fort Portal (administrative headquarters), Rubona, Rwimi, and Kijura.

Counties and Sub-counties: Bunyangabu County – Buhesi, Kibiito, Kisomoro, Rwimi, Bateebwa; Kabonero, Kibiito (Town Council), Rubona (Town Council) and Rwimi (Town Council); Burahya County – Bukuuku, Busoro, Hakibaale, Karambi, Karangur, Kasenda, Kicwamba, Kijura (Town Council), Mugusu, Ruteete; Fort Portal Municipality – Eastern Division, Southern Division, and Western Division.

Main Language: Rutooro.

People: Batooro.

Economic Activities: Agriculture with emphasis on:
   (i)   Food crops: Sweet potatoes, maize, cassava, beans, soyabean, groundnuts, sunflower, yams and bananas.
   (ii) Cash crops: Coffee and tea.
   (iii) Fruits and vegetables: Pineapples, passionfruit, tomatoes, onions and cabbage.

Banks: Stanbic Bank Uganda Ltd-1, Centenary Rural Development Bank –1, Crane Bank.

Area under Forestation: 55,424 hectares.

Animal Population: 67,115 cattle, 40,781 pigs, 13,510 sheep, 155,264 goats, 352,530 chicken, 8,990 ducks and 1,742 turkeys.

Co-operative Societies: Kabarole, Kamwenge and Kyenjojo have 203 registered primary societies.

Industries: Manufacture of bread and confectionery, soap, garments, jaggery, furniture, lime, chalk, saw milling and processing of tea and coffee.

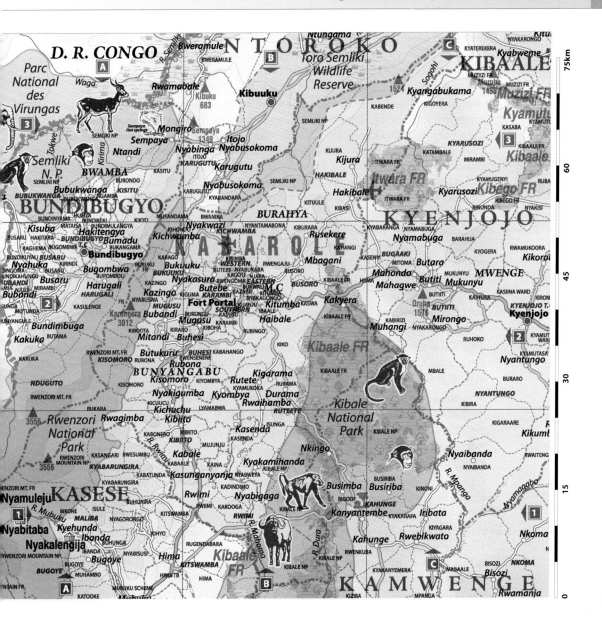

Education Services: Primary schools: 167 – 139 government, 27 private and 1 community. Enrolment 106,886 – 52,973 male and 53, 913 female. Primary school teachers: 2,020 – 1,028 male and 992 female. Available furniture is adequate for 80,168 pupils.

Secondary Schools: 35 schools - 14 government, 20 Private and 1 community. Secondary School Enrolment: 19,104 students – 9,936 male and 9,168 female. Teachers: 1,020 – 795 male and 225 female. Available furniture is adequate for 15,204 students.

Tertiary institutions: 3 teacher training colleges, 1 national technical institute – Kichwamba, 2 Universities - Mountain of the Moon University and Uganda Pentecostal University.

Health Services: 3 hospitals (1 government - Fort Portal Regional Referral Hospital with 300 beds, 2 NGO– Virika Hospital with 318 beds and Kabarole Hospital with 70 beds), 2 health centre IV (all government), 18 health centre III. (13 government, 5 NGO), 31 health centre II (21 government, 7 NGO, 3 private).

Transport Network: The district has an inadequate feeder-road network. In some places the roads are in poor condition while in others there is hardly any road link. The road from Fort Portal to Kyenjojo is tarmac; the rest of the road network is murram. The road that links Fort Portal to Kasese is also tarmac. The western railway line to Kasese crosses the southern parts of the district. This was a vital means of transportation and facilitated the transportation of agricultural produce to markets in Kampala and beyond, hence the stopping of the train service has deprived the district of affordable means of transport.

Tourist Attractions: Fort Portal, the capital of Kabarole is situated at the foothills of the Rwenzori Mountains. Small, quiet and refreshing, it is one of Uganda's most delightful towns with polite, hospitable people. Tourist information can be obtained from the Kabarole Tourism Association which shares its office with Kabarole Tours on Moledina Street.

Fort Portal's highest hill, Kabarole Hill, is home of the palace of the *Omukama* (king) of Tooro. Written permission may be needed to visit this site.

The Karambi Tombs are the burial grounds of the Tooro royal family. *Omukama* Kasagama, *Omukama* Rukiidi III and *Omukama* Kaboyo are all buried here. On display are personal artefacts of the kings, including drums and spears.

The stalagmites and stalactites (locally known as Amabeere ga Nyinamwiru) in the limestone caves near Nyakasura school are also attractive to see.

Fort Portal is a good base for trips to the Kibale Forest, Magombe Swamp, Bigodi and Bunyaruguru Crater Lake Fields.

Some of the accomodation in Fortportal include the Mountains of the Moon Hotel, Rwenzori View Guest House, Riviera Inn, Soka Hotel, Continental Hotel, Wooden Hotel, Brightman Executive Lodge, Christian Guest House, Executive Lodge, and the New Linda Guest House. Camping is available at the Garden of Eden Campsite.

Additional Information: The district has high agricultural potential. There is some large scale farming though most of the peasants grow crops for subsistence. The limiting factor is that some farmers are not linked to the markets by road and this deprives them of a chance to earn an income.

Operational Radio Stations: Voice of Tooro, Radio West Ltd, World Evangelical Ministries and Radio Maria Uganda Association.

Key NGOs: Family Planning Association of Uganda, Uganda Women's Effort to Save Orphans, Uganda Project Implementation and Management Centre, Bunyagavu Workers' Association, Diabetic Association of Toro, Kabarole District Disabled People's Union, Kabarole District Farmers' Association, Kasese Town Council Women Group, Rural Women's Development Agency, Toro Kateebwa War Veterans Associates, Burungu Kweteerana Group.

<table>
<tr><td>

District leaders:
Chairperson – Mr Rwabuhinga Richard
Chief Administrative Officer (CAO)
  – Mr Nyende Juma
Deputy Chief Administrative Officer
  (DCAO) – Vacant
Town Clerk (Fort Portal Municipal
  Council) – Mr Ambrose Jimmy Atwoko
Mayor Fort Portal Municipality
  – Mr Edison Ruyonga Asaba

</td><td>

Members of Parliament:
Fort Portal Municipality
  – Mr Ruhunda Alex
Burahya County
  – Mr Stephen Kagwera Kasaija
Bunyangabu County
  – Mr Adolf Kasaija Mwesige
Woman MP – Ms Businge Rusoke Victoria

</td></tr>
</table>

Kamwenge District

Kamwenge was formerly part of Kabarole District. It became a district in 2000. The present-day districts of Kabarole, Kamwenge, Kyegegwa and Kyenjojo constituted Kabarole District which came into existence in 1980. Before that Tooro District constituted of the three plus present-day Kasese District.

Location: It borders the districts of Kyegegwa and Kiruhura to the east, Kabarole and Kasese to the west, Kyenjojo to the north, Ibanda to the south and southeast, and Rubirizi to the southwest.

Area: 2,411 sq. km.

Climate and Relief: It lies at an approximate altitude of 1,585m –3,962m above sea level, with rainfall totalling 750mm –1,000mm per annum and low temperatures not exceeding 19°C.

Population: 303,900 people – 159,400 female and 144,500 male, with a density of 126 persons per sq.km.

Major Towns: Kamwenge (administrative headquarters); Trading Centres – Kahunge and Nyabani.

Counties and Sub-counties: Kibaale County – Biguli, Bwizi, Kabambiro, Kahunge, Kamwenge (Town Council), Kamwenge, Nkoma; Kitagwenda County – Buhanda, Kanaraa, Kicheche, Mahyoro, Ntara, and Nyabani.

Main Languages: Rukiga, Rutagwenda and Rutooro.

People: Bakiga, Batooro and Batagwenda.

Economic Activities: Fishing in Kitagwenda, Batagenda Cattle rearing, agriculture with emphasis on:
(i)   Food crops: Maize, sweet potatoes, groundnuts, bananas, millet and sorghum.
(ii) Cash crops: Coffee, tea, cotton on a small scale.
(iii) Fruits and vegetables: Tomatoes, cabbages, pineapples and onions.
(iv) Fishing in Kitagwenda
(v)   Cattle rearing

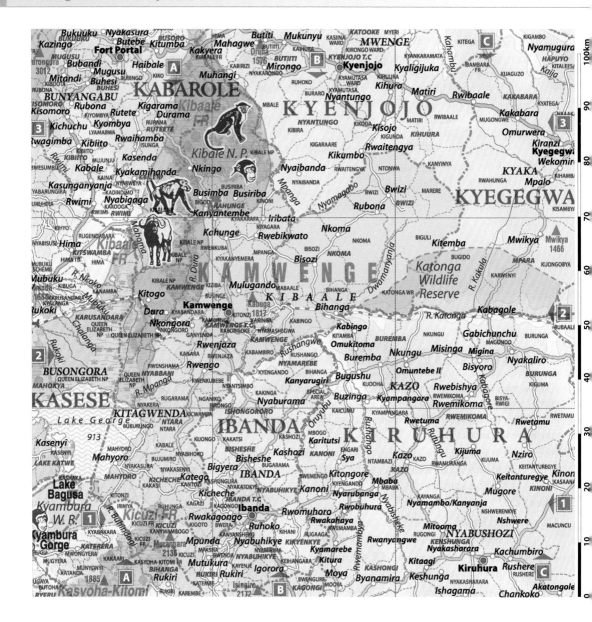

Area under Forestation: 52,574 hectares.

Animal Population: 120,906 cattle, 34,280 pigs, 26,239 sheep, 154,422 goats, 11,237 ducks, turkeys 363 and 339,191 chicken.

Co-operative Societies: Kamwenge, Kabarole and Kyenjojo have 203 registered co-operative societies.

Industries: Saw-milling, furniture making in Mpanga Forest and brick making.

Education Services: Primary schools: 225 – 149 government, 56 private and 20 community. Enrolment: 87,982 – 44,141 male and 43,841 female. Primary school teachers: 1,714 – 1,208 male and 506 female. Available furniture is adequate for 61,183 pupils.

Secondary Schools: 26 - 10 government, 10 Private and 6 community.

Secondary school enrolment: 8,113 – 4,989 male and 3,124 female. Teachers: 461 – 375 male and 86 female.

Health Services: 2 health centre IV - (all government), 8 health centre III - (7 government, 1 NGO), 19 health centre II - (13 government, 6 NGO)

Tourist Attractions: Kibaale Forest National Park – The Kibaale Forest provides a rich and unique habitat for more than 250 species of animal and over 300 types of birds. The animal species include 11 primates, including black and white colobus monkeys and chimpanzees. Monkeys can be spotted from the road and viewing of chimpanzees is the main tourist attraction. The group of chimps in the Kanyachu community is probably the largest in Kibaale Forest numbering about 45. There are excursions to see chimps twice a day from Kanyachu tourist site.

Sebitole Tourist Centre offers nature walks, bird watching, food, drinks, and accomodation in bandas and camping facilities.

Bigodi Wetland Sanctuary and Magombe Swamp is managed by Kibaale Association for Rural Development, a community based organisation that supports eco-tourism initiatives.

Magombe Swamp is towards Bigodi.

Operational Radio Stations: Radio Kamwenge FM Ltd and Western Broadcasting Services Ltd.

Key NGOs: Peace Foundation, Youth Alliance to Combat AIDS, Tech. for Rural Animal Power, Kaduido NGO Network, Kabarole Kitagwenda Progressive Farm and Ranch, District Economic Development Association, Kitagwenda Community Initiative Development Agency, Manyoro Youth Control Group, Parents Concern for Young People, Kamwenge Catholic Development Agency.

District leaders:	**Members of Parliament:**
Chairperson – Mr Kamasaka Robert	Kitagwenda County
Ag Chief Administrative Officer (CAO)	– Mr Nulu Byamukama
– Mr Frank Ntaho	Kibale County
Deputy Chief Administrative Officer	– Mr Frank Kagyigyi Tumwebaze
(DCAO) – Vacant	Woman MP
Town Clerk (Kamwenge Town Council)	– Ms Nshaija Dorothy Kabaraitsya
–Mr Nuwagaba	

Left: A crater lake in Tooro region of western Uganda. Right: The hilly terrain of Bundibugyo.

Kasese District

Kasese District is part of the former Tooro District which, at independence had been Tooro Kingdom. Under the 1974 provincial administration Rwenzori District was carved out of Tooro. In 1980, Rwenzori District was renamed Kasese District.

Location: It borders the districts of Kabarole and Bundibugyo to the north, Bushenyi District to the south and the Democratic Republic of Congo in the west.

Area: 3385 sq. km.

Climate, Relief and Vegetation: It lies at an approximate altitude of 912m at Lake Edward and 5,110m at the top of Rwenzori Mountains. It has characteristics of the savannah type of climate. As one moves away from the giant Rwenzori Mountains, the vegetation ranges from the afro-alpine type to short, savannah grass.

Population: According to the 2009 population projection, the district has 658,400 people – 342,100 female and 316,300 male, with a density of 194 persons per sq.km.

Main Towns: Kasese (administrative headquarters); Trading Centres – Kilembe, Katwe, Bwera and Hima.

Counties and Sub-counties: Bukonjo County – Bwera, Ihandiro, Isango, Karambi, Kisinga, Kitholu, Kyarumba, Kyondo, Mahango, Mukunyu, Nyakiyumbu, Mpondwe/Lhubiriha (Town Council); Busongora County – Bugoye, Bwesumbu, Buhuhira, Kitswamba, Kyabarungira, Maliba, Karusandara, Hima (Town Council), Kilembe, Lake Katwe, Katwe-Kabatooro (Town Council), Muhokya, and Rukoki. Kasese Municipality – Bulemba, Central, Nyamwanda Divisions.

Main Languages: Rukonjo and Rutooro.

People: Bakonjo and Batooro.

Economic Activities: The district is both industrial and agricultural. Mining of cobalt, copper, sulphur etc. is concentrated at Kilembe.

   (i)   Food crops: Beans, maize, cassava, Irish and sweet potatoes, bananas, groundnuts, peas, yams and finger millet.

   (ii)   Cash crops: Coffee and sugar cane.

   (iii)   Fruits and vegetables: Pineapples, passion fruit, tomatoes, onions and cabbage.

Banks: Stanbic Bank Uganda Ltd-1, Centenary Rural Development Bank Ltd –1.

Area under Forestation: 108,756 hectares.

Animal Population: 97,243 cattle, 31 donkeys, 85,812 pigs, 24,890 sheep, 227,518 goats, 6,687 rabbits and 752,800 chicken, 45,036 ducks and 4,694 turkeys.

Co-operative Societies: 66 registered primary societies with Nyakatonzi Union at the district level.

Industries: Manufacture of mattresses, limestone and white chalk, cement, carpentry, furniture, processing of tea, coffee, salt, and cotton ginning.

Education Services: Primary schools 432 – 271 government, 116 private and 45 community. Enrolment: 19,0308 – 93,674 male and 96,634 female. Primary school teachers: 4,284 – 2,706 male and 1,578 female. Available furniture is adequate for 131,468 pupils

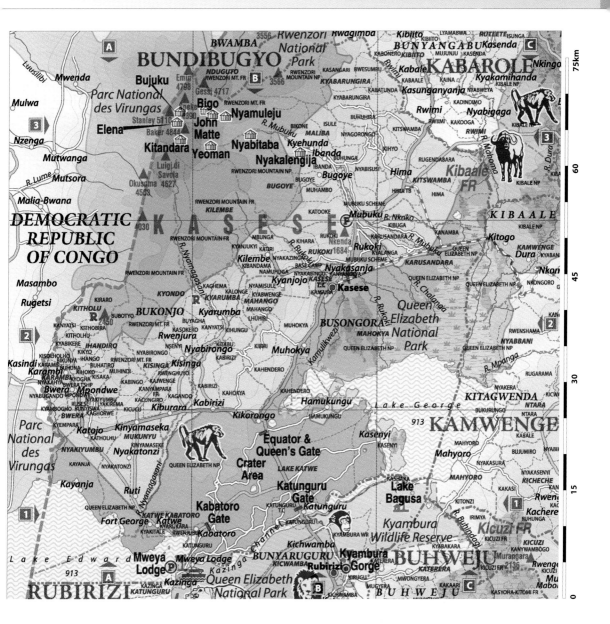

Secondary schools: 60 schools -17 government, 24 private and 19 community. Secondary school enrolment: 28,100 students – 15,499 male and 12,601 female. Teachers: 1,515 – 1,279 male and 236 female. Available furniture is adequate for 19,865 students.

Tertiary institution: 1 technical institution, 1 teacher training college. 1vocational institute – Fort Portal Clinical Officers.

Health Services: 3 hospitals (1 government– Bwera Hospital with 100 beds, 2 NGO – Kagando Hospital with 220 beds, and Kilembe Mines Hospital with 110 beds); 3 health centre IV (1 government, 1 private, 1 NGO); 28 health centre III (23 government, 5 NGO); and 63 health centre II (45 government, 4 NGO, 14 private).

Transport Network: The district has tarmac roads linking it to Kabarole and Bushenyi districts. The road from Kasese town to Kilembe is also tarmac. Hima and Muhokya towns lie on the tarmac stretch that links Kasese town to Kabarole and Bushenyi districts, respectively. The advantage the district has is that of the tarmac road cutting through its centre and all the feeder-roads linking to it. The district still lacks good feeder-roads, especially close to the border with the DRC. Even the few roads that exist are in poor condition, apart from those near the border town of Bwera.

Kasese is also linked by railway to the rest of the country. Kasese town marks the end of the western railway line, but due to the break down of rail services for years now rail transport is not available.

Kasese Airfield – Kasese Airfield is a designated entry and exit point. This airfield is served by a 1,570m x 30m grass runway, which is in good condition. River Nyamwamba seasonally floods and causes operational hazards. Information regarding the operational limits of the runway is always notified to Air Traffic Control by the resident airfield staff. The airfield terminal building is in fair condition. The airfield is linked to UTL, MTN and Celtel mobile telephone services. Public payphones are also available in town. The Civil Aviation Authority provides H. F. radio communication. The airfield is 1 km from Kasese town.

Tourist Attractions: Chambura Game Reserve which is now incorporated in the Queen Elizabeth National Park; Maramagambo Forest and Queen Elizabeth National Park. Hotel Margherita offers reasonable accommodation with bed and breakfast.

Kazinga Channel at Katunguru – a natural channel that connects Lake George to Lake Edward, had a large number of hippopotami and a variety of birds.

The Queen Elizabeth National Park lies across the Equator in the southwest of Uganda. It is bordered to the southwest by Lake Edward and to the northwest by Lake George. The Park covers an area of 1,987 sq. km.

The northern sector of Queen Elizabeth National Park is the most visited national park and game drives are possible and has Mweya Lodge to accommodate visitors. There are hyenas, buffaloes, Uganda kobs and down the Kazinga Channel are Nile monitor lizards. The most elusive of animals, the leopard, lives in this area, but is extremely diffcult to spot.

There are seven crater lakes, only four are accessible – Katwe, Kikongoro, Munyanyange (an alkaline lake) and Nyamunuka meaning "stinking", so named because of the strong smell of sulphur emitted from the water. Lake George and Lake Kikongoro are attractive sites.

The 10 km Kyambura Gorge is formed by a river that flows off the Kichwamba escarpment.

Lake Katwe's salt industry is 700 – 800 years old and is the main source of income among the Katwe inhabitants. So is fishing.

Mountain Rwenzori in the Rwenzori Mountains National Park lies along the border of Uganda and the Democratic Republic of Congo rising to a height of 5,109m (Margherita Peak of Mountain Stanley). The range is about 100 km in length and 50 km wide. The Rwenzoris have a large diversity of plants and trees.

Climbing the Rwenzoris – The Rwenzori Mountains Services, based at the Saad Hotel on Rwenzori Road, in Kasese, maintain the huts and trails and hold the concession to provide accomodation, porters, guides and rescue services. Climbing the Rwenzoris takes six days.

Additional Information: The copper smelter and Hima Cement Factory are found here. The district is accessible by road, rail and air.

Kasese District has both agricultural and industrial potential. There are a number of industries in the district, which have greatly contributed to employment. The Lake Katwe Salt Project has taken long without bearing full results. The project would make a significant contribution to the welfare of the people in terms of employment if it was modernised. Nevertheless, the local people are still practising rudimentary mining of the salt which helps them make a living.

Agricultural production is high, owing to the rich soils and reliable rainfall. But the lack of proper information about markets denies the farmers the opportunity to sell their crops. Most of the agricultural produce from Kasese has a market in urban centres in the region and in Kampala District. Passion fruit is one of the main crops from Kasese and is sold in most urban areas in the country. Kasese's position on the border with Congo means there is cross-border trade.

Operational Radio Station: Lion of Juda and Diocese of South Rwenzori.

Key NGOs: African Network for the Prevention and Protection Against Child Abuse and Neglect Uganda Chapter, Banyo Development Foundation, Ikongo Rural Development Association.

District leaders:	Members of Parliament:
Chairperson – Mr Mawa Muhindo	Bukonjo County East
Chief Administrative Officer (CAO)	– Mr Yokasi Bihande Bwambale
– Mr Giles Kihika	Busongora County North
Deputy Chief Administrative Officer	– Mr Nzoghu M. William
(CAO) – Vacant	Bukonjo County West
Town Clerk (Kasese Municipal Council)	– Mr Chrispus Walter Bazarrabusa
– Mr Wilson Musaba	Kiyonga
Ag. Town Clerk (Katwe/Kabatoro Town	Busongora County South
Council) – Mr S. Balaba	– Mr Kafuda Boaz
Town Clerk (Hima Town Council)	Kasese Municipaity – Mr Mbahimba James
– Mr Swizen Mugyema	Woman MP – Ms Winfred Kiiza
Mayor Kasese Municipaity	
– Mr Godfrey Kabanga	

Left: King of the Rwenzururu kingdom, Omusinga Charles Wesley Mumbere. Right: Kazinga Channel, western Uganda.

Kibaale District

Kibaale District was carved out of Hoima District in 1991. At independence in 1962, present-day Hoima, Masindi and Kibaale made up Bunyoro Kingdom. Following the abolition of kingdoms in 1967, it became Bunyoro District. Under the 1974 provincial administration, the district was divided into North and South Bunyoro districts. In 1980, South Bunyoro was renamed Hoima District from which Kibaale was later created.

Location: It borders the districts of Hoima to the north, Kyankwanzi to the east, Mubende to the southeast, Kyenjojo and Kyegegwa in the south and Kabarole and Ntoroko to the west.

Area: 4,387 sq. km.

Climate, Relief and Vegetation: It lies in a savannah climatic zone with moderately low rainfall and high temperatures. Vegetation consists of short grass and isolated bush.

Population: According to 2009 projections the district has 571,000 people – 291,200 female, and 279,800 male, with a density of 130 persons per sq.km.

Major Towns: Kibaale (administrative headquarters); Trading Centres – Karuguza and Kagadi.

Counties and Sub-counties: Bugangaizi West – Bwanswa, Kakindo, Kasambya, Nyarweyo, Birembo; Bugangaizi West – Kisiita, Nkooko, Mpasaana; Buyaga West – Burora, Bwikara, Kyakabadiima, Kyaterekera, Mpeefu, Muhorro, Ndaiga, Rugashari, Ruteete; Buyaga East – Kagadi, Karanda, Kiryanga, Kyanaisoke, Kyenzige, Mabaale, Kagadi (Town Council), Pachwa; Buyanja County – Bubango, Bwamiramira, Kibaale (Town Council), Kyebando, Matale, Mugarama, Nyamarwa, and Nyamarunda.

Main Languages: Runyoro and Rutooro.

People: Banyoro and Batooro.

Economic Activities: Mainly agriculture with emphasis on:
  (i)   Food crops: Rice, maize, sweet potatoes, beans, ginger, millet, sorghum, cassava, irish potatoes, yams, cow peas, pigeon peas, groundnuts and simsim (sesame).
  (ii) Cash crops: Coffee, cotton, tea and tobacco.
  (iii) Fruits and vegetables: Pineapples, tomatoes, onions and cabbage.

Animal Population: 174,926 cattle, 153,512 pigs, 24,329 sheep, 199,572 goats, 879,032 chicken, 34,194 ducks and 2,140 turkeys according to 2008 statistics.

Co-operative Societies: 124 primary societies.

Banks: Stanbic Bank Uganda Ltd –1.

Area under Forestation: 167,044 hectares.

Education Services: Primary schools: 561 – 274 government, 221 private and 66 community. Enrolment: 161,551 – 80,864 male and 80,687 female. Primary school teachers: 3,674 – 2,448 male and 1,226 female. Available furniture is adequate for 114,830 pupils.

Secondary schools: 52 schools - 15 government, 27 Private and 10 community. Secondary school enrolment: 17,257 – 9,637 male and 7,620 female. Teachers: 962 - 815 male and 147 female.

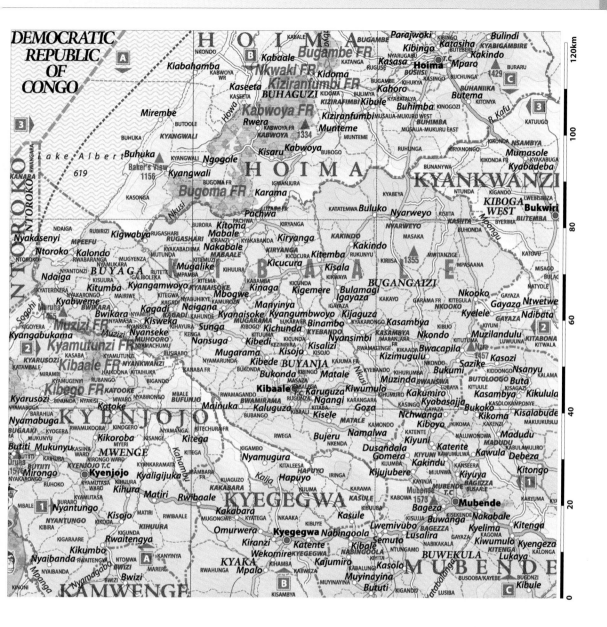

Health Services: By the end of 2006 there were:- 1 hospital (government - Kagadi Hospital with 100 beds), 4 health centre IV (3 government, 1 NGO), 19 health centre III - (15 government, 4 NGO), and 22 health centre II (10 government, 12 NGO)

Tourist Attraction: Kibaale Forest Reserve.

Operational Radio Station: Kagadi Kibaale Community Radio and Uganda Rural Develop and Training Programme

Key NGOs: African Medical Research Foundation Uganda, VSO Uganda.

District leaders:
Chairperson – Mr George W. Namyaka
Chief Administrative Officer (CAO)
　– Mr Dustan Balaba
Deputy CAO – Vacant
Town Clerk (Kibaale Town Council)
　– Mr Simon Kandole

Members of Parliament:
Buyanja East County – Mr Besisira Ignatius
Buyaga West County
　– Mr Barnabas Tinkasimire Ateenyi
Bugangaizi East County
　– Ms Mabel Lilian Bakeine Komugisha
Bugangaizi West County
　– Mr Kasirivu Baltazar Kyamanywa
　Atwooki
Woman Representative
　– Ms Nabbanja Robinah

Kiryandongo District

Kiryandongo was part of Masindi District as Kidanda County. It became a district in 2010 when Kibanda County was elevated to district status. The provincial administration, Bunyoro District, was divided into North Bunyoro and South Bunyoro. The former became Masindi District in 1980.

Location: Kiryandongo District borders the districts of Apac to the east, Nwoya to the north, Buliisa to the west, Masindi to the southwest and south, and Nakasongola to the southeast.

Area: 3,626 sq. km.

Climate, Relief and Vegetation: It lies at an altitude of between 621m – 1,158m above sea level in a savannah climatic zone, with temperatures averaging over 25°C and rainfall 100mm – 1,000mm per annum. Vegetation is punctuated by short grass and shrubs.

Population: Based on the population projection for 2009, there are 265,300 people - 130,000 male and 135,300 female, with a density of 73 persons per sq.km.

Major Towns: Kiryandongo (administrative headquarters), Kigumba and Bweyale; Trading Centre – Masindi Port.

Counties and Sub-counties: Kibanda County – Kigumba, Kigumba (Town Council) Kiryandongo, Kiryandongo (Town Council), Bweyayle (Town Council), Masindi Port, and Mutunda.

Main Language: Runyoro.

People: Banyoro.

Economic Activities: Mainly agriculture with emphasis on:
　(i)　Food crops: Maize, finger millet, beans, cassava, simsim (sesame), groundnuts, sorghum, peas, Irish potatoes, sweet potatoes and bananas.
　(ii)　Cash crops: Tobacco, coffee and cotton.

(iii) Vegetables: Tomatoes and cabbage.

(iv) Ranching.

Banks: Stanbic Bank Uganda Ltd –1.

Area under Forestation: 446,398 hectares.

Animal Population: Based on the 2008 statistics, the districts of Kiryandongo and Masindi had 213,402 cattle, 233,423 goats, 24,943 sheep, 87,616 pigs, 1,007,182 chicken, 39,362 ducks and 1,843 turkeys.

Co-operative Societies: Kiryandongo and Masindi have 89 registered primary societies with Bunyoro Growers Union at the district level.

Industries: Pit sawing, saw milling, printing, cotton ginning, metal fabrication, furniture making, processing of hides and skins, oil and grain milling.

Education Services: Primary schools: 95 schools – 74 government, 15 private and 6 community. Enrolment: 60,776 – 31,324 male and 29,452 female. Primary school teachers: 1,031 – 717 male and 314 female. Available furniture is adequate for only 33,494 pupils.

Secondary schools: 16 schools – 4 government, 9 private, 3 community. Secondary school enrolment: 6,528 students – 3,854 male and 2,674 female – Teachers: 277 - 227 male and 50 female. Available furniture is adequate for 5,986 students.

Tertiary institutions: 1 college – Kigumba Co-operative College.

Health Services: 1 hosptial - (government - Kiryandongo Hospital with 104 beds); 7 health centre III - (5 government, 2 NGO); 10 health centre II - (8 government, 2 NGO).

Transport Network: Masindi Airfield – The airfield is served by a grass-surface runway which is 2,010m x 30m. Water at the airfield is provided from an underground tank. The Civil Aviation Authority provides H.F. radio communication. The airfield is 5.1 km from Masindi town. Masindi Hotel offers reasonable accommodation with bed and breakfast. Transportation from the airfield to town can be provided by taxi.

Tourist Attractions:

Part of Murchison Falls National Park and Karuma Wildlife Reserve are found in this district, Kaniyo Pabidi Park is part of Murchison Falls National Park. Highlights of the park include mighty mahogany and iron wood trees. Ocassionally, lions, leopards and buffaloes can be seen and Pabidi Hill offers views over Murchison Falls Park, Lake Albert and the Democratic Republic of Congo.

Busingiro and Kaniyo-Pabidi are eco-tourism sites with natural trails, special interest walks, chimpanzee tracking and a range of inexpensive bandas and camping facilities.

The Royal Mile is a wide avenue of trees with abundant wildlife.

Lake Kanyege is at the forest edge with water birds and clouds of butterflies.

Operational Radio and TV Stations: Christian Life Ministries, Uganda Broadcasting Corporation Radio, Masindi Broadcasting Service, Earnest Publishers and Uganda Broadcasting Corporation Television.

Key NGOs: Actionaid Uganda, MS Uganda, VSO Uganda, Uganda Women's Effort to Save Orphans.

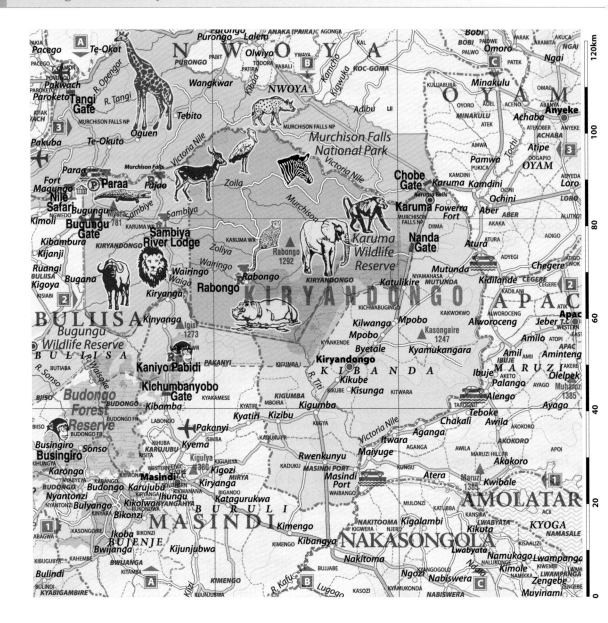

District leaders:
Chairperson – Mr Moru B. Constantine
Chief Administrative Officer (CAO)
  – Vacant
Deputy Chief Administrative Officer
    (DCAO) – Godfrey Ogwang Okello

Members of Parliament:
Kibanda County
  – Mr Owori Otada Amooti
Woman MP – Ms Kahunde Helen

Kyegegwa District

Kyegegwa was formerly part of Kyenjojo District, which came into existence in 2000 after being carved out of Kabarole district. It existed as Kyaka County until 2010 when the county was elevated to district status.

Location: It borders Mubende to the east, Kyenjojo and Kamwenge to the west, Kibaale to the north, and Kiruhura to the south.

Area: 1,747 sq. km.

Climate and Relief: It lies at an approximate altitude of 1,585m – 3,962m above sea level, with rainfall totalling 750mm –1,000mm per annum and temperatures around 19°C.

Population: According to the 2009 projections, the district has 140,300 people – 70,600 female and 69,700 male with a density of 80 persons per sq.km.

Major Towns: Kyegegwa (administrative headquarter); Trading Centre – Kakabara.

Counties and Sub-counties: Kyaka County – Hapuuyo, Kakabara, Kasule, Kyegegwa, Kyegegwa (Town Council), Mpara, Ruyonza Rwentuha.

Main Languages: Rutooro and Rukiga.

People: Batooro and Bakiga.

Economic Activities: Agriculture with emphasis on:
(i)   Food crops: Sweet potatoes, maize, cassava, bananas, groundnuts and sunflower.
(ii) Cash crops: Coffee and tea.
(iii) Fruits and vegetables: Pineapples, tomatoes, onions and cabbage.

Area under Forestation: 142,062 hectares.

Animal Population: Kyegegwa and Kyenjojo have 184,537 cattle, 1 donkey, 73,345 pigs, 38,235 sheep, 254,966 goats, 579,743 chicken, 6,712 ducks and 598 turkeys.

Industries: Furniture making, saw milling and brick making.

Education Services: Primary schools: 53 – 38 government, 11 private and 4 community. Enrolment: 38,534 – 19,583 male and 18,951 female. Primary school teachers: 632 – 413 male and 219 female.

Secondary schools: 9 – 6 government and 3 private. Enrolment: 2,453 – 1,507 male and 946 female. Primary school teachers: 632 – 413 male and 219 female. Available furniture is adequate for 528 students.

Health Services: 1 health centre IV (government), 7 health centre III (6 government, 1 NGO), 6 health centre II (all government).

Tourist Attractions: The 207 sq. km Katonga Wildlife Reserve which was gazetted in 1964, as a game reserve provides a wide range of wild game. A large proportion of the reserve is wetlands – either permanent or seasonal. Katonga is one of the few places in Africa with a large population of the extremely shy and reclusive sitatunga antelope, whose favoured habitat is papyrus swamps. Other mammals include elephant, hippo, black and white colobus monkeys, olive baboons, the Uganda Kob, water buck, duiker and reedbuck. Over 150 bird species have been recorded here.

The Sitatunga Trail offers the best opportunity to spot the timid antelope.

The Kyeibale Trail is a circular trek through the scrubland into the remnants of forests, passing through interesting rock formations and caves used for shelter by the animals.

The Kisharara Trail traverses the savannah to the wetland canal and passes through a variety of eco-systems.

The Wetlands Canal Trail is a 2 km ride through the reed and papyrus swamp, guided by a local boat operator and accompanied by a ranger, allowing the best opportunity to spot mammals such as the otter and an abundance of birds including kingfishers and storks.

Operational Radio Station: Kyenjojo Development Radio.

Key NGO: Integrated Rural Development Initiatives.

Kyenjojo District

The district was formerly part of Kabarole District, comprising Kyaka and Mwenge counties. Kyenjojo district came into existence in 2000, when the two counties previously part of Kabarole, were given district status. The district was reduced in size when Kyaka, one of its counties was made an independent district in 2010.

Location: It borders the districts of Kyegegwa to the east, Kabarole to the west, Kibaale to the north and Kamwenge to the south.

Area: 2,352 sq. km.

Climate and Relief: It lies at an approximate altitude of 1,585m – 3,962m above sea level, with rainfall totalling 750mm –1,000mm per annum and temperatures around 19°C.

Population: Basing on the 2009 projections, the district has 337,000 people – 170,900 female, 166,100 male with a density of 143 persons per sq.km.

Major Towns: Kyenjojo (administrative headquarter), Butunduzi, Katooke, Kyarusozi; Trading Centre – Butiiti

Counties and Sub-counties: Mwenge County – Bufunjo, Bugaaki, Butunduzi, Katooke, Kigaraale, Kisojo, Kyarusozi, Nyabuharwa, Nyakwanzi, Butiiti, Kihuura, and Nyantungo, Butunduzi (Town Council), Katooke (Town Council), Kyarusozi (Town Council), Kyenjojo (Town Council).

Main Languages: Rutooro and Rukiga.

People: Batooro and Bakiga.

Economic Activities: Agriculture with emphasis on:
   (i)   Food crops: Sweet potatoes, maize, cassava, bananas, groundnuts and sunflower.
   (ii) Cash crops: Coffee and tea.
   (iii) Fruits and vegetables: Pineapples, tomatoes, onions and cabbage.

Area under Forestation: 142,062 hectares.

Animal Population: Kyenjojo and Kyegegwa have 184,537 cattle, 1 donkey, 73,345 pigs, 38,235 sheep, 254,966 goats, 579,743 chicken, 6,712 ducks and 598 turkeys.

Co-operative Societies: Kyenjojo, Kamwenge and Kabarole have 203 registered co-operative societies.

Industries: Furniture making, saw milling and brick making.

Education Services: Primary schools: 186 – 130 government, 27 private and 9 community. Enrolment: 85,220 – 43,051 male and 42,169 female. Primary school teachers: 1,354 – 860 male, 494 female.

Secondary Schools: 18 - 8 government, 9 Private and 1 community. Secondary school enrolment: 7,311 – 4,116 male and 3,195 female. Teachers: 336 - 280 male and 56 female.

Enrolment in secondary schools. Private: 7,311 – 64,116 male and 3,196 female. Teachers: 336 – 280 male and 56 female.

Health Services: 2 health centre IV (all government), 11 health centre III (7 government, 4 NGO), and 13 health centre II (7 government, 6 NGO).

Tourist Attractions: The 207 sq. km Katonga Wildlife Reserve in the neighbouring district of Kyegegwa, attracts tourists to Kyenjojo District. Kyenjojo District is also a transit stop-over for tourists destined for Kibale and Rwenzori National Parks.

Operational Radio Station: Kyenjojo Development Radio, Voice of Tooro.

Key NGO: Integrated Rural Development Initiatives.

District leaders:	Members of Parliament:
Chairperson – Mr James Byamukama	Mwenge County North
Chief Administrative Officer (CAO)	– Mr Muhumuza David
– Mr Moses Kanyarutokye	Mwenge County South
Deputy Chief Administrative Officer	– Mr Aston Peterson Kajara
(DCAO) – Vacant	Woman Representative
Town Clerk (Kyenjojo Town Council)	– Ms Timbigamba Lyndah
– Mr Fred K. Rwabutoro	

Masindi District

It was part of former Bunyoro District. At Independence, Bunyoro was a kingdom. When kingdoms were abolished in 1967, it became Bunyoro District. In 1974, the provincial administration divided Bunyoro District into North Bunyoro and South Bunyoro. The former became Masindi District in 1980.

Location: Masindi District borders the districts of Kiryandongo to the east and northeast, Nakasongola and Nakaseke to the southeast, Gulu to the north, Kyankwanzi to the south, Hoima to the southwest and Buliisa to the west.

Area: 3,927 sq. km. (including Buliisa District)

Climate, Relief and Vegetation: It lies at an altitude of between 621m – 1,158m above sea level in a savannah climatic zone, with temperatures averaging over 25°C and rainfall 100mm – 1,000mm per annum. Vegetation is punctuated by short grass and shrubs.

Population: Based on the population projection for 2009 there are 560,000 people 278,800 male and 281,200 female with a density of 142 persons per sq.km.

Major Towns: Masindi (administrative headquarters); Trading Centres – Butiaba, Kigumba and Kiryandongo.

Counties and Sub-counties: Bujenje County – Budongo, Bwijanga; Buruli County – Kimengo, Miirya, Pakanyi. Masindi Municipality – Central Division, Karujubu Division, Kigulya Division, Nyangahya Division.

Main Language: Runyoro.

People: Banyoro.

Economic Activities: Mainly agriculture with emphasis on:
  (i)   Food crops: Maize, finger millet, beans, cassava, simsim (sesame), groundnuts, sorghum, peas, Irish potatoes, sweet potatoes and bananas.
  (ii) Cash crops: Tobacco, coffee and cotton.
  (iii) Vegetables: Tomatoes and cabbage.
  (iv) Ranching.

Banks: Stanbic Bank Uganda Ltd – 1, Crane Bank.

Area under Forestation: 446,398 hectares.

Animal Population: Based on the 2008 census, Masindi and Kiryandongo have 213,402 cattle, 233,423 goats, 24,943 sheep, 87,616 pigs, 39,362 ducks and 1,843 turkeys.

Co-operative Societies: 89 registered primary societies with Bunyoro Growers Union at the district level.

Industries: Pitsawing, saw milling, printing, cotton ginning; manufacture of jaggery, furniture making, processing of hides and skins, oil and grain milling.

Education Services: Primary schools: 115 schools – 98 government, 16 private and 1 community. Enrolment: 65,089 pupils – 33,077 male and 32,012 female. Primary school teachers: 1,301 – 633 male and 668 female. Available furniture is adequate for 41,704 pupils.

Secondary schools: 24 schools – 7 government and 17 Private. Secondary school Enrolment: 12,189 students - 6,901 male and 5,288 female. Teachers: 638 – 488 male and 150 female.

Tertiary institutions: 1 technical institution and 1 teacher training college; 1 national teacher's college – Masindi, Nyabyeya Forestry College

Health Services: 1 hospital - government - Masindi Hospital with 100 beds.), 1 health centre IV (government); 8 health centre III - (7 government, 1 NGO) 23 health centre II - (22 government, 1 NGO).

Transport Network: Masindi Airfield – The airfield is served by a grass-surface runway which is 2,010m x 30m. Water at the airfield is provided from an underground tank. The Civil Aviation Authority provides H.F. radio communication. The airfield is 5.1 km from Masindi town.

Tourist Attractions: On Kihande Hill is Kihande Palace, the palace of *Omukama* (King) of Bunyoro. Masindi Hotel offers reasonable accommodation with bed and breakfast.

Excursions to Lake Albert can be made from Masindi. One can head for the town of Butiaba Port on Lake Albert.

The information centre for Murchison Falls National Park is found in Masindi opposite the Town Council offices.

Budongo Forest Reserve is the largest area of unexploited mahogany forest in East Africa, with huge trees growing up to 60m high. About 700 chimpanzees live in the forest. Other primates are the black and white colobus monkeys, the red tailed monkeys, the blue monkeys, potto, baboons and the vervet monkey. Bird life is excellent with 366 species recorded. There are spectacular views from Butiaba over Lake Albert and the Blue Mountains of the Democratic Republic of Congo, on the western shore of the Lake.

General information on the reserve can be obtained from Nyabyeya Forest College, Masindi.

Lake Kanyege is at the forest edge with water birds and clouds of butterflies.

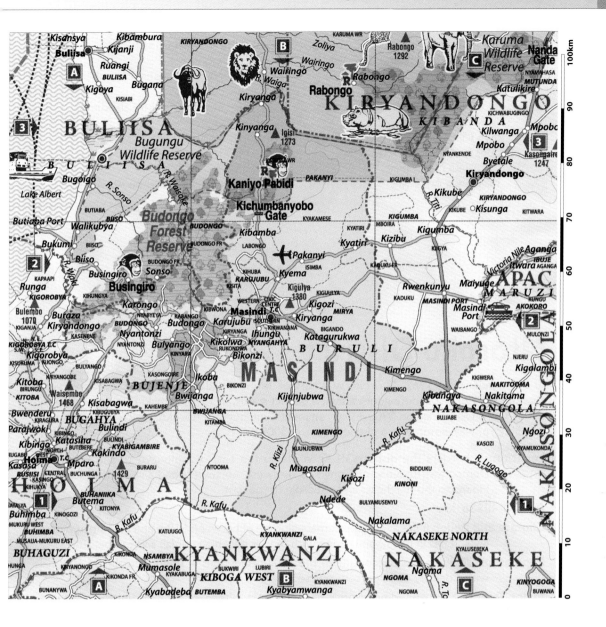

Operational Radio and TV Stations: Christian Life Ministries, Uganda Broadcasting Corporation Radio, Masindi Broadcasting Service, Earnest Publishers and Uganda Broadcasting Corporation Television.

Key NGOs: Actionaid Uganda, MS Uganda, VSO Uganda, Uganda Women's Effort to Save Orphans, Nature.

District leaders:
Chairperson – Mr Isingoma M.K. Wilson
Chief Administrative Officer (CAO)
   – Mr Aggrey Fredric Ngobi
Deputy Chief Administrative Officer
   (DCAO) – Vacant
Ag. Town Clerk (Masindi Municipal
   Council) –Mr Dauda Chwa
Mayor Masindi Municipality
   – Mr Joshua Amanyire

Members of Parliament:
Buruli County
   – Mr Nyiira Zerubabel Mijumbi
Bujenje County
   – Ms Labwoni Masiko Kabakumba
   Princess
Masindi Municipality
   – Mr Monday Ernest Apuuli
Woman MP
   – Ms Jalia Bintu Lukumu Abwooli

Ntoroko District

At independence in 1962, Ntoroko was part of Tooro Kingdom. When the kingdoms were abolished in 1967, Tooro Kingdom attained district status. In 1974, Semliki District was carved out of Tooro District and in 1980 it was renamed Bundibugyo. Ntoroko, which was a county in Bundibugyo, was elevated to a district status in 2009.

Location: It borders the districts of Kabarole to the east, Bundibugyo to the south, the Democratic Republic of Congo to the west, northwest and and north; Kibale and Hoima to the northeast and Kabarole to the east.

Area: 1,403 sq. km.

Climate and Relief: It lies at an approximate altitude of between 619m and 3,556m above sea level. It lies in the savanna zone with moderately high rainfall and temperatures.

Population: 70,900 people according to the 2009 projections – 36,500 female, 34,400 male with a density of 50 persons per sq.km.

Major Towns: Kibuuku (administrative headquarters), Ntoroko; Trading Centres – Karugutu and Ntungama.

Counties and Sub-counties: Ntoroko County – Butungama, Bweramule, Kanara, Karugutu, Nombe, Rwebisengo and Kibuuku (Town Council).

Main Languages: Rwamba and Rutooro.

People: Bamba and Batooro.

Economic Activities: Agriculture with a bias towards:
   (i)   Food crops: Maize, cassava, beans, sweet and Irish potatoes, soya bean, yams, groundnuts and bananas.
   (ii) Cash crop: Cocoa, vanilla and palm oil.
   (iii) Fruits and vegetables: Tomatoes, cabbages and onions.
   (iv) Fishing on the southern end of Lake Albert.

Area under Forestation: 74,084 hectares.

Animal Population: As of 2008, Ntoroko and Bundibugyo districts had 163,913 cattle, 14,692 pigs, 14,824 sheep, 131,765 goats and 312,931 chicken, 27,645 ducks and 519 turkeys.

Co-operative Societies: 51 registered primary societies.

Industries: Cocoa processing, construction and carpentry, brick making. Cocoa fermenting is the biggest single industry and it involves about 52 people.

Banks: Stanbic Bank Uganda Ltd – 1.

Education Services: Primary schools: 41 schools – 35 government, 5 private and 1 community. Enrolment: 15,433 pupils - 7,770 male and 7,663 female. Primary school teachers: 302 – 220 male and 82 female.

Secondary schools: 2 schools (all government). Secondary school enrolment: 728 – 456 male and 272 female. Teachers: 28 - 24 male and 4 female.

Health Services: 1 health centre IV (government), 2 health centre III (2 government), 3 health centre II (all government). Private/NGO – 2 dispensaries, 6 clinics.

Transport Network: A murram road network that meanders over rugged terrain. Transport to the district is a big problem.

Tourist Attractions: Semliki National Park which contains Sempaya Hot Springs, the Semliki Forest Reserve, the Rwenzori Mountains National Park.

Semliki Valley Wildlife Reserce, hikes at the foothills of the Rwenzoris and the Amabere Caves and Waterfalls.

Additional Information: Ntoroko District has rich soils and reliable rainfall. But agricultural practice in the district is basically small scale. The hilly terrain in the greatly restricts the use of machines for large scale farming.

Land tenure is mostly customary.

The farmers face difficulties in marketing their produce because of the poor road network. During the rainy season, transport is problematic and the farmers cannot reach the market easily.

There is some trade between the district and border areas of the Democratic Republic of Congo. But the densely forested borderline in some places and absence of roads frustrates large scale trade.

There are small industries in Ntoroko mainly for cocoa processing.

The district became a main route for rebel infiltration from 1996 – 2000. The Allied Democratic Front (ADF) operated in some parts of the district, forcing people to flee their homes, hence interrupting agricultural activities Normalcy has returned following the defeat of the ADF.

Key NGOs: Actionaid Uganda, World Vision Uganda, Abanya Rwenzori Mountaineering Association, Uganda Red Cross, North Rwenzori Rural Community Agriculture and Conservation Link, Self Care Bundibugyo, National Association of Women Organisations in Uganda, Baghendera Farmers' Organisation for Organic Farming, Bundibugyo Association of Women Living with AIDS, Green Dove Puppeter for Adolescent Awareness, Thukolendeke Disabled Group, Mataisa Womens Group, Community Hygiene and Sanitation Promoters Association.

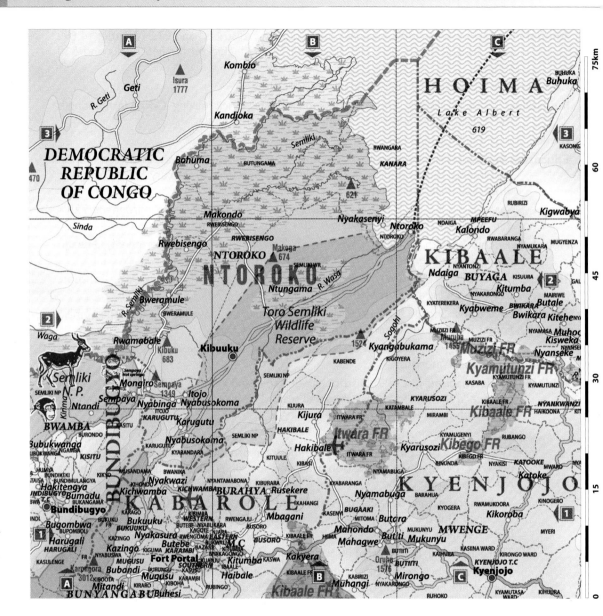

District leaders:
Chairperson
 – Mr Kamanywa Timothy Mugera
Chief Administrative Officer (CAO)
 – Vacant
Deputy Chief Administrative Officer
 (DCAO) – Asaba Allan Ganafa

Members of Parliament:
Ntoroko County
 – Mr Bahinduka Mugarra Martin
Woman MP – Ms Mujungu Jennifer K.

Districts Index

This index includes the following: places and areas — Districts (*Dist*), Counties (*Cy*), Divisions (*Div*), Municipal Councils (*M/C*), Subcounties (*S-Cy*), Town Councils (*T/C*), Parishes (*Par*), Wards (*Ward*), district headquarters (e.g. **Kaliro**), towns and village settlements — as well as spot heights (*h*); islands (e.g. *Kuiye*, *Is.*); rivers (e.g. *Buhindagi*, *R.*), swamps (e.g. *Lubigi Swamp*), lakes (e.g. *Opeta*, *L.*), gulfs (e.g. *Napoleon Gulf*), bays (e.g. *Wazimenya Bay*), channels (e.g. *Damba Channel*), passages (e.g. *Ugana Passage*), falls (e.g. *Karuma Falls*), springs (e.g. *Kanangorok Hot springs*), dams (e.g. *Nalubaale Dam*); Forest Reserves (*F/R*); National Parks (*N/P*), Wildlife Reserves (*W/R*), National Park headquarters (*P/Hq*), Sector headquarters (*S/Hq*), Ranger Outposts (*R/O*), camps/huts (*camp*), Park Gate (e.g. *Katunguru Gate*), historical and other places of interest.

How to use this Index

The entries are listed in a strict alphabetical order.

1. Each entry is followed by its description, but is preceeded by its map reference and page number in which map it is located e.g. **B1**237 Tanda Pits, that is vertical grid B and horizontal grid 1 on page 237.

2. The square reference is colour coded to match the regional grouping for further ease in locating it.

3. Districts and district headquarters are shown in the index in Bold Type and reference is to the page and square respectively where the area is to be easily found e.g. 162 **MANAFWA** and **B2**162 **Bubulo**.

4. Where entries could not be shown on the map because of congestion, they are shown in the index and reference is made to areas shown e.g. Baronger *Ward* which is not shown but is found in Railways *S-Cy* appears as **B2**55 Baronger *Ward* (Railways *S-Cy*).

5. When entries with the same name share the same grid reference on a map, the areas where they are located are shown to differentiate them, e.g. **C3**123 Kachonga *Par* (Kachonga *S-Cy*) and **C3**123 Kachonga *Par* (Naweyo *S-Cy*).

B143 Adeknino *Par*
B255 Adekokwok *Par*
B255 *ADEKOKWOK S-Cy*
A263 Adel *Par*
C350 Adelogo *Par*
C343 Aderolong *Par*
C259 *Adibu, R.*
B163 Adigo *Par*
C132 *ADILANG S-Cy*
B132 Adilang
C155 *Adip, R.*
B36 Adjugopi
B36 Adjumani Central *Ward*
6 **ADJUMANI** *Dist*
F101 **ADJUMANI** *Dist*
B36 *ADJUMANI T/C*
B36 **Adjumani**
A343 Adok *Par*
C336 Adonyimo *Par*
C336 Adonyimo
B110 Adraa *Par*
B310 Adripi *Par*
B36 *ADROPI S-Cy*
B340 Aduk
C240 *ADUKU S-Cy*
C240 Aduku
B3173 Adul *Par*
A210 *ADUMI S-Cy*
A210 Adumi
B36 Adunipi
B261 *ADWARI S-Cy*
A261 Adwari
B243 Adwila *Par*
B343 Adwoki *Par*
B243 Adwoki
B150 Adyang *Par*
B150 Adyeda *Par*
B240 Adyeda *Par*
B263 Adyeda *Par*
B163 Adyegi *Par*
B255 *ADYEL S-Cy*
B232 *AGAGO Cy*
32 **AGAGO** *Dist*
I91 **AGAGO** *Dist*
B265 *Agago, R.*
A240 Aganga *Par*
A240 Aganga
A1148 Agaria (Island) *Par*
B250 Agege *Par*
B132 Agelec *Par*
B232 Agengo *Par*
B223 Agermach
C236 Agikdak *Par*
B2173 Agirigiroi *Par*
B2173 Agogomit *Par*
B3148 Agolitom *Par*
A246 Agonga *Par*
B3106 Agonga *Par*
C259 Agonga *Par*
B2183 Agora *Par*
B353 Agoro Agu Forest *Par*
C353 *AGORO S-Cy*
C353 Agoro
B2173 Agu *Par*
B2173 Agu
B1183 Agugul
B2176 *AGULE Cy*

B1173 Agule *Par* (Kobwin *S-Cy*)
B2176 Agule *Par* (Agule *S-Cy*), see **B1173**
B3148 Agule *Par*
B3173 Agule *Par*
B2176 *AGULE S-Cy*
B2176 Agule
B3106 Aguliya
C263 Agulurude *Par*
B355 *AGUR S-Cy*
B2186 Agu16 Aguruu A *Ward*
B2186 Aguruu B *Ward*
A2148 Agurut *Par*
C138 Agwar-Yugi *Par*
B243 *AGWATTA S-Cy*
A243 Agwatta
B246 Agwee *Ward* (Laroo *S-Cy*)
B26 *Agwei, R.*
B343 Agwiciri *Par*
C340 Agwiciri *Par*
B218 Agwok
B310 *AII-VU S-Cy*
C3106 Airabet *Par*
B3167 Aisa *Par*
B155 Aito
C238 *Aiyuge, R.*
C210 Ajai *W/R*
B2106 Ajaki *Par*
B3106 *Ajaki, R.*
B232 Ajali *Par*
B3173 Ajello *Par*
B2173 Ajeluk *Par*
A2176 Ajepet *Par*
B363 Ajerijeri *Par*
B3173 Ajesa *Par*
B2144 Ajesai
B210 *AJIA S-Cy*
B210 Ajia
B110 Ajibu *Par*
B112 Ajipala *Par*
B210 Ajiraku *Par*
B340 Ajok *Par*
A210 Ajono *Par*
A210 Ajono
B134 Ajonyi *Par*
B36 Ajugopi *Par*
B1148 Ajuket *Par*
B2173 Ajuket *Par*
C363 Ajul *Par*
B218 Akaba
B110 *Akaba, R.*
A1148 Akadot *Par* (Mukongoro *S-Cy*)
B2176 Akadot *Par* (Pallisa *S-Cy*), see **A3146**
B2186 Akadot *Par*
B163 Akaka *Par*
B1277 Akaku *Par*
B1148 Akalabai *Par*
B2100 Akalale *Par*
C340 Akali *Par*
C150 *AKALO S-Cy*
B150 Akalo
B255 Akangi *Par*
B255 Akano *Par*

B218 Akanyo
A248 Akara *Par*
B2173 Akarukei *Par*
B3173 Akarukei *Par*
B2284 Akatoma
B2277 Akatongole
B1277 Akayanja *Par*
C2284 Akeirungu
B3173 Akeit *Par*
B240 Akere *Par*
A2106 Akeriau *Par*
B2114 Akero *Par*
B3144 Aketa *Par*
B3144 Aketa
B240 Aketo *Par*
B255 Akia *Par*
B3148 Akide *Par*
C248 Akilok
B310 Akinio *Par*
B310 Akinio
A1148 Akisim *Par* (Kanyumu *S-Cy*)
B2176 Akisim *Par* (Akisim *S-Cy*), see **A1173**
B2176 *AKISIM S-Cy*
B2183 Akisim *Ward* (Soroti Eastern *Div*)
B248 Akobi *Par*
B3178 Akoboi *Par*
B240 Akokoro *Par*
B240 *AKOKORO S-Cy*
B140 Akokoro
C2106 *Akokoroi, R.*
B234 Akol *Par*
C336 Akol *Par*
C236 Akongomit *Par*
B236 Akongomit
C2106 Akoromit *Par*
B2183 *Akoyo, R.*
B121 Akpokoa
B2148 Akubui *Par*
B2173 Akubui *Par*
B363 Akuca *Par*
B2144 Akulet
B3148 Akum *Par*
C2106 Akum *Par*
B3148 Akum
B2114 Akuoro *Par*
B2114 Akuoro
B187 Akur, *(h)*
A234 Akura *Par*
B1144 Akurao *Par*
B143 Akurolango *Par*
C248 Akurumou *Par*
B297 Akuyam *Par*
A265 Akuyam
B2176 Akwamor *Par*
C343 Akwanga *Par*
B250 Akwiridid *Par*
C236 Akwon *Par*
B118 *AKWORO S-Cy*
B255 Akwoyo *Ward Ward* (Adyel *S-Cy*)
B210 *Ala, R.*
B253 Alaa *Par*
B234 Alai
B234 Alal *Par*

B2100 *Alamachar, R.*
B261 Alangi *Par*
B261 Alango *Par*
A248 Alango *Ward* (Kitgum *T/C*)
B134 Alanyi *Par*
C343 Alapata *Par*
B214 Alarapi *Par*
F101 *Albert Nile, R.*
E71 *Albert, L.*
B155 Alebere *Par*
34 **ALEBTONG** *Dist*
I81 **ALEBTONG** *Dist*
B234 Alebtong *Par*
B234 **Alebtong**
A218 Alego
C2144 Alekilek
C359 Alelelele
B2144 Aleles *Par*
C236 Alemere *Par*
C236 Alemere
A250 Alemi *Par*
B343 Alenga *Par*
B110 Alengbelo
B3178 Alengo *Par*
A240 Alengo
A110 Alenzu
B2106 Alere *Par*
B287 *ALEREK S-Cy*
B287 Alerek
A359 Alero *G/R*
B359 Alero Kal *Par*
B359 *ALERO S-Cy*
C359 Alero
B310 Alia *Par*
B221 Aliapi *Par*
A310 Aliba *Par* (Aroi *S-Cy*)
C210 Aliba *Par* (Rigbo *S-Cy*)
A116 *ALIBA S-Cy*
A116 Aliba
B240 Alido *Par*
A1148 Aligoi *Par*
B1114 Aligoi *Par*
C340 Alira *Par*
B112 Aliribu *Par*
B255 Alito Camp *Ward* (Ojwina *S-Cy*)
B250 Alito *Par*
B3106 Alito *Par*
B250 *ALITO S-Cy*
C350 Alito
A210 Alivu *Par* (Pajulu *S-Cy*)
A310 Alivu *Par* (Aroi *S-Cy*), see **B114**
B114 Alivu *Par*
B210 Alivu *Par*
B214 Alivu
B112 Alla *Par*
B2183 Aloet *Par*
B2183 Aloet
B234 *ALOI S-Cy*
A246 Alokolum *Par*
C234 Alolololo *Par*
C363 Aloni *Par*
B1144 Alukucok *Par*
B216 Aluru *Par*
B163 Alutkot *Par*

B2134 *ALWA S-Cy*
B2134 Alwa
C232 Awala
C218 Alwi *Par*
C218 Alwii
C243 Alwitmac *Par*
B240 Alworoceng *Par*
A240 Alworoceng
B2144 Alyakamer *Par*
B236 Alyecmeda *Par*
B155 *AMACH S-Cy*
B155 Amach
C2186 Amagoro A *Ward*
C2186 Amagoro B *Ward*
C2117 Amanang *Par*
B314 Amanipi *Par*
C259 Amar *Par*
C3106 Amasenike
C3106 Amaseniko *Par*
B210 Ambeko *Par*
B214 Ambidro *Par*
A2148 Amejei *Par*
B2183 Amen *Par*
C2106 Amero *Par*
C3134 Amidakar
B240 Amii *Par*
B240 Amil
B2106 Amilmil *Par*
B240 Amilo
B2114 Aminit *Par*
B2183 Aminit *Par*
B240 Aminteng
36 **AMOLATAR** *Dist*
H71 **AMOLATAR** *Dist*
C236 Amolatar *Par*
C236 **Amolatar**
C1106 Amolo *Par*
C2186 Amoni *Par*
B3121 Amonikakinei *Par*
A334 Amonomito *Par*
B134 Amononeno *Par*
B3106 Amootom *Par*
C218 Amor *Par*
C3134 Amoru *Par*
B2106 Amorupos
A261 Amoyai *Par*
B255 Amuca *Par*
B2106 Amucu *Par*
B343 Amuda *Par*
B397 Amuda
89 **AMUDAT** *Dist*
L71 **AMUDAT** *Dist*
C289 Amudat *Par*
C289 *AMUDAT S-Cy*
C289 **Amudat**
B134 *AMUGO S-Cy*
B234 Amugo
C363 Amukogungo *Par*
B2141 Amukol *Par*
C261 Amunga *Par*
B2106 *AMURIA Cy*
106 **AMURIA** *Dist*
J81 **AMURIA** *Dist*
B2106 *AMURIA T/C*
B2106 **Amuria**
38 **AMURU** *Dist*

117 **BUKWO** *Dist*
L61 **BUKWO** *Dist*
C2117 *BUKWO S-Cy*
C2117 **Bukwo**
C2117 *Bukwo, R.*
B2180 Bukyabo *Par*
B2180 *BUKYABO S-Cy*
B2180 *BUKYAMBI S-Cy*
B2153 Bukyangwa *Par*
C3243 Bulaga, *(h)*
B1119 *BULAGO S-Cy*
B1119 Bulago
A1245 *Bulago, Is.*
B2219 Bulagwe *Par*
A2162 Bulako *Par*
B2128 Bulamagi *Par*
B1128 *BULAMAGI S-Cy*
B2128 Bulamagi
B2327 Bulamagi
B2119 *BULAMBULI Cy*
119 **BULAMBULI** *Dist*
K71 **BULAMBULI** *Dist*
B2180 Bulambuli *Par*
B2136 *BULAMOGI Cy*
C3257 Bulamu *Par*
B2219 Bulamula *Par*
B2235 Bulando *Par*
B2128 Bulanga
B1171 Bulange *Par*
B2138 Bulange *Par*
B1171 *BULANGE S-Cy*
A2211 Bulange
B1171 Bulange
C3146 Bulangira *Par*
C2146 *BULANGIRA S-Cy*
B3146 Bulangira
B3138 *BULAWOLI S-Cy*
B2206 Bulawula *Par*
B3235 Bulayi *Par*
A2197 Bule *Par*
B1245 Bulebi
B2221 Bulema
B1275 Bulemba *Par*
C3309 Bulembo, *(h)*
B2237 Bulera *Par*
B3237 *BULERA S-Cy*
B2237 Bulera
C2112 *BULESA S-Cy*
B2112 Bulidha *Par*
B1112 *BULIDHA S-Cy*
C2197 Buligi
B2128 Buligo *Ward*
B2303 *BULIISA Cy*
303 **BULIISA** *Dist*
E81 **BULIISA** *Dist*
B2303 *BULIISA S-Cy*
B3303 **Buliisa**
B2245 Bulijjo *Par* (Kyampisi S-Cy), see C3257
B2245 Bulika *Par* (Nama S-Cy), see C2257
B3199 Bulima
B2309 Bulimya *Par*
C2309 Bulindi *Par*
C2309 Bulindi
B1211 *Bulingugwe, Is.*
B2197 Bulo *Par*

B2197 *BULO S-Cy*
B2197 Bulo
B2257 Buloba *Par*
B2257 Buloba
B2110 Bulobi *Par*
B2138 Bulogo *Par*
B2171 Bulolo
B3257 Bulondo
B2153 Bulongo *Par*
B3255 Bulongo *Par*
B2153 *BULONGO S-Cy*
B2153 Bulongo
C2138 Bulopa *Par*
B2138 *BULOPA S-Cy*
C2138 Bulopa
B2128 Bulowoza *Par*
A3164 Buluba
B2128 Bulubandi *Par*
B2128 Bulubandi
C3110 Bulucheke *R/O*
B2110 *BULUCHEKE S-Cy*
B2110 Bulucheke
B1119 Buluganya *Par*
B1119 *BULUGANYA S-Cy*
B2180 Buluganya
B2119 *BULUGENI S-Cy*
B2132 Bulugo *Par*
B3119 Buluguya *Par*
C2112 *BULUGUYI S-Cy*
C3112 Buluguyi
B2180 Bulujewa *Par*
B210 Bulukatoni
B3327 Buluko
B2169 Bulule *Par*
C2134 *BULULU S-Cy*
B2134 Bululu
B3192 Bulumagi
B2136 Bulumba *Par*
B2121 Bulumbi (Bulumbi S-Cy)
B2121 Bulumbi (Dabani S-Cy)
B2121 *BULUMBI S-Cy*
B2257 Bulumbu *Par*
B2257 Bulumbu
B2128 Bulumwaki *Par*
B2128 Bulumwaki
B1239 Bulunda *Par*
C2128 Bulunguli *Par*
B2138 Buluuya *Par*
B2136 Buluya *Par*
B2201 Bulwadda *Par*
C1247 Bulwadda *Par*
B2201 Bulwadda
B2180 Bulwala *Par*
B2257 Bulwanyi *Par*
B2121 Bulwenge *Par*
B3167 Bulweta *Par*
C1247 Bulyake *Par*
C3243 Bulyambidde
A3247 Bulyamusenyu *Par*
C2309 Bulyango *Par*
A2337 Bulyango
B2237 Bulyankuyege *Par*
B2192 Bulyankuyege
A2192 Bulyantete *Par*
C2167 Bumadanda *Par*
B2305 Bumaddu *Par*

B2305 Bumadu
B2180 Bumagabula *Par*
B2162 Bumagambo *Par*
B2167 Bumageni *Par*
B2180 Bumaguze *Par*
B2180 Bumaguze *Par*
B2110 Bumakita *Par*
B2110 Bumakuma *Par*
B2169 Bumalenge *Par*
B2180 Bumalimba *Par*
B2180 *BUMALIMBA S-Cy*
A3204 Bumangi
B2136 Bumanya *Par*
B2136 *BUMANYA S-Cy*
B2136 Bumanya
B2110 Bumasata *Par*
A2110 *BUMASHETI S-Cy*
B2119 Bumasifwa *Par*
B2180 Bumasifwa *Par*
B2180 Bumasifwa *R/O*
B2180 *BUMASIFWA S-Cy*
B1167 Bumasikye *Par* (Bumasikye S-Cy)
B2167 Bumasikye *Par* (Busoba S-Cy)
B1167 *BUMASIKYE S-Cy*
B1119 Bumasobo *Par*
B2180 Bumasobo *Par*
B1119 *BUMASOBO S-Cy*
A2162 Bumasokho *Par*
A2162 Bumatanda *Par*
B2110 Bumatanda *Par*
B2305 Bumate *Par*
B2180 Bumatofu *Par*
A2162 Bumatoola *Par*
B2180 Bumausi *Par*
B2180 Bumawosa *Par*
B2110 Bumayoka *Par*
B2110 *BUMAYOKA S-Cy*
B1164 Bumba *Par*
B2266 Bumbaire *Par*
B2266 *BUMBAIRE S-Cy*
B2266 Bumbaire
C2162 Bumbo *R/O*
B2162 *BUMBO S-Cy*
B2162 Bumbo
B2167 Bumbobi *Par*
B2167 *BUMBOBI S-Cy*
B2167 Bumboi *Par*
B2146 Bumiza *Par*
A2180 Bummudu *Par*
C2239 Bumoozi *Par*
C2128 Bumozi *Par*
B3119 Bumufuni *Par*
B1119 Bumugisha *Par*
C2126 Bumugoli *Par*
B1180 Bumukone *Par*
C2180 Bumulegi *Par*
B1162 Bumulika *Par*
B2121 Bumulimba *Par*
B2180 Bumuluwe *Par*
B3167 Bumuluya *Par*
B3162 Bumumali *Par*
B1180 Bumumulo *Par*
A2110 Bumusenyi *Par*
B2110 Bumushisho *Par*
B2110 Bumusi *Par*

B2162 Bumusomi *Par*
B2167 Bumutoto *Par*
B1167 Bumutsopa *Par*
B2167 Bumutsopa *Par*
B2162 Bumuyonga *Par*
B2110 Bumwalukani *Par*
B2119 Bumwambu *Par*
B2162 *BUMWONI S-Cy*
B2153 Bunabala
B1119 Bunabude *Par*
B2110 Bunabutiti *Par*
B2162 Bunabwana *Par*
B1162 *BUNABWANA S-Cy*
C3235 Bunado
B3153 Bunafu *Par*
A1281 Bunagana *Par*
A2281 Bunagana
B2110 Bunakhayoti *Par*
B1245 Bunakija *Par*
B3162 Bunambale *Par*
C3162 Bunambale
B2167 Bunambutye *Par* (Busiu S-Cy)
B2167 Bunambutye *Par* (Busoba S-Cy)
B3119 *BUNAMBUTYE S-Cy*
B2110 Bunamubi *Par*
A2110 Bunamukye *Par*
B2162 Bunamulunyi *Par*
B2257 Bunamwaya *Par* (Makindye S-Cy), see A1211
B2110 Bunandutu *Par*
B2162 Bunangabo *Par*
B2167 Bunanimi *Par*
C2162 Bunanyama *Par*
A2219 Bunanywa *Par*
B1167 Bunashimolo *Par*
B1119 Bunasufwa *Par*
A1123 Bunawale *Par*
A2180 Bundege *Par*
B2110 Bundesi *Par*
B2305 Bundibugyo Central Ward
305 **BUNDIBUGYO** *Dist*
C51 **BUNDIBUGYO** *Dist*
B2305 *BUNDIBUGYO T/C*
B2305 **Bundibugyo**
A2305 Bundikahungu *Par*
B3305 Bundikeki *Par*
A2305 Bundikuyali *Par*
A2305 Bundimbuga
B3305 Bundimulangya *Par*
A2305 Bundingoma *Par*
A3305 Bundinyama *Par*
B2162 Bunefule *Par*
B2284 Bunenero *Par*
B2284 Bunenero
C240 Bung *Par*
A246 *BUNGATIRA S-Cy*
B2123 Bunghagi *Par*
B2123 Bunghaji
B2167 *BUNGHOKO S-Cy*
B2167 *BUNGOKHO Cy*
B253 Bungu *Par*
B2270 Bungura
B2119 Bungwanyi *Par*

C1128 Buniantole *Par*
B1239 Bunjako *Par*
B1239 *Bunjako, Is.*
B1295 Bunono *Par*
B3221 *BUNTUNTUMULA S-Cy*
C2284 Bunutsya *Par*
B2164 *BUNYA Cy*
A1180 *BUNYAFWA S-Cy*
B1128 Bunyama *Par*
B2204 Bunyama *Par*
B2204 *Bunyama, Is.*
A2317 *BUNYANGABU Cy*
A2305 Bunyangule *Par*
C1128 Bunyantole
B2293 *BUNYARUGURU Cy*
B2171 Bunyenvu *F/R*
B2128 Bunyiiro *Par*
B2162 Bunyinza *Par*
A2323 Bunyiswa *Par*
B2123 *BUNYOLE EAST Cy*
A2123 *BUNYOLE WEST Cy*
B1272 *Bunyonyi, L.*
B1138 Bupandhengo *Par*
B2305 Bupomboli *Par*
B2162 *BUPOTO S-Cy*
B3108 Bupuchai *Par*
B2136 Bupyana *Par*
B2136 Bupyana
A248 Bura *Par*
A310 Bura *Par*
B214 Bura *Par*
B310 Bura *Par* (Aroi S-Cy), see A114
B3317 *BURAHYA Cy*
B2295 Burama *Par*
B214 Buramali *Par*
B1272 Buramba *Par*
B1272 Burambira *Par*
B1272 Buranga *Par*
A2298 Buraro *Par*
B2334 Buraro *Par*
C2309 Buraru *Par*
C3309 Buraza
B2275 Burema *Par*
B2275 Burema
A3277 *BUREMBA S-Cy*
A3277 Buremba
B2263 *BURERE S-Cy*
B2263 Burere
C1275 Burimbe, *(h)*
B2272 Burime *Par*
B2295 Burombe *Par*
B3305 Burondo *Par*
B1295 Burora *Par*
B2327 Burora *Par*
B2167 Burukuru *Par*
B2167 Burukuru *Par*
B2337 *BURULI Cy*
B3277 Burunga *Par*
B3277 *BURUNGA S-Cy*
B2270 Burungamo *Par*
B2270 Burungamo
B2317 Burungu *Par*
B1215 Busaale *Par* (Kayunga S-Cy), see A1138
B2243 Busaale *Par*
A2123 Busaba *Par*

C2232 Buyaga
B2323 Buyagha *Par*
B2162 Buyaka *Par*
B2167 Buyaka *Par*
B3112 Buyala *Par*
B2253 Buyamba *Par*
A2253 *BUYAMBA S-Cy*, see Kagamba (Buyamba) *S-Cy*
B2253 Buyamba
B2121 *BUYANGA S-Cy*
C2128 *BUYANGA S-Cy*
C2128 Buyanga
B2171 Buyange
B2204 Buyange, *Is.*
B2327 *BUYANJA Cy*
A3126 Buyanja *Par*
B3232 Buyanja *Par*
C1266 Buyanja *Par*
B1295 *BUYANJA S-Cy*
B2295 Buyanja
A2180 Buyaya *Par*
B1199 Buye *Par*
B3164 Buyemba *Par*
C1186 Buyemba
126 **BUYENDE** *Dist*
I61 **BUYENDE** *Dist*
B2126 Buyende *Par*
B2126 *BUYENDE S-Cy*
B2126 *BUYENDE T/C*
B2126 **Buyende**
B2132 *BUYENGO S-Cy*
B1257 Buyiga (Bulumbu *Par*)
B1257 *Buyiga, Is.*
B3253 Buyiisa *Par*
B2239 Buyijja *Par*
B2136 Buyinda *Par*
B2235 Buyinja *Par*
B3169 *BUYINJA S-Cy*
B3169 Buyinja
B1215 Buyobe *Par* (Kayunga *S-Cy*), see **A1**138
B2180 *BUYOBO S-Cy*
B1153 Buyola *Par*
B1153 Buyola
B3257 Buyonga
B2136 Buyonjo
B2204 Buyovu, *Is.*
C2164 Buyugu *Par*
B2221 Buyuki *Par*
B2221 Buyuki *Par*
B2153 Buyunze
B2180 Buzamani *Par*
B1138 *BUZAYA Cy*
C2293 Buzenga *Par*
A2217 Buzibweera *Ward*
B2211 Buziga *Par*
B2211 Buziga, *(h)*
C2192 Buziika *Par*
A3277 Buzinga
B2204 Buzongo *Par*
B2253 Buziranduulu *Par*
B2199 *Buziri, Is.*
B2257 Buzzi
C2327 Bwacapila
B1268 Bwahwa *Par*
B3211 Bwaise I *Par*

A3211 Bwaise II *Par*
A3211 Bwaise III *Par*
B3211 Bwaise
B2277 Bwalumuli
B1272 Bwama Islands *Par*
B3305 *BWAMBA Cy*
A2295 Bwambara *Par*
A2295 Bwambara
B3230 Bwami
B2253 Bwamijja *Par*
B2327 *BWAMIRAMA S-Cy*
B2232 Bwamulamira *Par*
B2128 Bwanalira *Par*
B2295 Bwanda *Par*
B1295 Bwanga *Par*
B3317 Bwanika *Par*
A1281 Bwanjebe
C2327 *BWANSWA S-Cy*
C2239 Bwanya
B2206 Bwasandeku *Par*
C3298 Bwayegamba *Par*
B1136 Bwayuya *Par*
B2221 Bwaziba *Par*
A2199 Bweema *Par*
A2199 *BWEEMA S-Cy*
A2199 *Bweema, Is.*
B1268 Bwenda *Par*
B1268 Bwenda
A2204 Bwendero *Par*
A2204 Bwendero
C2309 Bwenderu
B3284 Bwengure *Par*
B2284 Bwentama
B1320 Bwera *Par*
C2266 Bwera *Par*
A1323 *BWERA S-Cy*
A2323 Bwera Township *Par*
A2323 Bwera
B2255 Bwera
A2340 Bweramule *Par*
A2340 Bweramule
B3206 Bwesa *Par*
B3206 Bwesa
B3323 Bwesumbu *Par*
B2257 Bweya *Par* (Sissa *S-Cy*), see **B1**211
B2221 Bweyeyo *Par*
B2243 Bweyogedde *Par*
C2257 Bweyogerere *Par* (Kira *T/C*), see **C3**211
C2128 Bwigula *Par*
A2138 Bwiiza *Par*
A2138 Bwiiza
B1337 *BWIJANGA S-Cy*
B2337 Bwijanga
A2327 *BWIKARA S-Cy*
A2327 Bwikara
B3119 Bwikonge *Par*
A3119 *BWIKONGE S-Cy*
B2309 Bwikya *Par*
A3281 Bwindi *F/R*
B1275 Bwindi *F/R*
B1275 Bwindi Impenetrable *N/P*
A2272 Bwindi *N/P*
B2272 Bwindi *Par*
B3320 Bwizi *Par*

C3320 *BWIZI S-Cy*
B3320 Bwizi
B2284 Bwizibwera
B259 Bwobonam *Par*
C1263 Bwoga *Par*
A2289 *BWONGERA S-Cy*
A2289 Bwongyera
B2253 Byakabanda *Par*
A2253 *BYAKABANDA S-Cy*
B2253 Byakabanda
A2277 Byanamira *Par*
A2277 Byanamira
A2219 Byerima *Par*
B3253 Byerima *Par*
B2330 Byetale
B2183 Camp Swahili *Ward* (Soroti Northern *Div*)
B595 Campswahili Chini *Ward* (Moroto *M/C*)
B595 Campswahili Juu *Ward* (Moroto *M/C*)
B240 *CAWENTE S-Cy*
B240 Cawente
B340 Cegere *Par*
B340 *CEGERE S-Cy*
B316 Celecelea *Par*
B2272 *CENTRAL Div* (Kabale *M/C*)
B2211 *CENTRAL Div*
C216 Central *F/R*
B2183 Central *Ward* (Soroti Eastern *Div*)
B36 Cesia *Ward*
B1281 Chahafi *Par*
B1281 *Chahafi, L.*
B1281 *CHAHI S-Cy*
A240 Chakali
C191 Chakolomun
A312 Chakulya *Par*
B236 Chakwara *Par*
C2323 *Chalanga, R.*
B2108 Chali *Par*
A2263 *Chambura, R.*
C223 Chana *Par*
B2277 Chankoko
A293 *Chapeth, R.*
B221 Charanga *Par*
B3121 Chawo *Par*
B2141 Chebelat *Par*
B2141 Chebonet (Kapsinda *S-Cy*)
B2141 *Chebonet, R.*
B2148 Cheele *Par*
B243 Chegere
B340 Chegere
B2176 Chelekura *Par*
B2176 *CHELEKURA S-Cy*
B2144 Cheleuko *Par*
B2141 *CHEMA S-Cy*
B2150 Cheminy *Par*
B2141 Chemosong *Par*
B2117 Chepkwasta *Par*
B2117 *CHEPKWASTA S-Cy*
B3150 Chepsikunya
B2119 Cheptui
B2141 *Cheptui, R.*
B2141 Cheptuya *Par*

B2117 *CHESOWER S-Cy*
B2117 Chesower
A210 Chiaba *Par*
B1281 Chibumba *Par*
A2281 Chihe *Par*
B1284 Chikunda
C159 Chobe *Gate*
A2114 Chodong *Par*
B2289 Chondo
B248 *CHUA Cy*
A26 *CIFORO S-Cy*
B310 Cilio
B2211 Civic Centre *Par*
C138 Cubu *Par*
B259 Coorom *Par*
B1323 Crater Area
B253 Cubu *Par*
B210 Curu
B2121 Dabani *Par*
B2121 *DABANI S-Cy*
B2121 Dabani
A210 *DADAMU S-Cy*
B2144 Dadas *Par*
B1121 Dadira *Par*
A2180 Dahami *Par*
B2204 Danje
B112 Danya
B1221 Ddegeya *Par*
B2245 Ddundu *Par* (Kyampisi *S-Cy*), see **C3**257
B2192 Ddungi *Par*
A2253 Ddwaniro *Par*
A2253 *DDWANIRO S-Cy*
C2217 *DDWANIRO S-Cy*
B2243 Debeza
A2201 Degeya *Par*
B212 Degiba *Par*
B118 Dei
A116 Delu
A2199 Dembe
B2257 Dewe
B353 Dibolyec *Par*
C2330 Diima *Par*
C2255 Dispensary *Ward*
B2146 Dodoi *Par*
C2106 Dodos *Par*
C291 *DODOTH EAST Cy*
A291 *DODOTH WEST Cy*
B263 Dogapio *Par*
C2123 Doho *Par*
B243 *DOKOLO Cy*
43 **DOKOLO** *Dist*
I71 **DOKOLO** *Dist*
B2183 Dokolo *Par*
B243 *DOKOLO S-Cy*
B2106 Dokolo
B2183 Dokolo
C243 **Dokolo**
B293 *Dopeth, R.*
A121 *DRAJINI S-Cy*
A214 Draju *Par*
B214 Dranzipi *Par*

B212 Dricile *Par*
A210 Driwala *Par*
C216 *DUFILE (INDRIDRI) S-Cy*
C216 Dufile *Par*
C216 Dufile
B1235 Dumu
A2320 Dura
B1317 *Dura, R.*
B2317 Durama
C1327 Dusandala
B2320 *Dwamanyanya, R.*
C223 Dwonga *Par*
B36 *DZAIPI S-Cy*
A16 East Madi *W/R*
B26 *EAST MOYO Cy*
B2317 *EASTERN Div* (Fort Portal *M/C*)
B316 Ebwea *Par*
B110 Eceko *Par*
B310 Edayi *Par*
A110 Edrivu
B31 *Edward, L.*
B214 Egamara *Par*
B310 Ejoni *Par*
B243 Ekwera
C36 Elegu *Par*
B210 Eleku *Par*
A3323 Elena *Camp*
B316 Elenderea *Par*
C1119 Elgon, Mt. *N/P*
B110 Elibu *Par*
B2277 Embaare *Par*
A1305 Emin, *(h)*
B2114 Emokori *Ward*
A1272 Enchuya *F/R*
C2270 Endiizi
C2270 *ENDINZI S-Cy*
A3277 Engari *Par*
B1257 Entebbe Bay (Katabi *Ward*)
B1257 Entebbe Central *Ward*
B1257 *ENTEBBE DIVISION A S-Cy*
B1257 *ENTEBBE DIVISION B S-Cy*
B1257 *ENTEBBE M/C*
B1257 Entebbe
B210 Enyio *Par*
B1323 Equator and Queen's *Gate*
C210 Eramva *Par*
C210 Eramva
B310 Erea *Par*
B121 Erezeli
A210 Eruba *Par*
A210 Eruba
B238 *Erudzi, R.*
B218 Erusi East, *(h)*
B118 Erusi
A118 Erusi, *(h)*
B218 *ERUSSI S-Cy*
B255 *ERUTE Cy*
B255 Erute
B26 Esia *Par*
B236 Etam *Par*
B236 Etam
B314 Etoko *Par*

A1340 Itojo *Par*
B3289 Itojo *Par*
B3289 *ITOJO S-Cy*
A2340 Itojo
B3289 Itojo
B1171 Ituba *Par*
B3128 Ituba *Par*
B2153 Ituba
A216 *ITULA S-Cy*
B216 Itula
A3334 Itwara *F/R*
C3317 Itwara *F/R*
A240 Itwara
A2171 Ivukula *Par*
B3171 *IVUKULA S-Cy*
B2171 Ivukula
B1132 Ivunamba *Par*
B1128 Iwawu *Par*
B3112 *IWEMBA S-Cy*
B3112 Iwemba
B3171 Iwungiro *Par*
C2126 Iyingo *Par*
C2126 Iyingo
A1186 *IYOLWA S-Cy*
B1186 Iyolwa
B236 Izigwe *Par*
B2199 Izinga, *Is.*
B2171 Izirangobi *Par*
B2171 Izirangobi *Par*
B2132 Iziru *Par*
C3204 Jaana *Par*
C2180 Jackson's Peak, *(h)*
B1164 *JAGUZI S-Cy*
B1164 Jaguzi, *Is.*
B146 Jaka *Par*
B2293 Jakana Lodge *Camp*
B316 Jalei, *(h)*
C2108 Jami *Par*
B2257 Jandira
A1239 Jandiru
B223 *JANGOKORO S-Cy*
B240 Jeber
B3167 Jewa *Par*
B3239 Jeza *Par*
B3239 Jeza
B293 *JIE Cy*
B36 Jihwa *Par*
A110 Jiki *Par*
B310 Jilla *Par*
B255 Jinja Camp *Ward*
    (Ojwina *S-Cy*)
B2132 *JINJA CENTRAL Div*
B1132 Jinja Central East *Par*
132 **JINJA** *Dist*
I51 **JINJA** *Dist*
B1132 *JINJA M/C*
B1121 Jinja *Par*
B1132 **Jinja**
B2257 Jinja-Kalooli (Maganjo
    Par), see **A3211**
B2257 Jinja-Kawempe
    (Maganjo *Par*), see
    A3211
B2257 Jinja-Kijapan (Maganjo
    Par), see **A3211**
B2239 Jjalamba *Par*
B2257 Jjungo *Par*

B3323 John Matte *Camp*
C218 *JONAM Cy*
A223 Jopakubi
A218 Jopangira
A218 Jukia *Ward*
B323 Juloka *Par*
C2201 Jumbi *F/R*
B255 Junior Quarters *Ward*
    (Adyel *S-Cy*)
B123 Jupadindo *Par*
A223 Jupamatho *Par*
A218 Jupangira-Pawong *Par*
B121 Jurei, *R.*
B291 Kaabong Central *Par*
91 **KAABONG** *Dist*
J111 **KAABONG** *Dist*
B291 *KAABONG EAST S-Cy*
B291 *KAABONG T/C*
B291 *KAABONG WEST S-Cy*
B291 **Kaabong**
A2272 Kaara *Par*
C1247 *KAASANGOMBE S-Cy*
B3162 *KAATO S-Cy*
B1164 Kaaza, *Is.*
B1164 Kaaza, *Is.*
C2257 Kaazi
A1317 Kabaale *Par*
B1255 Kabaale *Par*
B2206 Kabaale *Par*
B2255 Kabaale *Par*
B2309 Kabaale
A3270 Kabaare *Par*
B2266 Kabaare *Par*
A3270 Kabaare
B2270 Kabaare
C2284 Kabagarami
B3277 Kabagole
B1268 Kabagoma
B3277 *Kabagore, R.*
B2317 Kabahango *Par*
B3164 Kabaingire *Par*
A2211 *Kabaka's Lake*
B2221 Kabakedi *Par*
B2253 Kabala *Par*
B2211 Kabalagala *Par*
B2211 Kabalagala
B3134 Kabalangi
B2272 Kabale Central *Ward*
    (Kabale Central *Div*)
272 **KABALE** *Dist*
C11 **KABALE** *Dist*
B2272 *KABALE M/C*
A1320 Kabale *Par*
B1257 Kabale *Par*
B2309 Kabale *Par*
B3257 Kabale *Par*
A2277 Kabale
B1317 Kabale
B2272 **Kabale**
B3257 Kabale
B2327 Kabalega *Par*
B2134 Kabalkweru *Par*
A2243 Kabalungi *Par*
B2327 Kabamba *Par*
A1243 Kabamba
B2320 Kabambiro *Par*
B2309 Kabanda

A2245 Kabanga *Par* (Ntenjeru
    S-Cy), see **C2257**
B2192 Kabanga *Par*
B2245 Kabanga
A2337 Kabango *Par*
B2253 Kabano *Par*
B1284 Kabarama *Par*
B2270 Kabare *Par*
B3284 Kabare *Par*
B2221 Kabaroga
B1284 Kabatanagi
B2232 Kabatema *Par*
B1323 Kabatoro *Gate*
B1323 Kabatoro
C3323 Kabatunda *Par*
A1243 Kabbo *Par*
B2117 *KABEI S-Cy*
B2176 Kabelai *Par* (Butebo
    S-Cy), see **A1114**
B2245 Kabembe *Par* (Nama
    S-Cy), see **C2257**
B2245 Kabembe
C3317 Kabende *Par*
B2134 *KABERAMAIDO Cy*
134 **KABERAMAIDO** *Dist*
I71 **KABERAMAIDO** *Dist*
B2134 Kaberamaido *Par*
B2134 *KABERAMAIDO S-Cy*
B2134 **Kaberamaido**
B2272 Kabere *Par*
A3270 Kaberebere
B2270 Kabeshekere
B2141 Kabeywa *Par*
B2141 *KABEYWA S-Cy*
B2195 Kabigi *Par*
B3245 Kabimbiri *Par*
B1295 Kabingo *Par* (Rubabo
    Cy)
B2295 Kabingo *Par*
    (Rujumbura *Cy*)
A2323 Kabingo *Par*
B2266 Kabingo *Par*
B2320 Kabingo *Par*
B3270 *KABINGO S-Cy*
A3277 Kabingo
B2270 **Kabingo**
B1128 Kabira *Par*
B2253 *KABIRA S-Cy*
B2286 *KABIRA S-Cy*
A1289 Kabira
B2253 Kabira
B2286 Kabira
A2334 Kabirizi *Par*
B2323 Kabirizi *Par*
B2323 Kabirizi *Par*
B2323 Kabirizi
C2192 Kabizzi *Par*

A2270 *Kabobo, R.*
B2176 Kaboloi *Par* (Pallisa
    S-Cy), see **A3146**
A2235 *KABONERA S-Cy*
A1317 Kabonero *Par*
C2243 Kabosi *Par*
A2211 Kabowa *Par*
A2243 Kabowa *Par*
A3192 Kabowa *Ward*
C3230 Kaboyo
C3257 Kabubbu *Par*
B2275 Kabuga *Par*
B2320 Kabuga, *(h)*
C2192 Kabugoga
A2270 Kabugu *Par*
B2268 Kabujogera (Kagongo
    Par)
A1148 Kabukol *Par*
B3235 Kabukulwa
B3221 Kabukunga
C2126 Kabukye *Par*
B2232 *KABULA Cy*
B2232 Kabula
B2243 Kabulamuliro *Par*
C1221 Kabulanaka *Par*
B2201 *KABULASOKE S-Cy*
B2201 Kabulasoke
C1255 Kabulasoke
A1245 Kabulataka, *Is.*
    (Mpunge *Par*)
C2237 Kabule *Par*
C3257 Kabumba *Par*
B3257 Kabumba
B2108 Kabuna *Par*
A1243 Kabunde
B2289 Kabungo *Par*
C3221 Kabunyata *Par*
C3221 Kabunyata
B1277 Kaburegyeya
B2320 Kaburisoke *Par*
C2150 Kaburoron
C1249 Kabusinde
A3253 Kabusota *Par*
C2257 Kabuuma (Busabala
    Par), see **B1211**
B1237 Kabuwambo *Par*
B3253 Kabuwoko
A2270 *KABUYANDA S-Cy*
A2270 Kabuyanda
C2270 Kabuyembe
B1114 Kabwalin *Par*
C2176 Kabwangasi *Par*
    (Kabwangasi *S-Cy*), see
    B1114
C2176 *KABWANGASI S-Cy*
C2176 Kabwangasi
A2146 Kabweri *Par*
C2146 *KABWERI S-Cy*
B2332 Kabweza *Par*
B2298 Kabwohe *Par*
B2298 Kabwohe
C2298 *KABWOHE/ITENDERO*
    S-Cy
B3253 Kabwoko *Par*
B2295 Kabwoma *Par*
B2309 Kabwoya *F/R*
B2309 *KABWOYA S-Cy*

B2309 Kabwoya *W/R*
B1309 Kabwoya
B2243 Kabyuma *Par*
B1295 Kacence *Par*
B1148 Kacha *Par*
B2176 Kachabali *Par* (Petete
    S-Cy), see **A1114**
A1148 Kachaboi *Par*
B2114 Kachaboi *Par*
B2148 Kachaboi
A2114 Kachabule *Ward*
A2176 Kachango *Par*
A2176 Kachango
B2114 Kachede *Par*
A2253 *KACHEERA S-Cy*
B3148 Kachelakweny *Par*
B2268 Kachende
A2253 *Kachera, L.*
A1320 Kacherere (Kagazi *Par*)
A2272 Kacherere *Par*
A2272 Kacherere
B293 Kacheri *Par*
B293 *KACHERI S-Cy*
B293 Kacheri
B2173 Kachinga *Par*
B2176 Kachocha *Par* (Petete
    S-Cy), see **A1114**
B2108 Kachomo *Par*
B2108 *KACHOMO S-Cy*
C3123 Kachonga *Par*
    (Kachonga *S-Cy*)
C3123 Kachonga *Par* (Naweyo
    S-Cy)
B3114 Kachonga *Par*
C3123 *KACHONGA S-Cy*
C3123 Kachonga
B1114 Kachumbala *Par*
B1114 *KACHUMBALA S-Cy*
B1114 Kachumbala
B2277 Kachumbiro
B1114 Kachumi
B243 Kachung *Par*
B243 Kachung
B1114 Kachuru *Par*
    (Kachumbala *S-Cy*)
C2176 Kachuru *Par*
    (Kabwangasi *S-Cy*), see
    B1114
A2277 Kachwabagole
B3114 Kacoc *Par*
A2323 Kacungiro *Par*
A2272 Kacwamuhoro
B197 *KADAM Cy*
C197 Kadam, *(h)*
B2146 Kadama *Par*
B2146 *KADAMA S-Cy*
B2146 Kadama
A1148 Kadami *Par*
B2108 Kadatumi *Par*
B2108 Kadenge *Par*
B291 *KADEPO S-Cy*
A1148 Kaderin *Par*
B2173 Kaderun *Par*
B2108 Kaderuna *Par*
B2108 *KADERUNA S-Cy*
B2176 Kadesok *Par* (Opwateta
    S-Cy), see **B1173**

B2277 Kikaksi
B2247 *KIKAMULO* S-Cy
B2247 Kikamulo
B1247 Kikandwa *Par*
B2243 Kikandwa *Par*
C3237 Kikandwa *Par*
B2237 *KIKANDWA* S-Cy
B2237 Kikandwa
B3245 Kikandwa
A3295 Kikarara *Par*
A3295 Kikarara
A2192 Kikaula *Ward*
B3211 Kikaya *Par*
C2230 Kikenene *Par*
A3281 Kikimo
B2317 Kiko *Par*
B2132 Kiko
B2132 *Kiko, R.*
C2270 Kikoba *Par*
A3281 Kikobero
B1334 Kikoda *Par*
C2249 Kikoiro *Par*
C3249 Kikoiro *Par*
C3257 Kikoko *Par*
A3270 Kikokwa *Par*
B3243 Kikoloto
B2337 Kikolwa
B1221 Kikoma *Par*
B3243 Kikoma *Par*
B2164 Kikoma
B3243 Kikoma
C2255 Kikoma
A3219 Kikonda *F/R*
A3219 Kikonda *Par*
B236 Kikondo *Par*
C2239 Kikondo *Par*
A2295 Kikongi *Par*
B236 Kikongoro
B2289 Kikoni *Par*
B2289 Kikoni *Par*
C1217 Kikooba *Par*
B2219 Kikooma *Par*
B2334 Kikoroba
B1323 Kikorongo
C2247 Kikubanimba
A2221 Kikube *Par*
B2330 Kikube *Par*
B2330 Kikube
B3243 Kikukula
B3243 Kikulula
B1334 Kikumbo
B1284 Kikunda *F/R*
B1272 Kikungiri
B2272 Kikungiri
B2253 Kikungwe *Par*
C1128 Kikunyu *Par*
B2270 Kikunyu
B3249 Kikuta
A2289 Kikuto
B2337 Kikwanana *Par*
B1215 Kikwanya *Par* (Kangulumira S-Cy), see **A2132**
B2327 Kikwaya *Par*
A1192 Kikwayi *Par*
B1268 *KIKYENKYE* S-Cy
A2323 Kikyo *Par*

B3305 Kikyo *Par*
B1247 Kikyusa *Par*
C2221 *KIKYUSA* S-Cy
C238 KILAK *Cy*
B265 Kilak *Par*
B265 *KILAK* S-Cy
B265 Kilak
B238 Kilak, *(h)*
B3323 *KILEMBE* S-Cy
B2323 Kilembe
B2253 Kilembwe
B1153 Kiloba *Par*
C2197 Kilokola *Par*
B2330 Kilwanga
B3237 Kilyookya
B2249 Kimaga
B1132 Kimaka *Par*
A2162 Kimaluli *Par*
B1215 Kimanya *Par* (Nazigo S-Cy), see **A1138**
B3235 Kimanya *Ward*
B3235 *KIMANYA/KYABAKUZA* S-Cy (Masaka M/C), see **C1195**
C2337 Kimengo *Par*
B1337 *KIMENGO* S-Cy
C2337 Kimengo
B3245 *KIMENYEDDE* S-Cy
B2245 Kimenyedde
B1192 Kimera *Par*
A1245 *Kimi, Is.*
A214 Kimiru *Par*
B3249 Kimole
B3303 Kimoli
B2253 Kimukunda *Par*
A1237 Kimuli *Par*
A2253 Kimuli *Par*
A2253 Kimuli
C3257 Kimwanyi *Par*
B1275 Kinaaba *Par*
B2327 Kinaga
A2253 Kinaku
B1219 Kinakulya
B2126 Kinambogo *Par*
B2211 Kinawataka
B3211 *Kinawataka, R.*
B212 Kingaba *Par*
C3230 *KINGO* S-Cy
B2275 KINKIIZI *Cy*
B2334 Kinogero *Par*
C2309 Kinogozi *Par*
A2289 Kinoni *Par*
B2192 Kinoni *Par*
B3320 Kinoni *Par*
C2243 Kinoni *Par*
C3230 Kinoni *Par*
A3247 *KINONI* S-Cy
B2277 *KINONI* S-Cy
B1284 Kinoni
B2201 Kinoni
B2277 Kinoni
C3230 Kinoni
B2232 Kinunka
B2232 *KINUUKA* S-Cy
A2253 Kinyabu
A1323 Kinyamaseka
A1323 Kinyamaseke *Par*

B3337 Kinyanga
A2337 Kinyara *Par*
B3247 *KINYOGOGA* S-Cy
C1255 Kinywamazzi *Par*
B3186 Kipangor *Par*
B248 *Kipinyo, R.*
C2257 Kira *Par* (Kira T/C), see **B3211**
C2257 *KIRA* T/C
C2257 Kira
B26 Kiraba *Par*
B3206 Kiragga *Par*
C2309 Kiragura *Par*
A2281 Kirambo
B1263 Kiramira *Par*
B2327 Kiranzi *Par*
B2332 Kiranzi
A2317 Kiraro *Par*
A2323 Kiraro *Par*
B3215 Kirasa *Par*
C3167 Kirayi *Par*
C2199 *Kiregi, Is.*
C2257 Kireka *Par* (Kira T/C), see **C2211**
C2257 Kireka
B2221 Kireku *Par*
B2237 Kireku *Par*
B2221 Kireku
B1247 Kirema *Par*
B2286 Kirembe *Par*
B2286 Kirera *Par*
B1171 Kirerema *Par*
A2186 Kirewa *Par*
A2186 *KIREWA* S-Cy
A2186 Kirewa
B2272 Kirigime *Ward* (Kabale Southern Div)
C2327 Kiriisa *Par*
B1146 Kirika *Par*
B2146 *KIRIKA* S-Cy
B189 *Kiriki, R.*
B1275 *KIRIMA* S-Cy
B1275 Kirima
B2275 Kirima
B3305 *Kirima, R.*
B2235 Kirimya *Par*
B2235 Kirimya
B2247 Kirinda *Par*
B2305 Kirindi *Par*
C1215 Kirindi *Par* (Nazigo S-Cy), see **B1138**
B2275 Kiringa *Par*
C2239 *KIRINGETE* S-Cy
B1192 Kiringo *Par*
C2257 Kirinya *Par*
C2201 Kiriri *Par*
C2201 Kiriri
B3257 Kirolo
B255 Kirombe *Ward* (Adyel S-Cy)
A246 Kirombe *Ward* (Layibi S-Cy)
C2211 Kirombe
B2334 Kirongo *Ward* (Kyenjojo T/C)
B3199 Kirongo
B1232 Kirowooza *Ward*

B187 Kiru *Par*
B187 Kiru
B1211 Kiruddu
C2293 KIRUGU *Par*
B2204 *Kirugu, Is.*
277 **KIRUHURA** *Dist*
D31 **KIRUHURA** *Dist*
B2277 **Kiruhura**
B3253 *KIRUMBA* S-Cy
B2230 Kirumba
A2243 Kirume *Par*
B2249 Kirumi
B3281 *KIRUNDO* S-Cy
C2201 Kirungi
A2217 Kirurumba *Ward*
B2119 Kirwali *Par*
B3141 Kirwoko *Par*
B2243 Kiryajjobyo *Par*
B1219 Kiryajobyo *Par*
B3257 Kiryamuli *Par*
330 **KIRYANDONGO** *Dist*
G81 **KIRYANDONGO** *Dist*
B2330 *KIRYANDONGO* S-Cy
C3303 *KIRYANDONGO* S-Cy
B2330 **Kiryandongo**
C3309 Kiryandongo
B2327 Kiryanga *Par*
B2337 Kiryanga *Par*
B2327 *KIRYANGA* S-Cy
B2327 Kiryanga
B2337 Kiryanga
B3337 Kiryanga
C2309 Kiryangobe *Par*
A3219 Kiryanongo *Par*
B2195 Kiryassaaka *Par*
A2108 Kiryolo *Par*
B3237 Kiryooka *Par*
B3249 Kisaalizi *Par*
C2237 Kisaana *Par*
C2237 Kisaana
B1272 Kisaasa *Par*
B2253 Kisaasa *Par*
B3211 Kisaasi
C2309 Kisabagwa *Par*
C2309 Kisabagwa
B3255 Kisabwa
B2195 Kisagazi *Par*
B2217 Kisagazi *Par*
B3243 Kisagazi *Par*
B2195 Kisagazi
A2138 Kisaikye *Par*
A2323 Kisaka *Par*
B2327 Kisala
B3243 Kisalabude
B2327 Kisalizi
B3232 Kisaluwoko *Par*
B2332 Kisambya *Par*
C2243 Kisana
B2334 Kisangi *Par*
C3230 Kisansala *Par*
B3303 Kisansya
B1309 Kisaru
B2132 Kisasi *Par*
A2171 Kisega *Par*
B1247 Kisega *Par*
B3112 Kiseitaka *Par*
B2243 Kisekende *Par*

B2230 *KISEKKA* S-Cy
B2119 Kisekye *Par*
B1327 Kisele
B2211 Kisenyi I *Par*
B2211 Kisenyi II *Par*
B2211 Kisenyi III *Par*
C2249 Kisenyi *Par*
B2293 Kisenyi
C2284 Kisenyi
B2298 Kishabya *Par*
B2289 Kishami *Par*
A1272 Kishanje *Par*
C2284 Kishasha *Par*
B2275 Kishenyi *Par*
A2270 Kishenyi
A3270 Kishuro *Par*
B2303 Kisiabi *Par*
B2192 Kisiimba *Par*
C1171 Kisiiro *Par*
B2195 Kisiita *Par*
C3327 Kisiita *Par*
B1295 Kisiizi *Par*
B1295 Kisiizi
B2136 Kisiki
B2257 Kisimbiri *Ward* (Wakiso T/C), see **A3211**
B2257 Kisimbiri
B1247 Kisimula *Par*
B3136 Kisinda *Par*
B2257 Kisindye
A2323 *KISINGA* S-Cy
A2323 Kisinga
A1123 Kisiro
B2337 Kisita *Par*
C2239 Kisitu *F/R*
B3305 *KISITU* S-Cy
A2243 Kisizili
B1171 Kiso
C3221 Kiso
B2247 Kisoga *Par*
C2201 Kisoga *Par*
B1195 Kisojjo *Par*
B1219 Kisojjo *Par*
B2327 Kisojo *Par*
B1334 Kisojo
B2327 Kisojo
A1243 *Kisojo, R.*
B2186 Kisoko *Par*
B2186 *KISOKO* S-Cy
B2186 Kisoko
A2323 Kisolholho *Par*
B1219 Kisolooza *Par*
A2317 Kisomoro *Par*
A2317 *KISOMORO* S-Cy
A2317 Kisomoro
281 **KISORO** *Dist*
B11 **KISORO** *Dist*
B2281 Kisoro North *Ward*
B2281 Kisoro South *Ward*
B2281 *KISORO* T/C
B1284 Kisoro
B2281 **Kisoro**
B2186 Kisote
A3211 Kisowera
A3171 Kisowozi *Par*
B1138 Kisozi *Par*

B2173 Kokong *Par*
B1144 Kokorio *Par*
B1144 Kokorio
B2215 Kokotero *Par*
B2114 Kokutu *Par*
B197 Kokuwaum *Par*
B3141 Kokwomurya *Par*
B250 KOLE *Cy*
50 **KOLE** *Dist*
H81 **KOLE** *Dist*
B250 **Kole**
B2114 Kolir *Par*
B2114 *KOLIR S-Cy*
B2114 Kolir
B3173 Koloin *Par*
B2211 Kololo *Airstrip*
B2211 Kololo I *Par*
B2211 Kololo II *Par*
B2211 Kololo III *Par*
B2211 Kololo IV *Par*
C3239 Kololo *Par*
B3211 Kololo, *(h)*
B3211 Komamboga *Par*
B295 Komaret *Par*
A210 Komite *Par (Pajulu S-Cy)*
B2173 Komodo *Par*
C2106 Komolo
B1114 Komuge *Par*
B291 Komuria *Par*
B223 Konga
B2117 *KONGASIS Cy*
B1114 Kongatuny *Par*
B2211 Konge
C2239 Konge
B1114 Kongoidi *Par*
A1284 Kongoro *Par*
B293 *Kongorututui, R.*
B2178 Kongoto *Par*
B2141 Kongowo *Par*
B1114 Kongunga *Par*
B2148 Kongura *Par*
C2239 Konkoma *Par*
B2150 Kono *Par*
A2253 *KOOKI Cy*
B1232 Kooki *Ward*
A1245 *Koome Channel*
B1245 *KOOME ISLANDS S-Cy*
C2201 Koome *Par*
C2201 Koome
B1245 *Koome, Is.*
B2173 Kopege *Par*
B191 Koputh
B3114 Koreng *Par*
B2144 Koritok *Par*
B246 *KORO S-Cy*
B146 Koro
C343 Koroto
B2117 Kortek *Par*
B2117 *KORTEK S-Cy*
B389 Kosika
B297 Kosike *Par*
B395 Koten, *(h)*
B1114 Kotia *Par*
B293 Kotido Central *Ward* (Kotido *T/C*)
93 **KOTIDO** *Dist*

J101 **KOTIDO** *Dist*
B293 Kotido East *Ward* (Kotido *T/C*)
B293 Kotido North *Ward* (Kotido *T/C*)
B293 *KOTIDO S-Cy*
B293 *KOTIDO T/C*
B293 Kotido West *Ward* (Kotido *T/C*)
B293 **Kotido**
B2108 Kotinyanga *Par*
B2114 Kotiokot *Par*
B2100 *Kotipe, R.*
B293 Kotyang *Par*
B1114 Koutulai *Par*
B287 Koya *Par*
B265 Koyo *Par*
A310 Kubo *Par* (Adumi *S-Cy*), see **A114**
B218 Kuchwiny
B218 *KUCWINY S-Cy*
B218 Kucwiny, *(h)*
C2186 Kuitangiro *Par*
B2204 *Kuiye, Is.*
B2106 Kuju *Par*
B2106 *KUJU S-Cy*
B2106 Kuju
B3211 Kulambiro, *(h)*
A263 Kuluabura *Par*
B259 Kuluamuka *Par*
B312 *KULUBA S-Cy*
B212 Kuluba
A210 Kuluva *Par*
B210 Kuluva
B253 Kuluye *Par*
B2173 Kumel *Par*
B2148 *KUMI Cy*
148 **KUMI** *Dist*
K71 **KUMI** *Dist*
B2148 Kumi *Par*
B2148 *KUMI S-Cy*
B2148 *KUMI T/C*
B2148 **Kumi**
A140 Kungu *Par*
A3253 Kunswa
C289 *Kunyao, R.*
B221 *KURU S-Cy*
B3128 Kusambika *Par*
B3245 Kwaba
C240 *KWANIA Cy*
H71 *Kwania, L.*
C2150 *KWANYIY S-Cy*
C2186 Kwapa *Par*
C2186 *KWAPA S-Cy*
C2186 Kwapa
B1114 Kwarikwar *Par*
B3150 *KWEEN Cy*
150 **KWEEN** *Dist*
L71 **KWEEN** *Dist*
A140 Kwibale
C310 Kwili *Par*
C2117 Kwirot *Par*
B3150 Kwosir *Par*
B2150 *KWOSIR S-Cy*
B2141 Kwoti *Par*
C2197 Kyabadaaza
B3219 Kyabadeba

A3201 Kyabagamba *Par*
A3201 Kyabagamba
B2284 Kyabaganyi
B2270 Kyabahesi *Par*
B2245 Kyabakadde *Par* (Kyampisi *S-Cy*), see **C3257**
B3263 Kyabakara *Par*
B2235 Kyabakuza *Ward*
B3235 Kyabakuza
B2243 Kyabalanzi *Par*
B2245 Kyabalogo *Par* (Nakisunga *S-Cy*), see **C2257**
A1340 Kyabandara *Par*
A2320 Kyabandara *Par*
B2298 Kyabandara *Par*
A2334 Kyabaranga *Par*
B3323 Kyabarungira *Par*
B3323 *KYABARUNGIRA S-Cy*
C2327 Kyabasajja
A2289 Kyabashenyi *Par*
B1219 Kyabasita
C2309 Kyabatalya *Par*
B3245 Kyabazaala *Par* (Ntunda *S-Cy*), see **A1138**
B3245 Kyabazaala
C3327 Kyabeya *Par*
C2309 *KYABIGAMBIRE S-Cy*
A3253 Kyabigondo *Par*
A2323 Kyabikere *Par*
B2270 Kyabinunga (Kagarama *Par*)
A1132 *Kyabirwa Falls*
B2270 Kyabishaho (Kyabishaho *Par*)
B2270 Kyabishaho *Par*
A1253 Kyabiwa *Par*
B2266 *KYABUGIMBI S-Cy*
C2272 Kyabuhangwa *Par*
C3298 Kyabuharambo *Par*
B2270 Kyabukube
A2295 Kyabureere *Par*
B1249 Kyabutayika *Par*
B1249 Kyabutayika
A2327 Kyabweme
B2323 Kyabwenge *Par*
C2219 Kyabyamwanga
B2257 *KYADDONDO Cy*
B3257 *KYADDONDO Cy*
A2289 Kyafoora *Par*
C3298 Kyagaju *Par*
B2284 Kyagaju
B3298 Kyagaju
C2284 *Kyahi F/R*
B2245 Kyajja *Par*
B2332 *KYAKA Cy*
A2327 Kyakabadiima *Par*
B2327 Kyakabanda *Par*
B3219 Kyakabuga *Par*
B2277 Kyakabunga *Par*
B2277 Kyakabunga
B2195 Kyakalenzi
B3337 Kyakamese *Par*
B1317 Kyakamihanda
B2320 Kyakanyemera *Par*

B2320 Kyakarafa *Par*
B2327 Kyakarongo *Par*
C2243 Kyakatebe *Par*
C2243 Kyakatebe
C2243 Kyakiddu
A1323 Kyakitale *Par*
B2253 Kyakonda *Par*
B2232 Kyakuterekera *Par*
C2323 Kyalanga *Par*
B2239 Kyali *Par*
B2334 Kyaligijuka
C2257 Kyaliwajala *Par* (Kira *T/C*), see **C3211**
C3257 Kyaliwajjala (Kyaliwajjala *Par*), see **B3211**
A1253 Kyaluganda *Par*
B2221 Kyalugondo *Par*
A2253 *KYALULANGIRA S-Cy*
B3247 Kyalusebeka *Par*
B1195 Kyamagoma
B2295 Kyamakanda *Par*
B2266 Kyamakungu
A2277 Kyamarebe
B2289 Kyamate *Ward*
B2206 Kyambala *Par*
B2206 Kyambala
A2323 Kyambogho *Par*
B2255 Kyambogo *Par*
B3211 Kyambogo *Par*
C1249 Kyambogo *Par*
C3257 *KYAMBOGO/BUSUKUMA S-Cy*
C2293 Kyambura *Gorge*
C3293 Kyambura *W/R*
A3277 Kyampangara *Par*
A3277 Kyampangara
B2270 Kyampango *Par*
B1221 Kyampisi (Bamunanika) *Par*
A3257 Kyampisi *Par*
B2245 *KYAMPISI S-Cy*
C2221 Kyampogola *Par*
B3334 Kyamugenyi *Par*
B2266 Kyamuhunga *Par*
B2266 Kyamuhunga
C2330 Kyamukangara
B2317 Kyamukoka *Par*
B2249 Kyamukonda *Par*
B2211 Kyamula
B2206 Kyamulibwa *Par*
B2206 *KYAMULIBWA S-Cy*
B2206 Kyamulibwa
B2298 Kyamurari *Par*
A2270 Kyamusheija
A3237 Kyamusisi
A2270 Kyamusoni *Par*
B2204 *KYAMUSWA Cy*
C2204 *KYAMUSWA S-Cy*
B1247 Kyamutakasa *Par*
B2334 Kyamutasa *Par*
B2334 Kyamutasa *Ward* (Kyenjojo *T/C*)
B3334 Kyamutunzi *F/R*
B2334 Kyamutunzi *Par*
A2235 Kyamuyibwa *Par*
B2249 Kyamuyingo *Par*

C2289 Kyamwasha *Par*
B2327 *KYANAISOKE S-Cy*
B2327 Kyanaisoke
B2272 Kyanamira *Par*
C2243 Kyanamugera *Par*
B2235 *KYANAMUKAKA S-Cy*
B2235 Kyanamukaka
B3284 Kyandahi *Par*
A1237 Kyandalo
A2270 Kyandaro
C3317 Kyangabukama
A2327 Kyangamwoyo
B3253 Kyango *Par*
B3249 Kyangogolo *Par*
B2327 Kyangumbwoyo
B3298 Kyangundu *Par*
A1309 Kyangwali *Par*
A2309 *KYANGWALI S-Cy*
A1309 Kyangwali
B3298 *KYANGYENYI S-Cy*
B1136 Kyani *Par*
B2253 Kyanika *Par*
B1281 Kyanika
B2239 Kyanja *Par*
B3211 Kyanja *Par*
B3235 Kyanja
B3211 Kyanja, *(h)*
B2323 Kyanjojo
B2323 Kyanjukyi *Par*
B2268 Kyankanga
B2334 Kyankaramata *Par*
B2330 Kyankende *Par*
B2249 Kyankonwa *Par*
B2195 Kyankoole *Par*
219 **KYANKWANZI** *Dist*
F61 **KYANKWANZI** *Dist*
C3219 Kyankwanzi *Par*
C2219 *KYANKWANZI S-Cy*
C2219 Kyankwanzi
C2219 Kyankwanzi
C2219 Kyankwanzi, *(h)*
B2235 Kyantale *Par*
C2235 Kyantale
A3257 Kyanuuna *Par*
B2153 Kyanvuma *Par*
B1215 Kyanya
C2270 Kyanyanda
C2284 Kyanyarukondo
B2286 Kyanzeire *Par*
B2268 Kyaritanga II (Kashungura *Par*)
B2270 Kyarubambura *Par*
B1272 Kyarubanda *Par*
B3270 Kyarugaju *Par*
A2289 Kyaruhanga *Par*
A1323 Kyarukara *Par*
B2323 *KYARUMBA S-Cy*
B2323 Kyarumba
A2298 Kyarushakara *Par*
A3334 *KYARUSOZI S-Cy*
A3334 Kyarusozi
B2295 Kyaruyenje *Par*
A3257 Kyasa *Par*
B2243 Kyasampawu *Par*
B1272 Kyasano *Par*
B2284 Kyashemeire

B389 Loroo *Par*
B389 *LOROO* S-Cy
B297 Lorukumo *Par*
B189 Losidok *Par*
C293 Losilang *Par*
B291 Losogolo *Par*
B297 Lotaruk *Par*
B191 Loteteleit *Par*
B1100 Lothaa
B291 Lotim *Par*
B295 Lotirir *Par*
C2100 Lotithan
B232 Lotome *Par*
C2100 *LOTOME* S-Cy
C2100 Lotome
C261 Lotuke
B291 Lotuke, *(h)*
A187 *LOTUKEI* S-Cy
B353 Lotuturu
B2272 Lower Bugongi *Ward* (Kabale Northern *Div*)
C195 Loyaraboth *Par*
A291 Loyoro Napore *Par*
B191 *LOYORO* S-Cy
B191 Loyoro
B287 Loyoroit *Par*
C210 Luba *Par*
A2132 Lubani *Par*
A2132 Lubani
C2327 Lubaya *Par*
B3257 Lubbe *Par*
A3221 *Lubenge, R.*
A2211 *Lubigi Swamp*
C2128 Lubira *Par*
B2272 Lubira
B2211 Lubiri *Airstrip*
B3219 Lubiri *Par*
B2192 Lubongo *Par*
B2239 Lubugumu *Par*
C2243 Lubumba
B2136 Lubuulo *Par*
A3211 Lubya *Par*
A2211 *Lubya, (h)*
B212 Ludara *Par*
B312 *LUDARA* S-Cy
B212 Ludara
B312 Ludaraha *Par*
B210 Lufe *Par*
C2199 Lufu *Par*
C2199 *Lufu, Is.*
B2245 Lufunve
B2201 Lugaaga *Par*
B1192 Lugala *Par*
C2197 Lugala *Par*
A1192 Lugala
C2169 Lugala
A2211 *Lugala, (h)*
A2289 Lugalama
B3192 Lugalambo
A1197 Lugali *Par*
A2253 Lugando
A2192 Lugazi Central *Ward*
A3192 *LUGAZI* T/C
A2192 Lugazi
B310 Lugbari *Par*
B310 Lugbari
B3257 Lugo *Par*

A1192 Lugoba *Par*
A3211 Lugoba
A2249 *Lugogo, R.*
B3164 Lugolole *Par*
B2253 Lugongo
B3257 Lugungudde *Par*
B1255 Lugusulu *Par*
B2255 *LUGUSULU* S-Cy
A3257 Luguzi *Par*
A253 Lugwar *Par*
C3239 Lugyo *Par*
A2272 Luhija
A221 Lui *Par*
A3323 Luigi di Savola, *(h)*
A2204 *Lujabwa, Is.*
B146 Lujorongole *Par*
B265 Lukaci *Par*
B2327 Lukara *F/R*
B2206 Lukaya Central *Ward*
B2206 *LUKAYA* T/C
B2206 Lukaya
B2243 Lukaya
B132 Lukee *Par*
B1167 *LUKHONGE* S-Cy
A3257 Lukoma
B1253 Lukoma
A2253 Lukondo (Kamukalo *Par*)
A2136 Lukotaime
A3204 Luku
B2211 Lukuli Nanganda
B2211 Lukuli *Par*
B2247 Lukumbi
B353 *LUKUNG* S-Cy
B221 Lukutua *Par*
B2257 Lukwanga *Par*
B132 Lukwangole *Par*
A248 Lukwar *Par*
B246 Lukwir *Par*
A248 Lukwor *Par*
C146 Lukwor *Par*
B3204 Lulamba *Par*
B1257 Lulongo
B1138 Lulyambuzi *Par*
A3221 *Lumansi, R.*
B2153 *Lumbuye, R.*
B2121 Lumino *Par*
B2121 *LUMINO* S-Cy
B2121 Lumino
C265 Luna *Par*
B1245 *Lunfuwa, Is.*
A2211 Lungujja *Par*
B2217 Lunya
B3199 Lunyanja *Par*
A1121 Lunyo *Par*
B1121 *LUNYO* S-Cy
A1121 Lunyo
B1221 Lunyolya *Par*
B2108 Lupada *Par*
B112 Lurujo *Par*
B112 Lurujo
B212 Lurunu *Par*
B2253 Lusaka
A2243 Lusalira
B2206 Lusango *Par*
B2206 Lusango

B2257 Lusanja (Kiteezi *Par*), see B3211
B3237 Lusanja *Par*
B2206 Lusasa *Par*
B1215 Lusenke *Par* (Busana S-Cy), see **A**1138
B1119 *LUSHA* S-Cy
B2243 Lusiba *Par*
B2230 Lusiti
B2230 Lusiti
B2164 Lutale
B2257 Luteete (Masooli *Par*), see B3211
C2247 Luteete *Par*
B3257 Lutisi *Par*
A3204 *Lutoboka Channel*
A3204 Lutoboka
C2169 Lutolo *Par*
C2293 Lutoto
C2243 Lutunku *Par*
C2255 Lutunku
B2153 *LUUKA* Cy
153 **LUUKA** Dist
I51 **LUUKA** Dist
C2199 *Luvia, Is.*
C2199 *Luvia, Is.*
B210 Luvu *Par*
C3239 Luvumbula *Par*
B2211 Luwafu *Par*
B2211 Luwafu-Makindye
B2239 Luwala *Par*
B3192 Luwala
C1255 Luwanga
B1219 Luwawu *Par*
A2192 Luwayo *Par*
B2221 Luweero Central *Ward* (Luweero *T/C*)
221 **LUWEERO** Dist
H51 **LUWEERO** Dist
B2221 Luweero East *Ward* (Luweero *T/C*)
B2221 *LUWEERO* S-Cy
B2221 *LUWEERO* T/C
B2221 Luweero West *Ward* (Luweero *T/C*)
B2221 **Luweero**
A2112 Luwoko *Par*
B2112 Luwoko *Par*
B2195 Luwoko *Par*
B2221 Luwube
B1219 Luwunga *F/R* (Kigando)
A2239 Luwunga *Par*
B2257 Luwunga *Par*
A2204 *Luwungulu, Is.*
B1219 Luwuuna *Par*
B3327 Luzaire *F/R*
B1138 Luzinga *Par*
B1138 Luzinga
C2211 Luzira *Par*
B2211 Luzira Prison's *Par*
B2211 Luzira
A2253 Lwabakooba *Par*
B3206 *LWABENGE* S-Cy
B3249 *LWABYATA* S-Cy
B3249 Lwabyata
B2239 Lwagwa *Par*
C1221 *Lwajali, R.*

A2199 Lwajje *Par*
A2199 *Lwajje, Is.*
A2253 Lwakalolo *Par*
B1162 *LWAKHAKHA* T/C
B1162 Lwakhakha
B1153 Lwaki *Par*
B2134 Lwala *Par*
B2186 Lwala *Par*
B2134 Lwala
C336 Lwala
B291 Lwala, *(h)*
A3253 *LWAMAGGWA* S-Cy
A3253 Lwamaggwa
B2217 Lwamata *Par*
B2217 *LWAMATA* S-Cy
B2217 Lwamata
B3253 Lwamba *Par*
B1167 Lwamba
B2136 Lwamba
A2253 Lwambajjo *Par*
B2219 Lwampala
C3249 Lwampanga *Par*
B3249 *LWAMPANGA* S-Cy
B3249 Lwampanga
B2204 Lwamuswa
C1255 Lwamwende
B2249 Lwanama
B2253 *LWANDA* S-Cy
B1121 Lwanda
B2253 Lwanda
A2253 Lwanga *Par*
C2239 Lwanga *Par*
A2253 Lwanga
B3169 Lwangosia *Par*
C3169 Lwangosia
B3112 Lwanika *Par*
C2217 Lwankonge *Par*
B2253 Lwankoni *Par*
B2219 Lwansama *Par*
C2243 Lwantale-Namiringa *Par*
B1138 Lwanyama *Par*
B2167 Lwasso *Par*
B2167 *LWASSO* S-Cy
A2146 Lwatama *Par*
B3171 Lwatama *Par*
B2232 Lwebigoye
C2219 Lwebisanja *Par*
B2219 Lwebisiriza *Par*
B1255 Lwebitakuli *Par*
B1255 *LWEBITAKULI* S-Cy
A2255 Lwemibu *Par*
A2243 Lwemivubo
A2255 *LWEMIYAGA* Cy
A3255 *LWEMIYAGA* S-Cy
A2255 Lwemiyaga
B3257 Lwemwedde *Par*
B2230 *LWENGO* Cy
230 **LWENGO** Dist
E31 **LWENGO** Dist
B2230 Lwengo *Par*
B2230 *LWENGO* S-Cy
B2230 **Lwengo**
B2253 *LWENKONI* S-Cy
A3255 Lwensankala *Par*
A1253 Lwensinga *Par*
C2255 Lwentale *Par*

B2255 Lwentale
B2217 Lwentanga
B1232 *LWENTODE* S-Cy
B2176 *Lwere, R.*
B2192 Lweru *Par*
A2197 Lwezo
B1245 Lwomolo *Par*
C2232 Lyakajula *Par*
C3232 Lyakajula
B3230 Lyakibiriizi *Par*
A2323 Lyakirema *Par*
A3253 Lyakisana *Par*
A1108 Lyama *Par*
C2146 Lyama
B1108 *LYAMA* S-Cy
B2317 Lyamabwa *Par*
A1243 Lyangoma
232 **LYANTONDE** Dist
E31 **LYANTONDE** Dist
B1232 *LYANTONDE* T/C
B1232 **Lyantonde**
B2110 Maaba *Par*
A26 Maaji *Par*
B1237 *MAANYI* S-Cy
A1237 Maanyi
A1237 Maawa *Par*
B2320 Mabaale *Par*
B2327 *MABAALE* S-Cy
B2123 Mabale *Par*
B2327 Mabale
B3206 Mabale, *(h)*
C2197 Mabanda *Par*
B2295 Mabanga *Par*
C3298 Mabare *Par*
C2255 Mabindo *Par*
B3192 Mabira *F/R*
B2284 Mabira *Par*
B2270 Mabona (Mabona *Par*)
B1268 Mabona *Par*
B2270 Mabona *Par*
B1268 Mabonwa
A1281 Mabungo *Par*
B2206 Mabuye *Par*
B2221 Mabuye *Par*
B2169 MacDonald Bay
B2108 Macholi *Par*
B2277 Macuncu *Par*
B2201 Maddu *Par*
A2201 *MADDU* S-Cy
B2201 Maddu
B2183 Madera *Ward* (Soroti Northern *Div*)
B210 *MADI OKOLLO* Cy
C353 Madi Opei
B253 Madi-Kiloc *Par*
C353 *MADI-OPEI* S-Cy
B2173 Madochpar
B3169 Madowa *Par*
B2243 *MADUDU* S-Cy
B2243 Madudu
B1132 Mafubira *Par*
B1132 *MAFUBIRA* S-Cy
B1132 Mafubira
C1275 Mafuga *F/R*
C1275 Mafuga *Par*
B2247 Mafunve
A1253 Magabbi

B2211 Mbuya II *Par*
B2211 Mbuya, *(h)*
B346 Mede *Par*
B36 Meliale, *(h)*
C2186 Mella *Par*
C2186 *MELLA S-Cy*
C2186 Mella
B248 Melong *Par*
B3257 Mende *Par*
B3257 *MENDE S-Cy*
B112 Mengo *Par*
B2211 Mengo *Par*
A2211 Mengo
B1245 Mengo
B3186 Merikit *Par*
B3186 *MERIKIT S-Cy*
B3186 Merikit
A2183 Merok *Par*
B212 Metino *Par*
C316 *METU S-Cy*
B316 Metu
B316 Metuli
B1281 Mgahinga Gorilla *N/P*
A1281 Mgahinga, *(h)*
B36 Mgbwere *Par*
A214 Michu *Par*
A310 Michu *Par* (Aroi *S-Cy*), see **A114**
B2221 Midadde *Par*
B212 Midia *Par*
B112 *MIDIA S-Cy*
B212 *MIDIA S-Cy*
B321 *MIDIGO S-Cy*
A321 Midigo
A2186 Mifumi *Par*
B1247 Mifunya *Par*
B3257 Migadde *Par*
A2239 Migamba *Par*
B3277 Migina *Par*
C3298 Migina *Par*
B3277 Migina
B1247 Migingye *Par*
B321 Migo *Par*
B2249 Migyera *Par*
B2247 Mijumwa *Par*
B2243 Mijunwa *Par*
B2255 *MIJWALA S-Cy*
C2255 *MIJWALA S-Cy*
B1146 Mikombe *Par*
A263 *MINAKULU S-Cy*
B263 Minakulu
A146 *Minakulu, R.*
B2128 Minani *Par*
A310 Mingoro
B36 Miniki *Par*
B1253 Minziro *Par*
B2284 Mirama *Par*
B2289 Mirama
B2289 Mirama
A2305 Mirambi *Par*
A3334 Mirambi *Par*
B1195 Mirambi *Par*
A3253 Mirebi
A2309 Mirembe
B2114 Miroi *Par*
B3284 Mirongo *Par*
A2334 Mirongo

B2337 *MIRYA S-Cy*
B2219 Misago *Par*
B2215 Misanga *Par*
B2195 Misanvu
B2237 Miseebe *Par*
B3126 Miseru *Par*
C1275 Mishenyi *Par*
B1237 Misigi
B2245 Misindye *Par* (Goma *S-Cy*), see **C2257**
B3277 Misinga
A3164 Misoli *Par*
B1253 Misozi
B2239 Mitala Maria
A2317 Mitandi
A210 Mite *Par*
C1255 Mitete *Par*
B2253 Miti *Par*
B2195 Mitigyera *Par*
B2255 Mitima *Par*
A2334 Mitoma *Par*
286 **MITOOMA** *Dist*
B21 **MITOOMA** *Dist*
B2286 *MITOOMA S-Cy*
B2277 Mitooma
B2286 **Mitooma**
B3284 Mitozo *Par*
B2253 Mitukula *Par*
C2197 Mitwetwe *Par*
B2237 Mityana Central *Ward*
B2237 *MITYANA Cy*
237 **MITYANA** *Dist*
G51 **MITYANA** *Dist*
B2237 Mityana East *Ward*
B2237 Mityana North *Ward*
B2237 Mityana South *Ward*
B2237 *MITYANA T/C*
B2237 Mityana West *Ward*
B2237 **Mityana**
B2253 Mityebiri *Par*
B2253 Mityebiri
C1253 Mizinda
A221 Mocha *Par*
B221 Mocha
C353 Modote, *(h)*
A395 Mogoth *Par*
C2117 Mokoyon *Par*
B221 Moli *Par*
B3186 Molo *Par*
B3186 *MOLO S-Cy*
C3186 Molo
C2146 Molokochomo *Par*
B3305 Mongiro
B212 Monodu *Par*
B2167 Mooni *Par*
A2277 Mooya *Par*
B2186 Morikiswa *Par*
B2186 Morkisuwa
B234 *MOROTO Cy*
95 **MOROTO** *Dist*
L91 **MOROTO** *Dist*
B295 *MOROTO M/C*
B253 Moroto *Par*
C291 Moroto *Par*
B295 **Moroto**
B295 Moroto, *(h)*
C261 *Moroto, R.*

B2117 Morowo/Kartok *R/O*
B146 Moru
B146 Moru, *(h)*
B297 Moruangibuin *Par*
B2183 Moruapesur *Ward* (Soroti Eastern *Div*)
A2106 Moruinera *Par*
A2148 Moruita *Par*
C297 Moruita *Par*
C297 *MORUITA S-Cy*
C297 Moruita
B3173 Morukakise *Par*
C2186 Morukatipe *Par*
C2186 Morukebu *Par*
B2176 Morukokume *Par* (Agule *S-Cy*), see **B1173**
B291 Morukori *Par*
B187 *MORULEM S-Cy*
C2100 Morulinga *Par*
C2100 Morulinga
B2106 Morungatuny *Par*
B2106 *MORUNGATUNY S-Cy*
B291 Morungole
B291 Morungole, *(h)*
C2100 Moruongor *Par*
B2148 Morupeded *Par*
B248 *Moruta, R.*
B348 *Moruto, R.*
A2277 Moya
B216 Moyo Central *Par*
16 **MOYO** *Dist*
F111 **MOYO** *Dist*
B316 *MOYO S-Cy*
B216 *MOYO T/C*
B316 **Moyo**
B2150 Moyok *Par*
B2150 *MOYOK S-Cy*
B1221 Mpakawero *Par*
B2138 Mpakitonyi *Par*
B2272 Mpalo *Par*
B2332 Mpalo
B2173 Mpama *Par*
A2327 Mpamba *Par*
C2239 Mpambire
C2239 Mpanga *F/R*
B2320 Mpanga *Par*
A1334 *Mpanga, R.*
B1332 *MPARA S-Cy*
B2272 Mparo
B2272 Mparo
C2309 Mparo
A2327 Mpasaana *Par*
B1268 Mpasha (Mpasha *Par*)
B1268 Mpasha
B2245 Mpatta *Par* (Ntenjeru *S-Cy*), see **C2257**
A2327 *MPEEFU S-Cy*
B2245 Mpenja (Kabanga *Par*)
B2245 Mpenja (Kiyoola *Par*)
C2201 *MPENJA S-Cy*
C2201 Mpenja
B3211 Mpererwe *Par*
B3211 Mpererwe
C2239 Mpigi A *Ward*
C2239 Mpigi B *Ward*
C2239 Mpigi C *Ward*

C2239 Mpigi D *Ward*
239 **MPIGI** *Dist*
G41 **MPIGI** *Dist*
C2239 *MPIGI S-Cy*
C2239 *MPIGI T/C*
C2239 **Mpigi**
B2217 Mpiita
C2237 Mpiriggwa *Par*
B2330 Mpobo
C2330 Mpobo
C2201 Mpogo *Par*
B2192 Mpogo
B1221 Mpologoma *Par*
B1171 *Mpologoma, R.*
B2245 Mpoma *Par* (Nama *S-Cy*), see **C2257**
B2245 Mpoma
A2323 Mpondwe *Par*
A2323 Mpondwe
B2176 Mpongi *Par* (Puti-Puti *S-Cy*), see **B3146**
A1237 Mpongo *Par*
B1215 Mpongo
A2219 *Mpongu, R.*
B3235 Mpugwe
B2204 *Mpugwe, Is.*
A2171 Mpulira
B1171 Mpumiro *Par*
B2245 Mpumu
B1132 Mpumudde *Par*
B2230 Mpumudde *Par*
C2232 Mpumudde *Par*
C2232 *MPUMUDDE S-Cy*
A2255 Mpumudde
B1132 *MPUMUDDE/KIMAKA Div*
B1268 Mpunda
B2257 Mpunga *Ward* (Wakiso *T/C*), see **A3211**
B1245 Mpunge *Par*
B2201 Mpunge *Par*
B1245 *MPUNGE S-Cy*
B1245 Mpunge
B1275 Mpungu *Par*
B2272 Mpungu *Par*
B1275 *MPUNGU S-Cy*
B2164 *MPUNGWE S-Cy*
B3164 Mpungwe
C1247 Mpwedde *Par*
B1150 Mt. Elgon *N/P*
B2117 Mt. Elgon *N/P*
B2141 Mt. Elgon *N/P*
C2110 Mt. Elgon *N/P*
C2167 Mt. Elgon *N/P*
C2180 Mt. Elgon *N/P*
C2162 Mt. Elgon *Par*
C1253 Mubanzi
B1245 Mubembe *Par*
243 **MUBENDE** *Dist*
F41 **MUBENDE** *Dist*
B2243 *MUBENDE T/C*
B2243 **Mubende**
B2243 Mubende, *(h)*
B3323 Mubuku *P/Hq*
B2323 Mubuku Scheme *Par*
B3323 Mubuku Scheme *Par*
C2323 *Mubuku, R.*

B297 *Muchilmakat, R.*
B248 *MUCHWINI S-Cy*
A248 Mucwini
C2180 Mude *Cave*
C3239 *MUDUUMA S-Cy*
C3239 Muduuma
B2327 Mugalike
B1272 Mugandu *Par*
B2281 Muganza *Par*
B2327 *MUGARAMA S-Cy*
B2327 Mugarama
B2284 Mugarutsya *Par*
B1337 Mugasani
C291 Mugei, *(h)*
A1239 Mugge *Par*
B3164 Muggi *Par*
B36 Mugi *Par*
C2108 Mugiti *Par*
C2108 *MUGITI S-Cy*
B3215 Mugongo *Par*
B2332 Mugongwe *Par*
B2277 Mugore
A3204 *MUGOYE S-Cy*
A3204 Mugoye
B2123 Mugulu *Par*
B2123 Mugulu
A2317 *MUGUSU S-Cy*
B2317 Mugusu
A2327 Mugyenza *Par*
A2263 Mugyera *Par*
B1272 Mugyera *Par*
B1289 Mugyera *Par*
B3323 Muhambo *Par*
C2272 Muhanga *Par*
B2272 Muhanga
A2334 Muhangi
B240 Muharuzi, *(h)*
A1281 Muhavura, *(h)*
A2323 Muhindi *Par*
B2281 Muhindura *Par*
A2298 Muhito *Par*
A2298 Muhito
B2323 Muhokya *Par*
B2323 Muhokya
A2327 *MUHOORO S-Cy*
A2327 Muhooro
C2117 Muimet *Par*
B1317 Mujunju *Par*
C2243 Mujunwa
B3284 Mukagyera
C218 Mukale *Par*
B2169 Mukani *Par*
A2270 Mukatojo
B2289 Muko *Par*
A2272 *MUKO S-Cy*
A2272 Muko
B1235 Mukobe
C2206 Mukoko *Par*
B2206 Mukoko
A1243 *Mukokomya, R.*
A3255 Mukole
A1148 Mukongoro *Par*
A1148 *MUKONGORO S-Cy*
A1148 Mukongoro
B1289 Mukoni *Par*
B2245 *MUKONO Cy*
245 **MUKONO** *Dist*

B3192 *NAJJEMBE* S-Cy
B3192 Najjembe
B2153 Nakabale
B2243 Nakabale
B2327 Nakabale
A1253 Nakabanga
B2126 Nakabira Par
B2257 Nakabugo Par (Wakiso S-Cy), see A3211
B2153 Nakabugu Par
B1138 Nakabugu
B2153 Nakabugu
B295 Nakadeli Par
C1255 Nakagongo Par
A2132 Nakakulwe Par
B2128 Nakalama Par
B2128 *NAKALAMA* S-Cy
A3247 Nakalama
B2128 Nakalama
B3192 Nakalanga Par
C3230 Nakalembe Par
B3211 *Nakalere, R.*
B3167 Nakaloke Par
B3167 *NAKALOKE* S-Cy
B3167 Nakaloke
B2171 Nakalokwe Par
B1138 Nakandulo Par
B3245 Nakanyonyi Par (Nabbale S-Cy), see C3257
C293 *NAKAPELIMORU* S-Cy
97 *NAKAPIRIPIRIT* Dist
K71 *NAKAPIRIPIRIT* Dist
B297 *NAKAPIRIPIRIT* T/C
B297 **Nakapiripirit**
B3100 *Nakaromarengak, R.*
B2245 Nakasajja
B1215 Nakaseeta Par (Kayunga S-Cy), see A1138
B2237 Nakaseeta Par
247 *NAKASEKE* Dist
G61 *NAKASEKE* Dist
B2247 *NAKASEKE NORTH* Cy
C1247 Nakaseke Par
B1247 *NAKASEKE* S-Cy
B1247 *NAKASEKE SOUTH* Cy
C1247 *NAKASEKE* T/C
C1247 **Nakaseke**
B1217 Nakasengere Par
B1255 Nakasenyi Par
C1255 Nakasera
B2211 Nakasero I Par
B2211 Nakasero II Par
B2211 Nakasero III Par
B2211 Nakasero IV Par
B2211 Nakasero, (h)
C1247 Nakaseta Par
A2243 Nakaseta
A3257 Nakaseta
B2232 Nakaseta
C1221 Nakaseta
C2237 Nakaseta
B2197 Nakasi F/R
B2249 Nakasongola Central Par
B2249 *NAKASONGOLA* Cy

249 *NAKASONGOLA* Dist
G61 *NAKASONGOLA* Dist
B2249 Nakasongola Eastern Par
B2249 *NAKASONGOLA* T/C
B2249 Nakasongola Western Par
B2249 **Nakasongola**
B1217 Nakasozi Par
B2232 Nakasozi Par
B3255 Nakatabo
B2230 Nakateete Par
C236 Nakatiti Par
B1221 Nakatonya Par
B3253 Nakatoogo Par
B2197 Nakatooke Par
B2110 *NAKATSI* S-Cy
B1215 Nakatundu Par (Kangulumira S-Cy), see A2132
B2183 Nakatunya Ward (Soroti Western Div)
B2128 Nakavule Ward
B3211 *NAKAWA* Div
B2211 Nakawa Inst. Par
B2211 Nakawa Par
B2211 Nakawa
A1243 Nakawala
C3221 Nakawomeka
B2257 Nakawuka Par
B2257 Nakawuka
A2192 Nakazadde Ward
B2237 Nakaziba Par
A3257 Nakedde Par
A291 Nakgusokopire R/O
A1239 Nakibanga Par
B2237 Nakibanga Par
B1237 Nakibanga
B2245 Nakibano Par
B1138 Nakibungulya Par
B2138 Nakibungulya
C2100 Nakicumet Par
B1257 *Nakifulube Bay* (Nalugala Par)
B3245 *NAKIFUMA* Cy
B3255 Nakifuma
B1128 *NAKIGO* S-Cy
B2128 Nakigo
C2221 Nakigoza Par
C2201 Nakijju Par
B2221 Nakikoota Par
B3257 Nakikungube Par
B295 Nakiloro
B2164 Nakirimira
B2232 Nakisaja, (h)
B2245 *NAKISUNGA* S-Cy
B2245 Nakisunga
B1153 Nakiswiga Par
B2219 Nakitembe Par
B2215 Nakitokolo Par
A3249 Nakitoma
A3249 *NAKITOOMA* S-Cy
B2270 *Nakivali, L.*
B3112 Nakivamba Par
B2211 Nakivubo Par
B2215 Nakivubo Par
B2211 *Nakivubo, R.*

C1128 Nakivumbi
B1257 Nakiwogo
B2235 Nakiyaga
B297 Nakobekobe Par
B2247 Nakonge Par
C2112 Nakongolo
A2211 Nakulabye Par
A2211 Nakulabye
B2138 Nakulyaku Par
B297 Nakuri Par
B3136 *Nakuwa, L.*
B2257 Nakuwadde (Nakabugo Par), see A3211
C2197 Nakuzesinge F/R
B293 Nakwakwa Par
B3100 Nakwamoru Par
B3100 Nakwamoru Par
B2123 Nakwasi Par
B3237 Nakwaya Par
B2230 Nakyenyi Par
B1171 Nakyere Par
B2215 Nakyesa Par
B2215 Nakyesanja Par
B3257 Nakyesanja Par (Nabweru S-Cy), see A3211
B2180 Nakywondwe Par
B3257 Nakyyelongoosa Par
C2132 Nalinaibi Par
B2119 Nalondo
B1132 *Nalubaale Dam*
B2146 Nalubembe Par
C2237 Nalubudde
C236 Nalubwoyo Par
C236 Nalubwoyo
B1132 Nalufenya Par
B1114 Nalugai Par
B1257 Nalugala Par
A2180 Nalugugu Par
B2128 Naluko Par
A2211 *Nalukolongo, R.*
B3249 Nalukonge Par
A2180 *NALUSALA* S-Cy
A1243 Nalusomba
C2243 Nalutuntu Par
C2243 *NALUTUNTU* S-Cy
B1247 Naluvule Par
B2257 Naluvule Par (Wakiso S-Cy), see A3211
B2138 Naluwoli Par
B2243 Naluwondwa Par
B2110 *NALWANZA* S-Cy
B1121 Nalwire Par
B2245 *NAMA* S-Cy
C2243 Namabaale Par
C2243 Namabaale
B3167 Namabasa Par
B236 Namabere
B2201 Namabeya Par
C2192 Namabu Par
B2162 *NAMABYA* S-Cy
B1215 Namagabi Ward (Kayunga T/C), see A1138
B1138 Namaganda Par
B2138 Namaganda Par

B2138 Namaganda
A2132 Namagera Par
A2132 Namagera
B3167 Namagumba Par
B2245 Namagunga (Namagunga Par)
B2245 Namagunga Par
B2245 Namaiba Par (Nakisunga S-Cy), see C2257
B3169 Namaingo Par, see Namayingo Par
B2138 Namaira Par
B2171 Namakoba
B2112 Namakoko Par
B3171 Namakoko
B3167 Namakwekwe Ward
B2153 Namalemba Par
C2128 Namalemba Par
C3128 *NAMALEMBA* S-Cy
C2128 Namalemba
B3215 Namalere Par
B1221 Namaliga Par
B3245 Namaliga Par (Kimenyedde S-Cy), see C3257
B2215 Namaliiri Par (Kasawo S-Cy), see C3257
B3245 Namaliiri Par
B3245 Namaliiri
B297 *NAMALU* S-Cy
B197 Namalu
C2211 *Namalusu, Is.*
B1327 Namalwa
B3245 Namanoga Par
B2153 Namansenda Par
B2245 Namanyama
B3167 *NAMANYONYI* S-Cy
B3192 Namanyonyi
B3245 Namanyonyi
A2138 Namasagali Par
A2138 *NAMASAGALI* S-Cy
A2138 Namasagali
B3128 Namasago-Nabitende Par
B236 *NAMASALE* S-Cy
B236 Namasale
B2112 Namasere Par
B2110 Namasheti Par
A3164 Namasiga
B2132 Namasiga
B2257 Namasuba (Bunamwaya Par), see B2211
B2245 Namataba (Namataba Par)
B2245 Namataba (Ntanzi Par)
B2245 Namataba Par (Nagojje S-Cy), see A3192
B2245 Namataba
B2167 Namatala Ward
B1108 *Namatala, R.*
B2192 Namatovu Par
B2136 Namawa Par
B1167 Namawanga Par
C1221 Namawogya

B2245 Namawojjolo Par (Nama S-Cy), see C2257
B2146 Namawondo Par
169 *NAMAYINGO* Dist
J41 *NAMAYINGO* Dist
B3169 Namayingo Par
B3169 *NAMAYINGO* T/C
C3169 **Namayingo**
B3245 Namayuba Par
B3215 Namayuge Par
C3169 Namayuge Par
A3257 *NAMAYUMBA* S-Cy
A3257 Namayumba
B2162 Namba
B2112 Nambale Par
B3128 Nambale Par
C3123 Nambale Par
B2167 *NAMBALE* S-Cy
B3128 *NAMBALE* S-Cy
B3128 Nambale
B3221 Nambeere Par
A1221 Nambeya
B1221 Nambi Par
B1162 *NAMBOKO* S-Cy
B2162 Nambola
B2108 Namengo Par
A2192 Namengo Ward
C1128 Namiganda Par
C3237 Namigavu Par
B3249 Namikka Par
B2245 Namilyango (Nantabulirwa Par)
B2138 Naminage Par
C3192 Naminya Par
A2211 Namirembe Par
B2215 Namirembe Par (Busana S-Cy), see A1138
B1215 Namirembe
A2211 Namirembe, (h)
C2243 Namiringa Par, see Lwantale-Namiringa Par
B2138 Namisambya I Par
B2138 Namisambya II Par
B2119 *NAMISUNI* S-Cy
A1132 Namizi Par
B2215 Namizo Par
B248 *NAM-OKORA* S-Cy
B248 Nam-Okora
B2164 Namoni Par
B197 Namorotot Par
B1215 Nampaanyi Par
A2180 Nampanga Par
A2180 Nampanga
B2219 Nampiki
B2249 Nampiki
B3123 Nampologoma Par
A2230 Nampongerwa
B2169 Nampongwe Par
B3257 Nampunge Par
B1134 Nampyanga
B218 Namrwodho Ward
B2245 Namubiru Par (Nama S-Cy), see C2257
B2128 Namufuma
B3245 Namuganga Par

B2253 Njara *Par*
B2317 Njara *Ward*
C3192 Njeru East *Par*
A3249 Njeru *Par*
C3192 Njeru South *Par*
C3192 *NJERU T/C*
C3192 Njeru West *Par*
B3253 Njeru
C3192 Njeru
A2305 Njule *Par*
B2332 Nkaaka *Par*
B3112 Nkaiza *Par*
B2221 Nkampa
A2217 Nkandwa *Par*
B1219 Nkandwa *Par*
B2266 Nkanga *Par*
B2239 Nkasi *Par*
B1327 Nkenda *Par*
B2323 Nkenda, (h)
B2253 Nkenge *Par*
C3204 Nkese, *Is.*
A3320 Nkingo
C3323 *Nkoko, R.*
A2192 Nkokonjeru *Par*
B1221 Nkokonjeru *Par*
B2215 Nkokonjeru *Par*
A2192 *NKOKONJERU T/C*
A2192 Nkokonjeru
B2201 Nkokonjeru
B2320 Nkoma *Par*
B3167 Nkoma *Par*
C2201 Nkoma *Par*
B2320 *NKOMA S-Cy*
B3167 Nkoma *Ward*
B2320 Nkoma
B3167 Nkoma
B3164 Nkombe *Par*
A2309 Nkondo *Par*
C2327 Nkondo *Par*
B2126 *NKONDO S-Cy*
B2126 Nkondo
C2327 Nkondo
A3255 Nkonge
B2221 Nkonge
A2320 Nkongora
A2289 Nkongoro *Par*
A2320 Nkongoro *Par*
C3230 Nkoni *Par*
A2192 Nkonkonjeru *Par*
B2128 Nkono *Ward*
C2327 *NKOOKO S-Cy*
C2327 Nkooko
C2126 Nkoone *Par*
B1204 Nkose, *Is.*
B2232 Nkote
A1239 *NKOZI S-Cy*
A1239 Nkozi
C3221 Nkudumali
B1257 Nkumba (Nkumba *Par*)
B1257 Nkumba *Par*
B2275 Nkunda *Par*
B3277 Nkungu *Par*
B3277 Nkungu
B2257 Nkungulutale *Par*
B3230 Nkunyu *Par*
B3230 Nkunyu

B2112 Nkusi *Ward*
B2327 *Nkusi, R.*
B2309 Nkwaki *F/R*
A1239 Nnindye *Par*
B221 Noko
B1277 Nombe II *Par*
A3289 Nombe
B3284 Nombe
B1277 Nombi
B2272 Noozi *Par*
B3286 North Maramagambo *F/R*
B2272 *NORTHERN Div* (Kabale *M/C*)
B295 *NORTHERN Div* (Moroto *M/C*)
B2257 Nsaggu *Par* (Sissa *S-Cy*), see **A1211**
B3192 Nsakya *Par*
B2217 Nsala *Par*
C2128 Nsale *Par*
C2201 Nsambwe *Par*
C2201 Nsambwe
B2211 Nsambya Central *Par*
B2211 Nsambya Estates *Par*
C1237 Nsambya *Par*
B2211 Nsambya Police *Par*
B2211 Nsambya Railway *Par*
A3219 *NSAMBYA S-Cy*
B2255 Nsambya
B2211 Nsambya, (h)
A2136 Nsamule *Par*
C1255 Nsangala
B2257 *NSANGI (MUKONO) S-Cy*
B2257 Nsangi *Par*
B2257 Nsangi
B3164 Nsango *Par*
B2245 Nsanja *Par* (Ntenjeru *S-Cy*), see **C2257**
B1221 Nsanvu *Par*
B3243 Nsanyu
B2268 Nsasi *Par*
A2323 Nsenyi *Par*
C2257 *Nsenyi, Is.* see **B1211**
B1277 Nshara *Gate*
B1277 Nshara
C2289 Nshenyi *Par*
B2270 Nshororo *Par*
B2266 Nshumi *Par*
B2277 Nshwere
B2277 Nshwerenkye *Par*
B2232 Nsiika *Par*
B3284 Nsiika *Par*
C2263 **Nsiika**
B1215 Nsiima *Par* (Nazigo *S-Cy*), see **B1138**
B2277 Nsikisi
B1257 *Nsinga Bay* (Zzinga/Buganga *Par*)
B2171 Nsinze *Par*
A2171 *NSINZE S-Cy*
A2171 Nsize
B2255 Nsoga *Par*
C2126 Nsomba
B3164 Nsone
B2270 Nsongezi
B3211 *Nsooba, R.*

B1215 Nsotoka *Par* (Kayunga *S-Cy*), see **A1138**
C2197 Nsozibbiri *Par*
B2243 Nsozinga *Par*
B2245 Nsuube-Kauga *Ward* (Mukono *Div*, Mukono *M/C*), see **C2257**
B2245 Ntaawo *Ward* (Mukono *Div*, Mukono *M/C*)
B3153 Ntaigirwa *Par*
A2126 Ntala *Par*
A3126 Ntala
B2201 Ntalagi *Par*
B2206 Ntale *Par*
A3277 Ntambazi *Par*
B3305 Ntandi
C2270 Ntantamuki
B2245 Ntanzi *Par* (Ntenjeru *S-Cy*), see **A2192**
B2245 Ntanzi
A1320 Ntara *Par*
A1320 *NTARA S-Cy*
B1272 Ntarabana *Par*
A2277 Ntarama
B2284 Ntare
A1281 Ntebeko *R/O*
A3281 Nteko *Par*
B1215 *NTENJERU Cy*
B2245 *NTENJERU S-Cy*
B1215 Ntenjeru *Ward* (Kayunga *T/C*), see **A1138**
B2215 Ntenjeru
B2245 Ntenjeru
B1219 Ntiba *Par*
B3215 Ntimba Island *Par*
B3211 Ntinda *Par*
B3211 Ntinda
B1215 Ntoke
B2197 Ntolomwe *Par*
B2245 Ntonto *Par* (Kyampisi *S-Cy*), see **C3257**
B3320 Ntonwa *Par*
B1337 Ntooma *Par*
B2340 *NTOROKO Cy*
340 **NTOROKO** *Dist*
C61 **NTOROKO** *Dist*
C2340 Ntoroko *Par*
C2340 Ntoroko
A2219 Ntunda *Par*
B3245 Ntunda *Par*
B3245 *NTUNDA S-Cy*
A2270 Ntundu *Par*
B2340 Ntungama
B2289 Ntungamo Central *Par*
289 **NTUNGAMO** *Dist*
C21 **NTUNGAMO** *Dist*
A2243 Ntungamo *Par*
B1275 Ntungamo *Par*
B2289 *NTUNGAMO S-Cy*
B2289 *NTUNGAMO T/C*
A3281 Ntungamo
B2289 **Ntungamo**
A2270 Ntungu *Par*
B1295 *Ntungu, R.*
B2275 Ntungwa *Par*
B3275 Ntungwe *Camp*

B3284 Ntura *Par*
B2255 *NTUSI S-Cy*
A2255 Ntuusi *Par*
B2255 Ntuusi
B1219 *NTWETWE T/C*
B1219 Ntwetwe
B1266 Numba *Par*
B2121 Nuyonda *Par*
A210 Nvio
B259 *NWOYA Cy*
59 **NWOYA** *Dist*
F91 **NWOYA** *Dist*
B259 **Nwoya**
A2320 *NYABBANI S-Cy*
B1317 Nyabigaga
A1320 Nyabihoko *Par*
A2289 *NYABIHOKO S-Cy*
B1281 Nyabihuniko
B2272 Nyabikoni *Ward* (Kabale Central *Div*)
B1284 Nyabikungu *Par*
A2340 Nyabinga
C2272 Nyabirerema *Par*
A2323 Nyabirongo *Par*
B2334 Nyabirongo *Par*
A2323 Nyabirongo
A2277 *Nyabisheke, R.*, see **C2268**
B3284 Nyabisirira *Par*
B3323 Nyabisusi *Par*
B3323 Nyabitaba *Camp*
B1295 Nyabiteete *Par*
B2295 Nyabiteete *Par*
B2266 Nyabubaare *Par*
B2286 Nyabubaare *Par*
A2295 Nyabubare *Par*
A3289 Nyabubare *Par*
C2293 Nyabubare *Par*
B2266 *NYABUBARE S-Cy*
B2266 Nyabubare
C3270 Nyabubare
A2323 Nyabugando *Par*
C2284 Nyabuhama *Par*
C2284 Nyabuhama
B2327 Nyabuhikye *Par*
B1268 *NYABUHIKYE S-Cy*
B2268 *NYABUHIKYE S-Cy*
B1268 Nyabuhikye
B2317 Nyabukara *Ward*
B3268 Nyaburama
B2289 Nyaburiza *Par*
B2272 Nyabushabi *Par*
A2289 Nyabushenyi *Par*
B1295 Nyabushenyi *Par*
B1277 Nyabushenyi
B2277 *NYABUSHOZI Cy*
A1340 Nyabusokoma
A2340 Nyabusokoma
A2317 Nyabuswa *Par*
B1317 Nyabweya *Par*
A3281 *NYABWISHENYA S-Cy*
A3281 Nyabwishenya
A2337 Nyabyeya (Nyabyeya *Par*)
A2337 Nyabyeya *Par*
C2270 Nyabyondo *Par*
B218 Nyacara *Ward*

B3106 Nyada *Par*
A148 *Nyadiang, R.*
B214 *NYADRI S-Cy*
B110 *Nyagak, R.*
C2263 *Nyagoma, R.*
B3323 Nyagorongo *Par*
A2305 Nyahuka
B212 Nyai *Par*
B212 Nyai
A1334 Nyaibanda *Par*
A1334 Nyaibanda
B2289 Nyakabaare *Par*
B2281 *NYAKABANDE S-Cy*
B2281 Nyakabande
B1284 Nyakabare *Par*
B1281 Nyakabingo *Par*
B2309 Nyakabingo *Par*
B2323 Nyakabingo *Ward*
A2272 Nyakabungo *Par*
A2289 Nyakabungo *Par*
B2272 Nyakagabagaba *Par*
A1284 Nyakagango
B118 Nyakagei *Par*
B118 Nyakagenyi
B2317 Nyakagongo *Ward*
B2295 *NYAKAGYEME S-Cy*
B2295 Nyakagyeme
B2272 Nyakagyera *Par*
A2270 Nyakahandagazi (Ntungu *Par*)
A1284 Nyakahanga
B1277 Nyakahita *Par*
B1277 Nyakahita
A2323 Nyakahya *Par*
A1284 Nyakaikara *Par*
B1295 Nyakaina *Par*
B3270 Nyakakoni *Par*
B3323 Nyakalengija *Camp*
B3277 Nyakaliro
B2298 Nyakarama *Par*
A2270 Nyakarambi *Par*
B1289 Nyakariro *Par*
A2327 Nyakarongo *Par*
A2334 Nyakarongo *Par*
B2323 Nyakasanga I *Ward*
B2323 Nyakasanga II *Ward*
B2323 Nyakasanja
A1320 Nyakasenyi *Par*
B2340 Nyakasenyi
B2298 Nyakashambya *Par*
B2272 Nyakasharara *Par*
B2277 Nyakasharara *Par*
B2277 Nyakasharara
B1268 Nyakashasha
B1277 *NYAKASHASHARA S-Cy*
B2277 Nyakashashara
B2272 Nyakashebeya *Par*
B3286 Nyakashojwa *Par*
B2275 Nyakashure *Par*
B2275 Nyakashure
C2272 Nyakasiru *Par*
A1320 Nyakasura *Par*
B2317 Nyakasura
B2286 Nyakateete *Par*
B2268 Nyakatokye *Par*
B2268 Nyakatokye

B1169 Rabachi *Par*
B2330 Rabongo
B2330 Rabongo, *(h)*
B2330 Rabongo, *R/O*
B165 Rackoko
C318 Ragem *Par*
C318 Ragem
B255 Railway Quarters *Ward* (Railways *S-Cy*)
B255 *RAILWAY S-Cy*
253 **RAKAI** *Dist*
F21 **RAKAI** *Dist*
B2253 *RAKAI T/C*
B2253 **Rakai**
B2186 Ramog *Par*
B318 Ramogi *Par*
B155 Rao *Par*
B221 Renda *Par*
B293 Rengem
B293 *RENGEN S-Cy*
B118 Rero *Par*
C210 *RHINO CAMP S-Cy*
C210 Rhino Camp
C210 *RIGBO S-Cy*
C210 Rigbo
B121 Rigbonga *Par*
A114 Rikabu *Par*
C193 Rikitae *Par*
A210 Ringili *Par*
C2117 Riwo *Par*
C2117 *RIWO S-Cy*
A310 Robu *Par* (Aroi *S-Cy*), see **B114**
A210 Robu *Par* (Manibe *S-Cy*), see **B114**
B114 Robu *Par*
B314 Robu *Par*
C310 Roga *Par*
A221 Rogale *Par*
B332 Rogo *Par*
C187 Rogom *Par*
C248 Rom
C248 Rom, *(h)*
B221 *ROMOGI S-Cy*
B221 Romogi
A2164 *Roseberry Channel*
B3303 Ruangi
A3255 Rubaale *Par*
A2289 *RUBAARE S-Cy*
B2284 *RUBAARE S-Cy*
A2289 Rubaare
B1295 *RUBABO Cy*
A3211 *RUBAGA Div*
A2211 Rubaga *Par*
B1132 Rubaga *Par*
A2211 Rubaga, *(h)*
B2272 *RUBANDA Cy*
A2272 Rubanda
B1295 Rubanga *Par*
B1277 Rubanga *R/O*
B3334 Rubango *Par*
B1277 Rubare
B1272 *RUBAYA S-Cy*
C2284 *RUBAYA S-Cy*
B1272 Rubaya
C2284 Rubaya
B3270 Rubeya

B1275 Rubimbwa *Par*
B3284 *RUBINDI S-Cy*
B3284 Rubindi
B2284 Rubingo *Par*
B2317 Rubingo *Par*
B2284 Rubingo
C2289 *Rubingo, R.*
B2293 **Rubiriizi**
A2327 Rubirizi *Par*
A2317 Rubona *Par*
B2317 Rubona
B3320 Rubona
B2186 *RUBONGI S-Cy*
A2270 Ruborogota *Par*
A2270 Ruborogota
A2281 Rubuguri *Par*
B2281 Rubuguri
C2284 Ruburara
B2286 Rucence *Par*
B1284 Ruchenche
C353 Rudi *Par*
C1268 Rugaaga *Par*
B2270 Rugaaga
C2270 *RUGAGA S-Cy*
B3270 *Rugaga, R.*
B1284 *RUGANDO S-Cy*
B1284 Rugando
A2320 Rugarama *Par*
B2284 Rugarama *Par*
B2298 Rugarama *Par*
C2272 Rugarama *Par*
A2289 *RUGARAMA S-Cy*
B2284 Rugarama
C2284 Rugarama
A2327 Rugashari *Par*
A2327 *RUGASHARI S-Cy*
C2293 Rugazi *Par*
B2268 Rugazi
C3323 Rugendabara *Par*
B2277 Rugongi *Par*
C2263 Rugongo *Par*
B2337 Rugongo *Par*
B2309 Ruguse *Par*
B3270 *Rugyeye, R.* (Kyarugaju *Par*), see **B1277**
C1275 *RUGYEYO S-Cy*
C1275 Rugyeyo
B2289 Ruhaama *Par*
B2289 Ruhaama
B2289 *RUHAMA Cy*
B2289 *RUHAMA S-Cy*
B2275 Ruhandagazi *Par*
C2275 Ruhandagazi
B2289 Ruhanga
B1289 Ruhara *Par*
B2266 Ruharo *Par*
B2284 Ruharo *Ward* (Kamukuzi *S-Cy*, Mbarara *M/C*)
A1289 Ruhega *Par*
A2270 Ruhiira *Par*
B2270 Ruhimbo
B2286 *RUHINDA Cy*
B2295 *RUHINDA S-Cy*
B2295 Ruhinda

B2270 Ruhira
A2334 Ruhoko *Par*
B2289 Ruhoko *Par*
B1268 Ruhoko
B2272 Ruhonwa *Par*
A2272 *Ruhuma, R.*
B3284 Ruhumba
A1320 Ruhunga *Par*
B2284 Ruhunga *Par*
B3289 Ruhunga *Par*
C1309 Ruhunga *Par*
B2284 Ruhunga
A2295 *RUJUMBURA Cy*
A2289 Rukanga *Par*
B3284 Rukanza
B1284 Rukarabo *Par*
A3289 Rukarango *Par*
B2286 Rukararwe *Par*
B2272 *RUKIGA Cy*
B2284 Rukindo *Par*
A2289 Rukiri *Par*
B2263 Rukiri *Par*
B1268 *RUKIRI S-Cy*
B1268 Rukiri
B2263 Rukiri
B2323 Rukoki *Par*
B2323 *RUKOKI S-Cy*
B2323 Rukoki
C2323 *Rukoki, R.*
A2298 Rukondo *Par*
A2337 Rukondwa *Par*
A1281 Rukongi *Par*
A3289 Rukoni *Par*
C2289 Rukoni *Par*
C2289 *RUKONI S-Cy*
C2289 Rukoni
B1277 Rukukuru
295 **RUKUNGIRI** *Dist*
B21 **RUKUNGIRI** *Dist*
B2295 Rukungiri East *Ward*
B2295 Rukungiri North *Ward*
B2295 Rukungiri South *Ward*
B2295 *RUKUNGIRI T/C*
B2295 Rukungiri West *Ward*
B2295 **Rukungiri**
B2327 Rukunyu *Par*
A2270 Rukurijo
B3270 Rukuuba *Par*
B2289 *Ruloha, R.*
B2293 Rumuli *Par*
B1289 Runara *Par*
C3309 Runga
C3298 Runyinya *Par*
B295 Rupa *Par*
B295 *RUPA S-Cy*
B295 Rupa
B2317 Rurama *Par*
B1277 Rurambira *Par*
B2286 Rurehe *Par*
B2317 Rusekere
A2323 Rusese *Par*
B2275 Rushaka *Par*
B2272 Rushaki *Ward* (Kabale Southern *Div*)
B1284 Rushambya
B3268 Rushango *Par*
A3277 *Rushango, R.*

C3268 *Rushangwe, R.*
B2295 Rushasha *Par*
C3270 Rushasha
B2284 Rushasha
B3295 *Rushaya, R.*
B1263 Rushayo *Par*
B2289 Rushebeya *Par*
B2281 Rushekye
A2289 *RUSHENYI Cy*
A1289 Rushenyi
B2277 Rushere *Par*
B2277 Rushere
B3286 Rusheregyenyi *Par*
B2266 Rushinya *Par*
B2275 Rushoroza *Par*
B2286 Rushoroza *Par*
B3298 Rushozi *Par*
C2284 Rushozi *Par*
C2284 Rushozi
B2277 Rusoga *Par*
A2281 Rutaka *Par*
B1281 Rutare *Par*
B1317 *RUTEETE S-Cy*
C1275 *RUTENGA S-Cy*
C1275 Rutenga
B3272 Rutengye *Par*
A2327 Rutete *Par*
B2317 Rutete
B2284 Ruti *Ward* (Nyamitanga *S-Cy*, Mbarara *M/C*)
A1323 Ruti
B1284 Ruti
B2272 Rutoma
B2272 Rutoma
B2286 Rutoma
B2284 Rutooma *Par*
C2266 Rutooma *Par*
B2272 Rutooma *Ward* (Kabale Northern *Div*)
B2284 Rutooma
B2295 Rutooma
B1275 Rutugunda *Par*
B3277 *Rutungu, R.*
A2289 Rutunguru *Par*
B2270 Ruyanga *Par*
B2270 Ruyanga
B1295 Ruyonza *Par*
A2289 Ruyonza
A2327 Rwabaranga *Par*
A1277 Rwabarata *Par*
A1317 Rwagimba
B2272 Rwahi
B2332 Rwahunga *Par*
B2317 Rwaihamba
B1334 Rwaitengya *Par*
B1334 Rwaitengya
B1263 Rwajere *Par*
B2268 Rwakagongo
A2277 Rwakahaya
A2270 Rwakakwenda *Par*
B1295 Rwakirungura *Par*
B2284 Rwakishakiizi *Par*
A2340 Rwamabale
A2327 Rwamagando *Par*
B2327 Rwamalenge *Par*
B2320 Rwamanja (Bisozi *Par*)
A2272 Rwamanyonyi, *(h)*

A3295 *RWAMBARA S-Cy*
B1284 *RWAMPARA Cy*
B2272 *RWAMUCUCU S-Cy*
B2295 Rwamugoma *Par*
B3284 Rwamuhiigi *Par*
B2298 Rwamujojo *Par*
B2334 Rwamukoora *Par*
B1277 Rwamuranda *Par*
B3277 Rwamuranga *Par*
A2270 Rwamwijuka *Par*
B2289 Rwamwire *Par*
A3289 Rwanda *Par*
B2275 Rwanga *Par*
B2275 Rwanga
C2270 Rwangabo *Par*
C2270 Rwangabo
B3340 Rwangara *Par*
B2286 Rwanja *Par*
C2270 Rwanjogyera *Par*
C3270 Rwantaha *Par*
B2284 Rwantsinga
B2263 Rwanyamabare *Par*
B2284 *RWANYAMAHEMBE S-Cy*
B2284 Rwanyamahembe
A2277 Rwanyangwe *Par*
A2277 Rwanyangwe
B1272 Rwanyena *Par*
B1295 Rwanyundo *Par*
A2281 Rwaramba *Par*
A2289 Rwashamaire *Par*
A2289 Rwashamaire
B2320 Rwebikwato
B2340 Rwebisengo *Par*
B2340 *RWEBISENGO S-Cy*
A2340 Rwebisengo
B2284 Rwebishekye *Par*
B3277 Rwebishya
B1327 Rwega *Par*
B3298 Rweibare *Par*
B1284 Rweibogo *Par*
B2289 *RWEKINIRO S-Cy*
A2277 Rwemamba *Par* (Kashongi *S-Cy*), see C1268
A2277 *Rwemambya, R.*, see C1268
A2277 Rwemengo *Par* (Kanoni *S-Cy*), see C2268
C2219 Rwemiganda *Par*
C2284 Rwemigyina *Par*
B3277 Rwemikoma *Par*
B3277 *RWEMIKOMA S-Cy*
B3277 Rwemikoma
B1277 Rwempongo
B2289 Rwempungu
B2293 *Rwempunu, R.*
B1272 Rwene *Par*
B1272 Rwene
B2317 Rwengaju *Par*
A2323 Rwenghuyo *Par*
A1320 Rwengiri (Kagazi *Par*)
A2320 Rwengo
B2289 Rwengoma *Par*
B2317 Rwengoma *Ward*
A3289 Rwengoma
B1268 Rwengorogoro
B1268 Rwengwe *Par*